Revolution in the Making of the Modern World

This volume seeks to re-evaluate the contribution of revolutions to the formation of modern, industrial societies and it questions whether ideas of revolution are still relevant in the postmodern and globalized world of the twenty-first century. Featuring contributions from some of the world's leading sociological and political thinkers on revolution, this book combines theoretical concerns with a variety of detailed case studies of individual revolutions. Subjects covered include:

- democracy and revolution from 1789 to 1989
- twentieth-century revolutions and theories of revolution, including Marxism, modernization and structuralist theories
- revolution in the Third World and the variable geometry of the paths to modernity
- Islamic revolutions and modernity
- the 1989 revolutions as "democratic revolutions" or "elite-led transitions"
- globalization, the nation-state and revolution
- empire and "democratic revolution"
- network society and revolution
- Islamic fundamentalism, international terrorism and revolution
- democratic revolution as a new form of revolution
- postmodern theories of revolution
- new social movements, identities and new figures of revolution

This is a significant contribution to the study of revolution and is essential reading for all students and scholars of the issue.

John Foran is Professor of Sociology at the University of California at Santa Barbara, USA.

David Lane is Senior Research Associate at the University of Cambridge, UK.

Andreja Zivkovic is Lecturer at the University of Hertfordshire, UK.

Revolution in the Making of the Modern World

Social identities, globalization, and modernity

Edited by
John Foran, David Lane,
and Andreja Zivkovic

Routledge
Taylor & Francis Group

LONDON AND NEW YORK

First published 2008
by Routledge
2 Park Square Milton Park Abingdon Oxon OX14 4RN

Simultaneously published in the USA and Canada
by Routledge
270 Madison Avenue, New York, NY 10016

Routledge is an imprint of the Taylor & Francis Group, an informa business

Typeset in Times New Roman by
Taylor & Francis Books
Printed and bound in Great Britain by
Antony Rowe Ltd, Chippenham, Wiltshire

British Library Cataloguing in Publication Data
A catalogue record for this book is available from the British Library

Library of Congress Cataloging in Publication Data
Revolution in the making of the modern world: social identities, globalization, and modernity / [edited by] John Foran, David Lane, and Andreja Zivkovic.
        p. cm.
    Includes bibliographical references and index.
    1. Revolutions. 2. Social change. 3. Globalization. 4. Group identity. I. Foran, John. II. Lane, David Stuart. III. Zivkovic, Andreja.
    HM876.R44 2007
    303.6′4–dc22   2007018405

ISBN 978-0-415-77182-5 (hbk)
ISBN 978-0-415-77183-2 (pbk)
ISBN 978-0-203-93346-6 (ebk)

Contents

Illustrations

Figures

Tables

Contributors

Asef Bayat is the Academic Director of the International Institute for the Study of Islam in the Modern World (ISIM) and ISIM Professor at Leiden University, The Netherlands. His most recent book is *Making Islam Democratic: Social Movements and the Post-Islamist Turn* (2007).

John Barber is a Fellow of King's College, University of Cambridge. His books include *The Soviet Home Front, 1941–45: A Social and Economic History of the USSR in World War II* (1991, with Mark Harrison) and *Life and Death in Besieged Leningrad, 1941–44* (2005, co-edited with Andrei Dzeniskevich).

Robin Blackburn is Professor of Sociology at the University of Essex and Distinguished Visiting Professor at the New School for Social Research in New York. His books include *The Overthrow of Colonial Slavery* (1988) and *Age Shock: How Finance is Failing Us* (2006).

Alex Callinicos is Professor of European Studies at King's College, London University. His latest books are *Equality* (2000), *Against the Third Way* (2001), *An Anti-Capitalist Manifesto* (2003), *The New Mandarins of American Power* (2003), and *The Resources of Critique* (2006).

John Dunn is Fellow of King's College and Professor of Political Theory at the University of Cambridge. His works include *Modern Revolutions* (1972, 1989), *The Politics of Socialism* (1984), *The Cunning of Unreason: Making Sense of Politics* (2000), and *Setting the People Free: The Story of Democracy* (2005).

John Foran is Professor of Sociology at the University of California, Santa Barbara. He is the author of *Fragile Resistance: Social Transformation in Iran from 1500 to the Revolution* (1993), and *Taking Power: On the Origins of Third World Revolutions* (2005).

Jeff Goodwin is Professor of Sociology at New York University. He is author of *No Other Way Out: States and Revolutionary Movements* (2001) and co-editor of *Passionate Politics: Emotions and Social Movements* (2001) and *Rethinking Social Movements: Structure, Meaning, and Emotion* (2004).

Fred Halliday is Professor of International Relations at the London School of Economics. He has written extensively on nationalist and revolutionary movements in the Third World, including *Revolution and World Politics: The Rise and Fall of the Sixth Great Power* (1999).

John Hogan is Reader in Industrial Relations at the University of Hertfordshire, UK. His publications within the fields of industrial relations, organization theory, and political science look at the implications of the internet for the politics and processes of organized labor.

Krishan Kumar is William R. Kenan, Jr., Professor of Sociology at the University of Virginia. His works include *1989: Revolutionary Ideas and Ideals* (2001) and the co-edited Sage *Handbook of Nations and Nationalism* (2006). He is currently working on nations, empires and identities.

David Lane is Senior Research Associate, Faculty of Social and Political Sciences, University of Cambridge. He is the recipient of a Leverhulme Trust Research award on transformation in Ukraine and Russia. His books include (with Martin Myant) *Varieties of Capitalism in Post-Communist Countries* (2006) and *The Transformation of State Socialism* (2007).

Ching Kwan Lee is Associate Professor of Sociology at the University of Michigan. She is the author of *Gender and the South China Miracle: Two Worlds of Factory Women* (1998) and *Against the Law: Labor Protests in China's Rustbelt and Sunbelt* (2007).

Valentine M. Moghadam is Professor of Sociology and Women's Studies and the Director of the Women's Studies Program at Purdue University. Among her books are *Modernizing Women: Gender and Social Change in the Middle East* (2003) and *Globalizing Women: Transnational Feminist Networks* (2005).

Antonio Negri has been an important figure in the movements of contestation in Italy since the 1960s. He is the author of many works of political philosophy, including notably, with Michael Hardt, *Empire* (2000) and *Multitude: War and Democracy in the Age of Empire* (2004).

Eric Selbin is Professor of Political Science and University Scholar at Southwestern University. He is the author of *Modern Latin American Revolution* (1999), various articles and chapters on matters revolutionary, and co-editor of New Millennium Books in International Studies.

Mark Selden is a research associate, East Asia Program, Cornell University and a coordinator of *Japan Focus*, an e-journal on Japan and the Asia Pacific. His books include *The Political Economy of Chinese Development* (1993) and *Revolution, Resistance and Reform in Village China* (2005).

Göran Therborn is Professor of Sociology at the University of Cambridge and has been co-director of the Swedish Collegium for Advanced Study.

His latest books are *Inequalities of the World* (2006), and *Asia and Europe in Globalization* (2006).

Harald Wydra teaches politics at the University of Cambridge, where he is a fellow of St. Catharine's College. He is the author of *Continuities in Poland's Permanent Transition* (2001) and *Communism and the Emergence of Democracy* (2006).

Andreja Zivkovic is a lecturer at the University of Hertfordshire, UK. He has published widely on the history and politics of Balkan labor movements, and on the time-space dimensions of collective action in the Information Age.

Acknowledgments

The papers collected in this book originate from a conference organized at King's College, University of Cambridge, UK, by John Barber, David Lane, and Andreja Zivkovic. We wish to acknowledge the generous support of the King's College Research Centre which made the conference possible and thank its convener, Professor Simon Goldhill, and the Provost of King's College and its fellows for providing a magnificent setting.

We also acknowledge the financial support given by the Monnet Centre and the Faculty of Social and Political Sciences of the University of Cambridge. Andreja Zivkovic graciously covered the conference expenses of Antonio Negri.

Molly Talcott, graduate student in Sociology at the University of California, helped enormously with the preparation of the manuscript. Danny Olmos, graduate student in Sociology at the University of California, tracked down a number of missing references for us. Harald Wydra and Marina Frasca-Spada translated Antonio Negri's chapter from the original Italian. We are greatly indebted to them.

We thank the University of North Carolina Press for permission to publish an earlier version of Jeff Goodwin's chapter that appeared as "A Theory of Categorical Terrorism," pp. 2027–46 in *Social Forces*, volume 84, number 4 (2006).

Preface

John Barber

This book presents the results of the conference held at King's College Research Centre, University of Cambridge, UK, in April 2005. While the ancient setting in which the proceedings took place might seem to present a striking contrast with their modern theme, there was in fact no place more appropriate, in Cambridge at least, to hold such a conference.

It would not be an exaggeration to speak of a "tradition" of studying revolution in Cambridge, beginning at King's College. It was here in October 1967 that two fellows of King's College, Martin Bernal and John Dunn, established the first seminar on the subject of revolution ever in Cambridge. Over the next two years the seminar convened fortnightly to discuss papers produced by its young members.

Directly or indirectly this had three particularly significant results for the study of revolution. The first was the international conference on revolution held in the Research Centre in July 1968. Rarely can an academic occasion have been so closely linked with contemporary events. Not only did the conference take place against the background of the dramatic processes taking place that summer in Berlin, New York, Paris, Prague, and elsewhere, but several of the participants came straight from taking part in these events.

The second was the creation of the Revolution paper in the first year of the new Social and Political Sciences Tripos by John Dunn in 1971. This course would play a central part in the teaching of politics in the SPS, and through its seminar, organized by John Dunn with, at different times, Paul Ginsborg, John Barber, Harald Wydra, and Andreja Zivkovic, taught generations of students to think critically about the theory and practice of revolution.

The third was John Dunn's book, *Modern Revolutions: An Introduction to the Analysis of a Political Phenomenon* (Cambridge: Cambridge University Press, 1972). This seminal work, together with his later articles on the subject, raised the study of revolution to a new level, making in the process a major contribution to the understanding of one of the salient features of modern history.

Since sponsoring the first initiative to establish the study of revolution at Cambridge, King's College has been the venue for many lectures, seminars, symposia, and workshops on this and related subjects, with participants ranging from Perry Anderson and Eric Hobsbawm to Michael Ignatieff and Mikhail Gorbachev. Committed as its Research Centre has always been to supporting research and debate on central issues of politics and society, it welcomed the opportunity to host the conference on revolution, class and modernity, and it warmly thanks the contributors to the resulting volume.

John Barber
King's College, University of Cambridge, Cambridge, UK

Foreword

Roads to modernity: revolutionary and other

Göran Therborn

Have revolutions made the modern world? Or has modernity made revolutions? At least in one significant case, it is rather the latter. It is a modern conception of knowledge, and its historians, which created the seventeenth-century scientific revolution of Bacon, Descartes, Newton, *et al.* Politically, however, it was the French Revolution, which created modernity. Or, better, the French upheavals of 1789–94 created the modern concept of revolution, as well as political modernity. The revolution, like the Thompsonian working class, was present at its own making.

If someone in the 1760s, 1770s, or 1780s wanted to find out the best knowledge of revolution, she went to the *Encyclopédie*, which summed up the wisdom of the Enlightenment. In the entry on "revolution" the reader would be referred to an extensive, well-informed article on ... clock-making. While "revolution" in the eighteenth century, or earlier, might include the meaning of disturbance or riot, its main meaning was recurrent motion. When Copernicus, in 1543, published his treatise, *On the Revolutions of Heavenly Bodies*, he was not adumbrating Star Wars. He was referring to the revolving elliptic motion of the planets. The prefix "re-" in revolution or re-form actually means back, rolling back (originally the stone in front of the grave of Jesus) and returning to the original form of the Christian community before the papacy, as was the intention of Luther and Calvin.

It was in the process of the French events that revolution acquired its modern meaning as a door to a new future. Reform was sometimes used synonymously with revolution in those years of upheaval, and finally settled its modern meaning in the ensuing struggles for parliamentary change in Britain (Therborn 1989).

The French Revolution was the key site of the European road to modernity. The alignment for and against a new society was internal, to France and to Europe. Against were the princes, the (bulk of) aristocracies, the established churches of all Christian denominations, many mercantile oligarchies, and the subjects and clients of those forces. For modernity were (mainstream) professionals, many religious dissenters, (the bulk of) urban artisans and shopkeepers, (a predominant part of) the new industrial bourgeoisie, sometimes farmers, and a varying part of the urban populace. The main point here is the internal divide, not its class character.

1789 also set in motion a European epoch of revolutions and counter-revolutions, the Restoration of 1815 and the Holy Alliance, with the international revolution of 1830, the continental revolutions of 1848, and their international repression, the lesser but still significant reverberations of the Paris Commune in 1871, and the new watershed of 1917, a process explicitly argued out in terms of the 1789–1871 European tradition. 1918 and the collapse of the Hohenzollern and Habsburg Empires were also experienced as a revolution. The approaching heat of its proximate flames also brought about the "Democratic Breakthrough" in Sweden. The Spanish Civil War, and the French war between Vichy and the *Résistance* were fought out for and against the revolutionary modernity of 1789. The reform communism of 1956 and 1968 was another part of this revolutionary legacy. On the other side of the divide, the Netherlands kept its Calvinist Anti-Revolutionary Party – against 1789 and all other revolutions, a key governmental party in the interwar period – till the 1970s.

The young rebels of the 1960s did not, in most cases, see themselves in this light. Revolutionary inspiration was more likely to derive from the Vietnam war, from the Cuban Revolution, and from Third World struggles generally, than from the tradition of 1789–1917. However, when the immediacy of socio-cultural change receded, that generation also turned to one variety or other of the communist heritage.

The implosion of European communism meant the end of this European tradition of revolution and counter-revolution. 1989 was certainly no revolution in the historical European sense, of opening social, economic, and political space to hitherto excluded social strata. Privatization, marketization, demobilization of parties and trades unions meant a massive narrowing of popular social space. But nor was it counter-revolution in the classical sense of popular political exclusion. On the contrary, the political space of debate and elections was broadened. Anti-communist "lustrum" legislation was put in place in the Czech Republic and in Poland, banning communists from public office, but there was no repetition of historical White Terror. The victorious anti-communists of 1989 were neither revolutionaries nor counter-revolutionaries. They had ended the cycle, proclaiming "a normal state," "a normal market economy," and a "return to Europe." That is, an adherence to a triumphant Western European modernity, but perceived as at most only tangential to the previous experience of revolutions and counter-revolutions.

At the same time, French liberals proclaimed the French Revolution as "terminated," a termination celebrated in the markedly post-revolutionary bicentennial festivities of 1989.

The recent wave of middle-class revolutions, supported and significantly financed by the United States, of Serbia, Ukraine, and Georgia, should be analyzed in a new register of "regime change," different from the European tradition of revolution and counter-revolution.

Revolution made modern Europe. But what about the rest of the world? *Meiji Ishin*, the opening of Japanese modernity, was certainly not a revolution, but nor was it a counter-revolutionary "restoration." The Meiji restoration started a reactive modernization from above, by a part of the historical indigenous elite. It was eminently successful, and provided a model to China, Siam, and, especially after 1905 and the Japanese defeat of Russia, to the Ottoman Empire. Bluntly put, Japan is the most successful example of modernity without revolution.

The Americas made their revolutions against their decadent, corrupt, and tyrannical European mother countries. But the settler colonies also asserted themselves against other external enemies of civilization and modernity, the natives, the slaves, the ex-slaves, and the *castas* (mixed blood). Brazil emerged out of no revolution, and the epic Mexican Revolution took place a century after independence, neither being part of nor igniting any hemispheric pattern of revolutions.

Anti-colonial armed struggles for liberation may often refer to themselves as revolutions. But set against a foreign enemy and fighting for national independence, they are very different, in their alignments and in their consequences, from the European kind of revolutions. And so are post-colonial civil wars, like those of Angola and Mozambique. Nowhere in sub-Saharan Africa have you had a social revolution. There were Arab revolutions, in 1952 in Egypt and in 1958 in Iraq, both militarily overdetermined, but clearly inaugurating profound social transformations, soon to lose their dynamic, though. Iran was modernized from above, by the power of the shahs. The Islamic revolution is singularly unique, as a successful religious revolution in modern times. It is also unique in combining an anti-modernist culture with a social, anti-oligarchic program, of which not that much materialized but enough to qualify the event as a revolution rather than a counter-revolution.

India and South Asia had no revolution, and neither an anti-colonial nor a post-colonial war – albeit a huge amount of communal violence. Indonesia did have an anti-colonial war, and some sort of a very bloody counter-revolution in 1965, but nothing really of a revolution.

The Chinese communists were defeated in their first attempts at revolution. They succeeded largely as fighters for national independence against the Japanese. While they certainly included a heavy revolutionary component, today it seems that the main legacy of Chinese communism is national independence and national strength.

By way of conclusion, it is fair to say that revolution made European modernity. Revolution set the course of the Americas, though the significance of revolution to modernity in Latin America is, at least, ambiguous. But it did not make modern Asia and modern Africa. Revolution turns out to be a surprisingly Eurocentric concept.

A completely different question pertains to the causal weight and efficacy of revolution with respect to the sociology of modern societies.

Here, European history has already muddied ideological waters. In spite of its politically and ideologically ambiguous seventeenth-century revolutions, Britain was clearly leading modern economic transformation and the Industrial Revolution. Parliamentary democracy with universal suffrage was pioneered in reformist Norway. In the nineteenth century and up to 1933, Germany came to lead in scientific advances, while Paris was the aesthetic "capital of the nineteenth century." In terms of gender relations, France was one of the end-lights of Europe. Marital equality took 65 years to travel from Stockholm to Paris.

In brief, modern European history showed the multiple paths of social change, and that the steep revolutionary *piste* was by no means the most rapid one to social change. The communist assault on patriarchy never maintained necessary perseverance, and its outcome fell far short of that of the much milder reform climate of Scandinavia. Nevertheless, after the implosion of economic planning and after the re-privatization of property, the curtailment of historical Eastern European and of Eastern Asian patriarchy remains arguably the most important, enduring legacy of communism.

The modern world was "made" in different ways. Along the lanes of science, art, economics, and politics, "revolution" had a very different impact.

As many authors of this volume predict, the world is most likely to see revolutionary regime change also in the future. But whether there will be revolutions making a new world is much more uncertain. Most of us probably agree that another world is possible as well as desirable. If it will become a reality, and if so how, are questions beyond the competence of social science.

1 Revolution in the making of the modern world

John Foran, David Lane, and Andreja Zivkovic

The modern era of revolutions, in the sense of "rapid basic transformations of a society's state and class structures ... accompanied and in part carried through by class-based revolts from below" (Skocpol 1979: 4), is widely considered to be over. Postmodernity, it is argued, is defined by an incredulity towards the metanarratives of progress and class characteristics of modernity (Lyotard 1984). With the emergence of post-industrial societies, the class-based forms of organization of traditional labor movements are held to have been replaced by various forms of identity politics, encapsulated in the idea of new social movements. In the era of globalization, the very concept of revolution as a struggle over state power appears redundant as global flows of money, power, and information increasingly outflank and bypass the nation-state. In Fukuyama's (1992) notorious formulation, we have reached "the end of history;" which is to say, there is no future beyond liberal-democratic Western capitalism.

The end of revolution? Well, no not quite. For in response to the convulsions of neo-liberal globalization and to the recrudescence of empire, we have seen the flowering of new concepts and models of revolution, taking their cue from the "new social subjects" and identities of the "Information Age." The most celebrated is Michael Hardt and Antonio Negri's concept of the multitude (Hardt and Negri 2000, 2004). In their view, revolution no longer involves the seizure of state power, but is rather the expression of the autonomy of a network of productive singularities. The concept of the multitude represents a central reference point in contemporary debate on the future of revolution. We are delighted to include in this collection an original contribution by Antonio Negri in which he directly responds to criticisms of the concept of the multitude from Etienne Balibar, Ernesto Laclau, and Francis Fukuyama and clarifies what he means by "revolution in a postmodern age;" a contribution that is hotly debated in the discussion of the future of revolution in this volume.

Even since Marx, the contradictions, the promise and horrors, of capitalist modernity, and the wars and revolutions brought about in the course of its extension across the globe, have been at the center of discussion of the origins and outcomes of modern revolutions. A classic literature on revolution, starting with Barrington Moore (1966) and culminating in Theda Skocpol (1979), sought to relate it to national and international modernization processes, focusing in particular on the revolutionary impact of interstate conflict and the resistance of traditional agrarian structures to state modernization. The time has come to re-examine this relationship under the lenses of modernity and postmodernity, casting it in broader perspective and speculating into the future. In particular, the contributors to this collection examine the degree to which the traditional narratives of progress characteristic of modernity can explain both modern revolutions and the future of revolution.

Another hallmark of the traditional approach, from Marx (Marx and Engels 1975–2005: XI, 99–197) to Eric Wolf (1969) and Jeffery Paige (1975), is the centrality of class in explaining revolutionary trajectories. The *Communist Manifesto* famously declares that the "history of all hitherto existing society is the history of the class struggle," a struggle that results "either in the revolutionary re-constitution of society at large, or in the common ruin of the contending classes" (Marx and Engels 1975–2005: VI, 482). More recent scholarship has widened discussion to include the question of social identities, especially in relation to the ideas of postmodernism and the post-industrial society. The significance of new perspectives, which center on gender, culture, ethnic group, nation, religion, and race, to the study of revolution is a major theme of this collection.

The attempt to relate revolution to world-wide processes of change has its roots in Marx's theory of capitalist development, which holds that capitalism "compels all nations, on pain of extinction, to adopt the bourgeois mode of production; it compels them to introduce what it calls civilization into their midst, i.e., to become bourgeois themselves. In one word, it creates a world after its own image" (Marx and Engels 1975–2005: VI, 488). Subsequently, theorists as diverse as Lenin (1964: XXII, 185–304), Trotsky (1967), Skocpol (1979) and Halliday (1999) have seen global processes of economic and military competition between states as central to revolutionary transformation. Since the 1990s, scholars have been heatedly debating the degree to which globalization is the best rubric for capturing the international dimension of revolution (see the perspectives collected in Foran 2003a), and this is a third axis of interpretation we will explore in this collection.

Modernity

The concept of modernity may be understood as a philosophical idea, as a particular type of society, or as a mode of experience (Callinicos 1999). The philosophical idea of modernity emerged at the end of the eighteenth century as a result of a change in the notion of historical time. Previously the past provided the total horizon of the future: beliefs, institutions, and practices were legitimated according to traditional models and principles.

Under the impact of the scientific revolution of the seventeenth century, the Enlightenment identified the application of scientific knowledge to nature and society with the progress of the human spirit towards greater rationality and better organization of both the social and natural worlds.

This "modern" idea of historical progress prepared the ground for the concept of revolution. But it was the French Revolution that announced the modern concept of revolution as novelty, breaking with the predetermined order of things, blasting open "a new horizon of expectations," leading forward to an unknown future (Koselleck 1985: 46). Revolution had come to signify both stages within a wider historical process of development and events in which people could participate as agents of progressive transformation. The scene was set for a world history in which the philosophical idea of modernity, the promise of emancipation from arbitrary authority, collided not only against the survivals of traditional authority, but increasingly against the relations of inequality and oppression inherent in particular forms of modern authority, as oppressed groups engaged in struggles for their own emancipation. Henceforth, historical progress would be linked to political revolutions whose objective is the social emancipation of all people, that is, social revolution.

Although drawing on the Enlightenment's idea of historical progress, the concept of modernity, considered as a historical stage in the development of human society, in the sense of industrial society, only fully emerged in the wake of the dual industrial and political revolutions at the end of the eighteenth century. The relentless, dynamic, and convulsive process of global development characteristic of modernity gives rise to a distinctively modern mode of experience:

> Constant revolutionizing of production, uninterrupted disturbance of all social conditions, everlasting uncertainty and agitation distinguish the bourgeois epoch from all earlier ones. All fixed, fast-frozen relations with their train of ancient and venerable prejudices and opinions, are swept away, all new-formed ones become antiquated before they can ossify. All that is solid melts into air, all that is holy is profaned and man is at last compelled to face with sober senses, his real conditions of life and his relations with his kind.
>
> (Marx and Engels 1975–2005: VI, 487)

As such modernity is infused by a diffuse but protean expectation of revolution, which colonizes everyday life, ranging from social and political upheavals to fundamental scientific or technical innovations. In this way modernity "refers us to our modern circumstances ... as an era of revolutions ... [and] a direct experience ... that can be subsumed under the concept of revolution" (Koselleck 1985: 40).

The three registers of modernity – as philosophical idea, type of society, or mode of experience – are not equivalent to one another (Callinicos 1999).

For Marx, it is the dynamic and destabilizing character of *capitalist development* that gives rise to the peculiar *experience* of modernity. By contrast, theorists of *industrial society* tend to see modernity as the type of society that realizes the philosophical idea of modernity (of scientific rationality and technological progress). In the academic study of revolutions the view of modernity as industrial society is reflected in the paradigm of modernization, according to which revolutions represent decisive episodes in the modernization of agrarian states and in the transition to industrial society. For Marxists, the concept of revolution cannot be limited to the birth of the modern, nor to the belated modernization of agrarian states. In fact, it is precisely the *experience* of the gap between the philosophical idea of modernity and its limited historical realization in the types of society created by capitalist modernization that creates the conditions for social revolutions beyond the capitalist mode of production.

For Marx, socialism is the "revolution's declaration of permanence;" in line with the philosophical idea of modernity, all historical expressions of revolution are considered finite and a pretext for further enlightenment. As Krishan Kumar notes in this volume, revolution forms a critical tradition of thought and experience within which the degeneration of the Russian Revolution and the disasters of the Chinese Revolution can be subjected to critique under the aegis of the idea of modernity and potentially redeemed by means of further revolutionary efforts. Today the idea that revolutions are "locomotives of history" (Marx), leading to more rational social worlds, has fallen under deep suspicion. After all, the postmodern condition demands that we express incredulity to the metanarratives characteristic of the modern.

In a similar vein, the contributors to this volume present important challenges to revolutionary concepts of progress. For John Dunn, revolution poses in their most acute form two basic questions in political understanding: how free are we to determine our fate as a political community and how far can we understand our political actions? Dunn charges social theory, in particular Marxism, with having failed to predict political agency or provide criteria for the exercise of political judgment, and is skeptical whether any theory of revolution can successfully marry these distinct registers, factual and normative.

Göran Therborn's foreword argues that the paths to progress and modernity in Europe were multiple, and that the revolutionary path was not necessarily the most rapid or deepest in extending modernity's promise of a universal right to shape one's political destiny. The convulsions of capitalist modernity opened up multiple processes of transformation; and revolution generated its cousin, reform, as part of a general impulse to plan the future.

The question of modernity and progress is also at the center of discussions of the 1989 events in Eastern Europe and the "Islamic Revolution," from Iran in 1979 to the present. Harald Wydra argues that 1989 breaks with the entire tradition of revolution since 1789 in that it does not present itself as a model for the future and enunciates no new political principle. Yet, the revolutions of 1989 inaugurated a new turn in the sense that revolution as regime change may occur as the result of a non-violent process of resistance. Nevertheless, the Eastern European revolutions of 1989 remain within the conceptual space of the modern concept of revolution, as progressive transformations extending the universal right to politics promised by modernity.

Michel Foucault, as Asef Bayat's chapter reminds us, described the Iranian Revolution as "the first postmodern revolution of our time," a revolution against universalizing secular modernity in the name of the restoration of "the golden age of Islam." By contrast, Bayat argues that the Iranian Revolution, and radical Islamicist movements more generally, are not the expression of some imaginary anti-modernism on the part of so-called "traditional classes," but rather reflect the "costs of the modern," in particular the exclusion of the middle classes from the opportunities of modernity.

Modernity as a type of society is most commonly identified with industrial society. It has been argued by theorists as diverse as Aron (1962), Bell (1973), Touraine (1971), Castells (1996, 1997, 1998), and Negri (Hardt and Negri 2000, 2004) that we have moved to a post-industrial society where scientific knowledge is the basis of wealth and social power. This view of modernity then easily lends itself to a modernization theory proper in which the forms of rationalization and system differentiation characteristic of Western modernity become a universal model that all societies are destined to follow. This line of argument limits revolution to societies undergoing the transition to modernity, and concludes that the post-industrial or postmodern society ends the modern era of revolutions, in particular revolutions as struggles for state power or as socialist revolutions. The postmodern revolution, on the one hand, loses its political referent and becomes coextensive with the technological revolution of the "Information Age," as in Negri's chapter in this collection; on the other hand, it becomes a movement that seeks to evade the oppressive forms of instrumental rationality and authority characteristic of modernity.

As John Foran notes in his chapter, in opposition to the modern concept of revolution as a violent struggle for state power, the "postmodern revolution" is said to be non-violent, and to involve "changing the world without taking power" (Holloway 2002). Its hallmarks include the bypassing of the centralized structures of the nation-state by decentralized networks, a shift of organizational axis from ideology to identity or community, and from the national to the global. For Negri, the informational networks of post-industrial society generate a new subject, the multitude, which produces not only goods and services, but also knowledge, communication and affects, that is, social life itself. Revolution, if it can be termed as such, is now coextensive with the production of life by this communicative, cooperative network. In this light, revolution is now no longer an event delimited in time and space that is identical with the destruction and reconstruction of state power, but an indefinite and indeterminate movement to undermine the state by seeking autonomy from it. Some (though not Foran or Negri) may well consider that what we have here is not so much a new concept of revolution as the internal disintegration of the concept of revolution, which now seems to bear a suspicious resemblance to the concepts of evolution and reform.

For Kumar, the fragmentation and privatization of everyday life through modern technology and the commodification of space characteristic of post-industrial society undermine collective identities and the capacity to undertake collective action. By contrast, Andreja Zivkovic and John Hogan point to the contradictory *potentialities* of the new information communication technologies (ICTs). The decentralized and distributed character of ICT networks potentially enable social actors to overcome spatial dispersal and fragmentation and, more generally, time-space poverty through asynchronous communication; and in this way evade the spaces of enclosure of the territorial and bureaucratic "iron cages" (the nation-state, the capitalist firm, bureaucratized labor movements, and political parties) characteristic of modernity. From this standpoint, revolution in the information age turns out to involve not so much a new concept of revolution (autonomy) or a new informational subject (multitude), but new time-space dimensions of collective action that facilitate the construction of revolutionary subjects striving to "complete" modernity, to fulfill its promise.

Identities

The second concept which runs through the book is that of identity. With the much trumpeted "death of class" in Western industrialized societies, contemporary social science has undergone a revolution in the understanding of identities. As noted by John Dunn, traditional scholars of revolution and social change such as Barrington Moore, Seymour Lipset, and E.P. Thompson, as well as Lenin, gave social class the central explanatory role. The classical revolutions in England, France, and Russia were *social* revolutions of one kind or another, in which, essentially, a rising class replaced an incumbent one through revolutionary struggle. By contrast, social identity refers to the way that people classify or associate themselves with others in the formation of social groups and collectivities. Identity, in this sense, is a primarily discursive or cultural construct, to be counterposed to social class as an objective patterning of social inequalities and life chances. Class now loses its explanatory primacy in determining struggles over the allocation of power and resources in society, and is trumped by and dissolves into identity; becoming merely one of a multiplicity of irreducible, social identities.

In this way, class effectively disappears from the study of collective identity and political action. The analytical focus of "group struggles" is now on "race, ethnicity, nationality, gender and sexuality" (Davis 2000: 4), and religion. The more traditional sources of group identity, R.G. Dunn contends, have shifted significantly in the "postmodern" age from the "social sphere" to the "realm of culture" (2000: 124). The commodification of culture "destabilizes" the individual and leads to "a disintegration of integrated, productivist roles as the subject becomes fragmented through new regimes of consumption and leisure" (R.G. Dunn 2000: 115). Social class differences, determined by occupation and wealth, have been diminished and replaced by lifestyle distinctions formed by market-driven consumption. The resulting "new social movements" – for example, the women's movement and the environmental movement – represent a shift from economic concerns and from official politics to questions of lifestyle, identity, and culture.

Whereas the "ruling class" in traditional analysis has been formed from social classes (nobility, bourgeoisie), analysis has now shifted to elites as movers of system change. Rather than revolution, "system" or "regime change" are the processes by which elites maintain their power. Domestic elite conflict, enabled by the weakness of incumbent state leaders, leads to "within system" challenges to the state structure. Sometimes, though not always, popular support is courted by ascendant elites. In other cases (in the Middle East, and the "colored" revolutions in Georgia in 2003, Ukraine in 2004, and Kyrgyzstan in 2005), the elites are exogenous interests collaborating with internal class or elite allies. The implications are clear: no significant *class* changes are necessary following regime change (Mau and Starodubrovskaya 2001: 332). Reforms, or "regime change" engineered by Western elites, lead not to revolution or the substitution of one class by another, but to the removal of one set of elites by another.

The writers in this collection reflect these intellectual divisions. Eric Selbin, in line with the postmodern turn from class to the consideration of identities as discursively constructed *narratives*, argues that stories are the "form, even the primary form of socio-political struggle." The narrating of revolutionary identity – how people use memory, history, and symbol to make sense of their circumstances – is seen as indispensable to the undertaking – and making – of revolutions. Similarly, John Foran privileges culture, in particular discursively constructed "political cultures of opposition," in the explanation of revolutions. Revolutions require the articulation and organization of subjective emotions, popular idioms, and political ideologies into popular and broad-based political cultures of opposition that can challenge for power.

For Krishan Kumar, the era of classical, class-based social revolution is over. In a post-industrial society that fragments and privatizes collective identities, the idea of a "world revolution" made by some type of "global proletariat" is pure fantasy. Instead he finds hope in the new social movements, in particular environmental or ecological movements linked to alter-globalization movements. Valentine Moghadam's chapter challenges the postmodern model of new social movements, each expressing closed, incommunicable "cultural" identities based on irreducibly different forms of oppression. The rise of the alter-globalization movement represents precisely an overcoming of relativistic concepts of "difference" or "identity" as a result of the shared experience and rejection of the generalization and extension of capitalist relations to all social, geographical, natural, and biological space. Thus, for the new transnational feminist movement, "each form of collective action is inevitably gendered, in terms of patterns of participation and leadership, concepts of masculinity and femininity, and notions of women's place and men's privileges." But, equally, it proclaims that women's emancipation cannot be divorced from a general revolution by all the oppressed against neo-liberal capitalism.

Bayat, Callinicos, Lane, and Lee and Selden still find traditional class analysis a major explanatory and normative variable. Alex Callinicos notes the social changes in the modern world which now "deprive the concept of a revolutionary subject – of the collective agent capable of carrying through systemic transformation – of any obvious class referent." However, he goes on to point to the restructuring of capitalism in a global context, involving the tendential planetary extension of wage-labor. Here he sees an emergent global working class as the "social basis from which any new revolutionary subject might be formed," though he concedes that the "objective" working class is far from having a collective identity. The transition from socio-economic "class-in-itself" to revolutionary "class-for-itself" has yet to be broached.

Asef Bayat utilizes class in his analysis of the Islamist revolutions. He sees the middle classes as playing a leading role in "all major social movements and revolutions in the region." The failure of secular, nationalist revolutions, the intensification of political oppression, coupled with the deepening of social inequalities following the turn to neo-liberalism, increasingly led sections of the middle classes to identify with revolutionary Islam. Bayat here rejects the kind of essentialist or hypostatized understanding of religious identity that is arguably implicit in postmodernism. Islam is neither inherently revolutionary or reactionary, democratic or undemocratic but is rather the complex and changing artifact of Muslim communities experiencing both the opportunities and costs of capitalist modernization.

While Ching Kwan Lee and Mark Selden acknowledge the importance of class, they note the fragmentation and repression of popular movements which has taken place in China during its period of global market integration. While the conditions of class polarization grow under the transition to the market, revolutionary consciousness, or class identity is missing and "the rhetoric of resistance has shifted from a revolutionary language of class and class struggle to a liberal, contractual paradigm of legal rights and citizenship." In his discussion of the societies of central and Eastern Europe, David Lane contends that the transformations of the post-communist states should be analyzed as a revolutionary process promoted by and favoring class interests. Whilst conceding that other forms of self-identification (such as nationality) may be operating concurrently with class, he argues that the transformation of the post-communist countries has involved a revolutionary process in which endogenous and exogenous class forces have played a decisive role. These endogenous forces were sustained and led by an alliance between domestic reformist elites and international political elites who played a second major role in the collapse and, subsequently, in the transition to capitalism.

Antonio Negri seeks to reformulate class analysis. The multitude is a "class concept," but one that differs from the Marxist concept of the proletariat in both "extension" and "intension." With the rise of "immaterial labor," the working subject is exploited not simply in the factory, but at the scale of society as a whole. The multitude is a totality of multiple singularities in which differences coexist without being subsumed in "the common" material and social life that it creates. For Negri, this means that, operating on the "plane of immanence," the multitude becomes self-valorizing; that is, it already constitutes a revolutionary subject that has broken free from capitalism. The multitude thus transcends the framework of Marxist concepts of class and revolution: as a self-governing apparatus it is beyond the terms of class "in itself/for itself," socio-economic "contradiction/antagonism" and political "immediacy/mediation."

Andreja Zivkovic and John Hogan reject the idea that the decentralized, network society simply dissolves the traditional spaces and places of revolutionary politics into flows of information, money, and power. Their work points to the potentiality of decentralized ICT networks for resistance to the *really existing* territorial and organizational power structures of modernity. New time-space dimensions of collective action are brought into view that magnify the transformative power of social actors, thus contributing to the *formation* of revolutionary *class* subjects.

Globalization and the future of revolution

Many of the chapters in this book draw our attention to globalization as a factor conditioning the revolutionary process. By globalization we refer to (1) the new arrangements of production, now truly transnational, wherein goods and services can be produced in multiple locations, on tight deadlines, and delivered over great distances, (2) the development of communications and mass media that drive large sectors of the global economy and concurrently generate new needs and wants, (3) the speed and volume of financial transactions, and the volatility of the financial markets, (4) changes in the workforce and workplace, with sharp polarizations of class, race, nation, and gender, both between and within societies, (5) a new transnational elite or capitalist class, less rooted in national contexts, in command of the huge international corporations that dominate the world economy, (6) the rise of global regulating agencies like the World Trade Organization and the International Monetary Fund (IMF) which operate beyond the reach of national governments, (7) the emergence of such pressing global ecological threats as global warming, the accelerating depletion of easily extracted fossil fuels, and the adverse consequences of the biogenetic revolutions in food and medicines, and (8) the transformation of the bipolar antagonisms of the cold war into the opening of a new period of conflict defined by the militarized foreign policy of the United States and its aggressive search for global hegemony based on its construction of a "war on terror."

Many of our contributors address the question of how these intertwined phenomena influence the phenomenon of revolution in the modern world. In terms of the economic impact of globalization, the chapter on China by Ching Kwan Lee and Mark Selden portrays the dramatic transformation of a once revolutionary society from socialist to market driven in the last twenty-five years. Noting both class polarization across rural and urban areas, and the imbalance of power between the working classes and the ranks of officialdom (who overlap with the new economic elite), they see a potential for future political upheaval if these trends go unchecked, though one that is more likely to take the form of a struggle for democracy than a class-based revolution.

In his chapter on the Middle East, Asef Bayat suggests that globalization brings with it negotiation as well as confrontation, and that the realities of inequality do not automatically produce the capacity to redress them. Since the armed insurgencies offer little positive by way of social programs, a trend to non-violent Islamic reformism is likely to result, and, ironically, may lead to deeper social change. The future, he boldly concludes, may be democratic in the Middle East.

Democratic revolution in the Middle East has been proclaimed as the strategic doctrine of the U.S. empire. The neo-conservative doctrine of exporting "democratic revolution" by force of arms reminds us that the global extension of capitalist modernity, in the form of principles of popular sovereignty and national self-determination, was bound up with the extension of and resistance to the European and North American empires.

Robin Blackburn's chapter reconstructs the complex historical relations between revolution and empire. Societies that had been internally transformed by bourgeois revolution "thereby acquired social capacities that made economic, cultural, and territorial expansion possible ... If colonialism had a partly revolutionary impulse, it also invariably marked the limits of the transformative power of revolution, the geographical and social spaces that the bourgeois revolution could not penetrate." Colonialism brought highly uneven economic development, even de-industrialization in India and China, and tended to reinforce existing or institute new forms of exploitation and oppression, thus creating the foundations of anti-colonial national revolution. In Blackburn's view, the "democratic" U.S. occupation of Iraq is caught in the same contradiction. As in the colonial past, the furies of anti-colonial nationalism will compel the United States to introduce decolonization as a form of indirect imperial control. An unstoppable train of events has been set in motion that will unleash democratic revolution against imperial "revolution" in the Muslim world.

As Alex Callinicos points out, democratic revolution on the model of 1989, involving popular mobilization to achieve non-violent regime change and liberal market reform, has also been "distilled into a technique of imperial rule." In the "colored" revolutions in Georgia, Ukraine, and Kyrgyzstan, U.S. aid channeled to oppositional elites via a network of foundations and NGOs "helped effect political changes congenial to Washington." In this respect the global U.S. "war on terror" has unleashed a variety of social movements that are hard to classify as revolutionary in the traditional sense. Another – certainly the most dramatic contemporary expression of this, the rise of revolutionary terrorism, is considered in Jeff Goodwin's chapter, with particular reference to Al Qaeda.

The paroxysms of armed, neo-liberal globalization inevitably draw us to consider the future through the lens of revolution. Alex Callinicos poses the question explicitly in his title: "What does revolution mean in the twenty-first century?" Starting from the transnational structural context of the classical revolutions – the capitalist world economy and modern state system – Callinicos examines claims that globalization, with its qualitative increase in global economic integration, precludes the possibility of revolutionary transformation at the level of the nation-state (as implied by Hardt and Negri's concept of "Empire" as networked world capitalism). Rejecting such claims as exaggerated, he argues that "as long as global economic and political processes remain subject to what Trotsky called the law of uneven and combined development – which means certainly as long as capitalism exists," a space will also persist for national projects that might become revolutionary (as demonstrated by Chávez's Bolivarian Revolution).

The dream of moving to a global struggle, as theorized by Hardt and Negri, begs the question of the *strategy* required to realize the power of the global dispossessed. If the political economy of globalization has produced the largest working class in world history, under what conditions might that vast but unorganized group come to articulate a common revolutionary project? Callinicos sees glimmers of this at different points in the alter-globalization movement's set of projects – the protests in France in 1995 and 2006, the 2003 world demonstrations against the war in Iraq, the explosions in Bolivia in 2003 and 2005 that later brought Evo Morales to power.

On the other hand, a similar list of events is claimed for revolutionary projects other than that of classical Marxism and its universal class, the global proletariat. Antonio Negri and John Foran, to differing degrees, find the seeds of new modes of struggle in the shifting political cultures and practices that animate the Zapatista insurgency, the left-of-center governments that are coming to power in much of Latin America, and the global justice movement's attempts to translate these visions into a global network of radical social change. As Foran acknowledges, these movements are themselves divided over the key problem of modern revolutionary strategy, namely that of state power. Projects for autonomy and "changing the world without taking power" vie and conflict with projects that see the state as a mechanism and platform for the *reform* of the global system. It is clear that the question of the global advance of revolutionary movements has by no means escaped the familiar alternative inscribed in the narratives of progress of modernity – the problem of reform or revolution.

With respect to the problem of global revolutionary coordination, Andreja Zivkovic and John Hogan draw attention to the global space opened by new ICTs, a terrain of interaction that permits the global dispossessed, those traditionally poorly resourced, marginalized, excluded, and silenced, to organize and shape history. It is argued that the case of the UK Liverpool dockers' dispute of 1995–1998 demonstrates the new global powers of organizing, auditing, indexing, and accounting, diffused in ever more popular forms through the new distributed technologies of communication.

Taking his cue from the rise of a global justice movement, Fred Halliday examines the legacy of communist ideals of revolutionary internationalism for the future of revolution. In his view, the failures and perversions of communist internationalism in the twentieth century cannot be explained according to the dogma that asserts the primacy of nationalist over internationalist forms of social identification. Rather than nationalism overwhelming internationalism, the revolutionary state itself nationalized internationalism. Overcoming this problem requires more than pious professions of faith in the revolutionary mission of a "global multitude," or in "global civil society." It demands a confrontation with the problem of the modern interstate system, the traditional forge of revolution as "international civil war."

Halliday reminds us that, notwithstanding the neo-liberal orthodoxy, globalization has not marked a decisive break in the territorial and state-centered logic of modernity. In fact, 9/11 has revealed a new, post-cold war imperialist world order of economic and military competition between states. In this case, Lenin's perspective on imperialism as an "epoch of wars and revolutions" may once again represent a possible terrain on which the future of revolution is played out. From a different perspective, Negri also argues that the central problem for the new revolutionary subjects is that of counter-revolutionary imperialist war. But this means that it is not possible for the movements to simply assert their "autonomy" from the "horror without end" of state violence (Lenin 1964: XXII, 103–7), midwife to a "heavy artillery" of commodities that batter down all Chinese walls (Marx and Engels 1975–2005: VI, 488). If this is correct, the modern concept of revolution as the conquest of state power would still remain the unsurpassable and interminable horizon of futures beyond capitalism.

The authors in this collection for the most part suggest the classical concept of revolution no longer has any stake in our collective future. For John Dunn, revolution may well have a future in terms of the continued salience of regime collapse, but not of regime reconstruction as understood within the 1789–1917 tradition of revolution; nor in terms of a realistic political hope of an alternative and better collective future. But is this just another way of saying that we are witness to a transitional period in which the traditional terms of reference have collapsed or become reversed? As Alex Callinicos notes, "reform," traditionally designating collective projects to regulate capitalism, now signifies the limitless extension of capitalist social relations; while "revolution," involving the idea of social subjects taking control over their collective destinies, today degenerates into an imperial technique for imposing liberal, market capitalism by force of arms. For Krishan Kumar, this indeterminacy in the meaning of revolution, as the classical revolutions recede from cultural memory and become pure history, means that we cannot even be sure that we are dealing with the same phenomena any more.

It is here that John Dunn sounds a note of caution, lest we be tempted to throw the baby of revolution out with the bathwater of the past of the classical revolutions. Even if the idea that the era of revolutions is over is correct this does not show "how closed the framework of collective life has become anywhere at all." Precisely because we live in an era in which "all that is solid melts into air, all that is holy is profaned" in the fires of armed capitalist globalization, in which revolutionary movements have re-emerged at a new global level, magnified by the new ICTs and informed by new concepts of revolution – it would seem foolish to write off the idea of revolutions as sudden, violent, and fundamental transformations of social and political orders. The debate on revolution, with its promise of healing the wounds of modernity by means of "radicalized Enlightenment" (Habermas 1986: 158), is far from over.

Part I

From 1789 to 1989

Revolutions in Europe

2 Understanding revolution

John Dunn

In a few short months, in the year 1789, the people of France set their stamp ineffaceably on a political idea which has loomed over the history of the world ever since. Throughout its life, it has been an idea which prompted bitter disagreement on its political merits. But today, for the first time in more than two centuries, opinion divides sharply over whether or not it is a political idea whose time has now gone forever. Depending on just what we take the idea itself to mean, we are bound to continue to disagree vividly with one another on the answers we give to that question. What should be beyond dispute is that the answer matters – and matters not just as the prospective extinction of their very own endangered species might matter to a zoologist, through the prospective loss of an extant professional subject matter, but because the idea itself carries a heavy weight of political significance. There are doubtless some perspectives on politics from which that judgment could be coherently denied. But the least that one could say about them is that they would have to be very *eccentric* perspectives, as well as robustly indifferent to the texture of political experience: not just anti-Romantic (which might be a political virtue), but hardened or disabused enough to view the political hopes and fears, the pride and suffering of immense numbers of human beings over many decades with relaxed indifference or open contempt. To anyone whose experience of politics is more direct and importunate, it is scarcely a perspective they could actively entertain on their own behalf. They could *think* about it, of course, and even register potential cognitive advantages of economy or precision it might offer. What they could not do is to adopt it for their own.

The very idea of a science of the social was largely shaped by the impulse to take the measure of revolution as a collective experience: fathom its causes, rein in its formidable powers of destruction, and discipline collective judgment on how to seize the opportunities and forestall the dangers which it threatened (Nisbet 1970; Hawthorn 1976). From Pierre-Louis Roederer's lectures in the summer of 1793 on the *science sociale* (Roederer 1853–1858, VIII: 129–305; Scurr 2000, 2004) to Francois Furet's decades long campaign to lay the ghost of 1789 (Furet 1981; Furet 1999) and Francis Fukuyama's sprightly invocation to bring its "history to an end" (Fukuyama 1992), aspirants to subject political life to the rubric of professionalized cognition and aspirants to change the human world forever on the vastest scale have shared an involuntary common subject matter. For each of these markedly discrepant groupings, it has long been a very nice judgment when it was wise to let go, to recognize a form of thought grown old or a style of political aspiration which can be sustained further only in utter cynicism. Neither tragedy nor farce is ever far from the human condition. Each has run through this history prominently, marking it indelibly throughout. It has always been hard to judge the balance between tragedy and farce at all accurately, even in retrospect. But it is hard today to resist the suspicion that over the last few decades the balance has shifted decisively in favor of farce.

Some venerable perspectives on revolution will be unaffected by that shift. One, which has been very actively entertained ever since 1789 is a realist focus on state threatening, state defense, state destruction, state refashioning or even recreation. It was a perspective which long preceded the events which turned this late eighteenth-century French word into a global political cynosure, and altered its meaning dramatically in doing so. What broke France's *ancien regime* was a cumulative fiscal predicament which it lacked the political capacity to escape, a predicament which itself arose from over a century of France's impressive global self-aggrandizement as a state (Sonenscher 1997). There was no better defined realist component of state jeopardy by the last quarter of the eighteenth century than the core logic of that predicament; and it had dominated the concerns of leading French statesmen for decades (Hont 2005; Brewer 1989). In that sense, nothing could be further from the truth than that France's great revolution was lightning from a clear sky. What was new in 1789 was the direct tie between this objectifying and instrumental perspective on the French state, its situation and capacities, with an uncontrollably extended interrogation of the population at large on just how it imagined and felt about its own relations with the state to which it was subjected. It was that abrupt conjunction, best expressed in the themes which run through Sieyès's three great pamphlets (Sieyès 2003; Forsyth 1987), which set the agenda of world politics for the next two centuries, and in terms which may (or may not) now have run their course.

Historians – many of them figures of remarkable historical insight, awesome scholarly command, and very considerable moral force – have pored over the months which led up to the fall of the *ancien regime* ever since. Politicians of varying vitality, scruple, and imaginative reach, have had to do so from the outset, extending their range of examples as the generations went by. More recently, the professionalized social sciences, sociology, political science, at the margins even economics, have chipped in their personal contributions. But it is striking how little cumulative success any of these epistemic competitors have had in licking this formidable subject matter obediently into shape. We are not collectively evidently any closer than we were in early 1790 to taking the measure of what was happening in France at that time; and our failure to do so is increasingly hard to distinguish from our more general failure to master our own political predicament: to see clearly what it really is, or make it what we could possibly wish it to be (Dunn 2000).

Revolution raises in the most acute and painful form the two most fundamental questions in political understanding: how free ever are we to shape our own lives together on the scale of a political community; and how far do we ever understand what we are doing in politics, or what in failing to act, we are contributing decisively to bringing about? Plainly these are not questions which revolution can help us to answer, however sanguine we might be over the net benefit, utilitarian or symbolic, which a particular revolution might contrive to provide to most of those whom it affects. The two most discouraging answers – that we are never free at all to shape our lives on the scale of a political community, and never have the blindest comprehension of what we are really doing in politics, let alone of the practical implications of what we are failing to do, are each hallowed themes of counter-revolutionary persuasion (Hirschman 1991), though it is hard to see why their implications should be any less dismaying for revolution's enemies than they plainly must be for its more devoted friends. From the judgment that politics and society are alike from an individual point of view – that they are fated, rather than opportunities for agency – nothing follows validly for what any of us has good reason to do, and not much even for what we have good reason to refrain from attempting to do. Politics and society, on the most banal understanding, give us all the opportunities for agency we ever have. There is no clear categorical boundary between our fates and the lives we contrive to live.

What made revolution, this hitherto less than charismatic word, such a potent presence in modern political history was the burden of relatively determinate political hope it carried for some (and the weight of fear for others which necessarily accompanied that hope): the hope, for those who needed a very different schedule of life chances from those which the *ancien régime* had dealt them, and the fear of those whose lives, as Talleyrand observed, were sweet enough already, and who could reasonably suspect that those lives would be changed into something distinctly less agreeable if revolution in any sense went through and lasted (cf. Staël 1819: I (1), 187). This defined a political battleground for prospective winners and losers which divided them fiercely by tastes and interests and expectations, and forced them to choose sides accordingly and fight hard on behalf of their own judgments, or prescind helplessly from that judgment and submit themselves instead unflinchingly to an apparently whimsical and often brutal fate. It also put a level of pressure on the distinction between tastes, interests, and expectations under which those load-bearing conceptual contrasts (the basis on which each of us puts whatever shape we do contrive to sustain onto our own lives as individuals) buckled and collapsed under the strain.

The political thinker who saw this most clearly, and from the outset, was Edmund Burke (Burke 1989); and if we accept nothing else at all from his existentially singular vision of politics, and we could hardly in good faith still espouse much of it, we should at least recognize that in this respect he was overwhelmingly right. Burke, of course, disbelieved in that burden of political hope with all the electrifying imaginative energy at his command. But what that visceral revulsion positioned him to see was something every bit as consequential for those who felt or feel quite differently: that there are terrible political risks, and savage political costs, to revolution conceived as a political option, a strategy for changing a political, social and even economic order by overthrowing and replacing it in open combat. For Burke, at best an ambivalent devotee of the *ancien regime* in France or even England, this insight carried a clear political moral: "This is to play a most desperate game" (Burke 1989: 233). As a political strategy, revolution so seen is a reckless gamble, and a gamble where no one concerned needs to play at all, and where it must always be true that other and drastically less reckless options lie quite readily to hand, at least for the regime and for its subjects considered as a whole, if not necessarily for any particular individual or grouping amongst them. This is a good deal more discerning about the downside risk of any attempt to reconstruct a society through the exercise of political power under the conditions of acute struggle, than it is about the prospects of enlightened political reform in any regime which stands much chance of crumbling under internal attack.

To see the space of modern politics as a continuing choice between revolution, reform, and a more or less stolid continuity has become the official liberal *weltanschauung*. Its guiding insight is to privilege, resolutely but not uncunningly, the reform option, in distant homage to Aristotle. These are the three possibilities. Which would *you* prefer? But for all its practiced slyness, it is less than illuminating as a gloss on the politics of anywhere in particular at any particular time. No potentially sovereign political unit, or prospectively self-sufficient site of social membership, in the era since Burke wrote, has credibly faced a real option at any given point between setting off on a wholly new path, devising, and adjusting in a neat and controlled manner to, a less malign and dysfunctional set of collective arrangements, or carrying on imperturbably in the old way. On that point at least Lenin's classical formula of "Left-wing Communism, an infantile disorder" was entirely correct: "Only when the *'lower classes' do not want* the old way, and when the 'upper classes' *cannot carry on in the old way* – only then can revolution triumph" (Lenin 1947: II, 621).

We can be quite certain that incumbent regimes will continue at intervals to prove unable to go on in the old way. If we take their serial failure to do so, the sequence of their collapses, as our criterion for the continuing pertinence of revolution in contemporary politics, this is a professional academic subject matter in little danger of imminent extinction. Indeed we can scarcely yet conceive a political world in which it does become extinct. Some of the more readily foreseeable collapses will have very large consequences, not least in the vicinity of the Persian Gulf. The liberal *weltanschauung* naturally offers no specific against such collapses – merely, in better or worse faith, its generic political recipe of enlightened reform, the adoption of the now canonical political and economic institutions and practices of the West by societies hitherto able to exclude at least the former. You can see that proposal as the shrunken residue of political hope, as a practical judgment on which the United States of America has mysteriously established a global intellectual property right which it does not hesitate to enforce, or as an essentially prevaricatory façade to a realist politics of practical subjection, indifferent to the fate of the great majority of human beings anywhere at all. You can also see it, more charitably and perhaps more accurately, just as a symptom of extreme cognitive confusion at what should be the very apex of unmistakably the most powerful state on earth. The political formula of electoral democracy proffered incontinently to Afghanistan, Iraq, and some components of Palestine is a particularly poignant current instance of the intellectual and practical instability of our current approaches (Dunn 2005). Compare the lapidary verdict of the battle-scarred Walid Jumblatt on the New Middle East: not Condoleezza Rice's, but "Darkness everywhere" (Wallis 2006: 6).

What we need to recognize here reaches well beyond the evident disarray of American grand strategy, or the blatant infelicity of a political format which has rendered *"après-moi le deluge!"* a principle of situational rationality in second-term American presidential politics. Above all it is the impact on how we should think the politics of revolution, of the deflation and partial deconstruction over the last few decades of any more expansive conception of political hope. One response to this dismaying outcome is to retreat into increasingly hermetic muttering, in the pretense that we can already see clearly how hope can be resuscitated (even if we do not care to disclose this clearly to anyone else). This is neither a novel nor an odd response to catastrophe. But it is scarcely impressive as a political program.

With the privilege of hindsight, it has proved to be a mistake to suppose that the weight of animosity an oppressed population feels towards its oppressors, even orchestrated by political entrepreneurs of the utmost acuity, dedication, nerve, and pertinacity, can transpose fluently into building an unmistakably superior form of collective life. The political imagery of righteous vengeance on the bad, old, and increasingly ineffectual is as evocative today as it has ever been. What has lost credibility, perhaps everywhere, and certainly in all societies which are not still dominated by one or other great-tradition religion, is the picture of a plainly better collective future, close at hand and readily within our grasp, which disposing of the bad and old will enable us to reach. You can put different names to this outcome. But you can only coherently *deny* it by conjuring up, and rendering fully credible, a proxy for the hope that has gone: by showing what that hope can now consist in, and why it is therefore epistemically reasonable to anticipate its arrival, whether promptly and universally, or with painful tardiness and all too sporadically across the world. It is easy enough today, as it has always been throughout the historical past, to pick out the weight of animosity towards incumbent regimes in very many settings. It remains easy enough to see why the majority of the world's living population should still view the terms which history has set to their lives as ugly and coercive in very many ways, and why they should hate the ugliness and resent the coercion enough to fight back sooner or later, as best they can. But the mimetic effect which has run through the history of revolution from 1789 until today needs something more than the impulse to punish to keep it alive. Retribution is one of the deeper seated of human impulses; but it remains a very poor strategy for molding the future to one's advantage.

You can, of course, see the history of revolution across time quite largely as a history of political defeat, in which after the first thrilling collapse of the old and bad, the truly good, or very best, has somehow lost out again and again to the distinctly less desirable, or even to goals and practices and social and economic forms every bit as objectionable as those which they replaced. But this is not a politically intelligent way in which to see it, since it casts the light in quite the wrong place. Much political defeat plainly is just a matter of misfortune or adverse circumstances, and some simply of clumsiness or feebleness on the part of the defeated. But the defeats that matter, especially the long series of parallel defeats which by now forms the dominant pattern of modern revolutionary experience, trace something quite different: the failure of the orientating beliefs of the political movements which have in due course lost. What was vitally wrong in these beliefs was their key causal judgment; and the site of that judgment was their synoptic conception of the basis on which to build evidently more eligible political, social, and economic orders within which to live together. Shorn of epistemically credible conceptions of that kind, the tradition of modern revolution itself cannot hope to go on in the old way.

The idea of a social science has always had pronounced weaknesses, issuing not merely from individual and remediable human limitations, but also from an unsteady and ineliminable oscillation between the sane and decent purpose of interpreting the human world the way it really is and the fantasy or pretension of viewing it quasi-magically from somewhere securely outside and above it. At its most impressive that idea has served admirably to inspire and organize the attempt to take the measure of this long history. But it cannot honestly be claimed that on this exacting terrain the idea of a social science has often appeared at its best. In terms of intellectual or even moral prudence there must be something to be said for social scientists in future choosing to bite off no more than they can sanely hope to chew. But that is a defensive and somewhat narcissistic verdict. Any view of social science as occasioned by challenge, and not merely emboldened by social complicity and industriously nurtured local consensus, must resist the idea of surrendering this battlefield to its temporary political victors and their acolytes. To see it simply as the site of an experience which is now over might prove a sophisticated and even an accurate assessment. What it could not prove is either a stimulus or an aid to judging seriously together how closed the framework of collective life has now become anywhere at all, let alone everywhere. To judge that, as human populations are obliged to continue to try to as best they can, this long painful history of misery, disappointment, folly, and betrayal must be seen steadily alongside its equally long history of courage, hope, daring, patience, and insight; and the two must be balanced accurately against one another. Historians can be as partisan as anyone else. But the greatest among them have long felt the challenge of that effort to balance; and the votaries of social science need to learn to feel it just as keenly.

If we look at the matter from that angle there can be few domains where the social sciences have failed as badly as they have in meeting the political challenge to improve our collective judgment not within routine politics but in the face of the undeniable perils and the always more elusive opportunities of acute political crisis. Over the last half century, under the rubric of social science, a number of very capable and instructive works of social science have focused on revolution more particularly and sought to learn cumulatively from doing so (Moore 1966, 1978; Skocpol 1979, 1992; Tilly 1978; Goldstone 1991; Mayer 2000; Goodwin 2001). None has sought to provide a coherent record over time of their own inquiry as a heuristic exercise in political judgment (cf. Dunn 1972; 1980; 1985: 68–118; 1989; 1990; 2003). This is an occasion for regret in itself. It would be especially perverse and regrettable to infer from it the futility of any such exercise in judgment or the inevitable frustration of every ambitious conception of political good (conclusions, it is worth noting, which also contradict one another quite explicitly).

The cognitive extremity of such judgments is more a matter of scale than it is of any special and intrinsic opacity in revolution as a subject matter. It comes out just as acutely in efforts to gauge the basis and solidity of contemporary American ascendancy in comparison with its historical predecessors (Porter 2006; James 2006; Maier 2006), as it did in the grandest Enlightenment texts which essayed a similar scale of judgment: Edward Gibbon's *Decline and Fall of the Roman Empire* and Adam Smith's *Inquiry into the Nature and Causes of the Wealth of Nations* (Gibbon 1994; Smith 1976). It is not that sociology, history, or political science have failed at a type of venture at which international political economy has since convincingly triumphed. No body of professionalized social, economic, or political cognition has plainly succeeded where the human scale and moment of what we need to understand is even remotely comparable.

There are several lessons to draw from this intellectual and practical record. One is the extreme undesirability of organizing attempts to understand politically important phenomena through protocols for validating the findings of inquiry, rather than through a sharpened focus on their political implications. The key to understanding politics is capturing political significance, not superimposing on political phenomena chosen for their tractability an illusory conception of analytic translucency (Dunn 2000). In the professional historiography of all major revolutions that purpose has at least been duly honored, and a great deal of illumination garnered along the way. But only one major political and intellectual tradition has sought to pull those many separate and often parochial historiographies together and read them systematically as a record of epochal and global political experience. Marxism has long been unmistakably a protagonist of these historiographies. In the last century and a half it has also entered lavishly and often with singular indiscretion into the histories they strove to record and understand. Within the mode of historiography it has frequently done at least as well as any rival at each of these tasks, and shaped the world view of elites across the globe by doing so. Where its contribution has proved comparatively disappointing, even set beside those of less frankly politicized versions of social science, has been in disentangling within its engagement allegiance and antipathy from causal belief. By now it seems clear that that failure is less an outcome of the understandable desire to evade political blame and pass it comprehensively on to the enemy than from a deep unclarity within the Marxist vision of politics itself about the causal weight to be assigned to political agency and political judgment as such. For well over half a century it accumulated a formidable scholastic repertoire for finessing this ambiguity, to complement the lengthy history of political confusion and indecision which had preceded it.

It is a lot to ask Marxism's surviving champions (few in their first youth) to go back and try to do better; but there would be considerably more than nostalgia to be won from making the trip back, and it is hard to see where else within the modern professional academy any other substantial grouping is likely to muster either the motivation or the capacity to do better. To do so would require courage, patience, and immense energy. It would also require an explicit foreswearing from the outset of the fideist element in Marxism: the presumption that entering the confession yields privileged insight into a superior and humanly accessible future on a basis which does not need to be (and perhaps cannot be) clearly explicated to anyone still outside it. It is always far easier in politics to judge what not to do than it ever can be to judge quite what should be done (Dunn 2000). Consider the rebuke of Mme de Montmorin, wife of the minister for foreign affairs, to the jubilant Germaine de Staël as the 1200 deputies to the Estates General processed through Versailles *en route* to Mass on the eve of their opening session: "*Vous avez tort de vous rejouir, il arrivera de ceci de grandes désastres à la France et à nous*" (Staël 1819: I (1), 187). In revolution this banal insight becomes of overwhelming urgency. For almost a century Marxists sought to distract others from the importance of this inconvenient asymmetry; and even the sharpest of them assuredly contrived to confuse themselves quite badly by doing so. We shall never master the political lessons of revolution unless we can own up frankly to our shared political and social incapacity for precognition, and most of all over what most deeply matters to us. Very early in its modern history a dashing revolutionary leader offered a striking recipe for closing the gap: *"De l'audace, de l'audace, toujours de l'audace"* (Danton 1910: 52). Lenin himself took it up in suitably Napoleonic translation: *"on s'engage, et puis on voit."* But no revolutionary has made a secure cognitive advance in this respect on Georges Danton, and his recipe remains grimly insufficient.

Turning more concretely towards the future (and leaving the social sciences firmly behind) two large questions arise directly from the history of modern revolution, whether or not the grand optimistic strand which runs through that experience is now definitively over. One is a question of regime vulnerability, and the prospects for reconstituting for the better the regimes that go down. Regime change is going to go on, however unlikely it may be to do so on terms dictated from the White House, let alone on bases remotely intelligible to the latter's incumbents. Whether or not Britain remains a monarchy in ten years' time (which does not greatly matter one way or the other), Saudi Arabia is exaggeratedly unlikely still to be one in fifty years' time. The transition there is unlikely to prove amicable. Revolution is more than regime collapse or destruction. But it requires one or the other if it is to occur at all; and the record of revolution over the past century is still the best framework we have for analyzing the causal determinants of regime collapse, and the fusion of endogenous with exogenous forces with domestic political clumsiness and misfortune which brings the latter about (Dunn 1980).

What is hardest to see, looking forwards, is not the conditions which render regimes vulnerable, but the bases on which and the constituents with which new regimes of any durability can be constructed. Up to the year 1916 it was quite unclear that regime collapse could itself suffice to generate a new form of regime, although many had long confidently asserted that it held that potentiality, and the events of 1905 in Russia itself had already raised hopes on the other side of the world that it would soon prove able to do so (Price 1974). For over half a century from 1917 the attempt to emulate the Russian experiment with local improvements stimulated experiment and initiative across the world and transformed world politics by doing so. That particular model has now failed in its own heartland and appears to have run its course, though it has left behind it one of the two most potent, dynamic, and consequential regimes in the world (Nolan 1995, 2004). No one for the present can know quite what that survival means for the population of China or anywhere else.

Equally imponderable and every bit as disconcerting to the presumptions of Western social scientists or religious and political leaders is the continuing presence of other great-tradition world religions. Since the Iranian Revolution it has been very clear that Islam at least can still furnish an imaginative basis and a social and political medium through which to challenge a failing regime with unique intensity. The conditions of Iran differ in crucial ways from any other segment of the Islamic world (Abrahamian 1982; Mottahedeh 1987; Arjomand 1988); and despite vigorous attempts no subsequent Islamic challenge to regime incumbency has succeeded with comparable decisiveness or durability (Kepel 2004). Here too it remains hard to judge the prospective significance of a proven source of political power. But there are already a number of definite lessons to be drawn. One is the practical significance, even in extremis (and revolutions generate and are constituted by lengthy passages of extremity) of access to a quite different structure of rationality from those of material welfare (Gambetta 2005; and on a very different scale Huntington 1996). A second, more formally, is the continuing centrality of drastic and inherently unforeseeable political innovation and invention, and the consequent certainty that history will continue to surprise us (MacIntyre 1973; Dunn 1980). A third, almost equally abstract, is the practical importance for regime reconstruction of bases on which human beings can have good reason to identify, cooperate with, and even in some measure trust one another on a very large scale under conditions of acute stringency. Regimes can be challenged, and highly vulnerable regimes can even go down, in the face of very temporary coalitions of the resolutely unwilling. To build a new regime of any durability something more adhesive is required than an infinite will to coerce, eked out by hazily apparent complementarities of material interest. Very possibly it will prove unavailable in the future, as it very largely has in the past. But if we wish to gauge the possibility of revolution in the future, that is what we should be looking for.

3 Revolution and democracy

The European experience

Harald Wydra

Ever since the end of communism, the term "democratic revolution" has become synonymous with sudden, comprehensive, and non-violent regime change. The peaceful negotiated revolutions in East European countries such as Poland, Hungary, the German Democratic Republic (GDR), or the "velvet revolution" in Czechoslovakia in 1989 were followed more than a decade later by democratic revolutions in Serbia in 2000, the Georgian revolution of the Roses in 2003, and the Orange Revolution in Ukraine in 2004. These events not only achieved regime change in a peaceful manner but also transformed the modern concept of revolution. With the exception of Romania, they lacked the large-scale violence characteristic of the French, Russian, or Chinese revolutions. The people bringing down the Berlin Wall or forcing Czech communists to step down in November 1989 were not self-declared counter-revolutionaries against the Soviet-type regimes originally established by the October Revolution. The political challengers of the "old regime" did not look for a new society but seemed to be predisposed to "craft democracies." In this vein, 1989 saw double-rejective revolutions, aiming at rejecting communist rule domestically and foreign influence from the Soviet Union (Holmes 1997). They were also anti-revolutions in a wider sense, marking the end of belief in the tradition of revolutionary socialism inspired by Enlightenment thought and the desire of human emancipation by acts of revolution (Sakwa 2001: 162).

The conceptions of revolutionary or socialist democracy forged in the revolutions of 1789 and 1917 developed a universalism that remained more or less taken for granted practically until 1989. The political success of communism after the October Revolution vindicated the universal claim of the socialist strand of democracy introduced by the French Revolution. Similarly, interpretations of revolutions before 1989 were largely concerned with forward-looking expectations directed at political outcomes. Much of the best scholarship has interpreted revolutions with a view to underlying progressive forces of historical development such as modernization or state centralization (Skocpol 1979; Tilly 1993). With the decay of Soviet communism, liberalization and democratization became the historical forces that seemed to guide political development.

The peaceful negotiated revolutions in Eastern Europe and the implosion of the Soviet Union make the link between revolution and democracy somewhat paradoxical. The concept of democratic revolution is biased towards the political elements of constitutional democracy, having all but forgotten the social foundations of revolution. As a result of the failure of revolutionary communism in the Soviet Union the concept of revolution was "democratized." "Revolution" was deprived of its eventful character of sudden and violent regime change by conscious collective human action. It became detached from history and "universalized," symbolizing timeless protest against oppression (Kumar 2001: 196). Similarly, the end of communism has "universalized" the victory of democracy, making "democracy" arguably became the foremost goal of political development in the world. Therefore, the observer at the beginning of the twenty-first century may rightly assume that the victory of democracy has been the most consequential political development in the twentieth century. The potentiality of and the obstacles to democratization seem to be determined not by different points of departure but by a common destination and the imperative of convergence (Przeworski 1991: xii).

This "universalization" of revolution and democracy has obscured the primacy of revolutionary action in shaping democratic aspirations. One tends to forget that revolutions aim at sudden and lasting reversals of power structures, usually achieved by violence on a large social scale, but mainly interrupting the "normal" course of politics, which consists of the rules, norms, and values that define a system of political organization. The proclaimed universal victory of liberal democracy has obscured the fact that the evolution of democracy both as an idea and a constitutional form of government has not been a goal of history, but an "accident" in a historically contingent process (Michels 1987: 183–5). Although the institutional origins, for instance, of American democracy are to be found in the American Revolution, its evolution was not predetermined. A victory of the Southern Federation in the civil war might have led to the establishment of the Southern plantation system, entailing a scenario where the United States would have been in the position of some modernizing countries today, with a *latifundia* economy, a dominant anti-democratic aristocracy, and a weak and dependent commercial and industrial class, unable and unwilling to push forward toward political democracy (Moore 1966:112–15).

This paper links revolutionary conjunctures analytically to the formation of democratic consciousness. Taking the examples of European revolutions in 1789, 1917, and 1989, it argues that revolutions are not only effects of overarching historical forces such as state centralization, modernization, liberalization, or democratization. Rather, they themselves are causes of change, as they produce new states of consciousness and acts of symbolization. There is some truth in Marx's idea that matter determines consciousness. As the central place of war and violence in human affairs suggests, internal psychological states are always related to major material and structural transformations. States that succumb to revolutionary challenges are heavily burdened by material crises such as the state fiscal crisis, food scarcity, social misery, or external war. Yet, revolutionary consciousness in historical reality needs to be liberated from dogmatic statements about a law-like regularity of history or prescriptions about the correct revolutionary consciousness. Revolutionary situations display a rationality that needs to be understood from within the lifeworld of actors that are confronted with unexpected turns of events. The point is to evaluate dispositions of actors with regard to the rupture with the former "system," not with regard to abstract assumptions about future goals of historical development. From the perspective of the post-1789 meaning of revolution, the French revolutionaries of the first hour were unrevolutionary (Tackett 1996). While the Eastern European dissidents before 1989 were not democrats or revolutionaries in any common understanding of the concepts, their action was subversive to the old regime and promoted practices of democratic participation.

Revolution and democracy: A dramatic approach

Recent work has applied a dramatic perspective to democratization, thus linking the social context of uncertainty to the theatrical, performative, and expressive features of actors (Whitehead 2002: 36–64). The theatrical analogy not only allows for a defense against the imposition of "prefabricated" categories but is consistent with the moved history of democracy, which until the late nineteenth century was virtually a term of abuse (Dunn 1993). Despite its origins in ancient Greece, it was a particular series of dramatic and sudden social upheavals at the end of the eighteenth century that marked the age of democratic revolution (Palmer 1959). The French Revolution popularized democracy by weaving the egalitarian Christian notion of the value of human beings into the Enlightenment tradition of the emancipation of man. The French Revolution is considered as the birthplace of democratic politics, less because of Robespierre's radical definitions of total democracy, but because it introduced democracy and republicanism as a hypothetical ideal at the level of political imagination.

Borrowing a term from social anthropology, revolutionary events are "liminal" experiences where the dissolution of political and social structures blurs hierarchies of political agency, establishes multiple sovereignties, dissolves identities and social roles, and enhances the desire for vengeance. In revolutionary conditions, equality can be likened to what Marcel Mauss termed "total equality" (Mauss 2001: xxv-xxx), comprising not only political, but also economic, juridical, moral, social, aesthetic, or psychological realities. Revolutionary conjunctures suspend the bounded uncertainty of power relations prevailing in "normal" times, producing dual power arrangements or counter-revolutionary dynamics (Mayer 2000). Revolutionary events may force leaders to comply with the constraints set by unexpected and socially significant courses of action. Yet, in the boundlessness of action, the intentions of revolutionaries are often thwarted as the actor is never merely a "doer" but always and at the same time a "sufferer" (Arendt 1958: 190–1). Besides the dissolution of established institutions and structures, revolutions reverse meanings, representations, and symbols by establishing myths of origin or cults of personalities.

The birth of modern democracy in the French Revolution was such a liminal experience, set in the dramatic context of the downfall of absolutist monarchy and the revolutionary conflict of antagonistic forces. In Claude Lefort's terms, this democratic moment consists of the dissolution of "markers of certainty" and the attendant emptiness of the space of power (Lefort 1986a: 28). Whereas before the nineteenth century, political society relied on largely determined relations between corporate parts of society, the revolutionary rupture introduced radical indeterminacy by disentangling the legitimate basis of political power, the sources of moral and legal norms, and the production of knowledge. The democratic revolution in France transformed power structures that were incorporated in two kinds of bodies, the body of the king and the corporate social body (Lefort 1986b: 300–5). In monarchies, power was incorporated in the body of the king, as the body of the king gave body to society. Conversely, democratic rule is not entitled to incorporate or appropriate power, as the exercise of power becomes subject to a periodical competition for this power. Being the rule of the people in their own interest, power in a democracy emanates from the people but belongs to *nobody*. This empty space of power comes along with the "disincorporation" of individuals who are separated from corporate bodies or "natural" hierarchies to become the smallest units of the new type of social relations. This double disincorporation of the social body and the monolithic political body makes uncertainty about power a crucial feature of modern democratic states.

Rather than assuming a timeless "model" of democracy, the rule of the people in their own interest depends on shifts in subjectivity, consciousness, and symbolization of specific events that mark contests for power. The constitution of power in a revolution means not the limitation but the foundation and correct distribution of power (Arendt 1963: 146–8). As revolutionaries cannot base political models of representation and political participation on predetermined givens, their main goal is to legitimate their initially unconstitutional status. Sieyès's distinction between constituent power and constituted power suggested that the authority of the constituted power could not be guaranteed by the constituent power, as the latter was prior to the constitution itself (Sieyès 2003: 136–7). The exercise of real power by government had its roots in the nation as the constituent power, which was supposed to be formed solely by natural law and not subject to legal prescriptions formulated in positive constitutions. The national will as the origin of all legality, therefore, would always be seen as relying not on a differentiated social order regulated by law, but on a national spirit articulated under exceptional circumstances.

In revolutionary situations, the equality of conditions takes on a meaning beyond an understanding of equality of estimation, which would imply legally enforceable equal treatment and equal respect for everybody (Lefort 1986b: 301–3). Democratic equality is thus not only the object of a belief or a legal prescription laid down in democratic constitutions, which entitles people to political rights. Rather, it provides human relationships with meaning in so far as it becomes irreversible on the level of thought, even though in reality many inequalities subsist. On the one hand, social radicalization in revolutionary situations provides individuals with the idea of similarity, which entails the illusionary image of a collective identity, the people. On the other hand, equality emerges in the capacity of centralized state power. The state as a distant agency maintains the law of its construction, the power representing society as unique, simple, providential, and creative (Lefort 1986a: 242–4).

Indeed, after the French Revolution democracy became increasingly associated with a state of expectation, which claimed to satisfy newly constituted needs in order to justify its meaning (Koselleck 1985: 82). The revolutionary transformations of the concept of democracy involved mob rule, incivility, and violence before ushering in the Napoleonic empire, a cycle that confirmed historical precedents of the closeness of democratic conditions with authoritarian forms of government. In Antiquity, for instance, the establishment of the Athenian *polis* or of the Roman Republic followed upon tyranny. Their collapse entailed the building of an empire. Democracy in modernity originated from revolutions (the English, the French, and the Russian) that marked the culmination of the development of the three major ideological movements of the modern age: Protestantism, the Enlightenment, and socialism. In the early twentieth century, the crisis of the liberal state was accelerated by mob rule, which would facilitate the emergence of totalitarian rule in Russia and later on in Nazi Germany. The October and the Nazi revolutions confirmed the potential contagion of regime types, as the tyrannical autocracy of Bolshevik communism and Nazism were the one viable end to mob rule. After 1945, the foundation of post-fascist democracies in Germany, Italy, or Japan, was achieved by a temporary constitutional dictatorship.

The revolutionary tradition of democracy: France and Russia

If the outbreak of revolutions provokes the dissolution of authority structures, revolutionaries are obliged to fill the empty space of power by acts of symbolization that maintain new forms of collective representations for the people through rituals, commemorations, and a public consciousness. It is an achievement of the age of democratic revolution that the modern conception of representation includes the symbol "people" in two meanings, both as legitimizing the government and as being represented (Voegelin 1987: 38–41). In his Gettysburg address of 1863, Abraham Lincoln characterized democracy as the government of the people, by the people, and for the people; here the "people" absorbs three dimensions whose simultaneity is the result of a sequence of several crises. It designates articulated political society, its representatives, and the membership that is bound by the acts of the representative. By contrast, in medieval language the "people" could simply be distinguished as the "realm" and the "subjects." In the aftermath of the Magna Carta, the "people" originally meant only a rank in society without any possibility or aspiration for articulating representation. While the representation principle "king in parliament" preserved differences of rank, it already symbolized the relationship of head and member in one body politic.

As recent work has argued, revolutionaries are not predisposed towards a clear-cut ideological or organizational form of government but take decisions often in reaction to social processes in the empty space of power. Crowd violence and social effervescence prompted decisions and new acts of symbolization that only became possible in the situational reality of revolutionary events (Sewell 1996; Figes and Kolonitskii 1999; Wydra 2006). The French Revolution of 1789 became a politically constitutive act because it merged the formerly different dimensions of the people as a social reality with that of a political subject. The beginning of "democratic politics" in France after 1789 included crowd violence, mob rule, and insurrectionary peasant violence (Markoff 1998). The attack at the Bastille on July 14, 1789, for instance, endowed the concept "people" with a new meaning (Sewell 1996). The interpretation given to an act performed by insurrectionary crowds and collective violence was the basis on which the National Assembly forced the king to consent to the legitimacy of this constitutive act. Similarly, the Great Fear as the most astonishing mass panic in recorded history was hugely important for the legislative act of abolishing feudalism and privilege by replacing them with the equality before the law. The National Assembly had to interrupt negotiations on the constitution and the declaration of rights on August 4, 1789, because of the pressing situation of how to deal with increasing disorder in the provinces.

This symbolic sanction of spontaneous crowd violence at the Bastille as a legitimate act of popular sovereignty or the abolition of feudalism was achieved in the absence of "democrats." Both in the American and the French Revolutions, the self-perception of key actors was not that of democrats, let alone "liberal democrats" in the sense of the late twentieth century (Palmer 1959: 13–21). In the first age of democratic revolution there were no "democrats," while the Age of Aristocracy, as long as it was unchallenged, heard nothing of "aristocrats." The new concept of revolution with the idea of sovereignty of the people was not primarily based on revolutionary dispositions of heroic individuals but shaped in the situational reality of the contingent social context.

Tocqueville's famous point about the inevitability of the revolution testifies to the growing opportunities for political action against the established elite but brackets the formation of dispositions during the revolutionary event. The French revolutionaries did not have a choice between an imaginary and a potentially viable political project but between alternative imaginary constructions of the social and political world (Sewell 1994). Initially, the aim of the French revolutionaries was not the reversal of the ancient regime but its reconstitution. The period 1789–1790 was dominated by moderates who were keen to avoid counter-revolution and who pursued the establishment of constitutional government. Not only did the representatives of the third estate not have socially homogeneous backgrounds but they also lacked a revolutionary disposition, even as an ideological standpoint (Tackett 1996).

The French Revolution emancipated the "people" as a political subject but, in turn, subjugated individuals to more control by the centralized state than the old regime (Tocqueville 1988). A lasting effect of the French Revolution was that democracy lost its fixation on the constitutional realm and became equivalent to a new organizational form for the large modern state and its attendant social practices of equality such as in the rule of law, representation, citizenship (Koselleck 1985: 82). The long shadow of Thermidor initiated the radical egalitarian turn of the French Revolution as the figures of Gracchus Babeuf and Filippo Michele Buonarroti provided democracy with a meaning of a fiercely divisive political category as opposed to the victory of the order of egoism in the United States (Dunn 2005: 119–47). In the wake of the French Revolution, democracy became a possible form of domination, a central historical movement that was to draw more and more attention by the crowds (Furet 1998: 71–90). The beginning of "democratic politics" in the French Revolution, therefore, should not be seen as animated by a pre-existing democratic consciousness prior to the revolution.

If the Bolshevik revolution is judged by its political outcomes, it is undeniable that these were "totalitarian" and non-democratic. The collapse of Tsarist authority in February 1917, however, entailed a formidable authority vacuum, "institutionalized" in the dual power arrangement in March 1917. It would hardly have occurred to any observers in late 1916 to dispute the socialists' claim to belong to the "democratic club." The political rejection of the "bourgeois" occurred under liminal conditions of mob rule during the Russian Revolution of 1917 with its two peaks in February and October. While democracy was originally associated with a universal political concept and constitutional safeguards against dictatorship, the radical polarization of society in 1917 imposed a logic of class antagonism on democracy, thus giving it a quasi-dictatorial meaning (Figes and Kolonitskii 1999: 122–4). In revolutionary Russia, the term *demokratiia* soon became an exclusive social term, which reflected the growing domination of the idiom of class in 1917. *Demokratiia* was almost universally understood to mean "the common people" – and its opposite was not "dictatorship" but the "bourgeoisie" or indeed the whole of privileged society.

This socialization of the word "democracy" undermined attempts by Russian democratic leaders to impose the ideals of 1789 on to the realities of 1917. In the absence of a national consciousness, there was no real cultural or social foundation for the liberal conception of democracy in Russia, at least not in the midst of a violent revolution. Workers were capable of understanding the language of political democracy, but they did not choose to think of democratic power in the language of "constitutions" and "parliaments." As a consequence, the October Revolution introduced the dictatorship of the proletariat as the symbol for socialist democracy. Lenin's contempt for parliamentary democracy is well known. The "final" political outcome of the October Revolution was a totalitarian institutional-organizational framework, based on a political religion that was to become "administered" by a new political class. In terms of political communication, however, it developed a democratic terminology. Democratic centralism, originally introduced for the purpose of curbing the power of the Central Committee, became a hierarchically top-to-bottom principle of strict inner party discipline after 1934 (Kotkin 1995: 546). Communist leaders claimed to embody true democracy not because of a substantial contribution to political democracy but because this claim was part of the existential struggle for legitimizing power domestically and for achieving international recognition.

As quite a few authors have argued, the Russian Revolution was much foreseen and announced, but hardly inevitable (Kotkin 1995; Pipes 1998). Professional revolutionaries in Russia did little in preparing revolutions but it is the outbreak of the revolution that liberated them from wherever they happen to be – from jail, the coffee house, or from the library (Arendt 1963: 259). Rather than being representative of a major social group, the Bolsheviks followed a zigzag path with haphazard coalitions and attuned their strategies, often due to chance events. Despite the Bolsheviks' drive to the monopolization of the political space, however, the Mensheviks acknowledged the more "democratic" feature of Bolshevism in comparison to Tsarism, as the existence of a leftist Bolshevik government pushed the position of the Constituent Assembly to the right (Dallin 1974). As Prince Lvov remarked in 1923, Russia belonged more than ever to the people, although the Bolsheviks had betrayed the people and turned them into slaves. The popular masses supported a Soviet regime that integrated people of their kind into the apparatus, thus giving the impression of being theirs (Figes 1996: 815–16).

In Lenin's view, the Soviet regime was democratic in terms of enacting majority rule. Discarding the Western "liberal" conception of majority rule through representation inside the institutional apparatus of the state, he considered the people as a sociological entity, potentially participating in the work of government. Faithful to the Marxian idea that the revolutionary class of the proletariat has no class interest, under the dictatorship of the proletariat the people are not any longer separated by division inside society, and the division between society and state has also been removed.

For Lenin, majority is therefore based on the identity of the vanguard party with the proletarian people. The new power as the dictatorship of the overwhelming majority could and did maintain itself only by winning the confidence of the great masses, only by drawing, in the freest, broadest, and most energetic manner, all the masses into the work of government (Lenin 1964: XXXIV, 351).

The "anti-revolutionary" revolutions of 1989/1991

The revolutions of 1989 showed the conspicuous absence of charismatic actors, eschatological recipes, messianism, or teleological intentions. No new utopia of progress shone at the horizon of expectation but the overall feeling was the conservative "return to normality." Contrary to the class of 1945 or to the class of 1968 who had a certain set of ideals and a certain vision of society, the class of 1989 is not to be found (Ash 2000: 402). Whereas ten years on from 1917, there was already a rich literature on the actors, methods, and motivations of the October Revolution, a decade after 1989 accounts of the events of 1989 and their aftermath were relatively scarce, often reducing actors to objects of history as a reified actor (Kenney 1999). In this conspicuous absence of an ideological agenda for a future political order, the "actors" have become historical forces such as "modernization," "democratization," or "globalization."

1989 seemed to enact what Tocqueville had observed for 1848; that the monarchy fell "before rather than beneath the blows of the victors, who were as astonished at their triumph as were the vanquished at their defeat" (Arendt 1963: 260). Adapting Václav Havel's characterization of the Prague Spring in 1968, the revolutions of 1989 can be seen not as arising as a spontaneous happening but as the result of a gradual awakening, a sort of creeping opening of the hidden sphere of society (Havel 1985: 43). Being ardently desired but out of reach, democracy in Eastern Europe before 1989 was an empire of the mind, tinged with eschatological expectations, and pregnant with hazy images of total freedom, which were contingent upon the cultural context in society. Bereft of constitutional guarantees for and institutional practices of democratic participation, regime criticism came originally from inside a Marxist discourse. After the disillusionment of 1956 and 1968, intellectuals such as Leszek Kołakowski in Poland, but increasingly dissidents not attached to Marxist revisionism, formulated aspirations of equality and freedom. In the words of the Hungarian writer and dissident, György Konrád's view of the Polish revolution of 1980 identified *Solidarność's* unexpected vigor and popularity with democratic participation. He wrote that

> democracy is on our minds: it is what we crave the most because it is what we lack the most, in every sphere of activity, in our economy and culture as much as in politics – and especially in those areas where we

meet face to face and can look in the eye the people who make the decisions in our name and order us to carry them out.

(Konrád 1984: 142)

The division of two worlds in the bipolarity of the cold war enhanced the attraction of democratic images. As of the late 1940s, the totalitarian paradigm had equated the Soviet Union with the total externalization of evil. Meaning the polar opposite of democratic, the concept "totalitarian" simultaneously designated and disapproved of one-party states and mass terror but also presented Western democracy as the center of all virtue. Democracy turned from a constitutional form of government to a "good society," a normative aggregate, standing for an alternative civilizational truth. Western democracies drew much of their own legitimacy as the "good society" from a pervasive fear of contagion with communism and its ensuing stigmatization as the "empire of evil." Ironically, the dominant claim for the victory of liberal democracy after 1989 has transposed the assumption about the inevitability of communism by "liberalizing" the Marxist paradigm of transition to communism and projecting a teleological expectation for democracy (Guilhot 2002).

It is tempting to take the "availability" of the democratic model in the West as the proof for the inevitability of the revolutions of 1989. Yet, despite an increasing legitimacy crisis and instances of carnivals of revolution (Kenney 2002), the revolutionary outcomes of 1989 could hardly be anticipated. It is an irony of history that the arguably two foremost actors of regime change, the Polish *Solidarność* movement and Mikhail Gorbachev, were not intent on debunking communism.

In Poland, the opposition forces on the eve of the round-table negotiations in early 1989 had no transformative interest. The central objective of the *Solidarność* opposition was the relegalization of the trade union. Throughout the two months of negotiations between February and April, however, the gap between the opposition and the regime was drastically reduced and top party negotiators came to perceive the *apparatchiks* as "them," while including themselves with their partners from the trade union movement in an "us" category. This understanding among elites in a "revolution from above" was facilitated by a spontaneous community of mutual forgiving among former enemies. Yet, when the *Solidarność* opposition unexpectedly won a triumphal victory in the semi-free elections of June 1989, its leaders were completely disconcerted, lacking any strategy, and overwhelmed by the symbolic victory which would bring them power effectively.

Gorbachev's program of democratization had at its core a bid for a renewal of the representative nature of the party. The democratic renaissance in the Soviet Union at the end of the 1980s was primarily interested in giving back genuine accountability to the "people" by reviving the Soviets in the republics as representative organs. The increasing pressure on party officials to compete for office in a society where "class interests" had been systematically abolished, however, led to an intense practice of "hyper-democracy." Consistent with Gorbachev's early statements, *perestroika* prioritized cultural change with a focus on attitudes, psychology, and consciousness. Democratization under *glasnost* and *perestroika* thus did not only require the formal accountability of officials but the "pluralism of opinions" and systemic criticism, which realized an equalization of status between officials and the masses (Breslauer 2002: 67).

The demonstrations in late October and November 1989 in Czechoslovakia were overshadowed by quite determined interventions by riot police and kept many students in a state of fear. The violent attacks by riot police on some 50,000 students gathered on Wenceslas Square on November 17 prompted a spontaneous meeting the following day, when 2,000 people returned to lay flowers in commemoration. The brutality of November 17 became a mobilizing force for further demonstrations and the goal of a general strike on November 27. Despite the increase to 200,000 on November 20, and to half a million demonstrators on November 25, the crucial issue was the decision of workers to participate in the general strike that finally prompted the disintegration of the party and the victory of the revolution (Petersen 2001: 249–53). Quite differently from Poland, the Czechoslovak mass demonstrations symbolized the radical separation of the pure community of "us" from the dangerous and polluting elements of "them." The rhetoric of the Velvet Revolution maintained popular perceptions of clear-cut categories, helping to establish concepts such as democracy, freedom, humanity, and non-violence as synonymous with the Czechoslovak people against the regime.

The sudden end of communism was followed by the quick obliteration of 1989 in post-1989 political discourse. The very events of 1989 have entered into the no-man's land of mythical pasts, failing to become the models for new national holidays. The dissolution of the symbols of democracy and the disenchantment with the new order can be attributed to the end of romantic images of democracy, Europe, or the market. The crucial question, however, concerns the animating forces of the non-violent regime change. Here, the practices of resistance, rebellion, and revolution before 1989 are important for understanding the emergence of democratic revolution.

The infrapolitics of democratic revolution

The democratic revolution of 1989 relied upon forces that were neither democratic nor revolutionary in the accepted sense of the terms. The "democrats" were not democrats in the sense of a professional elite competing for votes in a system of government. Neither were they revolutionaries in terms of the Jacobin–Bolshevik insurrectionist version of revolution. The strategy of subversion did not aim at seizing state power but at denouncing the incivility of communism. Yet I would argue that 1989 was the result of a struggle for conquering the empty space of power by encouraging the people to claim their rights to democratic participation. Prior to the institutional breakdown of communism in 1989, the "people" had to become a political subject without institutionalized opportunities for democratic participation. As Rousseau suggested in his paradox of sovereignty, the founding of a general will as the precondition for sovereignty and democratic participation would be paradoxical. In his view, for an emerging people to follow the fundamental rules of statecraft embodied in the general will, the effect (social spirit) would have to become cause, and cause (good laws) would have to become effect. The problem is how to establish either condition without the previous attainment of the other upon which it depends (Rousseau 1993: 193–5). In a twentieth-century version of Rousseau's paradox, C.B. Macpherson argued that there will be no more democratic participation without a prior change in social inequality and in consciousness but the changes in social inequality and consciousness cannot be achieved without a prior increase in democratic participation (Macpherson 1977: 100).

As James Scott has suggested, politics is not just about openly declared dominance and revolt but also about the "disguised, low-profile, undeclared" resistance of subordinate groups (Scott 1990: 198–9). Between quiescence and revolt, there is a complex reality of infrapolitics, i.e. negotiations and interplay between the public and the hidden transcript (Scott 1990: 2–5). The public transcript reflects existing relations between dominant elites and subordinates. Out of prudence or fear, the latter's public performance will usually be – with rare exceptions – aimed to comply with the expectations of the powerful. The hidden transcript instead consists of speeches, gestures, and practices that occur offstage and defy the consensus of existing power relations established in the public transcript, thus contradicting or inflecting it. Produced for a different audience and under different constraints of power than the public transcript, the hidden transcript assumes the form of political struggle when frontal assaults are impossible or highly unlikely to succeed. From this perspective, it seems more accurate to see the realities of power not as a straightforward division between the state and society, between the powerful and the subordinate, but rather acknowledge a tension between compliance and potential of acts of resistance. Thus, deference and consent may only be a preliminary form of subversion. The revolutionary power of infrapolitics developed in the "hidden" sphere, exerting constant pressure on existing power arrangements, much as a body of water might press against a dam (Scott 1990: 219). The amount of pressure varies according to the degree of shared anger and indignation but also on the degree to which parts of the hidden transcript leak through and increase the probabilities of a complete rupture.

The ethical individualism of dissidence was "anti-political" as it renounced violence as the defining attribute of the modern state. Leadership would assume not a political but a moral stance, favoring non-violent, existential approaches to resistance against oppression. Anti-politics did not want to overthrow the state but to undermine communism by strategies of individual detachment from the contagious elements of communist power. The failure of the Prague Spring in 1968, for instance, had taught that the struggle for political authority should be located not in the sphere of the state, nor of society, but in the existential dimension of people's lives. By destroying any sphere of public space and meaningful political alternatives, communist systems caused the center of gravity of any potential political threat to shift towards the existential and the pre-political (Havel 1985: 44–51). In such an environment, political impulses could hardly come from politicians in the communist establishment, let alone from "professional revolutionaries," but had to come from outsiders.

In this vein, breaking the silence from the vantage point of the "hidden sphere" is not only a psychological release for the one who speaks on behalf of others, it is also a moment of political electricity. The compulsory emigration of Solzhenitsyn, for instance, was not due to his power position but rested on his writings that were a "dreadful well-spring of truth" with the risk of "incalculable transformations in social consciousness," which in turn might one day produce political debacles unpredictable in their consequences (Havel 1985: 42). Havel's essay "The Power of the Powerless" was not a treatise destined to gather dust but had considerable impact on activists in other countries, making it politically more significant in Poland than in Czechoslovakia. As Zbigniew Bujak, later on a prominent *Solidarność* activist remembered how, "this essay reached us in the Ursus factory in 1979 at a point when we felt we were at the end of the road .... Reading it gave us the theoretical underpinnings for our activity. It maintained our spirits; we did not give up, and a year later, in August 1980 – it became clear that the party apparatus and the factory management were afraid of us. We mattered. And the rank and file saw us as leaders of the movement" (Gleason 1995: 187–8). Bujak saw in the ultimate victories of Solidarity and of Charter 77 an "astonishing fulfilment of the prophecies and knowledge contained in Havel's essay."

The Polish self-limiting revolution in 1980 was profoundly anti-revolutionary if any meaningful classical conception of revolutionary class or vanguard party is applied. It renounced political action in the name of a partial entity such as the proletarian class but aimed to revive the Polish nation (*społeczeństwo*) as a realm outside the state. The emergence of an independent, self-organizing trade union movement *Solidarność* in the summer of 1980 came to constitute a "second Poland" where the sheer size of almost ten million Poles provided a unique platform for affirming the subjectivization of the Polish nation (*podmiotowość społeczeństwa*). Prior to 1980, the combined effort of intellectuals, workers, and the Catholic Church merged romanticism and religious spirituality with the action of the working class that propagated a democratic utopianism in the concept of *Solidarność*. The trade union movement adopted the tradition of the democracy of the gentry – the only form of democracy to have taken strong root in Poland – that was endowed by an ideal of unanimity and a corresponding image of a unitary and single national will. Thus, the concern for an idealized past became a structuring principle for *Solidarność* that was based more on myth than on reality (Walicki 1988: 10–13).

The revolutionary power of consciousness

Revolutions confirm Michel Foucault's point according to which humanity does not progress from combat to combat before arriving at universal reciprocity, where the rule of law would replace warfare. Rather, humanity installs each of its violence in a system of rules and thus proceeds from domination to domination (Foucault 1984: 85). Durable political authority requires transforming violence into effective social bonds. In Norbert Elias's terms, the change in the pattern of people's "we-and-they feelings," of identification and exclusion, of shared and collectively recognized attitudes such as trust, self-restraint, and mutual respect was a primary condition for the development of democracy in modern nation-states (Elias 1996: 144–7). Nevertheless, modern democratic states pursue power politics very much on Machiavelli's lines, not in the name of princely self-interest but in the name of a nation. While sovereignty in monarchies focused on feelings of loyalty and attachment from person to person, modern nation-states in the wake of the French Revolution relied to a much higher degree on attachments to symbols of the collectivity.

Yet, as Paul Ricoeur has argued, no political act ever conforms to the standard of being legitimate in terms of reflecting the previous consent of a sovereign authority (Ricoeur 1984: 254). As a political act always lacks full legitimacy at the moment of its enactment, sovereignty occurs with a temporal gap between act and the consent that enables it. Revolutions in 1789 and 1917 produced acts of symbolization that sanctioned committed violence with the aim of creating myths of origin and concealing the violence that originated the revolutionary regime. The truly intriguing point about the French Revolution is not so much what kind of future it is headed for but that it has cast a spell on the imagination of later generations in terms of a myth of identity and of origin.

Unlike 1789, the infrapolitics of democratic revolution was based not on the concealment of violence perpetrated by Stalinism or by Soviet troops in Hungary in 1956 or Czechoslovakia in 1968, but on the commemoration of its victims and the growing conviction that true reform could only be achieved by non-violent action. Gorbachev and his major allies were part of the generation of the 1960s (*shestidesiatki*) whose perceptions of social and political reality were largely shaped in the aftermath of 1956. Indeed, de-Stalinization brought about a transformation in the communicative context, which – although vague, limited, and contradictory – was mediated by the focus on socialist legality and in a not insignificant way revived the category "democracy" (Urban *et al.* 1997: 36). The intellectual thrust of democracy was the Soviet dissident movement that already in its letter to the Soviet leaders on March 19, 1970, prefigured what was to become the language of Gorbachev's *perestroika*. Gorbachev's commitment to non-violence (*'nye streliat'*) became a central principle of his action at the head of the Soviet communist party.

In Eastern Europe, 1956, 1968, and 1980 produced authority vacuums and situations of dual power where the party establishment temporarily not only lost a substantial proportion of its membership but, in particular in Hungary and in Poland, the control of the state. They also created countless social memories, which became powerful markers of national independence but also of democratic aspirations. Similarly, the *Solidarność* revolution in Poland, ethical individualism in Czechoslovakia or anti-politics in Hungary were not born as idealist projects but developed specific forms of infrapolitics as responses to the experienced humiliation of aborted revolutions.

The 1956 revolution in Hungary prefigured the recent democratic changes in Hungary, as the memory of thirty-year-old events and the chance that demands of that time might be satisfied, acted as a considerable integrating force. The democratic breakthrough between March and June of 1989 consisted of a considerable shift from a dichotomy between officialdom and the opposition towards a growing self-inclusion of party hardliners into the opposition (Kenney 2002: 261–5). The reburial of party leader Imre Nagy – executed after October 1956 – on June 16, 1989, was not a revolutionary situation with a confrontation between "us" and "them"; rather the authorities orchestrated this mass event in order to re-appropriate a heritage they had been despising for more than thirty years. This reburial as a performative act before 250,000 people was the climatic moment that uniquely symbolized Hungary's negotiated revolution.

The Soviet intervention in Czechoslovakia on August 21, 1968, produced a strong resistance movement underpinned by a spontaneous and deep solidarity of the overwhelming majority of the population (Eidlin 1980: 93–156). The bonding effect of manifestations of solidarity among citizens for the next six days invigorated personal responsibility and friendly relationships in society where the absence of dissenters brought pride and satisfaction in a common enterprise. Quite unexpectedly, defeat before military repression gave rise to the strongest formulation of powerful spiritual action, which would remain a symbolic marker of national protest (Kenney 2002: 244–9).

After the proclamation of martial law in Poland in December 1981, *Solidarność* became illegal but maintained an overwhelming symbolic presence in terms of flags, slogans, plaques, and flower crosses which maintained the memory of suffering and promised the expected re-emergence of the trade union. The we-image of a collective subject survived the period of martial law because it was preserved through the individual I-images of the leaders of *Solidarność* and the Polish people. *Solidarność* continued to enjoy a high moral reputation, which was maintained through regular decentralized gatherings in multiple secret communities in the "hidden sphere," under the shelter of the Catholic Church (Wydra 2006: 176).

The infrapolitics of democratic revolution in Eastern Europe indicate that democratization processes not only result from the "classical" revolutionary effects of violence, bureaucratic rationalization, and institutional differentiation (Weber 1980: 657–8). While institutional accounts focus on the revolutionary force coming from the technical means of disciplining, controlling, and rational goal setting by the state, charismatic authority consists of beliefs of revelation and heroic creativity. Such beliefs revolutionize from inside as they grasp the spirit of human beings before shaping institutional order and the material world. France and Russia clearly confirm this insight. While they were persecuted religious institutions, the revolutionaries in France and after October produced political religions. According to Tocqueville, the French Revolution was also a religious revolution as far as it took the French citizen in an abstract way as a representative for other nations and cultures much as religion takes man in an abstract way with regard to transcendence (Tocqueville 1988: 105–9). Seeking practical solutions to Rousseau's paradox, the French revolutionaries answered by replacing the divine right of kings with what Edgar Quinet called a people-God (*peuple-Dieu*) (Lefort 1986a: 176). They had followed Rousseau's observation that, to establish the validity of man-made laws, one actually would need gods (Arendt 1963: 184). On the one hand, the people were to become citizens, i.e. subjects who would govern themselves. On the other hand, to substitute a secular principle for the belief in divine right, they would need to inspire an awesome, almost mystical, authority. This radical reorientation of political purpose drew not on pre-existing theoretical principles, but required the mobilization in people's minds and hearts of a belief, if not of a cult, of the impossible.

Similarly, the revolutionary messianism of Bolshevik communism found fruitful soil in messianic ideas in Russia, where the symbol of the Third Rome was turned into a national program of salvation (Duncan 2000). This merger of different programs of salvation by revolutionary messianism largely accounts for why an atheistic ideology would be successful in a deeply religious, orthodox country (Berdyaev 1961). The October Revolution gave rise to a theocracy of the vanguard party, combined with the dogmatic defense of communist orthodoxy and a civil religion of Marxism–Leninism, aimed at the redivinization of society. Although the Bolsheviks led a merciless battle against religion and the clergy, their techniques of power were permeated by Orthodox Christian practices, techniques of self-fashioning such as self-sacrifice, and the transformation of a telos of Christian sainthood into hero worship and hero identification (Kharkhordin 1999: 263). Adapting the English maxim "my country, right or wrong" Trotsky underscored that history did not provide another way to prove the correct line than to go with and through the party. Against the claim of the dictatorship of the proletariat to be rule by the people, the techniques of communist power all but eliminated the influence of the "people" on political choices (Kharkhordin 1999).

Although anti-politics in Eastern Europe was dismissed by many due to its manifest denial of reforming the political system of communist government, it revealed the emptiness of power as it credibly suggested an existential alternative to the logic of communist power. Its democratic character consisted in influencing social spirit and consciousness by a choice for a different conduct of life and ethical individualism. Bereft of the possibility of institutional reforms, the infrapolitics of democratic revolution aimed at providing new markers of certainty by distancing people spiritually from the contagious overall influence of communist bureaucracy and the totalitarian lie (Konrád 1984: 231). The dangers of such a revolution of the spirit are evidently in the lack of accountability of such elites in a system of constituted power. Renouncing the power politics of collective class or nation the moral code of the anti-revolution was not only subversive of the communist state but also of state government in general (Sakwa 2001: 174).

The anti-revolutionary revolutions of 1989 and 1991, therefore, contradict common-sense understandings not only of revolutions but also of power; they relied upon a commitment to non-violence and they did not address the state as the political space of action. The dissidents of Charter 77 pursued a strategy of liberation from the "total" image of a class or a nation, thus renouncing the temptation of divinizing a social collectivity. Reminiscent of Odysée Barrot's assessment of how the Paris Commune in 1871 related to the French Revolution, it could be argued that 1989 (like 1871) as a political revolution was a reaction against the social revolution of 1793 with its "total" tendency of *"une et indivisible"* and the authoritarian imposition of one model (Arendt 1963: 266).

A critic, however, might well argue that this type of subversion of communism was unrealistic in its aspirations and of a vague, utopian quality at best. Developing democracy under communism relied, to a significant extent, on an urgent hope to attain an undifferentiated good, generated by images of the West that exerted a spell on Eastern consciousness and imagination. Such visions of democracy, however, must not be considered as a mendacious version of reality. Indeed, also in the western hemisphere democracy has gained acceptance not despite but *because* of its utopian bent. Modernity revived the Greek term of democracy that prescribes an impossible form, making democracy first and foremost a normative word, not *describing* a thing, but *prescribing* an ideal. This somehow romantic vision of freedom accounts for the linkage between original Athenian democracy and modern democracy, but also for the power of the image of democracy on Eastern European dissidents. Democracy consisted of a diffuse and urgent hope that human political arrangements may come to be more a matter of committed personal choice and less a matter of enforced compliance (Dunn 1993: 256).

Conclusion

Recovering the primacy of the revolutionary event, this piece has argued that European revolutions in 1789, 1917, and 1989 cannot be simply seen as effects of an objective historical development towards a universal idea of democracy. Against the dominant tendency to universalization of concepts, the focus on the historical rupture suggests that 1989, in some ways, turned 1789 on its head. In 1789, the revolutionary rupture dissolved markers of certainty, thus starting "democratic politics." Before 1989, the infrapolitics of democratic engagement prompted the "anti-revolutionary" revolution that ended the revolutionary cycle started in 1789 and continued in 1917. The revolutions in France and Russia "liberated" the enormous powers of the social reality of the people, creating powerful images of democratic equality to come. Similarly, they enacted revolution as an abstract agent for the emancipation of man or the monolithic entity of the "people-as-one" (Lefort 1986b: 273–98), searching for salvation as a final goal of history. These forms of the "deification of the people" in France after 1789 and the dogmatic cult of the dictatorship of the proletariat after 1917 in the Soviet Union came along with unprecedented violence against the people as a consequence of relentless processes of bureaucratization and state centralization. Conversely, the "democratic revolution" in Eastern Europe drew quite considerably on "pre-political" elements such as symbols and memories. Turning against the ideals of 1917, the revolutions of 1989 accomplished more of a restoration in the sense that Eastern European countries recovered what they had lost by returning to Europe. The important point, however, is that this return was not inevitably induced by the sheer power of the Western model of democracy but by a contingent process in which democratic dispositions shaped up in response to the existing incumbent regime. The Eastern European revolutions fulfilled such visions of democracy not only as given from outside but also as a result of forms of democratic participation in the infrapolitics of democratic revolution.

4 "Transformation" of state socialism or class revolution?

David Lane

An earlier generation of social scientists viewed major forms of social change in terms of class and social revolution.[1] By the end of the twentieth century, such approaches, if not completely extinguished, were smoldering. Social class, as a major mover of social change was "dead." John Dunn, writing in 1972, anticipated many current interpretations when he said that the "history of twentieth century revolution ... is ... a commentary on the falsity of ... Marxism" (1972: 19).[2] This paper will contend that such pronouncements, which since the end of state socialism have reached triumphalist dimensions, are untrue or at least grossly overstated.

Systemic breakdown followed by system transfer is the most usual explanation of the process of transition from communism in Eastern Europe. State socialism had "major systemic incompatibilities caused by the absence of both a market and a mechanism of conflict resolution ... . Because institutional arrangements deprive state socialism of the capacity to channel self-interested behavior into socially beneficial performance and condition its survival on the base of direct coercion, the whole concept of a politico-economic order is fundamentally flawed" (Kaminski 1991: 16, 3). An implication of this position, either shared consciously or, more often, assumed by most analysts of the post-communist societies, is that if the coercive powers of the totalitarian state were removed, a political and economic *tabula rasa* would be revealed on which the favored Western institutions of democracy and markets might be freely constructed. As Janos Kornai has asserted: "The socialist system was a brief interlude, a temporary aberration in the course of historical events .... [T]here is no alternative to the 'capitalist system'" (1998: 2, 40). In this paradigm, there is no need for political actors, let alone classes; revolution, involving the conscious overthrow of one system by another, is not necessary. The "system transfer" position assumes that state socialism was a fundamentally defective system and that a neo-liberal policy of markets, private property and competition in economy, and competitive polyarchy legitimized as "democracy" in the polity, would be a strategy to transform the ailing societies into prosperous democratic states (see, for example, Lipton and Sachs 1992: 350–4).

The form of social change was not a revolutionary one. Charles Tilly echoes many commentators when he says that the changes in Central and Eastern Europe "lacked the multiple features of the past's great revolutions; ... violence, class base, the charismatic vision, the faith in politics as an instrument of constructive change and resistance of old power-holders to removal" (1993: 234). He defines a revolution in terms of the transfer of state power, and the "depth of revolutionary situations" (ibid). He differentiates between the Soviet Union, Czechoslovakia, the GDR, and Yugoslavia which had revolutions (in the sense of the transfer of state power) but in the other East European states the situation was "marginal," "uncertain," or "doubtful" (1993: 235). The analysis of the transformation of the state socialist societies has not been in terms of theory of revolution or revolutionary actors. Many prominent Russian commentators also consider the outcomes of reforms to be a "social transformation" of state socialism (rather than a move to capitalism), the agents of which are particularly the endogenous "ruling elite" and the "higher bureaucracy" (see, for example, Zaslavskaya, 1999: 149).

An alternative approach is taken by those who insist that the collapse and transition which follows should be interpreted in the context of revolution, if not as a revolution itself. The discussion in these revolutionary scenarios is in terms of state breakdown, the reconstitution of new states and their elite structure (see particularly, Goldstone 1998: 96). Claus Offe, Leslie Holmes and Jack A. Goldstone all maintain that the post-communist countries have experienced a "comprehensive revolution" (Holmes 1998: 167–70). Holmes's argument is that state socialist societies have moved from one-party systems with command economies to multiparty ones with "increasingly privatized and marketized economies .... All this represented *a rapid and fundamental change of system*, which is ... the most basic and universal definition of ... revolution" (Holmes 1997: 131, italics in original). For Claus Offe, the East European revolutions lacked aims, and any "prescriptive 'ex-ante' revolutionary theory. ... This upheaval is a revolution without a historical model and a revolution without a revolutionary theory" (Offe 1996: 30, 31). Jack A. Goldstone conceives of the changes of 1989–1991 as "a major revolution" (Goldstone 1998: 96).

Valerie Bunce's account is in terms of "economic decline (and redistribution), the international system ... mass protest, and, especially, nationalism loomed large in ... the departure of socialist dictatorships from the European stage" (Bunce 1999: 152). On the status of the changes as revolution, she is equivocal, considering that the Eastern European transitions "diverged from the historical norm" (they were peaceful and the old elite survived), though she rather hesitantly concludes that they "would still seem to qualify as revolutionary events" (Bunce 1999: 152) and she concedes that, "The revolutions that brought down socialist dictatorships were remarkably similar to the classic revolutions of the past" (Bunce 1999:155). Russian writers, such as Vladimir Mau and Irina Starodubrovskaya, classify the "recent events in the USSR and Eastern Europe" as "liberation revolutions" removing constraints "which fettered social development" (Mau and Starodubrovskaya 2001: 324–5).

These approaches, however, lack societal (rather than elite) actors; they focus on the revolutionary events rather than on underlying causes and social and economic consequences. For Mau and Starodubrovskaya, "class analysis ... is not applicable to revolution" (2001: 324–5). Following writers like Tilly, they emphasize the link between revolution and a weak state, which stems from the "fragmentation of society" (Mau and Starodubrovskaya 2001: 328).[3] In the accounts of transformation, one has no indication of what social groups are likely to pursue and gain from, or oppose, a policy of marketization and privatization – common objectives of all the elites of post-communist societies. Revolution is conceptualized as being "state centered." In other words, the collapse or breakdown of the state and the replacement of the incumbent rulers is sufficient to define a revolutionary change. A distinction is made between revolutionary situations and revolutionary outcomes (Tilly 1993: 234). Tilly (who sets the scene for many others) defines a "revolution" as "a forcible transfer of power over a state in the course of which at least two distinct blocs of contenders make incompatible claims to control the state, and some significant portion of the population subject to the state's jurisdiction acquiesces in the claims of each bloc" (1993: 8). To the extent that the change from state socialism was a "top-down social transformation" it did not qualify as a revolution (1993: 9).

However, ambiguity arises when writers confine their analysis of revolution to "revolutionary situations" as they do not differentiate between a *coup d'état* and system change. Consider West and East Germany after the Second World War: both qualified as new states with significantly different political leaderships following state breakdown and both had a "top-down" transformation. But East Germany constituted a revolution, as significant economic, political and social changes followed in the new political regime. When defining a revolutionary *change*, one needs to consider structures before and after the revolutionary events. Revolutionary "outcomes" are crucial as they involve, to use Goodwin's terms, a fundamental transformation of "economic, cultural and associational arrangements" (see, for example, Goodwin 1997: 30, note 1). This article contends that the transitions from state socialism are revolutions in this sense, though the extent of change varies between different societies.

But other commentators conclude that post-communist societies have not experienced revolutionary outcomes. Stephen White has summarized their arguments (White 2003: 421–6). It was not a social revolution because the ruling groups were not renewed: the *nomenklatura* continued in power. The moving power was the "socially and politically marginalized intelligentsia" (White 2003: 422) which sought reform of an authoritarian and bureaucratic system, not a revolution. Capitalism was not introduced (or reintroduced) in Russia because of the continued presence of state ownership and the absence of a bourgeoisie. Finally, the changes have lacked the characteristic "democratic" political shell of capitalism.

The "death of class"

The lack of any class analysis in the major theoretical accounts of the "transition from communism" follows from two main suppositions. First, the contention that class, as a form of identification as well as an explanatory concept, is increasingly irrelevant in post-industrial society. Clearly, there can be no class-based revolution if society is lacking in social classes. Second, the peculiar "classless" structure of state socialism portrayed both in "totalitarian" and Western Marxist accounts.

In Western political science and sociology, the "demise of class" as a form of social identification is not new and goes back at least to a 1959 paper of Robert Nisbet (1959: 11–17). The decline of class has been associated with the development of post-industrial theories of politics. The erosion of the primary sector and the enormous fall in the number of workers in mass-production industry led, it is claimed, to the decomposition of the working class and with it the basis of class consciousness. In post-industrial society, its distinctive knowledge and technological basis give rise to a consumer society, in which status groups become a focus of identification, and gender, ethnic and regional concerns become a site of political conflict. Class as an independent factor determining political attitudes and political "inputs" simply withers away. As Jan Pakulski and Malcolm Waters put it: "[P]ost-communist politics cannot be usefully analyzed using the class paradigm" (1996: 146; see also 58–9 and 146–7). Moreover, it is asserted that national and ethnic cleavages underpin political behavior (1996: 147).

Within the totalitarian paradigm, which conditioned much of Western writing (and even more so in the post-communist states) on state socialism and its transformation, the social system was considered to be socially undifferentiated, and sociologically "classless." Totalitarianism ended classes which were replaced by an undifferentiated mass. Classes, as forms of association, did not exist due to the atomization of society. For David Ost, "class sensibility remains weak," for Richard Rose *et al.* "communist rule . . . made traditional social structural cleavages of limited significance" (Ost 1995: 182; Rose *et al.* 1997: 807). Moreover, the sudden imposition of market forces disrupted the formation of a class consciousness.

A rather different view (but with similar conclusions) is taken by those who see class not as an independent factor, but as one dependent on political parties and political ideology. I call this a "political mode" of class analysis. Traditional European social-democratic and communist ideology identified parties with the working class, leading their supporters to label themselves as "working class." The term "middle class" was adopted historically by bourgeois parties to legitimate themselves against working-class parties. In this paradigm, class identity becomes a consequence of political party formation not a cause of it. This was the view taken by Lenin, in his plea for a party of a "new type" to bring consciousness to the working class. The implication here is that the lack of political party ideology will enfeeble class identification and differentiation. The United States is an example of how "classlessness," in this sense, is generated by an ideologically vacuous party system.

It is true that parties identified with classes were not a legacy of the state socialist system. Political parties have been nascent in the post-state socialist period. This is made clear by Lipset who contends that, in post-state socialist conditions, parties have lacked ideologies and ties to social classes (Lipset 1994). In addition, the discrediting of the Communist Party and its ideology as a vehicle for the working class, coupled to the lack of a bourgeoisie, as a support for bourgeois parties, both led to weak party-class identification.

The process of transformation itself has also led other thinkers, from quite different viewpoints, to adopt a similar approach to the analysis of class structure. Like Tatiyana Zaslavskaya, cited above, Ivan Szelenyi and his associates have suggested a technocratic-intellectual class approach (Eyal *et al.* 1998). However, their actors are "the technocracy," "bureaucracy," and intellectuals. "Class formation," it is contended, is "under way" in neo-liberal systems (Czech Republic, Hungary, Poland), whereas in "patrimonial systems" (Russia, Ukraine) there is a "dominant estate" structure (King and Szelenyi 2001: table 1). In their discussion of "classes and elites," Eyal *et al.* make clear that they are concerned with "intra class or more precisely *inter-elite* struggles" (Eyal *et al.* 1998: 18). Hence rather than classes "in themselves" making politics, it is the other way around: different types of elites make classes. In doing so, they provide another version of the "political mode" of class analysis, identified above.

In this context, elites become a major focus as political actors. Michael Burton and John Higley (Burton and Higley 1987; Higley and Burton 1989) suggest that "elite settlements" are crucial to ensure effective leadership of the transformation process. An assumption underlying this thinking is that non-elites, the public, masses (labor, peasants, and intellectuals) are not mobilized and they allow elites to negotiate compromises. Interest articulation must be modified and "ideological neutrality" must be realized on the part of any counter-elite. This allows elites to come to agreement on fundamentals: on the ownership of property; on the definition of who constitutes the membership of, and has rights in, a nation-state; on how social and political change should take place and on international alliances and linkages. Elites then replace classes as movers of the transformation process (see Lachmann 1997: 78–9 on Eastern Europe).[4] Moreover, pursuing the "political mode" of class formation, political management by political elites ensures the absence of a critical class ideology as a consequence of party formation. Parties promote consensus and repress ideological opposition and, in doing so, suppress the rise of social classes.

A major problem here is to explain why the consensual political elites universally adopt the ideology and policy of markets, private property, and competitive party democracy. If dominant elites (as under state socialism) have the "capacity to appropriate resources from non-elites" (Lachmann 1997: 97), why should they support the "system transfer" of the uncertainty of the Anglo-American type of economic and political market institutions? Why not pursue a state-managed market system, leaving ownership unchanged? A class-based transition, I claim, explains why such a move has occurred.

Class and transformation: positive evaluations

I have shown above that in their analysis of the transformation process, Western political scientists decouple class as a motive force of social change. Others have argued, to the contrary, that classes are an important factor in the countries undergoing transformation. In this analysis one might distinguish three dimensions of class: first, the extent to which occupational groupings give rise to segmented groups with distinct patterns of life chances; second, the intensity to which such groups perceive of themselves as classes; and third, the degree to which classes are linked to political ideology and class consciousness promoting class action. The first two dimensions are components in the sociology of stratification, and the third is integral in the analysis of revolution. To clarify this distinction, I shall refer to class in terms of stratification as "class strata." Classes promoting revolutionary action and linked in a Marxist type of class relations to the means of production, I refer to simply as "classes." The essence of all these approaches to class is that rational choice leads people to combine on a common class-strata basis to further their interests.

The industrial and social development of state socialism led to the rise of classes based on the occupational division of labor. In the post-socialist period, one might expect that marketization, in the context of privatization and the consequent redistribution of wealth and the replacement of administratively determined incomes by market-linked ones, would stimulate the rise of class strata. This more sociological understanding of class supposes that groups of people are conditioned by the interests they derive and share from a common economic position. Such positions give rise to levels of advantage and inequality (class strata based inequalities) and lead to the formation of interests defining attitudes to other classes and consequently to social change (class-based action) which may be defensive and reformist or aggressive and revolutionary. In a sociological approach, class strata and classes are determinants of parties and their ideological predispositions, not, as contended above, the other way around.

Sociologists (such as John Goldthorpe and Geoffrey Evans) define class in terms of an occupational position giving rise to different levels of inequality and life chances. This approach to class is distinguished by a concern for the "attributes" that members of class strata share in common (occupation, education, income). A stronger version of this paradigm sees such groups being organized for political action through parliamentary processes (S.M. Lipset, Robert Dahl, and K.M. Slomczynski). This may provide a basis for electoral competition and electoral democracy, not class conflict and revolutionary change.

The third type of class analysis emphasizes the ways in which classes make system and/or political change. In the works of Marx, Moore, and Weber, classes have a prominent role not only in politics but also in the process of revolution. There is a distinct linkage between social class and political behavior given by their class awareness ("class consciousness"). Classes are formed by market relations, and the ownership of assets, which is a wider concept than occupation. As Max Weber put it, "'property' and 'lack of property' are the basic categories of all class situations" (Weber 1961: 182). Classes then have a causal impact on behavior, outcomes are class determined.

In what sense then, may we understand the transformation process in post-communist societies as being characterized by class strata or class interests? In the following discussion I consider the transformation process to include: the precipitants of the collapse of state socialism, the process of change and the outcomes.

The first area of analysis is a concept of class mainly focused on inequalities and identities flowing from occupational position ("class strata"). These measure the conditions flowing from market position: the differential resources at the disposal of occupational groups – the extent that levels of income, conditions of employment and chances for advancement form distinct groupings. Geoffrey Evans and Colin Mills, on the basis of empirical research in Hungary and Poland in the early 1990s, contend that class position (evidenced by occupation) "is a marker for a wide range of inequalities of resources and conditions" (Evans and Mills 1999: 42). On the basis of empirical survey studies in nine Central and Eastern European societies conducted in 1993 and 1995, Evans found that members of the upper salariat had the advantage of higher education which enabled them to benefit from the transition period. The working strata (manual and agricultural) had significantly higher levels of unemployment, much worse career prospects and very much lower incomes. His data also clearly indicate significant differences between the relative life chances of the manual and non-manual groups: the top social strata benefiting from the changes, but the two working-class strata were made relatively worse off (Evans 1996: 232). Further evidence of the importance of class strata during the transformation in Poland is provided by the research of Kazimierz Slomczynski and Goldie Shabad (Slomczynski and Shabad 2000) in the early 1990s. Their findings point to people in different class strata sharing common participation in organizations and political orientations. Even in the study of electoral behavior, Szelenyi, Fodor, and Hanley contend that "during the first five years of postcommunism the significance of class ... *increased"* (Szelenyi *et al.* 1997: 196, italics in original), a conclusion echoed by Mateju and Rehakova (1997).[5]

As far as class identification is concerned, survey research confirms a positive association. In the Evans and Mills study (on Hungary and Poland 1993–1994), respondents were asked whether or not they thought they belonged to a social class (based on a list of class groups – "class strata" as defined above). Nearly 90 per cent answered affirmatively and placed themselves in a social class.[6] This indicates a high level of class awareness. In a study of nine Eastern European countries (1993–1994), Evans also showed a very close relationship between the self-allocated (subjective) and actual class position (Evans 1996: 236).

If we consider in combination social background, class strata inequalities and experience of transformation we find a high correlation between class position and support for, and opposition to, the free market and electoral democracy (Evans 1996: 239). While the upper class strata are agreed on the (positive) consequences of transformation, the working classes are strongly divided. Evans also calculated a regression index for economic ideology (as dependent factor) and social class and other variables (independent factors): free market against government intervention (providing employment, influencing income inequalities), public ownership versus private. The highest coefficient was that of class, followed by age (older supporting intervention) and gender (women supporting intervention). The standard beta coefficient was 0.19 for class strata, -0.14 for age, -0.08 for gender (Evans 1996: 243, 244).

Slomcynski's research also found that support and opposition to transformation varied clearly between social classes (class strata, as I have defined them). Farmers, service workers and factory workers show the least support for system change, and managers, experts and employers the greatest. Despite the widespread belief that age groups are disproportionately distributed in favor of (young people) or opposed to systemic change (the old), Slomczynski and Shabad (1996: 206) found that taking age into account did not affect the relationship either between assessment of socialism or support for state welfare. Class, they concluded, was a stronger predictor than other social stratification variables. They conclude that: "the large class differences in the assessment of socialism, approval of systemic change, and stance toward state paternalism ... challenge the 'death of class' thesis" (1996: 209).

For the more recent period of transformation, a comprehensive research project (national random sample of 1,800 respondents), which addressed many of the questions above, was carried out in Ukraine in the year 2000. When asked how much the respondents had in common with ten social groups, 83 per cent identified themselves positively with a social class (Kutsenko 2003: 197). Research into the circumstances of the respondents showed quite conclusively distinctly structured distributions of resources and life chances of these four major class groups (businessmen/entrepreneurs, intelligentsia, workers, peasants). There were clear class differences between the life chances of the respective social groups. Kutsenko also calculated the distribution of the respondents' evaluation of whether their opportunities had increased, remained the same, or decreased between 1991 and 2000. The average scores of the four classes showed a very steep downward gradient from the business/entrepreneurial group to workers and peasants, that is, the higher the social class the greater the opportunity (Kutsenko 2003: 211–14).

These studies all shown that class, in a social stratification sense, is a major break in the social structure. Class stratification is meaningful to actors: subjectively, they feel a sense of belongingness to a class group; objectively, access to resources (income, education), security and opportunity are linked to class position. Life chances are clearly class strata based.

Though these data are derived from studies with different methodological approaches, they provide a basis to establish that class strata have strong boundaries promoting distinct life chances and self-identities in post-communist East European societies. The period of transformation has been characterized by winners and losers which have a clear class-strata basis. The new bourgeois and entrepreneurial groups have gained disproportionately in terms of income, personal security and life chances, while the manual working class and peasantry have lost. The previous "socialist intelligentsia" has had mixed fortunes. There is a clear class strata divide about the desirability of, and benefits from, the radical political and economic changes which have taken place. What is lacking in these studies, however, is the role different classes have played in the process of revolution – classes (or class strata) as instruments in major historical change.

Marxist approaches

One would expect that self-defined Marxists would address this question. However, in respect to the "transformation" of state socialism, the present generation of Western Marxists shares much in common with the conclusions of the elite system-transfer school. Traditional Marxist analysis has had difficulty not only in explaining the class structure of Soviet-type societies, but also in detecting any class dynamic in the transformation from state socialism. Ownership of assets has been replaced by a more politically related concept of control over assets giving rise to the extraction of surplus value. Resnick and Wolff (2002) follow a long line of writers who contend that Soviet-type societies had always been on a continuum of capitalist societies, sharing a statist economy (Schachtman 1962; Cliff 1964; Haynes 1992; their critics – Trotsky 1957; Mandel 1958). In this paradigm, a dominant (state) capitalist class extracted surplus value, exploited the working class and redistributed the surplus product to different end-users and to itself. Control of the state apparatus is a crucial pivot of exploitation and domination. Class analysis is moved to the political realm – the term "elite" (members of the top party and state apparatuses) is often utilized to describe those who *control* the state.

An important consequence of this analysis is that the post-1989 trans-formations of the USSR and Eastern European societies are not revolu-tionary processes, but have more in keeping with the system change accounts. As Alex Callinicos has put it, the transformations are a shift between two types of capitalism (1991: 56) (state to multinational) and the process is not a revolution. "The transition from state capitalism to multi-national capitalism is neither a step forward nor a step backwards, but a step sideways" (Harman 1990: 82). Another implication is that in the transformation process, social structure and forms of class domination and exploitation need not change from the previous one. Control con-stitutionally vested in the state now passed into private hands. Not only the elites but also the ruling classes are reproduced.

From this standpoint, the "upheavals" in the post-communist societies could not be defined as Marxist revolutions. There was no ascendant class in Soviet-type societies. The bourgeoisie could not be ascendant, because it was already in power – as the ruling state capitalist class. As Resnick and Wolff put it: "This socialism [USSR and its satellites] was and remains a state form of capitalism. The last century's intense struggles, articulated as epic battles between capitalism and socialism, were conflicts between private and state forms of capitalism" (Resnick and Wolff 2002: 98). There could be no process of the "restoration" of capitalism, because capitalism was already in place (this point is trenchantly put by Ernest Mandel (1990: 43–65)). Take the analogy, made by Resnick and Wolff, of the class structure of Adenauer's Germany: it was the same as Hitler's and required no major changes in ownership and control of German industry after the Second World War. The Allied occupying forces simply replaced the Nazi political shell with a polyarchic one, legitimated in democratic terms. The dominant capitalist class, enfolded within the shell, remained the same. A similar type of legitimation, it is claimed, has taken place in the post-communist coun-tries, except the process has been an internal one: capitalist relations remain the same, the formal legitimacy, and type of ruling class differ. Arguments presented by Tatiyana Zaslavskaya, Stephen White, and Olga Kryshta-novskaya concerning the continuation of the *nomenklatura* are used to but-tress these viewpoints (see White 2003: 420–1).

This "autonomous state-centered" approach may be criticized from many points of view. There is a real difference, I believe, between capitalist coun-tries, such as Nazi Germany and the USSR. In the former, other non-Nazi elite interests were in place, such as the army and capitalist companies. Political change, even revolution, could come from interests within the state. However, as state capitalist theorists contend that there was a fusion of politics and economics in Soviet-type state capitalist societies, such opposing interests could not arise. The analogy of Resnick and Wolff to transition in Germany may also be faulted. If one compares the transition in East and West Germany after the Second World War, one finds qualitative differences. The East experienced a social and economic revolution, unlike that in the West: only in the former, was the private ownership of assets expropriated by the state. Moreover, something more than a quantitative change in the ruling class and governing elite took place following the dismemberment of the GDR – changes greater in scope than those in West Germany after 1945. Finally, if the ruling state capitalist class extracted surplus value which its members largely expropriated, then why was there a need to change from state capitalism to private market capitalism?

In the period of transformation, all the former Central and Eastern European and state socialist societies (Belarus is exceptional) have experienced significant structural changes involving the introduction of markets and privatization of economic assets. The supposed "elite" reproduction (i.e. of the *nomenklatura*) is misleading. First, the socialist *nomenklatura* comprised more than the previous ruling class, as it stretched to the lower ranks of society (such as trade union secretaries). And empirically, the transformation has been more than a simple elite reproduction. Second, under state socialism, the elites were legitimated by, and operated in, a completely different ideological, political, legal and economic context. Members of the political elites could neither create money through the financial system nor could they spend or export economic surplus which was severely circumscribed by the power structure in the former state system. There were no equivalents of Roman Abramovich: as he himself has put it, people in Russia do not understand how Western civil society enables people to spend their money exactly as they wish. As one of his followers pointed out to me: "Ambramovich can buy football fields wherever he likes and put his foot soldiers out to graze in England, Russia, or Japan, just as he chooses – that's freedom!".

Markets and competitive polyarchy, as forms of exchange and control, have to be analyzed in the context of the legitimation of different forms of private property – both domestic and international. I maintain that the evidence shows that a qualitative, not a quantitative change has taken place. Transition has involved a transformation of class and power structure, which was secured initially through the formation of economic markets and the redistribution of property rights.

Revolutionary change or transformation?

One might distinguish between two approaches to the analysis of revolution. The first is that of "revolutionary situations" in relation to state power. As noted above, this scheme has been used to cast doubts on the status of the East European transformations as revolutions. Mass base, violent upheaval, ex-ante ideological vision, mobilized social movements and actors with conscious revolutionary goals were lacking. It is asserted that the transfer of political power was a consequence of political leadership failure (intentional or unintentional) and systemic breakdown. The state was weakened to a point of disintegration in which alternative political elites were able to seize power. The initial transfer of power had the character of a regime change, even a putsch. To the extend that it was followed by a social transformation driven from above, it was not a revolution. In this paradigm, classes are not identified as players, the transformation is essentially a top-down process led by elites.

A second approach is to consider not only the way that state power is transferred between blocs of contenders but also societal outcomes of the consequent changes. From this point of view, despite the qualifications of the first school, a revolutionary transition to capitalism occurred. The new regimes – strongly influenced by and modeled on external actors – set their goals on the construction of polyarchic political systems (electoral democracies), economic and social markets, and private property, set in an ideology of possessive individualism. To a considerable extent, though not without internal differences between societies, they have succeeded.

Even if it is recognized that social classes (class strata) were formed during, and benefited from, the process of transition, their role as movers in a revolutionary movement is more problematic. Those who identify classes in the transition process do not explain their role as agents of change. Slomczynski and Shabad, for example, address the problems of class strata divisions and social inequality, and the role of elite reproduction or circulation (Slomczynski and Shabad 1997). While their points about class identity are well taken, they neither show how class-strata interests led to the overthrow of state socialism nor to their role in the construction of capitalism. Their analysis is rooted in the paradigm of systemic transformation (a "class-strata" paradigm).

The analysis of who drives the policy of transition has focused on elite behavior. Rather than framing the discussion of social change in the context of classes and revolution, "transitions" are depicted as the consequences of more or less negotiated settlements between elite actors, involving pacts, agreements and constitution making. As one writer on revolution and elites has put it, the objectives of ruling elite configurations are to maintain their "organizational autonomy" and "exploitative relationship" (these are the two "vital interests" for ruling elites according to Lachmann 1997: 97, note 2). This does not tell us what policies they may adopt to do so, or why in the first place incumbents of power should transform their economic and political institutions. After all, the totalitarian perspective on power relations ensures, if nothing else, complete control of organizational autonomy and an exploitative relationship of the ruling elite over the mass. "Elites" do not share similar interests and have no common ideology.[7] Yet in all the former state socialist societies, similar macro policies in the economy, polity and foreign affairs have been adopted.

My contention is that underpinning elite behavior lie class interests. If a (revolutionary) class dimension has been present, it needs to be shown how elites are linked to classes and how they were motivated to embark on a policy of building capitalism. The role of different elites (and their class-strata position) in the appropriation of the process of property transfer has been indicated above. Their consequent ownership of productive assets is a crucial indicator of class interest. How then were classes and class strata involved in a process of revolutionary transition to capitalism?

Traditional class analysis locates the "nation-state" as the site on which revolution and class conflict are located. Both the bourgeoisie and the working class are national in form. This perspective has informed the state-centered approach to revolution, prioritizing state collapse rather than class interest. The former state socialist societies had no social classes and thus they could not have been a causal element in breakdown.

The Marxist perspective has attributed to the state two functions: in a national economy, it is an apparatus of capitalist class domination; in the world system of states, it secures the interests of national capitals. The policy of states then will vary depending on the relative strength of national or international interests.[8] In the state socialist societies, despite some inroads of trade and commercial intercourse with the West (particularly in Central Europe), there was no inward penetration and outward spread of capital. State socialist societies were on the semi-periphery of the capitalist world system (for substantiation see Lane 2006: 138–44). The dominant Western capitalist classes were excluded from the apparatuses of the state socialist societies (possibly explaining the political hostility of the hegemonic Western states led by the United States). A Marxist state-centered account would not identify any international revolutionary class forces – in the sense of an ascendant class motivated to change ownership relations – within the state socialist formation. Such international commercial activities that existed were under the control of the administrative state apparatuses.[9] Hence there was no latent Marxist ascendant internationally linked class here trying to get out to form a new dominant capitalist class. In my own view, to identify classes as forces of revolutionary change, one must widen the understanding of internal "national" classes, and also conceive of class as an interstate phenomenon. The role of classes in transition may be analyzed in terms of two domestic reform orientated class strata and an external globalized and globalizing capitalist class. Internal to state socialism there were class strata in the sense that they share a similar market position and their members had similar life chances (as described above). They were not classes in a Marxist sense derived from the traditional relationship to the means of production, creating or taking economic surplus, but they were motivated to support systemic change. First, that identified by writers such as Szelenyi and state capitalist theorists: being an administrative stratum with *control* of economic assets. Second: an "acquisition" stratum constituted of individuals with personal skill assets (the professional classes or the "intelligentsia") which they sought to valorize on an economic market. These class strata should not be conflated into the *nomenklatura*, which was not a class grouping but a list of positions subject to party and state nomination and/or veto.

Both these class strata sought to increase the significance of the bourgeois distribution of resources through strengthening, extending, and profiting from, the market. Some, in the Central European countries, supported reforms which would weaken the state, if not destroy it. Grzegorz Kolodko, for example, has shown that in Poland groups within the opposition, favored "reform" which would lead to economic deterioration "and ultimately lead to the end of the socialist order" (Kolodko 2000: 28). He cryptically calls this "the politics of 'the worse, the better.'" This is not evidence that "the state" at this juncture already contained within it a dominant capitalist class (as in the Western Marxist scenario); rather it indicates that counter-elites were in position to subvert the socialist state.

Under state socialism, these potentially ascendant class strata were unable to articulate an ideology of capitalism involving privatization of property and a comprehensive move to a market world system. They were denied the right to organize or articulate a counter ideology. (Ideological change had to be legitimated at the top by incumbent elites rather than insurgent counter-elites.) They were also ambiguous as to whether they sought such a revolutionary change. In the early period of transformation under Gorbachev, the internal administrative and acquisition strata supported "the market," but not a move to the privatization of state owned assets. This is clearly illustrated by the voting of the elites of these groups. In the Supreme Soviet of the RSFSR, in July 1990, voting on the "Silaev reforms," which introduced a market in Russia, had the support of over 70 per cent of the government and party elites, as well as over 80 per cent of deputies who had a professional or executive background (see voting data in Lane and Ross 1999: 129–33). However, when one considers privatization, government and party elites were divided. In December 1990, the vote on the introduction of private property was defeated, with nearly 70 per cent of the political elites voting against it; of the professional strata, however, under 40 per cent voted against (Lane and Ross 1999: 129–33). Clearly some (such as the incumbent administrative/executive elite in the oil industry) would have welcomed a move to capitalism, but not those in enterprises which would be unable to compete with capitalist firms. It seems very unlikely that the domestic political elites alone, even under Yeltsin, would have had the motivation to abolish their power under state socialism to move to the uncertain system of capitalism.

The global dimension

Moreover, as these economies were autarchic and economically independent from global capitalism, transnational corporate interests were not present at the state level. A crucial link was formed between reformist political elites and international elites supporting the introduction of capitalist-type market and political reforms. Here the political leadership of Gorbachev was a crucial factor in forming an alliance with the hegemonic Western political powers and the global political elites. As noted by Valerie Bunce (see also Lane 1996, especially 176–83), "Gorbachev assumed that the resistance to reform was so substantial and the problems of Soviet socialism so considerable that the only solution was to build a domestic–international coalition for reform that spanned the Soviet Union, Eastern Europe and the West, and that involved a virtual revolution from above" (Bunce 1999: 62). Outsiders were crucial allies to Gorbachev. As an adviser to Gorbachev (Andrey Grachev) has put it: "The task of [his foreign policy] was not to protect the USSR from the outside threat and to assure ... internal stability but almost the opposite: to use relations with the outside world as an additional instrument of internal change. He wished to transform the West into his ally in the political struggle against the conservative opposition he was facing at home because his real political front was there" (Grachev 1995: 3).

The exchanges between internal political and economic elites with global and international ones were crucial not only to levels of stability but also as potential movers of systemic change. Here, viewing the capitalist class as securing the national interest of capital through the nation-state, does not take account of the different constellations of capitalist power in different nation-states. The capitalist class has different components. Its driving forces have a global rather than a national base. While it is true that the class strata (including the working class) are constituted on a nation-state constituency, the hegemonic faction of the capitalist class has an international one.

The global capitalist class, through the global political elite, had a major effect on the collapse and the direction of transition. The international *political elites* were decisive backers, initially, of the move to political (democratic) and economic markets and, later, to privatization. It is important not to conflate the global political elites (the instruments of change) with factions of the capitalist class having a global reach.

The international hegemony of the United States has played a crucial role in the expansion of capitalism on a world scale. Not only did it subvert economically and politically the socialist states in the 1980s, but it provided an image and an ideology which has been irresistible to the masses. In this way an external agency provided the mass gravity for a popular revolution, initially hailed as a "move to the market" and to democracy. Rather than a global capitalist class operating in the former communist countries through intermediaries giving rise to a comprador type of capitalism, political alliances between internal political elites, particularly those sponsored by Gorbachev and Shevardnadze, and external members of the global political elites (George Bush, Helmut Kohl, Bill Clinton, Margaret Thatcher) were crucial agents of change. By global political elite, I mean international actors who help to shape global economic and political policy.[10] These include the chief executives of international economic and political organizations (such as the IMF and the Central Intelligence Agency (CIA)), leading professionals in non-government organizations with a global perspective, national politicians, and executives with a globalizing intent.[11] Note that here I posit not an economic class in a Marxist sense, but a wider concept of political elite. Political and economic elites are responsive to, but are separate from, the global capitalist class.

If one conceives of capitalism in an international, global perspective, the capitalist revolution in the post-communist countries was expressed through the international political elites. More specific conditions on the building of capitalism and its inclusion in the global order are to be found in the conditionality requirements of the IMF and other bodies, such as the Council of Europe and the European Union (EU). These had a significant and often unacknowledged effect on the internal economic and social policies of the post-communist countries. While Offe and others have noted the absence of a "prescriptive" ex-ante theory, the prescription followed the collapse of state socialism. The implantation of neo-conservative economic policies and political polyarchy has been a major objective of the hegemonic Western powers. "Economic democracy," envisaged in the Washington Consensus, involves individual rights to private property, privatization of enterprises, deregulation, a weak non-distributive state, and an economy open to the global market (see Williamson 1990, especially 8–17).

European agreements were conducted between the EU and the Central and Eastern European countries. As early as December 1990, the EU negotiated with Czechoslovakia, Hungary and Poland on the content of the agreement which was signed in December 1991. The agreements aimed to regularize relationships between the EU and the Central and Eastern European countries. These agreements were forerunners to the *acquis communautaire*; they covered free trade, financial and technical assistance, and encouraged the development of laws compatible with the single market – particularly state subsidies, and freedom of competition. In June 1993, at the Copenhagen Council Meeting, a commitment was made to opening up membership by the EU, subject to the fulfilment of the "Copenhagen Criteria."

The next major step was the codification of conditions in each of the applicant countries. No previous post-revolutionary government had the comprehensive transformative policy contained in the 31 chapters of *acquis communautaire* listing the laws, norms, and standards of the EU. The general conditions specified by the EU for future members from Central and Eastern Europe included:

Stability of institutions guaranteeing democracy, the rule of law, human rights and respect for and protection of minorities;
   The existence of a functioning market economy as well as the capacity to cope with competitive pressure and market forces within the Union;

The ability to take on the obligations of membership including adherence to the aims of political, economic and monetary union.

The administrative and judicial structures of countries intending to join had to be such that "European Community legislation transposed into national legislations [can be] implemented effectively."[12] It is here that the global capital class interest is most visible as this policy lays down conditions for the creation of capitalism and precludes the development of other forms of national socialism – communist, social democratic, and corporatist.

Conclusion

The "transformations" of the former state socialist societies of Central and Eastern Europe lacked some of the features of classical revolutions: violence, charismatic leadership, ideological vision, and resistance of power holders to removal. While some scholars often characterize the collapse and transition as a "revolution," most regard the transformation as a system change, accompanied by elite renewal and replacement. It is contended that the introduction of markets and privatization of property led to the creation of a capitalist class system. Distinctions are made between social class as a form of social stratification and personal identity and as a lever of political transition. It is demonstrated that both have relevance in the former state socialist societies. Underpinning the transition from state socialism were an undeveloped "acquisition" class and an ambiguous administrative class; these were latent ascendant classes. They were effectively constricted by the political environment of state socialism and were unable to articulate an ideology or to organize political opposition. Forming an alliance with the political elites of the hegemonic globalizing capitalist class, endogenous reformist political elites played a major role as agents of change. Capitalism was formed from above with support from below: its ideology, institutions and processes were defined by transnational organizations.

Acknowledgments

Acknowledgment is made to the Leverhulme Trust which supported this research.

Notes

1 Probably the most influential is Barrington Moore Jr (1967). Other writers in the Marxist tradition are Maurice Dobb, Rodney Hilton, and Paul Sweezy.
2 This paper is not concerned with the Marxist outcomes of revolutions, but with whether classes and class struggle are relevant categories of analysis.
3 Their view of revolution is very much of an elite (moderates, radicals) leading reform. Even the redistribution of property does not create new classes but "create the conditions for the formation of a new elite" (Mau and Starodubrovskaya 2001: 332).

4 Lachmann sees elite division in Eastern Europe (creating demands for transformation) as stemming from Gorbachev's policy in the USSR. He ignores divisions before this, for instance in Czechoslovakia in 1968, in Hungary in 1956 as well as the intense divisions within the Polish elites long before the 1980s.

5 They conclude that the association between class and party increased during this period (Mateju and Rehakova 1997: 537).

6 Moreover, many of those who did not were absent from the labor market at the time.

7 Mau and Starodubrovskaya, for example, who emphasize the role of elites, point to the fragmentation of the society and the rise of reforming elites. These, however, are very vaguely defined as "reformers," "radicals," and "conservatives" (2001: 337). For them revolution has no class base.

8 Turkey currently has a strong national focus, whereas the United Kingdom always has had a powerful international one.

9 The extent of administrative control of enterprises with Western business contacts may have varied between countries. Western companies, however, had little autonomous ownership of assets in the state socialist countries.

10 I define this group as a global political elite, rather than as a global political class. This is to avoid ambiguity in the use of the term class. It is similar in character to Mosca's idea of a political class.

11 The World Economic Forum might be considered the political elite of this political class. The leaders of the world's largest 1,000 globalized companies and 33 national leaders, often including the president of the United States, assemble at this meeting in Davos every January: see www.weforum.org.

12 European Union website: http://europa.eu.int/comm/enlargement/intro/criteria. htm#Accession criter.

Part II

Social identities, modernity, and new modes of struggle

5 Revolutionary internationalism and its perils

Fred Halliday

History and utopia

In the early years of the Soviet regime, the story was told of an incident at the Second, 1920, Congress of the Communist International, or Comintern, when without warning a delegation arrived from the recently established revolutionary regime in Mongolia. The members of the Soviet leadership were a bit taken aback by this event, and Lenin asked around anxiously to see if they could find someone to translate from Mongolian into Russian or, even better, into German, the official language of the organization. At this point one of the Bolshevik leaders, Karl Radek, already noted for his generally cosmopolitan outlook and experience, and in command of several languages, volunteered to do the job. Thus when the Mongol delegate came to speak, the Comintern audience were duly regaled with tales of the defeat of Great Han chauvinism, Japanese militarism, White Russian renegades, and so forth, as well as of the unrelenting struggle of the workers, peasants, and nomads of Mongolia against feudalism, Lamaism, and tribal fragmentation. The audience was enthused by this tale, and the Mongol delegate took his seat again. At this point Lenin turned to Radek and said: "Karl, that was excellent, but I did not know you spoke Mongolian." To which Radek replied: "I don't, in fact I do not know a word of the language. But I knew what they were going to say, so I thought I might as well help them convey this to the audience at the Congress." In this anecdote, true or false, is summed up much of the fate, of the good and bad, in the modern revolutionary concept of "internationalism." Spontaneous enthusiasm and solidarity on one side, calculated takeover by stronger states on the other, an appearance of common language and struggle masking very contrasted societies, interests, and cultures (Halliday 1999: chs 3 and 4).

The issue of internationalism is at once theoretical, historical, and actual: *theoretical*, because of the concepts and issues it encapsulates, because of its, often implicit, link to a conception of historical change, and because of its central, if protean, place within the overall conspectus of Marxist theory and politics in general, and the world capitalist system, in particular; *historical*, in that this ideal served for two centuries as one of the leitmotifs of revolutionary action and aspiration by states and movements alike; *actual*, because in the rise since the late 1990s of the anti-globalization movement, and the forging of a new loose band of militancy between radical Third World states, "internationalism" has once again come to be a proclaimed goal of anti-systemic politics across the world. In this last context, there is much room for inspiration, idealism, and hope, if also for cynical instrumentalization, but there is also a conscious, but unreflective, reference back to the internationalism of earlier times. If this current commitment is to bear greater fruit, and to avoid the pitfalls of earlier struggles, it must, however, be based on a critical, informed, reading of that past record: internationalism, precisely, because it is an ideal that recurs across history, requires realistic analysis and formulation. Utopian iteration serves little purpose.

Here, perhaps, it is apt to quote the fine remark of historian E.P. Thompson, that the task of the historian "is to rescue the [past] ... from the immense condescension of posterity" (1963: 12). In regard to matters of revolution in general, and to the principle and practice of internationalism in particular, that condescension takes two forms: on the one hand, a modish, complacent, post-1991 rejection of the revolutionary past, this latter dismissed as an illusion, failed God, or plaything of intellectuals; on the other, a romantic, uncritical and uninformed, resuscitation of ideals that have been associated not only with emancipation but also with much blood, mendacity, and coercion in modern times. We have to bear both parts of the history of revolution in mind, on the one hand that in the century just past, tens of millions of people adhered to, fought for, died for, these ideals, out of a rejection of the injustices of the world they witnessed; on the other, that these revolutionary upheavals themselves led to much further, and unnecessary, suffering, and universally to the creation of new forms of coercion, inequality, inefficiency, and waste of human and natural resources (for two books that capture the dual, utopian/coercive character of revolutions, see Borkenau 1963a and Camus 1992). All ended, on any sober criteria, in failure. As with the associated issues such as insurrection, armed struggle, revolutionary violence, party "discipline," collective ownership of the means of production, indeed that greatest of all modern mobilizatory myths, "revolution" itself, recuperation of past ideals should be matched by accuracy of historical record and clarity of critical and moral assessment. The last thing that is needed, in the face of the barbarities, wastage, fanaticism, and ideological superficiality of the contemporary world is an uncritical trumpeting of revolutionary platitudes, a Rip van Winkle socialism, or, in this case, internationalism that has learned nothing from the past and seeks set fair to teach little or nothing to the present.

Like nationalism itself, to which it is counter-posed, the term internationalism has never received clear, authoritative, definition or theorization within the writings of modern revolutionaries. If liberalism has done somewhat better in that Kant's essay *Perpetual Peace* at least lays out a historic vision coupled with moral urgency, all internationalist visions tend to be vague and, in Marx's sense of the term, "utopian." The solution in regard to nationalism has, however, been for social scientists and historians to come up with a module or set of necessary components which every nationalism must have a territory, a named people, a claim to independence, a flag, etc. (see Smith 1983: 21 for one example of the nationalist "module"). In regard to internationalism, the same approach can be taken. Such an ideological module is necessarily general, allowing of multiple alternatives within each, necessary, box, and all the more so because in its generic form internationalism is not necessarily an idea exclusive to Marxism or revolution: if it is taken as arising out of the French Revolution, and the globalizing politics of the nineteenth century, it can be taken to have several different forms: classically, three – liberal, revolutionary, imperial or hegemonic, to which can be added, in more recent times, postmodern and indeed religiously defined variants.[1]

In this vein, internationalism is a theory with at least four modular components: first, a conception of an international system that imposes a common structure of oppression on different peoples and nations; second, a conception of how, within that global structure, a revolutionary agent, at once national *and* global, is created, and charged with the responsibility of leading a challenge to that structure; third, that the growth through this process of increased internationalist consciousness is matched by the spread of objective processes, e.g. of communications, railways, planes, trade, and investment, that reinforce the international rise in consciousness; and fourth, that all of this, far from being lamented as the destruction of the specific, be it nation, tradition, or identity, is to be welcomed, and is indeed part of the broader emancipatory advance of humanity.

To a minimum degree, the Marxist theory of internationalism meets the requirements of this module, but this is a rather threadbare operation. Marxism has no monopoly on the concept of, and aspiration to, internationalism. Nor indeed is Marxism the only form of *revolutionary* internationalism, since anarchism, however inchoately, also proclaimed its rejection of national and state affiliation. Moreover, while Marxist and communist politics has always adhered to internationalism, it has never given it systematic historical, sociological, or theoretical formulation. Within Marxism no attempt was ever made to locate the incidence, let alone feasibility, of internationalism in terms of specific phases of development of modern politics, or capitalism. The international vocation of the proletariat is often asserted, but no serious argument advanced as to why this should be so, or indeed to deal with the problem that, on some evidence, it is the bourgeoisie that has been more capable of international economic and political mobilization than the working class. All the problems associated with internationalism in modern times, be it in liberal (the United Nations (UN), the European Union) or revolutionary forms, not least that of recognizing and reconciling different state, or "national," interests, are swept under the carpet – in theory as well as in practice as the evidence of Soviet policy in Eastern Europe showed for decades.

The starting point for this presumption but absence of theory is the lack of any serious engagement with internationalism, either as theory or as politics, within the classics of historical materialism. If you want a canonical Marxist discussion of the state, you can turn to *The Critique of the Gotha Programme* and *State and Revolution*, for the revolutionary party to *What is to be done?*, for imperialism to Lenin's 1916 study of that name. But for internationalism there is no such canonical reference, scattered reflections on the capitalist unification of the world from the 1840s (*German Ideology, Manifesto of the Communist Party*) being matched by equally scattered, and conjunctural, statements on internationalist activity and solidarity from the period of the First International itself. Lenin's reflections on the same topic, later collected in volume form, are equally unsystematic, immediate, and oftentimes rhetorical (Lenin 1967).

Like nationalism too, the term "internationalism" denotes two distinct entities, the *ideology* of internationalism, with its appeals of varying kinds to a broader human interest, and the *movement* or *practice* associated with it, be it by political parties and groups, or by revolutionary states. In one other important respect, the concept of internationalism matches, in counterpoint, the fate of the concept of nationalism: while the latter is, in essence, an ideology concerned with the internal, separate, and domestic, constitution of states and peoples, above all their self-determination and independence, nationalism has in practice spread across the world as a transnational force, crossing boundaries and cultures, to become *the universally accepted* normative code of modern politics. Nationalism is a module, not a theory; it is a loose, very loose, modular set of ideas, into which different peoples, movements, states, writers, sundry dreamers, and oftentimes murderers, can put whatever they want. Hence the brilliant observation, itself a reworking of the famous sentence by Marx and Engels, with which the Turkish writer on nationalism, Umut Ozkirimli, begins his most recent book: "The nationalists have no country" (Ozkirimli 2006). By contrast internationalism, which in its initial aspirations denied the efficacy of national or state boundaries, and aspired to a global unity of interest and organization, has, in the practice of twentieth-century revolutions, become an instrument of states. It has been defined by interests of state, even as it has, through the abuse by revolutionary regimes of the principle, served to stimulate contrary, nationalist, responses within the societies concerned. The transnationalization of nationalism has, therefore, been matched by the nationalization of internationalism. In this consists much of the dynamic, and not a little of the tragedy, of the politics of the past century.

If the French Revolution, though its internationalist export of revolutionary change to Germany, Italy, Russia, and Spain, and through its challenge to the monarchy of Britain, served to stimulate nationalism in all these states, the Russian Revolution achieved a similar, contradictory, result in the countries onto which it abutted – China to the east, Eastern Europe to the West, and Iran, Turkey and, latterly, Afghanistan to the south. Equally, within the socialist and communist movements, internationalism, far from serving as a principle that has united parties and movements in different countries, or as a means of adjudicating tensions between revolutionary states and movements still aspiring to take power, has, repeatedly, served as one of the main issues around which division has crystallized. In the communist tradition, internationalism has, in effect, become a catalyst of disunity. Thus the First International split apart in the early 1870s over the question of relations between anarchists and communists within the organization. The Second International broke up on the outbreak of the First World War, in August 1914 and with the adoption of nationalist pro-war positions, by all its major components. The Third International was contested, from within the USSR and outside, most notably by Trotsky and his followers, over its international line (Trotsky 1937). In the 1960s there transpired the Sino–Soviet dispute, a conflict within which issues of the "international line," in particular relations with the United States and nuclear weapons, were crucial. This protracted inter-communist polemic occasioned many charges that the other side had abandoned its internationalist position. Finally, in the two decades of decline of the European communist movement, from the Prague Spring and subsequent Soviet invasion of 1968, through the emergence of Euro-communism in the 1970s, to the final dissolution of the late 1980s, the issue of loyalty to, or critique of, the USSR and the right of individual communist parties to autonomy, was central. In the process of rejecting the orthodoxies associated with an earlier, "monolithic," era within the European communist movement, the two principles most associated with the old Soviet-controlled orthodoxy were "dictatorship of the proletariat" and "proletarian internationalism." Neither survived the collapse of official communism into the 1990s when, perhaps equalled only by the commitment to the equality of women, they were consigned to the dustbin of contemporary politics.

The principle of, or aspiration to, internationalism was thus both central to, and repeatedly abused and contested within, the history of the socialist and communist movements. Yet in both its early espousal and adoption, and in its later rejection, it was never clear what exactly was being proposed. Internationalism, in its popular and unpopular times, remained something vague, unanalyzed. And this has, paradoxically, remained the case since the collapse of Soviet communism. For while, in Eastern Europe and the USSR, the principle itself has been rejected, in favor of all the forms of nationalism, statism, and identity politics associated with post-communism, bloodily so in the case of the former Yugoslavia, within the anti-globalization movement, and in the rhetoric and policies of the remaining radical states, such as Cuba, Venezuela, and Iran, it has retained an important and apparently revived status. In the 2000s from Tehran to Porto Alegre a new generation of militants, and leaders, has come to espouse internationalism, in a way that is generically, but not in detail, claiming continuity with earlier epochs of revolutionary internationalism, but which, once again, avoids specific, concrete, let alone historically informed, and self-aware investigation of the concept. A more detached, and historically based, investigation of the fate of the term, its uses and abuses within the revolutionary tradition may, therefore, serve to cast light not just on what was for two centuries an important, almost permanent, feature of the radical tradition, but also on the ways in which, in the contemporary world, and in particular in the contestation of globalization, internationalism is once again playing the contradictory role, of aspiration and instrumentalization, that it was allotted long ago.

Formation of a myth: proletarian internationalism

The concept of internationalism, formally qualified as "proletarian internationalism" to distinguish it from its "bourgeois" or "liberal" forms, as well as from the ever present specter of proletarian "nationalism," lies, as we have seen, at the core of the Marxist and Leninist tradition. Along with the dictatorship of the proletariat and the revolutionary party it is, arguably, one of the three most important political concepts in that tradition. The term "internationalism" itself originated from the work of the First International, formally titled the International Working Men's International, established in 1864, and the words "internationalist" and "internationalism" first occur in English soon thereafter (1864 and 1877, respectively). Internationalism's most famous slogan, found at the end of the *Manifesto of the Communist Party* of 1848, "Workers of the world unite, you have nothing to lose but your chains," was to serve as the basis for the subsequent century and a half of communist commitment to this goal.[2] Although the First International itself was dissolved in 1874, the aspiration to internationalism continued and was to find concrete expression in the founding of the Third International, the Comintern, in 1919. This propounded not a federation of parties, as was the case with the IWA and the Second International, but a single, highly organized, global party, *in effect one world communist party,* comprised of those national groups, or sections, that affiliated on the basis of the "21 conditions" established by Moscow. The slogan propounded by Lenin, in the official language of the Comintern, summarized this program: *Weltklasse, Weltpartei, Weltrevolution* – perhaps best translated as "global class, global party, global revolution." From early times, however, the Comintern served as an instrument of Russian foreign policy and followed the various twists and turns dictated by the Communist Party of the Soviet Union, be they the alliance with "national democratic" forces in Asia dictated in 1920, the ultra-leftist "Third Period" of 1928, or the "United Front" of 1935 (see Claudin 1976).

The Comintern itself was dissolved in 1943, a measure taken by Stalin to appease his Western allies and, hopefully, remove one of the mobilizatory slogans of the Axis Powers (who were sometimes referred to as the "Anti-Comintern Pact"). In fact, the 1943 dissolution was in large measure deceptive: Moscow maintained, or sought to maintain, control of the major communist parties of the world through the 1940s, succeeding in most of Eastern and Western Europe, with the exception of Yugoslavia. Its greatest setback came after 1956 when the largest party in the world, the Communist Party of China, came increasingly to criticize Soviet policy and influence in China, leading to an open split in July 1963. The Chinese made much of the Soviet betrayal of internationalism, seen first of all as a militant opposition to the United States, but did not seek, except in a sporadic and bilateral way, to build their own, organized, international following. They had good relations with Albania, by now also in revolt against Moscow, and with some communist parties around the world, but never sought to build their own countervailing organization. Beyond the fact that Moscow was itself no longer sponsoring such an international organization, two other reasons for this abstention may be suggested. First, China's international following, in terms of organized parties as distinct from "Maoist" sympathizers and movements (e.g. in Portugal after 1974), was scattered and in real terms negligible. No party in Western Europe, Latin America, or Africa sided with them, and their international following was confined to some splinter (India, the Naxalites) or eccentric (New Zealand) parties in Asia. Second, the self-sufficiency, not to say solipsism, which characterized Chinese policy and world view in other respects may have also played a role here. A country like China, representing a quarter of humanity, felt no evident need to build up an international following as a means of bolstering either its security position or its prestige.[3]

In Western Europe the critique of Stalin offered by Khrushchev at the Twentieth Congress of the CPSU in February 1956, combined with the evident failure of Moscow to control the Chinese, encouraged a more gradual process of diversification, known first, as in the writings of Italian leader Palmiro Togliatti, as "polycentrism," later, in the late 1960s and onwards, as "Euro-communism." This autonomous communist movement did indeed reject some of the core tenets of the previous Moscow-led tradition, among them dictatorship of the proletariat and proletarian internationalism, the former being associated with centralized, even "totalitarian," dictatorship, the latter as pretext used by Soviet leaders to justify their invasions of Hungary (1956) and Czechoslovakia (1968).

Yet if the denunciation of Stalin in February 1956, and the subsequent invasions of Eastern European states were to undermine much of Western communist support for the USSR, the links were not broken entirely and some continued to proclaim loyalty to the old conception of internationalism. At the 1969 biannual conference of the Communist Party of Great Britain, the veteran intellectual and editor of *Marxism Today*, Palme Dutt, rose to his feet in the debate on the invasion in the previous year of Czechoslovakia to declare: "Comrades, in 1920 we stood firm over Georgia;

in 1939 we stood firm over Finland; in 1956 we stood firm over Hungary; and today we stand firm over Czechoslovakia" (the author attended the conference as correspondent of the radical paper *Black Dwarf*). Soviet financial aid, if only through subsided purchases of party publications, free trips to the USSR for "delegations," etc., continued well into the late 1980s. As late as 1988, in the dying months of Soviet control in Eastern Europe and when the Soviet model itself was discredited for all to see, Anatoly Dobrinin, veteran diplomat and now head of the international section of the CPSU, summoned representatives of the European communist parties to a meeting in Prague to study the "international lessons" of recent developments within the Soviet Union itself (*Le Monde*, April 16, 1988). All of this was accompanied by many attempts not to jettison internationalism, but rather to reinterpret it, and the traditions of solidarity and struggle therewith associated, in a more open, democratic light, "a new internationalism" open to non-communists, radical Christians, and others, when not to turn the very concept of internationalism, as association of free agents and peoples, against the Soviet record (Pajetta 1978). Gorbachev himself sought, in his writings and speeches, to defend a concept of internationalism, even as he emptied it of much, or all, of its earlier revolutionary content. Thus in his programmatic work, *Perestroika*, he calls for a new form of internationalism, based on cooperation between sovereign states and peoples (Gorbachev 1987). Ironically, just as in the dying years of communism the concept of "solidarity" was turned against it by a workers' movement in Poland committed to removing the communist party from power, so a range of new uses of the term, from the journal of Oxfam in Britain to the interventionist policies of the Reagan administration, sought to appropriate the term "internationalism."[4]

This record of organized engagement by the Soviet Union, in the face of pressure from both anti-communist and dissident communist states, forms, however, only a part, the more formal and visible part, of a much larger history of activity by the CPSU and other revolutionary states that can be seen as putting the commitment to internationalism into effect. It has long been commonplace, in the face of criticism of Soviet policy from within the revolutionary movement, be it by anarchists, Trotskyists or Maoists, or by Western observers who see all Soviet policy in terms of Moscow's pursuit of realpolitik, to question whether utopian aspirations and broad emancipatory goals played *any* part in the formation of Soviet policy and practice, internally or internationally. The same applies to the particular concept of internationalism and its implementation. The list of Soviet, specifically Stalinist, distortions of internationalism is a long one, starting from Stalin's famous 1928 definition of internationalism as "unswerving loyalty to the USSR." The list of actions that seem to confirm the treacherous, capitulationist, cynical in Soviet policy are many, chief among them being the Molotov–Ribbentrop Pact of August 1939, the failure to support the Warsaw uprising in August 1944, the invasions of Hungary and Czechoslovakia.

The more radical critics, such as Trotskyists, will include the "abandonment" of the German Revolution in 1923, the "capitulationist" line taken during the British General Strike in 1926, the failure to achieve victory in Spain in 1936–1939, the backing down in Cuba in the missile crisis of 1962, and much else besides. In Trotskyist eyes, though not of those who thought the USSR was capitalist all along, Gorbachev who made his peace with the West in the late 1980s and who, in so doing, unleashed the collapse of the communist system itself, was but one in a long line of bureaucratic leaders who, in the end, put the class interests of the Soviet bureaucracy before that of internationalist solidarity and confrontation with the capitalist world. The implications of all this for the study of internationalism are evident: it was but a slogan, without practical impact.

The internationalist record

Here, however, it is essential to recall the other part of E.P. Thompson's program, that of rescuing the past from the condescension of those who denied the impact of, and widespread support for, revolutionary politics in modern times. On closer examination, therefore, the wholly negative assessment, supposedly more revolutionary or "realist," of the seven decades of Soviet foreign policy, as but betrayal and realpolitik, and also of the foreign policies of other revolutionary powers, be they China or Cuba, is simplistic. It understates the degree to which revolutionary internationalism, that of states as distinct from that of classes, was a significant factor in the external relations of these countries and hence in the international history of the twentieth century.[5] Indeed the very same balance sheet, of aspiration, instrumentalization, commitment, and betrayal, can be drawn up in regard to the revolutionary impact of the French Revolution, as it is being written today, incomplete but clear in its broad trajectory, of the international policy of the most recent, but non-communist, revolution, that of the Islamic Republic of Iran. The key to assessing the international impact and foreign policy of a revolutionary state lies not in taking isolated incidents, of success or failure, of "principle" or "betrayal," these latter often abstracted from the realities of the moment, but in looking at how, over years and decades, such a policy evolves within the parameter of the "dual," diplomatic *and* revolutionary, policy. Given that no state has the capacity on its own to alter the character of international relations, or the internal political and socio-economic order of other states, revolutionary regimes cannot be judged, and condemned, in some moralistic way for their failure to set the rest of the world on fire. Rather, it has to be seen how, with the commitments they have, such states respond to the opportunities presented to them (see Halliday 1999: ch. 5).

The Bolshevik leadership were clear that, while the incidence of revolution in the rest of the world, and first of all Europe, depended on conditions within each country and the power of revolutionary forces there, they also had a need, indeed a duty, to promote and assist in whatever way they could, including in extreme cases, the sending of troops, the revolutionary forces in other countries. The USSR did not succeed in exporting revolution to Europe in the 1920s, but it certainly tried to do so in invading Poland in the summer of 1920 and in providing the aid it could, up to 1923, to the German Revolution. The role of Moscow in the Spanish Civil War of 1936–1939 has been the subject of much controversy, from anarchist and POUM critiques of the imposition of communist control on the republican militias and army, to right-wing denunciations, from Spain in the 1930s and, more recently, in U.S. commentary on recently released Soviet documents on the war. Yet what is evident is that the USSR did indeed try, amidst extremely difficult circumstances and far from its frontier, to bolster the Spanish republic. The conventional critique of Stalinist bureaucratization, reflected above all in Orwell's *Homage to Catalonia,* is true as far as repression of the independent left is concerned, but naïve when it comes to the military aspects of the war (see Hughes 1998 and Borkenau 1963b).[6] Similarly the right-wing, and Franquista, account misses the point that it was the very attempt by the nationalist forces to seize power in a coup in July 1936 that made the Spanish communist party, hitherto a small sect, into a national party, not the other way around.[7]

With the advent of the Second World War, of course, the international situation changed so dramatically that new opportunities to the West, with the retreat of the Nazi army, and east, with the rise of communist parties in China and in Vietnam, had arisen. Far from shying away from taking advantage of this general international crisis, and overriding the dissolution of the Comintern in 1943, the USSR proceeded to install communist parties in power across eastern Europe, or assist those with some real prospects of so doing (Yugoslavia, Albania, Czechoslovakia), while in East Asia it provided major, long-term, assistance to the Chinese, Korean, and Vietnamese parties that had so improved their own situation during the Second World War itself or, as in the case of Vietnam, in its immediate aftermath.[8] Nor did the Soviet commitment to assisting revolutionary parties and regimes across the world end with the stabilization of the world map in the early 1950s with the armistices in Korea and Vietnam. For all the cynicism and bureaucratic calculation that did indeed mark the USSR up to its demise, it remained committed to a competition with the West, across the world, and to support for states and movements that were struggling against, or resisting, the USA and its allies. The victory of the Vietnamese communists in reuniting their country in 1975, the long-term economic and military survival of Cuba, the prolonged political and guerrilla struggle of the African National Congress (ANC) in South Africa would all have been impossible without the sustained backing of the USSR into the 1980s in some cases.[9]

The commitment of revolutionary states to exporting revolution and assisting allies abroad is evident in other modern revolutions as well. China, as already noted, did not pursue, or seek to emulate, the kind of global political and military commitment that the USSR aspired to. It remained a regional power, confined in influence and aspiration to East Asia, and having only inspirational, and at times notional, relations with the various "Maoist" movements and parties that claimed guidance from Beijing: for example, neither the Maoist movement in Peru, *Sendero Luminoso,* nor the Marxist–Leninist guerrillas of Nepal were in any substantial sense armed, guided, or financed by the Chinese. Yet in regard to Indo-China the People's Republic did indeed play an important role, if only to ensure that Moscow did not monopolize alliances, and credit gained, with regard to the movements in Vietnam and Cambodia. While it is impossible to allocate the respective roles of the USSR and China in the 1975 communist victories in Vietnam, China, and Laos, it is evident that it was the aid *from these two states*, rather than just the effectiveness and heroism of popular mobilization, that contributed to the revolutionary victories.

For its part, Cuba played a significant role over more than two decades in promoting revolution in Latin America, at first with little success. The new Third World international organization set up in 1966 by Havana, the Organization of Solidarity of the Peoples of Asia, Africa and Latin America (OSPAAAL), soon ceased to have any active life, never held another international congress, and soon fell moribund under the control of a few, already established, states. The death of Che Guevara in Bolivia in 1967, apparently on a mission that was to link up with revolutionaries in Tucuman, the northern province of his native Argentina, symbolized the failure to export the Cuban model of guerrilla war. The overthrow of the Popular Unity government in Chile, in September 1973, appeared to mark the failure of the other, more political and electoral, strategy. Yet six years later, in July 1979, and with substantial Cuban military and political assistance, the Sandinistas took power in Nicaragua, while pro-Cuban forces were also strong in El Salvador and Guatemala. In a further twist of revolutionary fate, a decade later, there emerged in a major state of Latin America, Venezuela, a populist anti-American movement headed by Hugo Chávez, whose election in 1998 as president marked a major political, and financial, breakthrough for Cuba. Other states, notably Bolivia, were to follow (for the extent and costs of the Cuban role in Central America, see Castañeda 1993).

The greatest revolutionary internationalist commitment of the Cuban revolution did not, however, lie in Latin America at all, but across the Atlantic, in southern Africa. Cuba had, from the early 1960s, sought to build alliances with anti-imperialist forces in that continent, in Egypt and Algeria where radical regimes were already in power, and with guerrillas in the Congo, southern Africa, and the Portuguese colonies. When, in 1975, following the April 1974 revolution in Portugal, a major struggle broke out in Angola, with U.S.-backed forces of the FNLA (National Front for the Liberation of Angola) challenging the left-wing MPLA (Popular Movement for the Liberation of Angola), Cuba intervened decisively and on a large scale, sending thousands of combat troops across the seas to defend Luanda and the MPLA. There followed an extraordinary decade of military activity by Cuba in Angola itself and against the South African forces sent to combat it from Namibia. In the end, the Cubans and their allies won an astounding political victory, forcing the independence of Namibia in 1990 and, by humiliating South African forces on the ground, assisting the transition to majority rule in South Africa itself (see Gleijeses 2002).

This record of "internationalist" activity by revolutionary states may serve as a corrective to the two variants of historical condescension, a rebuke both to arguments which claim that no such commitment was ever sustained, and to those which present the external activities of these states in a generally favorable, disinterested light. On the one hand, there is the commitment, over decades, by the USSR to promoting communist parties seeking to take power, a commitment also met by the Chinese in regard to Indo-China, and by the Cubans despite their limited resources, in Latin America and Africa. But far from serving unalloyed emancipatory or democratic ends, this policy, when it became one of defence of such regimes, degenerated into one of supporting authoritarian parties and states. The actions that most alienated international public opinion, including many communists, were often those "internationalist" actions aimed precisely at shoring up like-minded communist regimes: Hungary in 1956, Czechoslovakia in 1968, and the most extreme, brutal but ideologically consistent, of all such actions, the despatch of the Soviet "Limited Contingent" to Afghanistan in December 1979. In the Cuban case the idealism of support in southern Africa contrasted with the dishonorable association with the Ethiopian Derg. China activated the unification of Vietnam *and* the consolidation of Khmer Rouge terror in Cambodia.

The contrast between these kinds of internationalist support is also evident in the relationship between the condition of these regimes domestically and their international activity: far from them following, as "realist" and Trostkyist critiques alike would suggest, a more cautious and accommodating policy the more they "degenerated" within, these states showed a capacity to pursue, sometimes at considerable cost to themselves, support for revolutionaries abroad even as their internal situations became more ossified and corrupted. Here the famous analogy of the fire in the field, taken by George Kennan in his long telegram of 1946 from the novel by Thomas Mann, *Buddenbrooks*, has particular appeal: in Kennan's view, revolutions were like fire in a field – as they spread, the core died out, but the fires the revolution had lit continued to spread further and further till in the end they too were extinguished. There could be no more graphic illustration of this than the situation of the USSR and Cuba in the 1980s, a few years before the communist system collapsed in its core states: while bureaucratization, demoralization, "stagnation," and so forth held sway within these countries, including in a now exhausted Cuba, their states were busy, according to their own lights, promoting or defending revolution and battling counter-revolution abroad, the Russians in a vain attempt to contain the forces of the Afghan mujahidin counter-revolution and so defend the government of the People's Democratic Party of Afghanistan, the latter to push back and defeat the armies despatched by Pretoria to control southern Africa. In the persistence of these internationalist endeavors, at considerable political and economic cost to the states so involved and in the light of their contrasting character and outcome, lies much of the paradox that has characterized revolutionary internationalism in modern times.

Internationalism in the twenty-first century: unanswered questions

The contemporary rendering of internationalism therefore faces a challenge both retrospective and prospective. On the one hand, it involves providing an accurate historical assessment of what internationalist politics has involved in modern times, such that neither the exaggerations of revolutionaries, past or present, nor the dismissals of twentieth-century revolutions by post-1991 complacency, can be accepted. But it also poses a challenge to contemporary analysis, and political activity, in that for this ideal to acquire greater impact on the contemporary world, its inherent difficulties, as well as its often manipulated past, need to be taken into account. It is conventional to argue that the failure of internationalism, revolutionary or liberal, over the past two centuries is due to the predominance of its rival, nationalism. It is in the failure to recognize the force of this ideology, the constitutive role it plays as the basis of legitimation and affect in the international state system and, not least, the onward sweeping of identity and community politics across the world in the wake of the end of the cold war, that, it is argued by many, from Anthony Smith to Tom Nairn, has determined the fate of internationalism. Marx's prediction of the 1840s, that workers are more and more turning away from their national affiliation, has proven to be resoundingly false in the world of the 1990s and 2000s as much as in the fragmentation of the Second International in 1914. Yet this is at once to concede too much to nationalism and to probe too little the weaknesses of internationalism: nationalism has proven to be a powerful tool for mobilizing feeling within countries and for opposing foreign domination, but it has made little or no contribution to the major changes of modern times, the growth of the world economy, of technology and communications, and, despite the best efforts of sympathetic theories and philosophers to splice intellectual content into it, has remained a threadbare moral and analytic system.

The failures of revolutionary internationalism lie not just in its rivalry with nationalism, but in the weakness of the very core propositions it has itself advanced, and its own failure to engage with the social and political realities of the modern world, not least that of the revolutionary movement, and the incidence of revolutions that it has claimed to reinforce. This failure may become clearer if we return to the four basic, modular, requirements of a theory of internationalism and assess how far revolutionary ideology and practice have provided adequate substantiation of each: a theory of global change and development; the identification of internationalist agency; the analysis of socio-economic developments that reinforce that agency; and the specification of an international good. In one sense, Marx and Engels, writing in the mid-nineteenth century, had it easy: before their eyes industrial capitalism was expanding across the globe, a new social subject had just emerged, expanding trade, migration, and communication were undermining state frontiers, and all of this was, plausibly, furthering the revolutionary socialist movement. Lenin took this further, recognizing the uneven but also fractural nature of capitalist expansion, supplementing the proletariat with other, peasant and national bourgeois, allies around the world, adding war as a major catalytic factor, and theorizing, and implementing, as Marx had never done, his conception of a global revolutionary party. As Marx did not, Lenin linked global analysis, imperialism, to global revolution, the Comintern. Yet at once the central problem of any theory of internationalism becomes clear, its tendency to simplify both the development of capitalism, and the politics associated with it. To be more than an abstract, disembodied ideal, a utopian proclamation from nowhere, or from one or two beleaguered radical capitals, internationalism has a political and social goal to articulate. It has also to link this to an understanding of the objective context in which this goal is to be articulated and achieved, namely that of the capitalist world market, and, much under-recognized by Marxists then and now, the fragmentation of the world into separate states. This latter characteristic of the international, the system of states, is not just some transient, or epiphenomenal, accompaniment of capitalism, but a constitutive ordering institution, with great economic, political, and ideological effects.

In this scheme, the assumed political outcome of economic and social change, the ever greater collaboration of the oppressed, led by the working class, itself reproduces the weakness of classical Marxism with regard to politics in that it ignores the existence and impact of states, and the very real, recurrent, and not accidental rivalries and conflicts that may arise in any international collaboration. Above all, it ignores the role of the state, this seen here not as the institution to be struggled against, but the chosen instrument of revolutionaries themselves in their struggle for global consolidation and advance. Here the insight of orthodox political sociology on the necessary reinforcement of state powers by modern revolutions can easily be extended to the realm of international solidarity and struggle, with consequences all too evident, from Lenin onwards (Skocpol 1979). The fundamental failure of revolutionary internationalism was not, therefore, that nationalism overwhelmed internationalism, but that the revolutionary state itself nationalized internationalism.

The contemporary world allows of no such easy, rhetorical, and world-historically light-minded generalizations as were vouchsafed to the authors of the *Manifesto*. We cannot simply recognize and, dialectically, respond to the spread of globalization and hail the emergence of a new, international, political subject, be it the "multitude" of Hardt and Negri, the assembled benign masses of "global civil society," or the reconstituted bloc of radical Third World states patronized by Chávez and Ahmadinejad. The challenge that confronted Marx and Engels, and liberal internationalists a century and a half ago still stands, namely that of countering the exploitation, inequality, oppression, and waste of the contemporary capitalist order with a radical, cooperative, international political order. This has been the goal of the assorted movements and institutions that have arisen from these traditions in modern times, from the International Working Men's Association and the Comintern, to their liberal and often scorned counterparts' international peace movements, the UN and the European Union. In many ways, the challenge is more urgent than it was in the nineteenth century, because of the environmental and demographic challenges we now face, and because those advancing internationalism have to elaborate a theory and politics that take account of the lessons of the past century and a half of thwarted internationalist endeavor.

Acknowledgment

This essay draws on research into problems of contemporary internationalism carried out under a grant from the Leverhulme Foundation, whose support is gratefully acknowledged.

Notes

1 I have formulated this at greater length in Halliday 1988. For all its differences of language and historical reference, radical Islamic internationalism also meets the demands of this module.
2 Even this slogan is open, in its context, to different readings, as in the light of the preceding paragraph it can be taken as an appeal to the workers of *each* country, separately, to unite, or "combine" (*Vereinigt Euch*) rather than to form one *single* world organization.
3 In 1978 I had occasion to meet in London the veteran Australian communist writer Wilfred Burchett, for a time in the 1960s and early 1970s one of the very few outside reporters to whom the Chinese gave access and interviews. I asked him how many people in China, out of 1.2 billion, were reasonably informed about the outside world. He paused for a minute and replied: "Around twelve, maybe less."
4 "Ronald Reagan Internationalist," *International Herald Tribune* editorial (no date). In a curious recycling of the original Marxist concept, the term "internationalist" has a long, and quite separate, history within U.S. politics, denoting someone, of left or right, who pursues an active foreign policy and relates the security, interest, and prosperity of the United States to such an engagement.
5 Someone who grappled with this issue, and who, despite his general stance of disabused statism and "realism," understood the power of internationalism as an ideology was the historian and international relations specialist E.H. Carr. His

1973 study of the foreign policy of the early Bolsheviks gives a vivid account of the politics and aspirations of the time. On the later development of this topic in his work, and the conflict between this theme and other more "realist" proclivities, see Halliday 2000.

6 For one sober corrective to the Orwellian account, see Hughes 1998. By far the best account of the Republican camp, and of the civil war as a whole in 1936 and 1937, see Borkenau 1963b.

7 The recently released Soviet documents are in Radosh *et al.* 2001. While there is no reason to question the authenticity of the documents reproduced, or their translation into English in this volume, the accompanying commentary is of little value, being a Cold War polemic that ignores the context of Spain at that time. That these, in themselves very interesting, documents on the Spanish Civil War should be published by an editor who does not know Spanish and has no scholarly background in the war, is itself an index of how politicized such archival work and publication has become.

8 The conventional, Western *and* Chinese communist claim, that after the defeat of Japan in August 1945 Stalin tried to prevent the triumph of the Chinese Revolution and was niggardly in his support of Mao, is belied by recent materials released from the Soviet archives. The new revelations on the outbreak of the Korean War in June 1950 show that, while Stalin was at first cautious about Kim Il-sung's wish to launch a war to capture the South, he in the end agreed to support it, as did, on his side, Mao Tse-tung.

9 It is conventionally argued, not least by the Cuban leadership, that the Soviet Union betrayed them in the denouement of the 1962 missile crisis. Much U.S. analysis stresses that Khrushchev "backed down." But this is to mistake the purposes of the Soviet deployment of missiles in Cuba in the first place. This had two purposes: a military one, to match U.S. deployment of Thor and Jupiter missiles near the Soviet border, in Turkey, in Khruschev's words "to put a hedgehog in Uncle Sam's pants;" second, and this was why the Cubans themselves were so keen to have the missiles, to deter another U.S.-backed invasion, a more effective variant of the Bay of Pigs fiasco of April 1961. The outcome of the crisis was, in fact, a victory for the Russians: while not formally committed to doing so, the United States did pull its missiles out of Turkey in 1963, and, while avoiding the formal guarantee not to invade that Moscow had requested, it in practice held to this commitment. The Cuban Revolution was saved from further major militant threat, and was thereby given a free hand to pursue its revolutionary policies in the rest of Latin America: see Halliday 1999: 200–2.

6 Durable inequality

The legacies of China's revolutions and the pitfalls of reform

Ching Kwan Lee and Mark Selden

Since the early 1980s, China has been hailed as the success story of post-socialist transition, shifting its revolutionary course via a reform that has generated the world's most dynamic growth over a quarter of a century and elevated it to the forefront of nations attracting foreign investment. Often eclipsed in this glowing picture are enduring, even exacerbated, structures of inequality and the vibrant forms of popular resistance these have spawned. In this chapter, we compare the structures of class and spatial inequality that were both transformed and created in the course of these epochs and the nature of the social upheavals of the revolutionary epoch from 1945 to 1970, and China's post-1970 market reform. Two key questions drive our analysis: What are the legacies of the Chinese Revolution for the pursuit of social equality? How has reform structured patterns of inequality and conflict?

We find a striking persistence of two major divides in modern Chinese society – the rural–urban hierarchy and the domination of the bureaucratic class over ordinary citizens within rural and urban societies – while noting their changing character across the two historical epochs. The transition from the national revolutionary era into one of global market integration has the paradoxical effect of localizing and fragmenting class conflicts and protests which in the previous era had at times taken the forms of cross-regional, large scale, party-initiated mass mobilization. The rhetoric of class and exploitation has given way to a liberal discourse emphasizing rights, legality, and citizenship at a time of exacerbated class and spatial inequality.

Revolutionizing class and spatial hierarchies, 1945–1970

Land reform and collectivization

Land reform and subsequent market controls eliminated the major polarized rural social classes rooted in differential land ownership and wealth, producing a striking homogenization of intra-village incomes and opportunities while enshrining an important new social divide between cadres and villagers. In the years 1946–1953, land confiscation and redistribution both partially satisfied the land hunger of the landless and land poor and toppled the rural elite, while establishing a class-struggle mode of mobilization politics that would be repeatedly invoked in subsequent campaigns throughout the revolutionary era. The results included roughly equal per capita land ownership within each village community and the rise to power of a local party leadership that emerged at the head of land reform and was committed to maintaining its results.

Collectivization transformed Chinese agrarian institutions and social processes in ways that land reform, which left intact a farming regime centered on the household, had not. The basic units of collective agriculture were teams of 20–30 households dominated by local cadres who directly controlled labor, the transfer of grain to the state, income distribution, and major parameters of social, cultural, and political life. Collectivization expanded the reach of the state, making possible extraction of a larger share of the agricultural surplus, substantial portions of which were transferred to industry and the cities through compulsory sales to the state at low fixed prices of collectively produced grain and cotton. For all its distinctive social and political dynamics, China nevertheless reproduced one of the standard trajectories of industrialization familiar from the dawn of the industrial revolution: the transfer of the surplus from agriculture and the countryside to industry and the cities. And with it, one of the central fault lines of social conflict.

The revolutionary processes of land reform and collectivization therefore homogenized the complex social structure of pre-revolutionary rural China into a two-class structure of collectivized villagers and cadres, the latter exercising a monopoly on political power reinforced through the allocation of labor, income distribution, and market control. In the formal "class" structure of the revolutionary period, class position was fixed by birth, on the basis of purported class position in the pre-land reform social landscape. The result was to create a frozen, hereditary, and misleading set of categories, more caste than class, that were said to define the socio-political hierarchy of virtue and its opposite. Landlords and rich peasants, stripped of the property and wealth that once defined their class position and designated as pariahs, constituted a new social stratum at the lowest echelons of the collective order. In this transvaluation of values, these class enemies and other "bad elements" would be repeatedly scapegoated and attacked in political campaigns that ritually sanctioned party power while humiliating the once powerful. This had the effect not only of reifying party leadership and depriving those defined as class enemies of citizenship within the village order, but also of concealing existing polarities of power.

Urban class structure

The party spearheaded a similar drive to transform the urban class structure through the expropriation of merchants and capitalists and the socialization of industry in the form of state and collective ownership. Where the rural class struggle was played out with ample violence in the midst of a civil war, however, nationalization of industry took place for the most part after the party's power was secure, and involved far less mass mobilization or violent confrontation. In the wake of socialization, urban workers enjoyed substantial welfare and income benefits that were the envy of villagers. Permanent workers in state-owned enterprises gained lifetime employment and a welfare package that included health care, housing, and generous retirement benefits. Only workers in core (mainly large) state-owned enterprises obtained the "big" welfare package that provided free health care for family members and many amenities, benefits unavailable to workers in smaller state enterprises and collective enterprises. Particularly after 1960, villagers were largely barred from finding work in cities, but even those who were able to find work as temporary and contract workers were largely excluded from urban welfare benefits (Walder 1986). Overall, the revolution conferred on urban workers as a group significant welfare and status gains, if not power, as the titular class in the "workers' state." This was a product both of the party's ideological profiling of social classes and of the material and security benefits that steadily widened the urban–rural and state–collective gap.

The deepest social divide in the cities was not within the ranks of workers but, as in the countryside, between workers and cadres. Disparity in income and benefits such as housing allocation and medical care between cadres and workers remained relatively small by international standards (Zhou 2004). But cadres monopolized political power, and they had access to scarce resources such as special shops, and services available only to the most privileged workers.

In short, the city, like the countryside, experienced an homogenization of diverse classes into a two-class system of working people ("the masses") and officials ("the cadres"), with significant gradations within each category but without the extremes of wealth and status characteristic of the pre-revolutionary order. If the pre-revolutionary class order rested heavily on differentiated positions with respect to ownership of the means of production and associated social relations, the primary class differences in revolutionary China pivoted on positioning with respect to the party–state.

Rural–urban divide

In 1960, when the Great Leap Forward failed, propelling China into famine, the party imposed a population registration (*hukou*) system that erected a great wall between city and countryside, locking rural people into their villages and cutting off most remaining intra-rural and city–countryside exchange, while the siphoning of the rural surplus to urban industry via compulsory grain sales at state-imposed low prices continued (Cheng and Selden 1994). A two-tier institutional and accumulation structure divided city and countryside, and set the stage for widening income and social inequality between them. To be sure, urban wages were set low, but the combination of cash incomes (rural people mainly earned income in kind), lifetime employment, pensions and health care (provided by the state for urban workers and employees only), and superior schools, all worked to the advantage of urban workers and employees.

The significance of the urban–rural divide is driven home with particular clarity by two sets of facts. First, nearly all of the millions who starved to death during the Great Leap famine – the most credible estimates ranging from 10 million to more than 20 million extra deaths – were rural people. Viewing city and countryside as a whole, urban per capita grain consumption dipped slightly in the years 1960–1963, from 201 kilograms per person in 1959 to an average of 187 kilograms in the years 1960–1963 before returning to previous levels. By contrast, rural grain consumption plummeted from 201 kilograms in 1958 to just 168 kilograms in the years 1960–1963 and did not return to 1958 levels until 1979 (Taylor and Hardee 1986). Second, in 1961 the state "sent down" (*xiaxiang*) 20 million urban workers, thereby shifting its burden of feeding and providing work for them in famine times to a countryside that already had a large labor surplus and confronted acute hunger. Promised restitution of their urban jobs once the famine ended, most would live out their lives in the villages to which they were sent. This first wave of "sent down" urban denizens would be followed by the dispatch to rural areas of close to 20 million urban junior high and high school graduates in the years between 1964 and 1976, ostensibly to bridge the urban–rural gap through their contributions as farmers to rural development, but at least as important, obviating the necessity for the state to provide jobs and benefits for them. To be sent down was to lose the largesse of the state.

In short, the revolution had brought the homogenization of both rural and urban social classes, reduction of wealth disparity, and alleviation of urban poverty. It had not, however, eliminated class or spatial divisions. Indeed, it had exacerbated the latter. The state policed social divisions, notably those between collectivized villagers consigned to agriculture, and urban workers and employees in state and collective enterprises. The former group subsidized the state, principally through compulsory sales at low fixed prices; the latter were subsidized by it, notably through subsidized food, housing, and welfare benefits.

Conflict and popular protest in the era of revolution

In transforming class and spatial relationships, the revolution sparked numerous conflicts, ranging from everyday forms of resistance to mass mobilization and collective violence. In the late 1940s and early 1950s, the party effectively mobilized poorer villagers and urban industrial workers in support of its primary revolutionary goals of land reform and nationalization of industry. These class conflicts, enacted across the length and breadth of China, resulted in the transformation of ownership and class relations, giving rise to new state–society relationships. Because these movements have been well documented elsewhere (Hinton 1966; Schurmann 1968; Selden 1979; Friedman *et al.* 2005), we focus here on movements that subsequently divided or directly challenged party leadership.

In the wake of collectivization and state restriction of markets, with the failure of the Great Leap Forward and the subsequent famine, and with mobility stifled by the *hukou* system after 1960, some villagers seeking to expand the scope of the household sector and the market and to flee extreme manifestations of collectivism, resorted to everyday forms of resistance (Perry 1986: 426). Risking public criticism, humiliation, and jailing, villagers withheld labor in collective production in favor of household plots or sideline activities and marketing, concealed production, and participated in theft, vandalism, and physical assault on rural cadres (Friedman *et al.* 2005; Bianco 2003; Zweig 1989). Such actions rarely took the form of direct challenges to the state, yet their cumulative effect was to undermine rural collectives and communes.

In the cities, the 1950s nationalization of industries triggered more than 10,000 strikes across the country, by far the most important taking place in Shanghai, China's industrial, financial, and working class capital and the historic nerve center of the working class movement. Perry (1994) documents the fact that in Shanghai, in 1957, strikes at 587 enterprises involved 30,000 workers, levels impressive even by standards of the great strikes of the years 1924–1927. Workers displaced or disadvantaged by nationalization were at the forefront of a strike wave decrying bureaucratism of cadres in the form of a vast increase in managerial personnel following nationalization, and demanding the recovery of wages and benefits cut during nationalization.

The sternest test of revolutionary leadership would come during the Cultural Revolution. The nationwide social movements that crescendoed and exploded violently during the Cultural Revolution originated and had their most far-reaching impact in the cities. While driven in part by national agendas choreographed by Mao and other party and military leaders, and by political struggles at the center in both city and countryside, rebellion was simultaneously fueled by popular grievances stemming from inequalities under the revolutionary regime. In the initial stage of the Cultural Revolution, protests in factories usually began as a top-down mobilization and counter-mobilization among permanent state workers along a cleavage between conservative and rebel factions that could be traced to higher levels in the party–state, with those closest to the incumbent party leadership hewing to loyalist positions while those with weaker ties to the party or with vulnerable class backgrounds gravitating to the rebel camp. Soon, however, disadvantaged workers pressed material demands such as higher wages, housing, job transfer, and urban residence (*hukou*). Illustrative of a level of militancy distinctive of that era were the national and regional organizations of temporary and contract workers that emerged in 1966 only to be crushed after receiving encouragement from Jiang Qing, Mao's wife (Walder 1996; Perry and Xun 1997).

In the countryside, behind the banners of class struggle were often to be found long standing hostilities among families, villages, and lineages over water rights, ancestral tombs, land, or lumbering rights, now cloaked in Maoist rhetoric that justified violence and vendettas both within and between communities. Village officials who were victimized by previous political campaigns saw in the Cultural Revolution an opportunity to take revenge and regain their power, while incumbent leaders sought to direct popular struggles against helpless bad-class households while seeking local and higher allies in factional competition (Unger 2002; Friedman *et al.* 2005). In the end, the Cultural Revolution did little to address the fundamental inequities of power, opportunity, and income in city and countryside. Indeed, the outcomes solidified the power of the party and military elite. Nevertheless, the heavy price exacted by the Great Leap famine, and the violence and turmoil of the Cultural Revolution led many within the party to question key components of the revolutionary agenda.

Reforming inequality, 1970–2005

Inequalities and social conflicts during the revolutionary epoch were framed within a state socialist strategy of mobilization spearheaded by a communist party exercising political monopoly, premised on a class struggle-based politics conducted in isolation from the world economy. By contrast, the reform period is notable for the growing salience of global and domestic capital in structuring inequalities and for an adjustment in the political style of a party bent on preserving its political monopoly with an emphasis on political stability. This section traces landmark measures that transformed the architecture of inequality through articulation of intertwined Chinese and global socio-political and economic processes.

Rural reform: from growth with equity to regional and class disparities

By the early 1970s, it seemed clear to the reform leadership that further development of the national economy required reviving the rural economy and improving the standard of living for the 80 per cent of the populace residing in the countryside so that the countryside could provide not merely an agricultural surplus but a vast market for the products of industry and a major source of exports. In the early 1970s, the state encouraged the development of rural collective industry. By the late 1970s, it had relaxed controls on the household sector and the market, and substantially boosted state purchasing prices for agricultural commodities. In addition, it provided incentives in the form of a multi-tier price system for crops, reopened and expanded the scope of rural markets, reduced taxes, raised the limits on private plots (from 5 per cent to 15 per cent of cultivated land), and gave greater autonomy to agricultural collectives to diversify, devise a new division of labor, and increase incentives through new compensation systems (Unger 2002). Villagers and local cadres both anticipated and seized the opportunity of this liberalization to press further and, eventually, joining hands with reformers in the ranks of state cadres and intellectuals, exercised pressures leading to decollectivization and the dismantling of the communes. The post-collective rural order pivoted on the combination of the household responsibility system in agriculture, that is, household contracts on land distributed equally to households on a per capita basis, and on the expansion of rural industry and markets.

The result was a rapid increase in agricultural output even as substantial labor moved into off-farm and extra-village industrial and trade activities that had been restricted. Grain output increased by one-third, oil crops more than doubled and cotton nearly tripled in just six years (Kelliher 1992: 139). Rural income increased one-and-a-half-fold in the same six-year period, for a net growth of 16 per cent per year, the product not only of higher returns on booming agricultural production, but also the result of surging rural markets and local industry in coastal areas (Sheng 2001: 7–11). The ratio of urban to rural per capita income, by one informed estimate, fell from 2.37 in 1978 to 1.7 in 1983 (Khan and Riskin 2001: 4). Just as the countryside had taken the lead in the period of revolution with land reform, the most profound institutional and structural changes occurred there in the early years of reform.

Industrializing and internationalizing rural China

From the early 1970s, more villagers turned to non-agricultural activities, including both local and regional village enterprises, group and private enterprises, and waged employment in rural and urban industries in coastal areas that provided much of the growth in China's exports and a magnet for foreign investors. One important source of wage income is rural industries, which are highly concentrated in coastal areas of Guangdong, Fujian, Jiangsu, and Shandong, areas that have become more suburban than rural with the surge of migration, industrialization, and exports. These provinces were the first beneficiaries of the Coastal Development Strategy, enjoying advantages of easy access to transportation (water and rail), foreign markets, and the capital of overseas Chinese, many of whom invested in native provinces or townships. Producing labor-intensive industrial products and processing agricultural crops, township and village enterprises (TVEs), many of them former brigade and commune workshops, became the engine of export-led growth for the Chinese economy from the 1970s to the mid-1990s, accounting for 32.7 per cent of China's foreign-exchange earnings and 41.6 per cent of total export earnings in 1993 (Zweig 2002: 121).

The scale of foreign direct investment (FDI), sometimes involving TVEs and joint ventures with village or state interests, was so significant that by the mid-1990s, a number of rural coastal areas were more internationalized and dynamic than many cities whose industries were dominated by state-owned enterprises. By 1998, 90 per cent of TVE exports were found in the coastal regions (Zweig 2002: 128). The TVEs, sometimes in alliance with the local state at township and county levels, provide vital examples of the emerging bureaucratic-business elite wedding regulatory power with capital, including Chinese private capital and international capital. By the late 1990s, local leaders had "privatized" between half a million and a million TVEs, turning these former collective enterprises into private, shareholding companies frequently dominated by former managers and local cadres, and in some instances drawing on international, particularly overseas Chinese, investments. The regulatory power retained by rural local officials in licensing, taxation, and customs made them critical partners for international and domestic businesses (Oi 1998). Workers in the privatized enterprises, however, faced increasing insecurity and often the loss of benefits and mounting competition from migrants.

The predatory local state in the agricultural hinterland

In stark contrast to the dynamic coastal areas, the agricultural heartland, the grain-producing central provinces, and the mountainous areas of the far west have been slow to develop rural industry and commerce or to attract foreign or domestic investment. In many instances, the problems associated with economic stagnation have been exacerbated by predatory local officials. In the central regions, overall income registered negative growth rates between 1984 and 1990, the very years in which economic and income growth in coastal areas exploded (Rozelle 1996). If uneven linkages to international trade and investment (centered in coastal areas) contribute to regional inequality, the government's regressive investment priorities and tax regime (favoring, at least until recently, the dynamic coastal areas over the stagnant inland region) also contribute to sharpening class and spatial inequality.

In 1995, the poorest rural decile's share of net taxes was twelve times its share of income, while the richest decile had a high negative rise of net taxes, that is, a net positive transfer from state and collective (Khan and Riskin 1996: 34). Agricultural taxes and levies accounted for 8 per cent of rural income in the central areas, compared to 3.9 per cent in more prosperous coastal provinces and 5.6 per cent in the West in 1996 (Bernstein and Lu 2000: 750). The roots of this cruelly inequitable tax burden lie in two components of the central government's reform strategy: let the rich areas (the coastal areas) prosper first, and fiscal decentralization. To create incentives for local governments and cadres to push for market reform, the center allows them to retain revenues for local development after remitting a contracted amount of taxation. But decentralization also implies local financing of public goods and local government payrolls, which, particularly in poor non-industrialized localities, has often taken the forms of coerced fund-raising, fines, and levies to support educational and welfare services that are frequently inadequate compared with those in prospering areas.

In brief, decentralization of fiscal responsibility has spawned growing income disparities between industrialized and agricultural rural areas. On the one hand, in interior regions, decentralization has weakened the control of the center over the conduct of local cadres who no longer fear anti-corruption campaigns and purges. The lack of political accountability and lack of market opportunity together aggravate the burden problem, even as the central government has attempted to cap a combined village and township tax level at 5 per cent of the average per capita income. On the other hand, in enterprising areas of the coastal provinces, the economic dynamism of rural industries relies on the entrepreneurship of local officials, forming what has been called "developmental communities" which rely on a formidable alliance of local officials, foreign capital, and domestic investors.

Rural–urban dualism

Aside from the recovery of land-use rights making possible subsistence production on family farms and the freeing of labor for other purposes, the biggest gain for villagers as a result of reform is arguably the increased freedom to seek waged employment in cities, suburbs, and rural areas. An estimated 80 to 100 million rural residents since 1985 have taken advantage of a relaxation of the household registration system coupled with the voracious demand for cheap labor created by the extraordinary flourishing of industry since the 1970s. Nevertheless, the potential of market forces to reduce the urban–rural income gap has been tethered by the continued official classification of citizens into the categories of rural or urban residents, and maintenance of a hierarchy of urban places with Beijing and Shanghai at its apex. The results include perpetuation of unequal entitlements, and vulnerability of rural registrants to police harassment and extortion to prevent eviction from the cities. Rural residents who succeed in finding urban jobs are not entitled to government-run pension schemes or housing allowances available to urban residents. Migrant workers do not have the right to send their children to urban schools, including those who lived and worked in cities for a decade or more (Solinger 1999). Their second-class status in the cities has led to an exploitative "bonded labor system" (Chan 2000), among whose features has been the frequent non-payment of wages. In short, the rural–urban dualistic social hierarchy has persisted throughout the reform era, providing subordinated labor for a new round of accumulation involving both domestic and global capital.

Urban reform and class polarization

Since the early 1990s, after a brief economic downturn that followed the bloody crackdown on the Tiananmen protests, the central leadership under

Deng Xiaoping pushed for a new round of "reform and opening" that unleashed sweeping institutional changes on Chinese cities. Most important was the privatization of state-owned industries. These policies eliminated the safety net previously enjoyed by urban, particularly state-sector workers, and created an unemployed urban population numbering in the scores of millions, a new urban underclass. This process strengthened the grip of the emerging bureaucratic-business elite whose wealth and power rested on its ability to combine political and financial capital. For the first time since the early 1950s, urban workers were forced to compete directly for low-end jobs with the sea of rural migrants whose vulnerability made them all the more eager to accept jobs on terms unthinkable to workers accustomed to the benefits and security of the socialist enterprise.

Unemployment and the urban poor

From the early 1990s, the Chinese state began cutting back on subsidies to loss-making state firms, eventually allowing leasing, contracting out, and sales of small state-owned enterprises through acquisitions and mergers. From 1997, after formally endorsing the policy of "grasping the big and letting go of the small" (that is, allowing the merger and acquisition of small and weak firms, as well as bankruptcy, while big firms in strategic sectors were reorganized), bankruptcy (averaging six thousand firms a year) and privatization brought about a rapid surge of unemployment. The numbers of laid-off workers in different types of unemployment, given euphemistic names like waiting for work, early retirement, or taking a long vacation, had quietly grown in the early 1990s. It leaped from three million in 1993 to a cumulative total of 25 million by the end of 2001.

The effect of unemployment has been devastating to ordinary workers, especially middle-aged women workers. Not only did workers experience the abrupt shattering of a compact with the state that rested on the bedrock of lifetime employment, unemployment has also frequently meant the permanent loss of welfare entitlements that were central to the socialist employment package and had been accumulated over a lifetime of labor. Even though the government has initiated a contribution-based new safety net, the system is so ineffectively and unevenly enforced that the most vulnerable workers in old industrial regions are also least likely to obtain benefits. By 2002, a new class of urban poor had emerged, estimated to be about 15–31 million, or 4–8 per cent of the urban population (Tang 2003–2004).

Privatization of state assets, foreign investment, and the bureaucratic-business alliance

Privatization of state-owned enterprises has simultaneously produced both the urban poor and a new elite. Taking advantage of their effective control over the assets of state-owned enterprises and the ambiguities of reform measures, managers and local officials illicitly transferred public property into their own hands on a massive scale (Qian 1996). A wide spectrum of tactics was used by managers and officials in the manufacturing, finance, and public utilities sectors to create new companies by stripping off the most profitable segments of existing state firms, building consortiums with non-state units to blur the ownership boundary of the new entity, operating covert twin businesses by stealing from the state company under their administration, or simply embezzling and misappropriating state funds (Ding 2000). Alternatively, the approved policy of "corporatization," i.e. transforming state ownership into a share-holding system, allows senior government officials directly to designate themselves as large shareholders.

In the process of commodifying, privatizing, and frequently embezzling state assets, FDI plays a pivotal role. From 1979 to 2002, $446 billion in utilized FDI made China the second largest recipient of FDI, behind only the United States. In 1999, 60 per cent of China's FDI inflows took the form of mergers and acquisitions (Gu 1999). In the process of privatization, workers' rights are almost invariably sacrificed as a condition for foreign takeover. Foreign–Chinese mergers and acquisitions typically involve massive layoffs from state-owned enterprises and failure to pay promised severance packages.

Finally, the commodification of urban land use rights has become another fertile ground for the growth of the new bureaucratic-business elite. Urban land is totally "state owned," or owned by government administrative or economic units. In the reform period, these "socialist land masters" began establishing development companies. Selling land use rights to commercial developers, they reaped huge fortunes (Hsing 2006). The loss of state land assets through illicit land use transfers since the late 1980s has been estimated in the range of 10 billion yuan per year. Between 1999 and 2002, documented illegal land sales totaled 550,000 cases involving 1.2 billion square meters of urban land (Sun 2004: 36).

In the period since the 1970s, China achieved rapid and sustained economic growth, breaking a pattern of income stagnation and producing significant income gains for a large portion of the population. However, measured by income distribution, China has evolved from being one of the world's most egalitarian societies on the eve of reform to becoming, by 1995, one of the most unequal in Asia, and then, by the early 2000s, in the world. The Gini coefficients for the country as a whole worsened at a stunning rate from 0.31 in 1979, to 0.38 in 1988, 0.43 in 1994, and 0.47 in 2004 (Li 2000: 191; Gu and Yang 2004: 222). Emerging trends of spatial, and particularly class polarization were the product of the commodification of labor, land, and capital, embedded in and enabled by an emerging alliance between domestic and international capital and the local bureaucratic elite.

Social conflict and unrest in the era of reform and internationalization

The reform agenda, notably the commodification of land and labor and enterprise privatization, have simultaneously stimulated economic growth and threatened the livelihood and security of segments of the rural and urban working classes. Many social conflicts spring from the fact that marketization is poorly regulated and the laws are unevenly enforced. However, thanks to the central government's promotion of legal reform, deemed necessary for China's globalizing market economy and its rhetorical flourish of "ruling the country according to the law" (*yifa zhiguo*), as well as its wish to remove the arena of conflict from the streets, aggrieved villagers and workers have attained a new rights consciousness. The result, however, has not only been growing litigiousness, but also a veritable explosion of direct and indirect testing of the still fragile legal system in the streets as well as in the courts. In recent years, civil disobedience and legal activism have taken forms in which class rhetoric and consciousness tend to yield to liberal discourses of rights and citizenship, even as the underlying class divisions are deepening.

Rural resistance

Until about 2000, the major grievances prompting mass action by villagers were "burdens," including taxes, levies, extraction of funds (for building schools or roads), penalties (e.g. fines for exceeding birth quotas), and compulsory assessments. By the early 2000s, land expropriation had become an additional incendiary issue in many provinces (Ho 2005: 16). Rural rebellions frequently begin when some villagers acquire details of the laws and regulations bearing on their interests and rights. When local cadres violate these policies, villagers write complaint letters, visit higher officials, expose local violations of central policies in the media, mobilize fellow villagers to withhold payment of illegal and arbitrary fees and taxes, and challenge such abuses as land theft. Confrontations between resisters and local cadres have resulted in protracted court battles and in small- and large-scale riots as well as violent crackdowns by local and provincial governments. In recent years, informal groups of rights activists have emerged in a number of localities. Shrewdly building networks across villages, even counties, relying on trust, reputation and verbal communication, they consciously avoid formal organizations with hierarchy, documents, and memberships (Yu 2003). Reports make clear that where protesting villagers succeeded in coordinating cross-village or cross-county actions, sometimes culminating in riots, armed police invariably cracked down.

As tensions rise, Beijing has repeatedly issued edicts urging local governments to lighten burdens and has sought to reduce central state taxation and abolish fees. Emphasizing the center's concern for the peasantry, and responding specifically to worsening conditions that precipitated rural riots in 1991–1992, the national legislature in 1993 adopted the People's Republic of China Agricultural Law. It gave farmers the right to refuse payment of improperly authorized fees and fines, and stipulated a 5 per cent cap on income tax. In 2000, the center inaugurated the tax for fee policy that aims at eliminating all fee exactions and retaining only a unified agricultural tax. Second, the central authorities passed laws to firm up farmers' land rights by extending their land contracts by 15 years in 1984, and then for another 30 years in 1998. Third, to enhance accountability, elections of rural committees have been instituted in many villages.

There is little evidence, however, that these efforts have had a significant effect on curbing the arbitrary powers of local officials, and still less that they been effective in empowering villagers in the face of the party's monopoly on formal power. Township manipulation of elections, where they do take place, is rife and village committees are incapable of providing a significant counterweight to officialdom. Assuaging popular discontent by initiating villager-friendly policies, moreover, has been carried out at the same time that the government progressively relaxed legal restrictions on commercializing and transferring rural land out of farmers' hands. This contradiction is at the heart of the continued increase in rural conflicts both in areas with stagnant rural economies and in prospering areas where inequalities of wealth and power may be all the clearer, and where the economic stakes, driven higher by the prospects of foreign investment, are all the greater.

Labor protests

Reform of state-owned enterprises, bankruptcies, massive unemployment, and labor rights violations triggered a rising tide of labor activism in the cities throughout the 1990s and beyond. Grievances of workers in both the state and private sectors focus mainly on an array of economic and livelihood problems, notably unpaid pensions and wages, layoffs, inadequate severance compensation, arrears of medical reimbursement, and non-payment of heating subsidies. The targets of worker grievances have been enterprise management and local governments. In numerous cases involving bankruptcies and privatization, workers voice opposition to official corruption and the illicit transfer of state assets.

Petition, arbitration, and protest are the most common worker strategies of action, sometimes pursued simultaneously. In 2003, 1.66 million laid-off, retired, and active workers participated in protests nationwide, accounting for 46.9 per cent of participants in the 58,000 incidents that the police recorded (Qiao and Jiang 2004). Blocking traffic, staging sit-ins, and holding demonstrations in front of government office buildings or enterprises have become legion. When workers make claims on the state, they invoke the rhetoric of legal rights and the law, much as do villagers. But workers' banners also demand subsistence rights (e.g. "We Want Jobs," "We Need to Eat, We Need to Exist"), often appealing to standards of justice harking back to socialist ideology and the social contract between the working class and the state that prevailed throughout the first four decades of the People's Republic (Lee 2002; 2003).

In contrast to the large-scale horizontal bonds formed by workers, students, and villagers during the Cultural Revolution, the mode of organization in contemporary labor protests is one of "cellular mobilization." Most urban protests are based on single work units or subgroups within those units, and rarely achieve lateral organization across factories, industries, neighborhoods, or cities. There have been a few exceptional instances in which workers veered away from cellular mobilization, displaying a capacity for broader class-based activism. Yet, once arrests of worker representatives from one factory occurred, popular support quickly collapsed. And once the government began conceding to some workers' economic demands, even the momentum for work-unit-based action was undermined (Lee 2007). Above all, once mobilization extends beyond a single village or enterprise, the state steps in quickly to crush the movement.

Labor unrest has been taken seriously by a regime that has made the maintenance of social stability, but not worker welfare or rights, among its top priorities. Many workers who have been involved in collective action report getting at least *some* response from the enterprises or the government, usually in the form of stopgap payment of back wages and pensions, almost never, however, reversing the layoffs, dispossession, or elimination of worker rights that had been their birthright for more than a generation. The central government has sometimes allocated emergency funds to localities with social insurance deficits and sought to ensure more effective social pooling.

Faced with mounting resistance, the Chinese regime has thus far successfully contained rural unrest and urban protests within their respective localities and repressed all incipient horizontal organization and leadership challenges. No broad alliances have emerged within countryside or city. The rural–urban divide embedded in the Chinese social structure is mirrored in the cleavage between villager and working-class rebellion. The dramatic standoff during the 1989 pro-democracy movement was the last time when sprouts of cross-class agitation emerged in the form of support for students and intellectuals on the part of workers and entrepreneurs in demanding political liberalization, clean government, and economic stabilization. The regime's violent crackdown on the movement led many engaged intellectuals to turn away from mass politics toward legal and constitutional reform, while many more scarcely skipped a beat in moving from the movement to the market, taking up various entrepreneurial activities or finding a lucrative niche in the bureaucratic-business elite. The vast majority of educated Chinese have been winners as a result of economic reform. For many, any political disgruntlement or collective sense of relative deprivation have given way to economic ambitions and upward social mobility facilitated by an ability to effectively navigate China's integration into the world economy.

Conclusion

Across the revolutionary and reform eras, economic and political inequalities in the form of class and spatial hierarchies have given rise to distinctive patterns of popular resistance. First, in the revolutionary period, political campaigns launched by the central party–state, its leadership unified in the 1950s but fractured by factional strife in the 1960s, provided impetus for the emergence of large-scale popular protests which were themselves fueled by social grievances rooted in class and spatial inequalities. Either by conscious cross-regional mobilization (*chuanlian*) or by the simultaneous occurrence of uncoordinated but similar activism across the country, villager and worker struggles spread across the nation, targeting policies emanating from the central authorities. In the reform era, decentralization and marketization have produced starkly uneven developmental outcomes across the country, fragmenting and localizing popular grievances and interests. The result has not been the elimination of protest but its dispersal in the form of cellular protests targeting local village leaders, enterprise managers, and local state officials while appealing for support from the center.

Second, just as market forces combined with state power have perpetrated or exacerbated class and spatial inequalities, and despite villagers' and workers' shared animosity toward a powerful and corrupt bureaucratic-business elite that has consolidated political and economic dominance, the rhetoric of resistance has shifted from a revolutionary language of class and class struggle to a liberal, contractual paradigm of legal rights and citizenship. A striking parallel in the evolving dynamic of rural and urban unrest may sow the seeds of significant change: legal reform in the context of political authoritarianism. The extreme imbalance of power between officialdom and the populace constitutes the major barrier to the realization of liberal legal rights in both the countryside and the city. The contradiction between an authoritarian legal system and an ideology of the rule of law may be the crucible for a radicalization and convergence of popular mobilization in a society with rampant and growing spatial and class inequalities.

Acknowledgment

We are grateful to Elizabeth Perry, Carl Riskin, and especially Dorothy Solinger for criticisms of earlier drafts of this article.

7   Is there a future for Islamist revolutions?

Religion, revolt, and Middle Eastern modernity

Asef Bayat

The forward march of Muslim militancy – from Iran to Lebanon, from Algeria and Palestine, and North Africa to South Asia, extending to the immigrant communities in Europe, and not to mention the transnational Al-Qaida – seems to confirm the view that the world is on the verge of Islamist revolutions. It is as though the late twentieth century has impregnated history to give birth to Islamic revolutions with the same intensity and vigor that the early twentieth century had produced socialist rebellions. Is globalization pushing religion, Islam, into the center stage of world radical politics?

This essay attempts to show that ours may be an age of widespread socio-religious movements and of remarkable social changes, but these may not necessarily translate into the classical (rapid, violent, class-based, and over-arching) revolutions. What most accounts of Islamism refer to do not signify Islamic revolutions, rather they point to heightened but diffused sentiments and movements associated, in one way or another, with the language of religiosity. Perhaps we need to rethink our understanding of "revolutions" in general and the Islamic version in particular. In the Muslim Middle East, the future is likely to belong to a kind of socio-political change that might be termed "post-Islamist revolution."

Modernity and revolutions

Revolutions and revolutionary movements are integral features of modernity, and the Middle Eastern experience is no exception. Modernity implies the solidification of the nation-states which forge material infrastructure, such as a modern army and conscription, education, and media through which people can "imagine" and develop a sense of nationhood (Anderson 1991). Nationalist movements are the likely outcome, if the nation is under colonial domination (Hall 1995). Furthermore, modernity is also characterized by the formation of modern centralized states, with the sole power of constituting laws and the monopoly of coercive powers over people whose rights (as citizens) within the framework of the nation-state are recognized. In short, it involves rule over people who hold rights. Modern states, in turn, not only enact laws to regulate dissent (establishing organizations, unions, procedures, and protection), they tend also to become the target of contention by political forces. Third, it is indeed under modern conditions that broader modular contentions become possible, when the localized and endemic struggles for parochial concerns give way to generalized and epidemic movements (Tarrow 1998; Hobsbawm 1959). Finally, (capitalist) modernity involves an overarching contradictory tendency, which is followed by deep-rooted contentions fostered by both the remaining old social classes and groups as well as historically novel ones (such as the new middle class, women, youth, etc). Here I am not referring to the Marxian labor-capital contradiction, even though it remains a fundamental one. I am rather pointing to a more general anomaly. Simply put, modernity both offers unparalleled opportunities for many people to thrive, forge identities, and get ahead in life, and yet it excludes and ravages the fortune of many others. Modern capitalist economy and science, urbanization, education, and the idea of citizenship are closely tied to the flourishing of new social groups such as the bourgeois, professional classes, youth, and women who foster a new social existence, habitus, and engender particular demands. At the same time, on the margin of modern political economy, ways of life, and institutions, lies a great humanity that is excluded from modern offerings, in terms of life chances, respect, equality, and meaningful political participation. Revolutions come as the outcome of the collective contention of such social beings whose often "partial interests," moral and material, converge and become the basis of collective identity and action. Revolutionary struggles target the state and are waged only within the confines of a particular nation-state.

As such, none of the above on its own may explain the actual making of revolutions. Revolutions are more intricate phenomena than mere structural contradictions and agency. The making of revolutions involves, in addition, a complex set of material, moral, cognitive conditions as well as political (internal or international) opportunities. One needs to determine how the potential revolutionaries perceive and interpret, their real or imagined misfortunes and marginalizations. And if they do so at all, whom do they blame as being responsible: themselves, God, the state, their immediate superior at work, or fate? Do they find possible ways to get out of their hardship such as reliance on family, kin, or traditional institutions of support? But if they opt for change, what kind of resources do they have in their possession to deploy as Tilly and others have wondered? (Tilly 1978). Finally, to what extent does a "structure of opportunity" allow for action, and how far are states able to withstand the demand of their citizens for change, and what (coercive or reformist) strategies do they deploy to undermine revolutionary movements? (Skocpol 1979).

Middle Eastern modernity and revolutions

These propositions find resonance also with respect to the modern Middle East, notably those countries with oil and other kinds of rentier economies.

Despite claims to be otherwise (see for instance Bromley 1994 and Khafaji 2004), Middle Eastern modernity has had its own particularities, even though it is by no means "peculiar" or "exceptional" as the orientalists would suggest. In the Middle East, the modernization process (character-ized by capitalist relations, national markets, human mobility, urbanization, new education systems, and modern national states) has by and large been a synthesis of both internal dynamics and colonial encounters (Hourani 1993). For Hisham Sharabi, this "hybrid" formation reflects "neo-patriarchy" defined as a mixture of "pseudo-modernism" and "patriarchy." And patriarchy is seen as a socio-cultural reality characterized by myth (rather than reason), religious (rather than scientific) truth, rhetorical (as opposed to analytical) language, authoritarian (instead of democratic) polities, communal (rather than civic) social relations and kin-based rather than class-based social relations (Sharabi 1988). Although Sharabi's neo-patriarchy focuses on the cultural dimension of modernity in the Arab world (ideas, behavior, and relations), its structural dimension in terms of the emergence of new social structures, social forces, economic classes, and social relations, has also been far reaching.

Thus, the gradual process of modernization inaugurated since the late nineteenth century and earlier has involved two contradictory processes. On the one hand, it has fostered opportunities for city dwelling, modern edu-cation, social mobility, and for new classes and groups such as new working and middle classes, women, and youth (who came to coexist together with the already existing merchants, artisans, and the religious elite, or ulema (the clerical class)). On the other hand, modernization has also triggered formidable challenges for the population. Restricted political participation (by both colonial regimes and post-colonial populist states), inequality, and exclusion from economic development (the poor and marginalized groups), political structures, and conditions of reproduction (of the power of the "traditional" groups, the Islamic institutions, the ulema, and their legiti-macy) account for the major challenges. At the same time, modernity fos-tered strong centralized states which commanded power over the populace and major economic resources. An overarching feature of Middle Eastern modernity has been the contradiction between social and economic devel-opment and political underdevelopment (Abrahamian 1982), a condition ripe for democratic revolutions. A modern economy, institutions, bureau-cracy, work relations, education, social classes, city dwelling, and modern public sphere have been accompanied by the states which have remained, by and large, authoritarian, autocratic, and even despotic (embodied in kings, monarchs, sheikhs, or lifetime presidents). Thus the modern middle classes have often played the leading role in all major social movements and revo-lutions in the region. The authoritarian character of the regimes has partly to do with the ruling elites' forging of a "traditional solidarity" based upon *asabiyya,* notably in the Arab states of the Persian Gulf (Salama 1990); but for the most part it has to do with their control over oil revenue, an asset that has given them not only monopoly over economic resources, but also political support of foreign powers who also look for a share in oil. The overwhelming power of these rentier states has been such that it has generated dissent from almost all segments of the population, including the affluent groups. No wonder Homa Katouzian sees the *mellat* (people)– *dawlat* (the state) divide as the principal line of demarcation in societies like Iran (Katouzian 1981), even though social conflicts within the category of *"mellat"* cannot be denied (Bayat 1994). Such centralized states often invoke analogies with Marx's "Asiatic mode of production" or Wittfogel's "oriental despotism."

No doubt many of these authoritarian regimes are the products as well as promoters of modernization, albeit not in the domain of the polity. Many of these states were either installed by the colonial powers (as in Jordan, Saudi Arabia, or other sheikhdoms in the Persian Gulf, as well as both Pahlavi shahs of Iran) or pushed to power by the rising classes. In their quest for modernization of their countries, the post-colonial regimes often encountered formidable conflicts with the power of land-owning classes who held power but resisted transforming themselves into the new bourgeoisie. In such circumstances, the modernizing regimes began a significant process of "revolutionary reform" often from above on behalf of the middle classes as well as the peasantry who then were to turn into smallholders or farm workers. In Egypt, Syria, Iraq, and Iran, the earlier political conflicts assumed the form of military coups representing the ascending classes, followed by massive social and economic transformation, nationalization, land reform, and populist dispensation in employment, education, and health (Khafaji 2005). Yet none of these revolutionary reforms entailed an inclusive polity and democratic governance. What they did was to produce and empower social forces which in later years were to target the very same states, this time in the name of Islam.

Modernity and agency: what sorts of Muslims rebel?

So what kinds of Muslims rebel in the age of modernity? Many accounts of Islamist movements see the basis of Muslim rebellion in reaction against modernity.[1] Beyond the perspectives of the Islamist ideologues, in general, two types of interpretation have attempted to explain the spread of religious politics in modern times. The "modernist" interpretations portray Islamism as reactive movements carried by traditional groups, whether intellectuals or the urban poor, against Western-type modernization. The movements are said to be anti-democratic and regressive in character. On the right, "the clash of civilizations," proposed by Bernard Lewis and shared by Samuel Huntington, manifests the framework within which the "anti-modern" character of such movements in their encounter with the Western modernity is assessed (Huntington 1996; Lewis 2002). On the left, one can point to Albert Melucci and Alain Touraine, among others, who express concerns about religious revivalism. "Regressive utopianism" and "anti-modern" are how they refer to religious movements including Islamism (Melucci 1996: 104; Touraine 1988: 64; Touraine 1998). The second type of interpretation views Islamism as the manifestation of, and a reaction to, postmodernity. In this framework, the movements represent a quest for difference, cultural autonomy, alternative polity, and morality against a universalizing secular modernity. Foucault described the Iranian Revolution as the "first post-modern revolution of our time," as the "spirit of a world without spirit" (Foucault 1987). For Giddens, it signals "the crisis of modernity" (Giddens 1987: 50).

There seems to be some plausibility in such observations. The global conditions in which most of these movements emerged and the discourses of such Islamist leaders as Abul-ala Mawdudi, Ayatollah Khomeini, Ali Shariati, Musa Sadre, Sayed Qutb, Rachid Qanoushi, and others attest to this tendency. Mawdudi's concept of *jahiliya*, a society characterized by the worship of man by man and the sovereignty of man over man, has been taken up by Sayyed Qutb in Egypt, Abdul Salaam Yassin in Morocco, and Ali Shariati in Iran, among others who lash out against Western liberalism, secular nationalism, and imperialism which come, in Yassin's views, in the name of enlightenment, reform, nationalism, and rationality (Shahin 1994: 173). Shariati's notion of "return to self" reflected Islamists' choice of Islam as an indigenous and all-embracing human alternative. While Mawdudi proposed some kind of "Islamic cosmopolitanism" to be governed by "theo-democracy" or a "divine democratic government," Shariati offered "divine classless society," and Sayyed Qutb, Islamic state and economy (see Shariati 1982, Mawdudi 1982, Sachedina 1983, and Haddad 1983). Ayatollah Khomeini called for "Islamic government," but went along with an Islamic republic.

What is not entirely clear about these observations is how their authors have come to their conclusions. It seems that many of the assumptions rest on texts, on the discourses of articulate leaders of the Islamist movements. If we understand movements not in a Bourdieuian sense of solid groups represented by leaders, but as heterogeneous entities with diverse layers of activism, ideas, and interests, then we will consider the variety of discourses embedded in a social movement, digging into what their constituencies really aspire. Living in and observing the Middle East for the past 20 years, I would argue that most of the Islamist rebels would probably be in favor of modern conditions, would wish to be part of these, and would desire to enjoy their offerings, if only they could afford their multi-faceted costs. But they simply cannot. The central problem, therefore, is not primordial animosity against what is modern; nor is it related to opponents' historical origins in that pre-modern classes, for instance, may oppose the modern order; after all the working class is a product of the modern capitalist economy, and yet has major conflicts with this economic and social formation. The question rather pertains to whether and to what extent individuals and groups have the capacity to handle modernity, so to speak, to function within, and benefit from it. The truth is that not everyone can afford to be modern. For modernity is a costly affair. It requires the capacity to conform to the kind of material, institutional-cultural and intellectual imperatives that many simply cannot afford. In other words, things would likely to be less volatile had the majority of the population been enabled to cope with the different costs of modern life. Let me elaborate.

In many Middle Eastern countries, a large segment of the educated middle class (college graduates, professionals, state employees, or unemployed intelligentsia) lack the material abilities to enjoy what modernity would otherwise offer them, such as decent shelter, and the possibility of forming a nuclear family with a good degree of autonomy from elders (UNDP 2002). So, many are compelled to stay under the protection of extended family, father, and elders, with all the constraining implications, and limiting the autonomy and individuality to which they often aspire. Many of them wish to possess, but cannot afford, the usual consumer commodities, or to travel to the places about which they often have great knowledge. Consequently, they are often pushed into the ranks of the poor and marginalized, in terms of life chances and consumption realms, while struggling hard to maintain a lifestyle and taste that matches their education and status.[2] Their acute *awareness* about what is available and of their inability to acquire this produces in them a constant feeling of exclusion and, what Barrington Moore called, "moral outrage" (Moore 1978). They are likely to be revolutionaries (on Iran and Egypt see Bayat 1998).

The urban poor often experience the same and higher degrees of material deprivation as the educated, but marginalized, middle classes. Yet this state of deprivation does not engender in them the same kind of political and moral outrage as among the middle classes. For unlike the middle class, the poor often live on the margin of modern offerings, be it rights at work, goods, entertainment, power, opportunities, and above all, information. The poor are immediately affected and frustrated by the complex modalities of modern working, living, and being (which requires, for instance, adherence to the discipline of time, space, and contract, etc.) which they do not possess. They often lack the capacities and the skill, both materially and culturally-behaviorally, to function within the prevailing modern regimented institutions. As a result, they remain largely on the periphery of modern institutions; in fact they tend to seek an informal way of life, in that they may not report to police to resolve disputes but resort to informal and local dispute resolution mechanisms; they may not borrow money from banks but resort to *gamaiyyat* or informal credit associations; they may not get married in municipalities but through local sheikhs. This does not mean that the poor are anti-modern traditionalists; rather it tells us how the conditions of their lives compel them to resort to informal ways of doing things (Bayat 2007b).

Nor are the Muslim poor necessarily anti-modern revolutionaries. Indeed instead of confronting the states, the poor often seek recourse in what I have called "quiet encroachment," referring to an individualistic lifelong struggle to redistribute life chances, by quietly encroaching on the propertied and powerful, whether private or public, for instance, by taking over public and private land to build shelters, squatting in vacated apartments, illegally using running water, electricity or phone lines, or occupying sidewalks to establish vending businesses at the cost of the local shopkeepers (Bayat 2002). But when the opportunity arises, the poor tend to make tactical alliances with revolutionaries, until their expected benefits dwindle, in which case they return back to the strategy of "quiet encroachment" (Bayat 1997a). Otherwise, as I have discussed elsewhere, the poor have remained largely divorced from Islamism as a political project. The experiences of Iran and Egypt demonstrate that Islamist movements neither invest in the poor as agents of political change, nor do the poor express a particular commitment to Islamist agendas. They tend to pursue an overwhelmingly pragmatic approach (Bayat 2007b). Thus, the conventional idea that the poor, especially rural migrants, represent a revolutionary class in pursuit of Islamism (because modernity uproots them, pushing them into a state of anomie) is empirically overstated (as with Lewis 1990, among others). The poor surely generate their own often kin-based ties and collectives, but these do not necessarily induce revolutionary communities, as some (for example, Denoeux 1993) tend to suggest.

Then, there are the rich – segments from the well-off classes, mostly the new rich (notably women) who do enjoy material well-being and economic status; they often adhere to globalized consumer behavior, ranging from consumer goods, education, and entertainment. Yet they lack the intellectual abilities to tackle the epistemological premises of late modernity, its multiple truths to which they are widely exposed precisely because of their privileged positions (traveling, global communication, access to global cultural and intellectual products, and living in global cities). They are disturbed by modernity's philosophical and existential uncertainties, its risks. They are troubled, for instance, by the normalization of the idea that there may or may not be a God, or that homosexual marriage may be legitimate. They are distressed at being bombarded by many "truths" showering from the satellite TV channels, by new "discoveries" that overturn established ethical paradigms. Such groups are likely to form their own moral communities, as spaces for existential security and certainty. Religion, Islam, can offer a core institutional and conceptual setting for such communities. In Egypt, for instance, thousands of *halaqat*, or the weekly informal gatherings of women to discuss religious rituals and injunctions, serve as moral communities where participants feel empowered to face the challenge of modern ethics (Hafez 2001; Mahmood 2005). These groups may not be revolutionaries, but are likely to support some kind of religious transformation of society.

To these critical modern classes may be added the traditional merchants, artisans, and the religious elites, members of the traditional religious establishments, the guardians of mosques and seminaries, who altogether may form a loose coalition of contentious classes in the modern Muslim Middle East. They tend to wage their collective struggle against secularist, often repressive and inefficient post-colonial regimes which have tended to rest on the support of the secular Western powers.

In the post-war period, popular classes in the Muslim Middle East were mobilized overwhelmingly around the secular ideologies of nationalism, socialism, or Ba'thism, which by the 1970s were superseded by illiberal capitalism. The Nasserist revolution of 1952 in Egypt mobilized the lower and middle classes to fight the remnants of colonial rule and to ensure social justice; it spearheaded a model of "Arab socialism" that swept the Arab world in subsequent decades. In 1961, a military coup overthrew an Imam-led medieval system which had ruled Yemen for centuries. Two years later, a revolt in Iraq brought the Ba'th Party to power. A secular nationalist movement secured Algerian independence from French rule in 1962, and the Libyan modern elites dismantled the Sinussi monarchical dynasty, establishing a revolutionary regime in 1969 (Khafaji 2005: 184). A precursor to these events was the nationalist movement led by the secular prime minister Muhamad Mosaddeq who nationalized the Iranian oil industry and inaugurated a secular democracy in Iran before he was overthrown by a CIA-engineered coup in 1953 (Halliday 1978). But by the 1970s, these secular ideologies seemed to be failing to deliver. Arab socialism (despite some important social outcomes) soon encountered insurmountable economic pressure, as in Egypt and Algeria. Secular nationalism fell to Nasser's defeat by Israel in the 1967 war, known as the *nekbah* (the catastrophe). Ba'thism lost to the despotism of Saddam Hussein and Hafez al-Asad. Capitalist experiments led to growing social inequality and exclusion, identified with Sadat's perceived "sell-out" in foreign policy and his heavy-handed internal policies. Then "political Islam" emerged with an enormous boost from the Islamic revolution of 1979 in Iran.

The place of Islam

Why political Islam? What is the place of Islam in these contentious conditions? Is Islam an inherently revolutionary religion, a religion of politics? Certainly the religious outcome of the Iranian Revolution reinforced among many observers the image of a highly politicized Islam in the age of modernity. Projecting from the outcome of the revolution to the process, even such careful scholars as Nazih Ayubi consider Islam a political religion due to the attempts of many of its adherents to control public morality (Ayubi 1995).

Initially, much of the attention focused on the Shi'i branch of Islam (the Iranian version) as more prone to revolution and protest than Sunni Islam.

This was so supposedly because Shi'ism represented a minority group, a "creed of the oppressed" and thus a "religion of protest." The story of the struggles of Imam Hussein (the Prophet's grandson) against the powerful and "oppressive" Ma'awiah, was to provide the doctrinal and historical basis for the imagined radicalism of Shi'ites. The writings of the Iranian Ali Shariati, a Sorbonne graduate, gave a particularly "scientific" legitimacy to the conceptualization of what he termed as "red" or revolutionary Shi'ism (Shariati 1980). In fact he brought the modern concepts of "class," "class struggle," and "revolution" into the Shi'i Islamic discourse, popularizing the battle of Karbala (where Imam Hussein fought against Ma'awiah) as the historical stage of a pre-modern revolution. Following Shariati, the Iran's Mujahedin Khalq organization, with an ideological blend of Islam and Marxism–Leninism, put revolutionism into practice by establishing a Latin American-type guerrilla organization in the 1960s (Abrahamian 1989). Hamid Dabashi's massive 1993 volume *Theology of Dissent* represents an exploration of this revolutionary character of Shi'i Islam in retrospect. Beyond Iran, the rise of Hizbullah in Lebanon in the late 1980s to the center stage of world radical politics, and its relentless struggle to oust Israeli occupation forces from Lebanon, further reinforced the revolutionary image of Shi'i Islam in the world, until September 11, 2001, when attentions were directed to Sunni Islam as the religion of violence and revolution.

In truth, Sunni Islam has also had some revolutionary elements. The Egyptian Hasan al-Banna, a leader of the oldest and largest Islamist movement in the Arab world, brought the concept of *jahili* state and society referred to earlier from the Indian Abul-alaa Mawdudi who himself was influenced by Lenin's perspective on organization and the state. His notion of Islamic "theo-democracy" was not very dissimilar to the model of a communist state. Al-Banna, however, was remarkably Gramscian in strategy (in "war of maneuver" and hegemony), even though there is no evidence as to whether he actually read Gramsci. More recently, in the 1980s, many Sunni Marxists (such as Tariq al-Bishri, Mohammad Emarah, Mustafa Mahmoud, Adel Hussein, Abdulwahab el-Massiri, and others) were turning to Islamism, thus bringing many Marxian visions and vocabularies into political Islam, projecting the latter as an endogenous Third World-ist ideology to fight imperialism, Zionism, and secularism.[3] However, it was the events of post-9/11 that mostly exonerated the revolutionism of Shi'i Islam, shifting attention to Sunni radicalism, notably its Wahabi version. Not only were all culprits in the 9/11 attacks Sunni Islamists, the rise of post-Islamist reformists in Iran in the late 1990s had already undermined essentializing assumptions about Shi'i revolutionism. Thus, the violent insurgency of the "Sunni triangle" in Iraq against the U.S. occupation is often contrasted with the "reasonable" Shi'ism of the Iraqi clerical leader, Ayatollah Sistani.

I have argued elsewhere that the revolutionary/reactionary, democratic/undemocratic character of religions, say Islam, should be seen not by reference to some "intrinsic" disposition of the faith, but to the historically conditioned faculties of the faithful. In other words, we should focus not on Islam as such, but on historical Muslims, who come to define and redefine their religion, both in ideas and practice, in diverse fashions. In short, it is Muslim populations, with their diverse moral and material interests, loyalties, and orientations that come to construct different types of Islam – revolutionary, conservative, democratic, or repressive (Bayat 2007a).

In this prism, the role of Islam in radical politics is important in at least two main respects. First, Islam can act, and has done so, as the ideological and moral structure within which contentious politics and revolutions are given meaning. Any act of contention first goes through the filter of the prevailing moral and communal values through which "injustice" is perceived, defined, and resisted, and where struggle assumes its meaning. Islam can provide that structure. Islamic codes and concepts can also be deployed, deliberately, to frame a revolutionary movement, that is, to justify, legitimize, dignify, and extend the appeal of movements. Muslim revolutionaries attempt to present Islam as an alternative social, political, moral, and even economic order. Having an alternative on the horizon constitutes a leap for contenders to further their struggles. The ideologues' representation of Islam as an alternative social order often remains at the level of generality. This might sound like a drawback, but it is in fact projecting a broad and ambiguous prospect that may ensure the covering over of differences in opinions and expectations and thus ensure unity. In the chaos of revolutionary hope, the generality of objectives ensures uniformity and guides action, leaving the potentially divisive details to the free imagination of each contender to construct their own ideal outcome.[4]

Islam may intervene in revolutionary struggles not merely as an ideology, frame, and model, but also as a harbinger of vested interests. In the Middle East, the "Islamic sector" (consisting of the religious institutions, mosques, shrines, madrasa, rules, rituals, tastes, and the associated personnel, property, and power) has historically been pervasive. Within it, the ulema, as the articulated gatekeepers, have served as the main legitimizing factor for Middle East rulers (Hourani 1993). The sector continues to reinvent itself in the face of modernity's challenges. Yet the advent of the modern state, citizenship, education, finance, and taxation has seriously undermined the legitimacy and power, as well as material gains and control of many functionaries, notably the "spiritual elites" involved in the religious sector. The ulema, as a status group controlling "spiritual property," could see their status, legitimacy, material gains, and especially their "paradigm power" (that is, the discursive field within which their authority is communicated, perceived, and internalized) was being eroded. The new education system deprived them of the role of sole transmitter of knowledge and literacy; the modern justice system pushed them aside from the helm of religious arbitration; the new taxation and financial institutions undercut their ability to raise religious tax (*sake, chums,* and *sadaqat*), while the modern states brought much

of the religious endowments (*mowqufaat*) under the control of the bureau-
crats, consequently seriously undercutting the financial independence of the
religious authorities. Associated with these changes, religious sensibilities
and the power that they bring to the religious elites are being challenged. In
short, Islam, in this sense, may move into the center of a revolutionary
struggle because of religious elites' vested interests. In the experience of
Iran, the Shi'i clerics who had managed to maintain their autonomy
(financially and politically) succeeded in retaining a good part of the religious sector independent from the diktat of the Shah's regime by relying on
various religious taxes and donations (*zakat*, *khoms*) from the faithful and
the revenue from the remaining endowments. But, the Egyptian ulema, and
with them much of the Islamic sector, were incorporated into the state
structure first by Mohammad Ali in the nineteenth century and later and
more fiercely by Nasser in 1960s. In Iran, the ulema became a major revolutionary force, while in Egypt, it was the lay Muslim activists, in the form
of the Muslim Brothers, who raised the banner of re-Islamization of Egyptian society and polity.

This is not to fixate Islam and the Islamic ulema as essential subjects of
revolutionary transformation. Indeed, "modernizing ulema" may well cohabit
and cooperate with Middle Eastern secular states. The top segment of
Egypt's religious establishment and its elites have for decades pursued a
policy of coexistence and cooperation with the government. Indeed, today
most regimes in the region enjoy the general blessing of the "establishment
Islam," as with Al-Azhar's top clerics in Egypt. In Iran, the clerical class is
deeply divided along political as well as doctrinal lines. The "traditional"
and "fundamentalist" ulema (as they are labeled in Iran) support a religious
state, while the younger generation, and those adhering to a "critical rationality," and who place "reason" at the center of the management of public
life, oppose the very idea of an "Islamic state." While the unity of political
and religious authorities tends to alienate at least a segment of the clerical
class, lay Muslims have expressed far greater distrust of an Islam that is
enticed by mundane political power. As the outcome of several elections in
the late 1990s showed, many women and the young in Iran feel more than
any other group the debilitating effect of the religious state in their daily
lives, at work, before the law, and in the public space. They are in the forefront of opposition against an Islam which, they see, has descended into an
office of power. Thus Islam may be both a factor of revolution and its
target. It can be not only the subject of revolution, but also its object.

Revolutions in the age of globalization

What is the future of Islamist revolutions in the age of globalization? Is
globalization conducive for the making of revolutions in general, and Islamist
revolutions in particular? I think that globalization may induce dissent,
social movements, and even revolts, but is antithetical to classical revolutions,

including the Islamic versions. Perhaps we need to revisit our understanding of "revolutions," looking at them in terms of more diffused and non-violent mobilization and as gradual processes involving long-term change. Their ultimate aim may not measure up to challenge the global system but is rather to negotiate with it.

Critics of globalization seem to be in general agreement that it leads to considerable instability and insurgency, in particular in the periphery of the world capitalist system (Hoogvelt 1997; Castells 1997). Nation-states get undermined by the normalized involvement of supra-national economic and political entities and structures in the national affairs of sovereign states. Neo-liberal economic policies, often directed by the creditor nations, the IMF and the World Bank, oblige the post-colonial populist states to retreat from their traditional social contract in offering subsistence provisions to their needy citizens. Not only do such retreats generate popular resentment against these regimes, they also open new space (left by the withdrawal of the state from the social sector) which is then filled by oppositional forces, such as the Islamist militants in the Middle East (Lubeck and Britts 2002). Many view the growth of "social Islam" as a front for political Islam resulting from such an absence of the state. In the meantime, the globalization of means of communication facilitates the internationalization of national conflicts, easy flows of information, and the forging of solidarities that extend beyond national boundaries. In addition, international political pressure, by governments, civil society, and supra-state institutions (e.g. the International Criminal Court, the UN Charter, and the Security Council, human rights organizations, and the like) are likely to reinvigorate movements for political change within the individual countries of the global South. Thus, with the decline of the "legitimating identities" of nationalism and socialism, according to Castells, contenders express their resistance against the global "network society" by forming autonomous "communities" around ethnic, cultural, and religious identities ("resistance identities"). These formations, what Castells calls "project identities," may not even remain defensive, but may develop into new identities that define their position in society and by so doing seek the transformation of the overall social structure (Castells 1997: 356–7).

The 1989 chain of revolutions in Eastern Europe, the Zapatista revolutionary movement connecting a local peasant rebellion to the international anti-globalization movement (Castells 1997), and most recently, the Ukrainian Orange Revolution of 2004 (which unlike the Zapatista movement was supported by the Western establishment and elites) all point to the power of the transnational linkage of dissent and solidarities, of models and lifestyles which seem to permeate through the national iron curtains (Tarrow 1998; Keck and Sikkink 1998). It is as though such momentous events of the turn of the twentieth century stand as a testimony to yet another "age of revolution," reinforcing the high hope of such post-war social theorists and activists as Hanna Arendt who saw "almost as a matter of course that the end of the war is revolution, and that the only cause which possibly could justify it is the revolutionary cause of freedom" (Arendt 1990: 17–18). Eric Hobsbawm retained such a high hope until the "halt" of the "forward march of labour" in 1978 (Hobsbawm 1981). And as late as 2000, David Harvey suggested, against the prevailing mood, that Marxism and notably the *Communist Manifesto* have never been as relevant to global conditions as today. At the outset of the twenty-first century, Harvey implied, the world is ripe to free itself from the shackles of capital (Harvey 2000).

However, it seemed that these theorists' "optimism of will" had over-shadowed their "pessimism of intellect." Arendt did not survive to observe the wave of revolutions against communism. Hobsbawm in reviewing his own history was to acknowledge, though "without apology," the "over-optimism" of those early years (2002). And Harvey was dismayed by the absence of interest in Marxism and the politics of revolution (Harvey 2000). If the idea of revolution for these observers was to free humanity from the diktat of capitalism, then the age of globalization seems to have made such a freedom ever more formidable. With the hegemony of capital and neo-liberal logic in every society and major sector, space for alternative social orders becomes restricted primarily and ironically to marginal areas and spaces, those on the exclusion zones of global capital and political order: the informal sectors, the barrios, the city escapes, household economies, and in terms of reviving cultural identities and ethnicities, within which some degree of autonomy is still maintained.[5] Indeed some post-development advocates consider these "pre-modern-communes" as the major alternative to the Western-imposed development model (Escobar 2001).

The point, then, is that a world *needing* a revolution is not necessarily the one that has the necessary forces to carry it out if the agents are figured by fragmentation, despair, individualism, and alienation. Harvey's merit lies not so much in spelling out revolutionary conditions, but in his attempt to offer "spaces of hope," the possibility of alternative ways of organizing society, economy, work, and ecology, to undercut the debilitating pessimism of will, or the prevailing idea that "there is no alternative."

What Harvey and Castells explore are not, nor do they aim for, agency and conditions for Marxian revolutions, but the constitution of dissent, social movements, and alternative ways of arranging work and life.

I incline to think that the logic of globalization (because it tends to frag-ment the popular classes through informalization, NGO-ization, and indi-vidualization, and because it transnationalizes both the objectives and actors of revolutionary movements) may be antithetical to the making of classical revolutions. It is true, globalization does engender radical changes, but not in the form of the rapid, violent, and nationally based revolts to transform the state and society, i.e. classical revolutions. For classical revo-lutions are actualized only within the confines of the nation-state; they come to fruition by mass revolts in which the national states become the ultimate target, because it is only within the limits of a nation-state that "rights" assume their concrete meaning, and around which dissent, mobilization, and action make sense. In addition, it is only within the confines of the nation-state that dissent finds a concrete focus, a recognizable target, and a manageable course of action. In other words, the question of revolution is ultimately tied to the question of the state – the way in which the states change (or do not change) determines whether a revolution has occurred, and what kind. If nation-based revolts lie at the core of classical revolutions, then the transnationalization of revolts, both in their agents and aims (e.g. struggles against the "West" or "global injustice") would deprive them of broad mobilization against a concrete national objective. In short, the idea of world revolution is ironically non-revolutionary.

The future of Islamic revolutions

Now, what of the future of "Islamic revolutions"? I think that the possibility of "Islamic revolutions" in the current age follows a more or less similar logic. Iran's earlier idea of "global Islamic revolution" beginning with Iraq clearly failed during the war with Saddam Hussein, because opposition against the Ba'thist regime did not come from within the country, but had a foreign element (Iran) which in turn instigated Iraqi nationalism. Since then, the revisionist idea of "Islamism in one country" has become the accepted strategy of the Islamic Republic. But there is more to the story of revolutions. Revolutions signify extraordinary change par excellence, rare moments of utopian visions and extreme measures, followed by compromise and conflicts to merge utopia and hard realities, thus leading to surging dissent from both within the revolutionary ranks and from without. The Islamic revolution involves particular incongruities by virtue of its distinctly religious ideology and moralist regime, which paradoxically rules over a modern citizenry through modern states. Although, the Islamic revolution in Iran caused dissent at home, it inspired and found friends among the Islamic movements in the Muslim world. But Islamic revolutions do not only inspire emulation; they also subvert similar happenings, because they make incumbent secular regimes (e.g. in Egypt or Algeria) more vigilant in suppressing potential revolts, and because their subsequent anomalies and retreat demonstrate that revolutions after all may not necessarily be desirable options. This pushes the nation-based Islamist movements into a state of perplexity and confusion where they vacillate between revolutionary utopia and realpolitik, between aspirations and limitations.

Yet, more significant trends seem to be under way in the dispositions of Islamism which lead it away from a revolutionary path. These trends are influenced by both the internal workings of the Islamist movements and global politics, in particular by post-9/11 events. One trend is what I have called "post-Islamization." It refers to the project and movements that want to transcend Islamism as an exclusivist and totalizing ideology, seeking instead inclusion, pluralism, and ambiguity. It is nationalist in project (as opposed to being pan-Islamist), and consciously post-revolutionary, post-idea-of-revolution, that is. It represents primarily a political project. In Iran, it took the form of the "reform movement" of the late 1990s, which was partly translated into the "reform-government" (1997–2004). A number of Islamic movements also exhibit some aspects of "post-Islamism." Witness the new pluralist strategy of the Lebanese Hizbullah in the early 1990s, leading to a split in the movement; the emergence in the mid-1990s of the Al-Wasat party in Egypt as an alternative to both militant Islamists and the Muslim Brothers; the pluralism of Islamic parties in Turkey (Virtue, and Justice and Development parties); the discursive shift in Indian Jamat-i Islami towards more inclusive, pluralistic, and ambiguous ideological dispositions; and the emergence in Saudi Arabia of an "Islamo-liberal" trend in the late 1990s seeking a compromise between Islam and democracy – each displaying diverse versions of post-Islamist trends in Muslim societies today (Alagha 2006; Ahmad 2005; Lacroix 2004). Most of these movements seek a secular state, but wish to promote religious societies.

Many movements in the Muslim world still aspire to establish an Islamic state, but wish to do so within the existing constitutional frameworks; they reject violent strategies and hope to operate within the prevailing political norms, invoking many democratic principles. Their Islamic state and economy find an overall compatibility with capitalism. The Muslim Brothers in Egypt and its offshoots in Algeria, Syria, Sudan, Kuwait, Palestine, and Jordan represent this trend. So do the locally based Party of Justice and Development in Morocco, as well as Arbakan's Rifah Partisi in Turkey. Even though, in classical terms, they are reformist, not revolutionary, movements, they tend to engender significant social and political change in the long run.

Global events since the late 1990s (the Balkan ethnic war, Russian domination of Chechnya, the Israeli reoccupation of the West Bank and Gaza, not to mention the post-9/11 anti-Islamic sentiments in the West have created among Muslims an acute sense of insecurity and a feeling of siege. This in turn has heightened religious identity and communal bonds, generating a new trend of "active piety," a sort of missionary tendency quite distinct from the highly organized and powerful "a-political Islam" of the transnational Tablighi movement. Inclined towards individualism, diffusion, and Wahabi-type conservatism, its adherents aim not to establish an Islamic state, but to reclaim and enhance their own individual ethical self, even as they strive to implant such an undertaking amongst others. Even though the mobilization of millions of Muslims against the Danish cartoons of the Prophet Muhamad in 2006 demonstrated a new type of ethical-political practice and protest, it also pointed to the globally disparate, reformist, and non-revolutionary character of the dissent.

It is largely the so-called "jihadi trend" which pursues armed struggle and terrorism. But even here, only a segment follows the project of overthrowing the Muslim regimes within a particular nation-state, and is in this sense revolutionary. For the most part, these groups are consumed by the idea of jihad as an end, perceiving the very process of struggle as an ethical journey, offering little in the way of projecting a future state, society, and economy. Many jihadi groups are involved in "civilizational" struggles, with the aim of combating an abstract "West," "infidel," and "corrupt." A reading of Bin Laden's messages reveals how his priority goes little beyond "uniting opinions under the word of monotheism and defending Islam" (Lawrence 2005; Devji 2006). Transnational and notoriously male in aim and organization (defending the global umma against an "unholy West"), Al Qaeda intrinsically lacks any sort of social and political program, and thus is unlikely to succeed in mobilizing a concerted national dissent against a concrete national state.

In the current status of widespread religious sentiments and movements in the Muslim world, the growth of democratic sensibilities and movements (secular or religious oriented) is likely to push Islamism into the post-Islamist course, paving the way, through "reformist" struggles, for a democratic change in which an inclusive Islam may play a significant role. The outcome might be termed "post-Islamist refolutions." In the end, the Iranian experience of 1979 may well remain as the first and last Islamic revolution of our time.

Notes

1 The next three paragraphs draw heavily on my article Bayat (2005).
2 Evidence for this argument is scattered. To begin with I have utilized my unpublished survey of some 199 middle-class, largely religious professionals in Cairo, 1990–1994, including an in-depth interview with a focus group of 15 professionals conducted by Dana Sajdi (1990). Published studies relevant to Egypt include de Koning (2005), Bayat (1997a), Abaza (2001), and Amin (2000). On Jordan see Beal (2000). On Iran see Bahdad and Nomani (2002) and Bayat (1997b).
3 Indeed as early as 1954, Bernard Lewis implied in an essay how the ethics of Islam were compatible with the spirit of communism: see Lewis (1954).
4 For the concept of "imagined solidarities" see Bayat (2005).
5 For a discussion of these spaces in the advanced capitalist countries see Amin and Thrift (2002).

8   Revolution, nationalism, and global justice

Towards social transformation with women

Valentine M. Moghadam

If class and revolution are intimately linked to modernity, so is "the woman question." Not only has women's emancipation been a defining feature of many revolutions, but the women's movement has been among the most successful social movements of the modern era, and feminists around the world continue to associate modernity with women's equality and rights.[1] Although some revolutions are identified with women's emancipation, others certainly are not, and understanding why has been a key question. The same with nationalism, that other feature of modernity that sometimes has been associated with revolution (as in the cases of Vietnam and Algeria). If the early part of the twentieth century was characterized by a kind of alliance between nationalists and feminists, the latter part saw distrust and distance. The rift between nationalist and feminist movements and goals is historically significant, and similarly requires explanation.

At the turn of the new century, possibilities for transnational collective action led to the emergence of a global justice movement, also known as the *alter-mondialisation* or alternative globalization movement. Transnational feminist networks (TFNs) have been centrally involved in this movement, and – in a replay of some of the radical revolutionary movements of the early twentieth century – women figure prominently among its leadership. However, feminists have expressed dissatisfaction with some of the movement's tactics and partnerships, and with the absence of an integration of gender justice in the movement's discourses on social justice and peace.

Drawing on Marxist, feminist, and world-system analyses, this chapter casts a historical and comparative perspective on the gendered nature of revolution, nationalism, and the global justice movement, the role and position of women, and feminism's ambivalent relationship with them. The social transformations called for by the global justice movement, I argue, are unlikely to occur or succeed without strong representation by women and without an agenda that integrates feminist demands for equality, autonomy, and rights.

Women, feminism, and revolution

Not all revolutions have served women well, nor have they resulted in women's empowerment and transformations in gender relations. Many feminist scholars have argued that revolutionary movements have tended to subordinate women's interests to "broader" revolutionary goals, and that revolutionary states often marginalized or excluded women from power and enacted legislation that emphasized women's family roles. In an early work, Sheila Rowbotham (1972) recovered women's roles from historiographical obscurity and emphasized women's participation as important to the course and outcomes of revolutions; later studies by Djamila Amrane (1991) and Cherifa Bouatta (1995) did the same for the Algerian Revolution. In her survey of socialist revolutions, Maxine Molyneux (1982) argued that they sought to harness women and the family, for reasons of production and reproduction, and in her analysis of the Nicaraguan revolution and its impact on women, she developed the concepts of women's practical needs versus their strategic gender interests (Molyneux 1985). In their separate work on Latin American revolutions, Karen Kampwirth (2002) and Julie Shayne (2004) have emphasized women's agency, demonstrating the central role played by women revolutionaries during the struggle, identifying a feminist revolutionary agenda, and showing how and why women revolutionaries subsequently forged a feminist identity and built new organizations.

Why do women and gender issues matter to the study of revolution? Elsewhere, I have defined revolutions as entailing economic, political, and cultural changes, and involving class and gender dynamics. Revolutions are attempts to rapidly and profoundly change political and social structures; they involve mass participation; they usually entail violence and the use of force; they include notions of the "ideal" society; and they have some cultural reference points. Thus far, revolutions have occurred in societies undergoing the transition to modernity. The major theories of revolution – Marxist class analysis, relative deprivation, and resource mobilization – have linked revolution to the dynamics and contradictions of modernization. A feminist account of revolution would similarly situate it in the contentions over modernity, and would point out, too, that notions of "the ideal society" are invariably accompanied by notions of "the ideal woman" as well as the "new or revolutionary man."

There is consensus among the "fourth generation" of scholars of revolution that in addition to the state, class conflict, resource bases, and the world system, cultural dynamics also should be investigated. Put another way, if revolutions entail rearrangements of economic production and social reproduction, then gender matters as much as class does, and this explains the prominent position of women's status, family law, and the prerogatives of men in the discourse of revolutionaries and the laws of revolutionary states. A body of prolific research on the position of women in revolutionary Russia, China, Vietnam, Cuba, Algeria, Afghanistan, Nicaragua, El

Salvador, Iran, and elsewhere strongly suggests that gender relations constitute an important part of the culture, ideology, and politics of revolutionary societies (for details and full references, see Moghadam 2003: ch. 3).

In previous work, I developed a model in which I classify revolutions by their gender outcomes, limiting the assessment to immediate outcomes.[2] This work was an attempt to bridge the divide between the feminist scholarship and the more mainstream study of revolutions. It sought to integrate gender analysis in the broader study of revolution, to recognize the social-structural salience of gender, and to differentiate revolutions by their gender outcomes (patriarchal or emancipatory). In my review of the great social revolutions and various Third World populist revolutions, I found two types of revolution and their implications for women and gender relations (Moghadam 1993, 1997). One group of revolutions falls into the "women in the family" or patriarchal model of revolution (the French Revolution, the Mexican Revolution, the Iranian Revolution), while others illustrate the "women's emancipation", or egalitarian model of revolution (the Bolshevik Revolution and some Third World revolutions that were explicitly socialist, e.g. Yemen, Afghanistan, and Nicaragua). These are ideal types, and it should be noted that in each case the revolution has had differential effects upon women, based on social class, race/ethnicity, and ideological divisions among women. Nevertheless, in the history of modern revolutions, the discourses and policies of revolutionary movements and states pertaining to women, the family, and citizenship fall into one or another of these two categories.

In the "women's emancipation" model, the liberation of women from the patriarchal constraints of family and community is an essential part of the revolution or project of social transformation. It constructs Woman as part of the productive forces and the citizenry, to be mobilized for economic and political purposes. Here the discourse is more strongly that of gender equality than gender difference. The first example, historically, of such a revolution is the Bolshevik Revolution in Russia, which especially with respect to its early years, remains the avant-garde revolution par excellence, more audacious in its approach to gender than any revolution before or since. Other revolutions that conform to this model – in some cases explicitly – include those of China, Cuba, Vietnam, Democratic Yemen, Democratic Afghanistan, and Nicaragua (socialist or populist revolutions) and the Kemalist revolution in Turkey (a bourgeois revolution).

The "women in the family" model of revolution excludes women from definitions and constructions of independence, liberation, and liberty, and sometimes expressly designates women as second-class citizens or legal minors. It frequently ties nationhood to patriarchal values, kin structure, and the religious order. It assigns Woman the role of wife and mother, and associates her not only with family but also with tradition, culture, and religion. The historical precursor of the patriarchal model was the French Revolution, which, despite its many progressive features, had an extremely conservative outcome for women. The French woman's chief responsibility in the republic was to be the socialization of children in republican virtues. In twentieth-century revolutions that had similarly patriarchal outcomes for women – notably Mexico, Algeria, and Iran – women were relegated to the private sphere despite the important roles they had played in the revolutionary movements. In these three cases, men took over the reins of power, associated women with family, religion, and tradition, and enacted legislation to codify patriarchal gender relations. Feminist studies in the 1990s on post-communist Russia and East–Central Europe (e.g. Heinen 1992; Einhorn 1993; Rueschemeyer 1998) would confirm that the immediate political and economic changes there, too, conformed to the patriarchal model of revolution. Scholars described rising unemployment among women, the resurgence of gender stereotypes, the emergence of porno-graphy and prostitution, a fierce battle over women's reproductive rights, the masculinization of the new political structures, and other political and economic losses for women in the aftermath of the "1989 revolutions."

What have been the determinants of such types of revolution and of their gender outcomes? Here ideology and social structure are equally salient. In general, where revolutionaries were guided by a modernizing and socialist ideology, the revolution was more likely to be emancipatory in gender terms. By contrast, where revolutionaries were guided predominantly by religious or nationalist ideology, patriarchal outcomes ensued. In addition, pre-existing gender relations (the position of women within the society and economy), and the place of women within the revolutionary movement strongly determined the gender outcome. In many revolutionary situations, pre-existing patriarchal gender relations were often carried over in the post-revolutionary situation, despite temporary disruptions in the course of the revolution, when women would take part in protests and struggles. This occurred less frequently, however, in cases where a "critical mass" of women had entered the public sphere in the pre-revolutionary situation, and when large numbers of women took part in the revolution and assumed decision-making and leadership roles.

Even where the prerequisites existed for an emancipatory revolution, gender egalitarian outcomes did not necessarily ensue. Apart from the strikingly avant-garde Bolshevik Revolution, and, to a lesser degree, the Chinese Revolution, most Third World revolutions lacked the capacity to alter concepts of masculinity and femininity, end the sexual division of labor, transform the public–private divide, and offer women full partnership in state building, economic development, and political decision making. The reason, I would argue, is largely structural – the absence of a sufficiently large pool of educated, employed, and politically aware women, and the non-existence or relative novelty of feminism. Feminism as a *global* phe-nomenon took off in the 1980s and peaked with the 1995 Fourth World Conference on Women (Moghadam 2005).

Women, feminism, and nationalism

Regions across the globe have seen nationalist movements of different types with varying class and gender dynamics, but in the interest of space as well as clarity I will focus on nationalism in South Asia, the Middle East, and North Africa.

In her now classic text, *Feminism and Nationalism in the Third World,* Kumari Jayawardena (1986) described the compatibility of and synergy between nationalist movements and feminist aspirations in the nineteenth and early twentieth centuries. The movement for women's emancipation in Asian feminism's first wave was acted out against a background of nationalist struggles aimed at achieving political independence, asserting a national identity, and modernizing society. For some of the independence and liberation movements Jayawardena analyzed, women's emancipation was an explicit objective; for others, it was a necessary component of the national goal of emancipation from feudalism, illiteracy, and backwardness. In general, women's activism in the anti-colonial movements was welcomed, and resulted in their inclusion in post-colonial state-building projects and in the adoption and implementation of favorable legal frameworks and social policies, including state-sponsored education for women and girls.

In addition to discussing feminism and nationalism in South, Southeast, and East Asia, Jayawardena showed that: in Turkey, "civilization" was equated with women's emancipation; in Egypt, reformism and women's rights were of a piece; in Iran, women's emancipation and modernization-from-above were considered parallel movements; and in her brief account of Afghanistan, she notes the failed attempt at women's emancipation and modernization on the part of King Amanullah. In all these, and the other Asian cases she documented, feminism and nationalism were complementary, compatible, and solidaristic.[3] In many cases, male feminists were instrumental in highlighting the woman question. Among the earlier generation of male women's rights advocates are: Egypt's Qassem Amin (author of the 1901 study *The New Woman*) and Muhammad Abduh (1849–1905); Iran's Malkum Khan (who in an 1890 issue of his journal, *Qanun* [Law], wrote an article advocating women's education) and Iraq's Jamal Sudki Azza Khawy (who in 1911 advocated doing away with the veil); Turkey's Ziya Gökalp and Mustafa Kemal Ataturk; Afghanistan's Mahmud Tarzi (1866–1935); and Tunisia's Taher Haddad (author of the 1930 text *Our Woman, Islamic Law, and Society*). Many other intellectuals, inspired by socialist or liberal political thought, advocated the emancipation of women through unveiling, elimination of seclusion, and formal education. In most cases, especially in the first half of the twentieth century, these ideas were used to call for revolt against corrupt, feudalistic governments. Anti-colonialism, nation building, and modernity constituted the frame within which calls for women's emancipation were made.

Although male reformers were instrumental in changing laws pertaining to women, women activists were crucial agents themselves of legal and political change. In the early modern period, well-known women activists included: Iran's Qurratul Ayn, the famous Baha'i leader who fought in battles and caused a scandal in the 1840s by going about unveiled; Sediqeh Dowlatabadi, who, like Qurratul Ayn, was a fierce nationalist opposed to concessions to the British and publisher of the short-lived *Zaban-e Zanan* ("Women's Tongue"); Egypt's Hoda Sharawi, who supported the anti-colonialist 1919 "revolution," formed the Egyptian Feminist Union in 1923, and dramatically threw her veil into the sea; and Turkey's Halide Edip (1883–1964), a nationalist who had served in Mustafa Kemal's forces.

Cherifati-Merabtine (1995) describes how women were integrated into the political parties of Algeria's revolutionary nationalist movement in the 1940s. The Algerian Women's Union was created in 1943 as an auxiliary of the Algerian Communist Party. Comprised largely of European women, it also included Muslim women leaders such as Abassia Fodil, who was later assassinated by the OAS in Oran. The Association of Algerian Muslim Women was formed in 1947, largely to protest colonial repression and to support the families of political detainees, and was linked to the MTLD-PPA, a party dedicated to the promotion of liberties and democracy. Both parties also campaigned for women's right to vote.

Clearly, revolutionary nationalism and first-wave feminism were allies in the project of Asian and Arab modernity. As Jayawardena notes, in the wave of decolonization that took place in the middle part of the twentieth century, many national leaders of the colonial world embraced nationalism and socialism as paths to modernity and progress; for their part, feminist leaders embraced the nationalist cause as the pathway to their own liberation. Nationalist ideologies offered a window of political opportunity for the advancement of women and their incorporation into the "body politic." Indeed, during the period of decolonization, political rights, including voting rights, were granted to women as well as to men.[4]

If nationalism and feminism were compatible in the first half of the twentieth century, their relationship became strained in the latter part. This was caused by discursive and political shifts in both movements, along with the transition from universalizing modernity to the fragmentation and inward-looking nature of postmodernity. Second-wave feminism's objectives of recognition and autonomy seemed to subvert the idea of the nation as an extended family, while its struggles for redistribution and power sharing through enhanced employment and political participation came to be seen as disruptive of the social order, still dominated by men. Nationalist movements came to be driven less by welfarist and developmentalist goals and more by cultural identity and assertion, along with the deployment of religious language and symbols. The new religio-cultural face of nationalism that spread in the latter part of the twentieth century – in the Middle East and North Africa as well as in South Asia – became less consistent with feminism than with patriarchy (see contributions in Kan-diyoti 1991 and Moghadam 1994a, 1995). In their struggles against what they saw as internal oppression and external colonialism (or, variously, imperialism, Zionism, and Western cultural invasion), the male leaders of religio-nationalist movements expected all members of their community to join, or at least to support, the movements. But women were divided, both for and against these movements. And thus feminism's second wave asserted itself in countries such as Iran, Algeria, Turkey, Tunisia, and Morocco.

The new nationalist projects, many of them imbued with fundamentalist notions, drew on and reinforced concepts of male–female difference. They constructed men as breadwinners and economic providers, and women as housewives and mothers who are the symbols of culture and tradition and the carriers of the collective "honor." When the new movements gained political power, as in the Islamic Republic of Iran in 1979, they formulated rights and obligations in ways that strengthened the masculinity of the public sphere and the femininity of the private sphere (Paidar 1995; Moghadam 2003a). While one may say that Islam always has been impor-tant to nationalism and national identity in the Muslim world, and espe-cially in the Arab region, the "holy warriors" of the late twentieth century wrapped themselves in "the mantle of the Prophet," in Roy Mottahedeh's apt title (1986), while other discourses – such as socialism or feminism – were rejected as illegitimate and alien. This put feminism and nationalism on a collision course. The adoption by many states of structural adjustment policies that ended proactive educational and employment policies, which had benefited women in the earlier development and "state feminist" period, further distanced Middle Eastern feminists from the nation-state and its project (Hatem 1994; Moghadam 1998: ch. 8).

Today, feminists and nationalists view each other with suspicion if not hostility, and nationalism is no longer assumed to be a progressive force for change – the panacea to problems of underdevelopment and social inequality, the path to a healthier and less dominated socio-economic order – as it was in the first half of the twentieth century. For example, in Eastern Europe and the Soviet Union, and especially in Yugoslavia and Russia, during the 1990s, nationalism had become a retrogressive phenom-enon in which various national groups and ethnic communities were pitted against each other, often violently. In addition, the new nationalist projects assigned to women the rather onerous responsibility for the reproduction of the group – through family attachment, domesticity, childbirth, and mater-nal roles. In some cases – such as in Sri Lanka, Chechnya, and Palestine – the nationalist movements assigned women more militant roles, whereby women were recruited, or volunteered, for the new tactics of suicide bomb-ings. While the movements glorified these women as martyrs and full parti-cipants in the nationalist cause, feminists have largely decried both the tactics and the movements themselves.

Why feminism and nationalism have gone their separate ways is clearly linked to the biological, cultural, and symbolic roles assigned to women in nationalist projects. In his celebrated book *Imagined Communities,* Benedict Anderson (1983) makes the simple but profound suggestion that nationalism is best viewed not as an ideology but as akin to kinship and religion. And as Nira Yuval-Davis has noted, nations often are perceived as "natural and universal phenomena with automatic ... extension of kinship relations" (1997: 15). If the nation is an extended family writ large, then women's role is to carry out the tasks of nurturance and reproduction. If the nation is defined as a religious entity, then the appropriate models of womanhood are to be found in scripture. When nationhood was recast in these terms in the latter part of the twentieth century, this had distinct implications for the social relations of gender, for the role and position of women, and for feminism's relationship to nationalism. Feminists – with their insistence on women's autonomy and control over their bodies – became anathema to religio-nationalists, and vice versa. When nationalists began to attack feminism as an alien, imperial ideology, the rift became complete.[5]

Fundamentalist nationalism versus developmentalist nationalism

Although in some ways the nationalist project and the religious fundamentalist project are different and in opposition, many of the movements associated with political Islam in the Middle East or with militant Hinduism in India cast themselves as a new type of nationalism. Given their emergence in the context of the post-Keynesian neo-liberal shift, the collapse of non-alignment, and the strengthening of the capitalist world order under the domination of the United States in the late twentieth century, fundamentalist movements could be seen as nationalist responses to changing domestic, regional, and international relations. These movements were able to mobilize cultural and religious discourses and resources partly because the secular movements appeared to be exhausted and unsuccessful, and partly because religious discourses already had a long history, extensive social base, and legitimacy. This was especially the case in Muslim countries, and thus the rallying cry became "Islam is the solution." In the fundamentalist discourse, Islam was the solution to domestic economic crises, political authoritarianism, imperialist and Zionist plots, and moral decay. As disappointment grew with the failure of the secular modernities of socialism or old-school nationalism to prevent the growing power of Israel and the defeat of Arabs, and as economic difficulties emerged, many Muslims turned to fundamentalism or followed men who preached a more political and militant form of Islam (see Moghadam 1994, where I situate the emergence of political Islam – including its cultural conflicts and gender discourse – in terms of international, economic, and political factors).

In contrast to the developmentalist nationalist movements of the earlier part of the twentieth century, the fundamentalist movements of the late twentieth century were less interested in crafting programs for economic and social development than in legislating Islamic laws and norms, including codes of public morality and restrictions on women's activities and dress. Although they have paid lip service to issues of social justice, fundamentalist movements have shown themselves to be (a) capable of co-existing with any type of economic arrangements, including neo-liberal capitalist, (b) concerned mainly with regulating citizens' religious and public behavior, and (c) preoccupied with women's comportment, dress, and position within the family. In this sense, Islamic fundamentalism exemplifies the shift from a developmentalist to a more culturalist nationalism, and from a revolutionary to a reactionary nationalism.

In turning to fundamentalism, the lower-middle-class men of the new religious movements were reacting in part to the growing visibility of women in public spaces and their social participation. In turn, religio-nationalist reactions fueled the women's movement. Women's struggles for equality, autonomy, and empowerment have been directed at laws, policies, and cultural understandings that exclude women and privilege men. In the Middle East, as elsewhere, women's social movements have sought the elaboration or extension of civil, political, and social rights for women (Berkovitch and Moghadam 1999).[6] As Jayawardena pointed out, women's struggles in various parts of Asia originated in the early twentieth century in nationally specific and indigenous ways. In the late twentieth century, women's struggles were taking place in less congenial national contexts, but in a new global environment that provided opportunities, support, and legitimation for the advancement of women. As such, women's movements have had both the opportunities and the resources to assume a more coordinated transnational strategy. Feminism itself has largely transcended an exclusive focus on issues within national borders and has assumed an internationalist stance. Thus in a further divergence with nationalism, women's social movements and feminist organizations operating across national boundaries have been helping to create a "global civil society" and the notion of "global citizenship" (Lister 1997). Solidarity across borders, critiques of state gender policies, and opposition to various forms of fundamentalism have become hallmarks of global feminism (Moghadam 2005).

Women, feminism, and the global justice movement

If the classic social revolutions and Third World populist revolutions were the products of the contradictions of early capitalism and "modernization from above," we may view the global justice movement of the new millennium as the contemporary expression of revolutionary mobilizing and the grassroots response to "globalization from above." Positioning themselves against both neo-liberal capitalism and the new American imperialism, the justice and anti-war movements exhibit core values of non-violent struggle, democratic practice, social justice, inclusiveness, peace, solidarity, and equality.

The new global social movement has shown tremendous promise and the potential to form a counter-hegemonic bloc in global politics, especially through the annual World Social Forum and its thematic and regional manifestations. Transnational feminist networks have been active in the movements and there seems to be a much higher participation of women in the global justice movement than was the case in past revolutionary movements. For example, in the first World Social Forum, women represented fully 54 per cent of participants (Vargas 2005: 108).

The era of globalization has brought forth both global capital and global social movements. The global justice movement combines a large number of transnational social movements as well as more locally based groups, who convene at the World Social Forum – the oppositional counterpart to the World Economic Forum – and at numerous regional gatherings. Between 2001 and 2004, the World Social Forum met in Porto Alegre, Brazil, and in 2005 it convened in Mumbai, India. The global justice movement is said to have "taken off" at the Battle of Seattle in late 1999, and was followed by a series of coordinated protest actions at the meeting sites of the world's financiers, trade negotiators, and politicians. The global justice movement's repertoire of collective action includes demonstrations against the World Trade Organization (WTO), anti-war rallies, and debates and networking at the World Social Forum and regional forums (Smith and Johnston 2002; Starr 2005).

Transnational feminist networks are involved with the global justice movement while also constituting a separate transnational women's movement. TFNs are structures organized above the national level that unite women from three or more countries around a common agenda, such as women's human rights, reproductive health and rights, violence against women, peace and anti-militarism, or feminist economics. They work with each other and with transnational human rights, and with labor, social justice, and environmental organizations to draw attention to the negative aspects of globalization, to try to influence policy making, and to insert a feminist perspective in global advocacy and activism.

Elsewhere I have analyzed the emergence of TFNs and described their activities, but, in brief, one group of TFNs arose in the 1980s to protest structural adjustment policies and their impact on women's socio-economic conditions and rights, while another emerged to protest religious fundamentalism and its patriarchal agenda for women. Both groups – as well as other types of TFN that similarly arose in the 1980s and expanded in the 1990s – utilize a human rights/women's rights frame in their anti-corporatist and anti-fundamentalist discourses. Development Alternatives for Women in a New Era (DAWN), Network Women in Development Europe (WIDE), and Women Living under Muslim Laws (WLUML) see themselves as part of the global justice movement but insert a distinctly feminist perspective into demands for economic justice (Moghadam 2005).

When TFNs proliferated in the 1990s, they helped to bridge the North–South divide among women activists that had been so prominent in the

1970s. They transcended the earlier political and ideological differences through the adoption of a broad feminist agenda that included a critique of neo-liberalism and structural adjustment policies as well as an insistence on women's reproductive rights, bodily integrity, and autonomy. Eventually, that common agenda took the form of the 1995 Beijing Declaration and Platform for Action, adopted on September 15, 1995, at the close of the UN's Fourth World Conference on Women. It contains language calling for gender-sensitive socio-economic development, an end to structural adjustment policies, the importance of the North's taking a lead with respect to sustainable consumption, and the goals of women's personal autonomy and their political and economic empowerment. Global feminists frequently refer to both the Cairo Plan of Action and the Beijing Platform for Action, as well as the UN's Convention on the Elimination of All Forms of Discrimination Against Women, in their national and international campaigns for women's rights. Inasmuch as most of the world's governments have signed on to these documents, they provide a useful legal and discursive tool, and global feminists frequently invoke their moral authority. Certainly these documents have helped to create an international climate more conducive to feminist aspirations and goals.

There is a long tradition of women's resistance to militarism and war, and women have been active in peace efforts since at least the time of Lysistrata. Resistance to neo-liberal capitalism and economic globalization by feminists and by ordinary women is somewhat newer, but should be unsurprising. Women, after all, have a stake in welfare regimes and rights-based development. Where these are denied – such as with the introduction of privatization of social services or with large-scale infrastructural projects (e.g. dam-building in India) that threatened the local ecology and livelihoods – women can be expected to organize and mobilize. Analysis of the gendered nature of globalization has revealed its heavy reliance on female labor, whether in industrial or service sectors. With women making up an increasing share of globally mobile labor, and with an increasing proportion of jobs taking on conditions associated with "women's work" – part-time, irregular, and temporary in both industrial and service sectors – it is clear that flexibilization, globalization, and feminization are interrelated. Trade agreements also threaten women in the commercial sector, as women owners are unlikely to be able to compete with cheaper imported products. TFNs insist on economic agreements and arrangements that are based on human rights, women's rights, and labor rights. Feminists recognize that the exploitation of female labor is integral to the functioning of the global economy, and they have been at the forefront of international critiques of structural adjustment and of neo-liberal capitalism's effects on poor and working women (see, for example, Naples and Desai 2002).

TFNs are adept at coalition building and WIDE in particular works with an array of social justice and anti-globalization actors in Europe and in developing countries. But they are impatient with non-gendered understandings of globalization or with inattention to women's human rights, including their reproductive rights. And they are critical of coalitions with groups that are hostile to gender equality or women's autonomy. Hence they have advanced the demand for *gender justice* along with economic justice and peace. The global justice movement differs from earlier anti-systemic movements such as revolutions and national liberation movements in a number of ways, but one striking feature lies in the extent of women's participation in its leadership and among its intellectuals. Among the most prominent women associated with the global justice movement are: the Indian ecofeminist and physicist Vandana Shiva; Susan George of ATTAC; Naomi Klein (author of the influential book *No Logo*); Medea Benjamin of Global Exchange and Code Pink; the ecofeminist Starhawk; and the famous Indian writer Arundhati Roy. In addition, TFNs such as DAWN, WIDE, WLUML, and the World March of Women were actively present at the World Social Forums in Brazil and in India, as well as in the regional forums. They have produced cogent analyses of the global economy and numerous reports that have shown how neo-liberal trade agreements violate human rights and women's rights. At the 2002 World Social Forum, the International Gender and Trade Network produced a statement pointing out that "in the current trading system, women have been turned into producers and consumers of traded commodities and are even traded themselves." They wrote:

> In solidarity with our sisters across the globe, we acknowledge that another world will be possible when systems of inequitable power among governments, among institutions, among peoples, and between women and men have been changed to represent the needs of the majority of people and not the market. ...
>
> IGTN representatives from Africa, Asia, Latin America, the Caribbean and North America here in Porto Alegre are calling for a halt to WTO, FTAA, the Cotonou Agreement and other regional negotiations that are inherently flawed and demand an alternative multilateral trading system that will include the incorporation of a democratic process, corporate accountability, gender and social impact assessments and a commitment to put human rights and social development at the core of all negotiations. Women have much to lose! Today, we women celebrate our power, our partnership and our vision for peace and social justice, and we will continue in the struggle because – ANOTHER WORLD IS POSSIBLE!
>
> (IGTN 2002)

Yet representatives of TFNs have coined the term "Porto Alegre Man" (DAWN 2002: 3) to deliberately underscore the role of "big men," in an echo of *The Economist*'s less conscious formulation about the transition from "Chatham House Man" to "Davos Man" (*The Economist*, February 2, 1997). Likewise, feminist reports of regional social forums have been critical of the absence of feminist concerns outside of explicitly feminist events. The main demands of the third European Social Forum (London, October 14–17, 2004) were "stop the war; no to racism; end privatisation; for a Europe of peace and social justice." Gender justice seemed outside its scope. One report noted that "outside of women's events, gender and women's issues were forgotten!" (Bach 2004). At the Africa Social Forum later that year (Lusaka, Zambia, December 10–14, 2004), women were in the minority because, in the words of the authors of a report on the forum, "the leadership of organizations and movements (i.e. those likely to represent organizations at international forums) are men," maintaining: "Essentially, we know that patriarchy and other forms of dominance are being re-inscribed within our movements for resistance .... As Shallo Skaba, an Ethiopian coffee worker stated at the Africa Court of Women, 'No one is looking for women's problems. No one considers all that women are doing'" (Alexander and Mbali 2004).

Catherine Eschle's examination of the role and position of feminism and feminists within the global justice movement finds that while women are certainly not marginalized from movement activities, feminism itself is not fully integrated (Eschle 2005). In her survey of key anti-globalization texts (e.g. Danaher and Burbach 2000b), she writes that feminists and feminism are rarely found in the authoritative movement texts, and that the texts "fail to recognize feminism as an integral presence within the antiglobalization movement" (Eschle 2005: 1747). Reviewing one text, she writes:

> [The authors] trace the outlines of a "global democracy movement" encompassing trade unions, the corporate accountability movement, "citizen empowerment" groups, and efforts to bridge the concerns of environmental groups and social justice struggles .... Their section on "dealing with diversity" has nothing on women or feminists. Although ecofeminists Starhawk and Vandana Shiva contribute to the collection, they do not write with an explicitly feminist voice. One contributor, Deborah James, acknowledges in a final chapter on the democratisation of the global economy the need to tackle gender inequalities.
>
> (Eschle 2005: 1746)

Later in her article, Eschle acknowledges that more recent publications, such as *We Are Everywhere* by Notes from Nowhere (2003), include many contributions by women and by feminists. She also writes that the World Social Forum has provided a space for non-economistic perspectives, which she finds more conducive to feminist interventions, and that the growing anti-militaristic discourse at the WSF has more affinities with feminism. Indeed, following the US/UK invasion of Iraq in 2003, the global justice movement coalesced with the growing global anti-war movement into a global peace and justice movement. This new, larger movement includes many feminist peace organizations, including the well-known Women's International League for Peace and Freedom (WILPF) and Code Pink. However, it also includes elements hostile to feminism. This was the source of the anger expressed by WLUML in a 2005 statement.

In an appeal/statement issued in February 2005 that was prepared for the World Social Forum in Porto Alegre and discussed at the Feminist Dialogues that immediately preceded the forum, WLUML decried the beginning of an "unholy alliance between a growing number of anti-globalization activists, human rights activists and progressive people in the West in general with Muslim fundamentalists, and the gradual abandonment of progressive democratic forces from within Muslim countries and communities." It is worth quoting from the statement in extenso:

> For more than two decades, women have identified one of the warning signs of fundamentalisms to be anti-women policies, whether it is the attacks on contraception and abortion in the USA and in Europe, or the imposition of dress codes and forced veiling and the attacks on freedom of movement and on the rights to education and work under Taliban-like regimes . . . . However, we are now facing a new challenge: what seemed to be clear politically when we were talking of far-off countries loses its clarity when fundamentalist policies come closer to Europe and the USA in the guise of "authentic" cultural identity, and the worldwide support once given to both victims and resisters of fundamentalism vanishes under the weight of considerations of [the] "right to difference" and cultural relativism.
>
> Disturbed by the discrimination and exclusion that affect people of migrant descent in Europe and North America, progressive forces in the West are keen to denounce racism – and rightly so. But subsequently, they often choose to sacrifice both women and our own internal indigenous democratic progressive opposition forces to fundamentalist theocratic dictatorship, on the altar of anti-racism. Or they censor their expressions of solidarity with us for fear of being accused of racism.
>
> Derailed by neocolonial invasions and wars, progressive forces are prepared to support any opposition to the super powers. We have already witnessed prominent Left intellectuals and activists publicly share the view that they could not care less if fundamentalist theocratic regimes come to power in Palestine or Iraq, provided that the USA and Israel get booted out. We have witnessed representatives of fundamentalist organizations and their ideologists invited and cheered in Social Fora. We have witnessed prominent feminists defend the "right to veil" – and this sadly reminds us of the defense of the "cultural right" to female genital mutilation, some decades ago.
>
> We call on the democratic movement at large, on the antiglobalization movement gathered in Porto Alegre, and more specifically on the women's movement, to give international visibility and recognition to

progressive democratic forces and to the women's movement within it, that oppose the fundamentalist theocratic project. We urge them all to stop supporting fundamentalists as though it were a legitimate response to situations of oppression.

(WLUML 2005)

What brought about this outcry included several anti-war rallies in London where speakers from Muslim groups invited to share the platform began and ended their talks with chants of "Allah-o Akbar," as well as the invitation extended to the European Muslim intellectual Tariq Ramadan, who had earlier made statements defending the veil as integral to Islamic identity.[7] Similarly, the French feminist Christine Delphy's defense of Muslim women's veiling was considered incomprehensible by WLUML.

Alexander Cockburn, Jeffrey St. Clair, and Allan Sekula have described the global justice movement as "less sexist" than older movements (cited in Eschle 2005: 1746), but feminists in the global justice movement have insisted that women's rights are human rights and that gender justice must accompany economic justice. There are tensions resulting from feminist dismay over the participation of religious fundamentalists in anti-war rallies, at the World Social Forum, and at the European Social Forum, and feminists' concern that gender equality and women's human rights could be marginalized in the interests of zealous inclusiveness.

Feminist groups continue to be a mainstay of the global justice movement. In March 2005, a large number of international women's groups met in New York during the Beijing + 10 special session of the UN, in a new mobilization established under the umbrella of the Global Call to Action Against Poverty (GCAP). The message to governments was that poverty is a women's issue and that feminist groups around the world would work toward the elimination of poverty among women. But while feminist groups tackle poverty, corporate arrogance, violence against women, and war, they do so within the framework of women's human rights. Thus they have insisted that women's sexual and reproductive health and rights are integral to women's capacity to enjoy and exercise their full human rights, including socio-economic rights. When global feminists mention unequal power relations, they are referring both "to sexual and reproductive rights and to the 'big boys' – the military and global economic establishment who control the security and trade agenda" (WIDE 2005). The April 2004 Women's March for Global Rights in Washington DC was a massive display of contemporary feminist concerns: threats to women's reproductive rights, attacks on their socio-economic conditions and rights, and sexual violence against women in the home and at the war front. At the Africa Social Forum that year, feminists called for both economic rights and personal autonomy for women:

Activists called for further strategizing on helping to make women economically independent. As one activist from the Gambia remarked, "we must make it possible for women to get a divorce if necessary, to have some measure of financial independence. In a global economy where women produce over 80% of resources, and yet own less than 20% of them, the battle for economic sovereignty for women will be long and difficult. However, we will work to assure that women are not further exploited by our own movements, and that we create means for economic independence as we can."

(Alexander and Mbali 2004)

Conclusions

The capitalist world system has often produced anti-systemic movements that cross borders and boundaries, while national-level class conflicts, political struggles, and the contradictions of modernity have similarly generated forms of collective action and social protest, notably revolutions, and national liberation movements. A key characteristic of the era of late capitalism, or globalization, is the proliferation of transnational social movements such as the global justice and anti-war movements. Each form of collective action is inevitably gendered, in terms of patterns of participation and leadership, concepts of masculinity and femininity, and notions of women's place and men's privileges. Revolutions, nationalist movements, and global justice/anti-war organizing have all relied on women's participation and support, but they have not necessarily taken on board women's demands and feminist concerns.

Julie Shayne (1999) has argued that a revolutionary movement is not truly successful if the subjugated position of women is not challenged, accounted for, and altered; and that revolutionaries are better off consciously including women and feminism as part of their revolutionary agenda. This means more than depending on women fighters. In the Eritrean national liberation movement, for example, one-third of the fighters were women, and those women fighters certainly made a difference to the success of the struggle. And yet, although gender relations during the struggle were radicalized, at least among the revolutionaries, post-liberation transformation in the broader society was limited (Connell 1998).[8]

Elsewhere, I have argued that domestic social changes and global processes alike have served to bring greater legitimacy to demands for women's participation, autonomy, and citizenship. As feminist ideas have spread and women's rights are on global and national agendas, revolutionary movements and state-building projects of the new century are more likely to incorporate women and feminism (Moghadam 2003b). I pointed to South Africa's ANC, the Zapatista movement in Mexico, and Northern Ireland's republican movement as contemporary examples of revolutionary movements and states that had incorporated feminists or women's rights goals. In these cases, the revolutionary ideology and women's major roles in the movements were far more amenable to emancipatory gender outcomes, and in South Africa had led to the conscious integration of feminist claims in the legal framework. These also were movements and states hailed as progressive throughout the world. At the time, they stood in stark contrast to Afghanistan, where the Taleban's repressive gender regime was receiving international opprobrium. The Taleban regime was a pariah state, shunned by the international community, recognized only by three states, and extremely unpopular domestically. The lesson seemed obvious. In an era of feminism and globalization, if revolutions or oppositional movements do not incorporate women and feminism, it will be to their disadvantage. They will be less likely to gain either national or international support.

Today, feminist futures seem anchored to the prospects of the global justice movement. But the reverse also is true. Can the global justice movement expand its social base without recognition of the critical role of women workers in the global economy? Can it count on the support of middle-class women without "mainstreaming" into its agenda feminist demands for reproductive rights and full autonomy? Can it maintain its integrity and its progressive social vision if it sidelines feminists in favor of religio-nationalists? As important as it is to build a worldwide movement against neo-liberalism and war, surely that movement is unlikely to withstand the ideological claims and the power of globalization and the new imperialism – such as the claim that free markets and "humanitarian invasions" are meant to liberate women – unless it is grounded in women's human rights. Meanwhile, the lessons of the past seem clear to feminists, who will continue to build their own movement while participating in others. I end with an apt observation by one TFN:

> Women are taking the lead and making a huge contribution to defining the international agenda in terms of human rights, macroeconomics, conflict/peace, and sustainable development. We have a valuable and unique perspective on these issues as women and as human beings. We recognize that feminism in one country is not sustainable – we need feminism on a global scale.
>
> (WIDE 1995: 3)

Notes

1 For example, in her discussion of competing gender frames in contentious Algeria, Doria Cherifati-Merabtine (1995) distinguishes the "Islamic female ideal" from the "modernist model."

2 I do not see any advantage in extending a revolution's timeframe indefinitely. In my analysis, a revolution is time bound and covers the period of uprising and – in the case of successful revolutions – the period of state building by the new revolutionary elite. "State building by the new revolutionary elite" is a conceptual shorthand that covers the formation of new economic, ideological, political, and juridical institutions and norms. This process is imbued with ideologies and relations of gender as well as those of class.

3 The specific cases are Turkey, Egypt, Iran, Afghanistan, India, Sri Lanka, Indonesia, the Philippines, China, Vietnam, Korea, and Japan.
4 The Egyptian case was somewhat complicated. Although women took part in the 1919 revolution, they were excluded from the drafting of the 1923 constitution and denied political rights. Later, following the overthrow of the monarchy and the establishment of a republic, they secured the right to vote in the 1956 constitution following protests and hunger strikes by leading activists such as Doria Shafik: see Badran 1995 and Hatem 2000.
5 I have discussed this at more length (Moghadam 2007), with examples from Algeria and Iran, in "Feminism and Nationalism in the Middle East," prepared for the festchrift for Kumari Jayawardena (Dehli: Kali for Women, 2007). See also contributions by Salma Sobhan on Bangladesh, Nahla Abdo on Palestine, and Cherifa Bouatta on Algeria in Moghadam (1995).
6 Women's relationship to contemporary religio-nationalist movements is a complicated one, especially in the Muslim world. Women from "traditional" or conservative households and communities, and from the lower middle-class tend to support religio-nationalism, partly in keeping with the political and ideological leanings of their male kin, and partly because of their own anxiety about the disruption of the familiar moral order. Feminists, in contrast, are more often found among the educated and secular middle classes. The size of the female proletariat is small in Middle East and North African countries (other than Morocco and Tunisia), and research on working-class political and ideological preferences is undeveloped or unavailable.
7 For a critique of Tariq Ramadan's Arabic-language statements, see Fourest 2004. Fourest – who also has authored a scathing critique of the French far-right nationalist leader Le Pen – notes that in one of Ramadan's cassettes he deliberately conflates "so-called secular Muslims" with "Muslims lacking Islam" (2004: 149). He also calls veiling a Muslim obligation and encourages young women to defend their right to veil, in part to protect themselves against the male gaze (see Fourest 2004: 212, quoting another cassette). At the first international congress of Islamic feminism, held in Barcelona in late October 2005, Zeinah Anwar of the Malaysian group Sisters in Islam told me that Tariq Ramadan had defended *hijab* at a meeting in Kuala Lumpur, leading to a spirited debate with the feminists of Sisters in Islam who are themselves not veiled.
8 Dan Connell writes of "one of the first post-war surprises in Eritrea" that "shortly after the shooting stopped in May 1991, men in many villages and towns formed secret committees to try to block women from participating in peacetime distributions of land" (Connell 1998: 189). Nonetheless, available statistics show that women held a 22 per cent share of parliamentary seats in 2004.

9 Stories of revolution in the periphery

Eric Selbin

Scan the news and it is evident that "revolution" remains a rough and ready descriptor for any number of instances in our (post)modern world. This seems particularly true of what even in this age of "globalization" might be construed as the periphery, those places at a remove, literal or otherwise, from the metropole, itself no longer so easily identifiable. The surprising persistence of "revolution" no doubt reflects the impressive array of factors, aspects, elements, and relationships of varying degrees, intensities, and durations which the term evokes.

This is not to ignore that "traditional" conceptions of revolution remain alive, where the ultimate goal is state power for the purpose of fundamentally transforming society; at this time of writing Nepal seems the most obvious instance, perhaps followed by the Philippines. But the past two decades have presented us with more nuanced cases: the complexities of the 1989–1991 Eastern European transitions, the saga of Chiapas since 1994, the ill-defined struggles in Colombia, as well as the various shades of what have come to be construed as "Islamic" revolutions.

Whatever else they may be, revolutions are fundamentally about people: created by people, led by people, fought and died for by people, consciously and intentionally constructed by people. This is not to deny the power of actually existing social, political, and economic structures; of ideologies; of the international situation; of milieu defining meta-narratives such as the Enlightenment, global(ized) capitalism and its co-relations (colonialism, imperialism, modernization, development, dependency, globalization); of tropes such as modernism or progress; or perhaps even the grand sweep of History. Yet, if the question is why revolutions happen here and not there, now and not then, and among these people and not those, we must focus on people and their worlds.

By what mysterious method are people moved into and through a revolutionary process? This question often and all too readily resolves into the familiar narrative wherein a unified "leadership" (commonly framed as some sort of vanguard) mobilizes and guides a population of followers (usually inscribed as "the masses") who have been immiserated by a small elite and their foreign allies; assuming they are victorious, these leaders then reconstruct state and society along new material and ideological lines. Regardless of its accuracy, this narrative is *the* story of revolution we have told for several hundred years now and are prone to retell, regardless of the circumstances. There is almost certainly something to this, yet it obscures and obviates more than it illuminates. In what follows, I will explore the possibilities opened up by a broader (and perhaps more nuanced) reading of this story. Specifically, I will "trouble" this time honored tale by focusing on the role of the stories that move people, and speculate what some of those stories might be.

Revolutions: an obligatory aside

People do not fight, risk their lives and those of their families, or put their hopes and dreams on the line lightly; dry, distant, theoretical concepts alone are unlikely to move them. Revolutions are often about commitment and passion and are at least as much cultural as social or economic in their "origins." Faced with the exigencies of everyday life and intolerable conditions, fueled by demands for justice, and driven by a dynamic of hope, people seek to change their world. Hence, the impetus for revolutions derives from injustice, impoverishment, the disenfranchisement of people, and the stories people tell of the liberty, freedom, and social justice they deserve and which promise them a voice in their present lives.

The endeavor here is to deepen the human and cultural aspects of our thinking about revolution, re-centering Tilly's (1978) focus on mobilization *with* people and what Paige (2003: 24) has recently described as their "metaphysical assumptions." Revolution here is construed as a conscious effort by a broad-based, popularly mobilized group of actors, formal or informal, to profoundly transform the social, political, and economic institutions which dominate their lives; the goal is the fundamental transformation of the material and ideological conditions of their everyday lives. This reflects a *process* of origination and subsequent struggle, and an *outcome*, the effort at fundamental transformation. When both elements are realized, we are more likely to consider them "great" or "social" revolutions; lesser degrees of success are often labeled political revolutions, rebellions, revolts, resistance, or other types of collective action.

The story of revolution

My contention is that what has been missing from our understandings of revolution and why they happen when and where and with whom they do is "story." We have largely ignored or derided the role and place of story and the working assumption seems to be that no "mere" story is sufficient and certainly not necessary to move a people into a revolutionary process. While it is doubtful that a story in and of itself is adequate – a tall order for any one factor – stories are absolutely, even crucially, necessary to revolution.

People are storytellers, narrators of their own lives and of the world around them: analysts and commentators, judges and juries, critics, reviewers and appraisers, intermediaries between this world and that, the makers and purveyors of history and of the world which they are embedded in. The stories we tell define us as people; we create, see, and manage the world through them. And when people create and coalesce around one powerful story, it is often a heady concoction and concatenation of names (particularly "heroes" and martyrs), dates, places, grievances, and methods, woven together into some sort of serviceable and usable (hi)story.[1]

"History" is the term commonly used to label that knowledge reservoir; once it was lore, stories, tales. While History has traditionally told stories of fact mixed with fiction – how could it do otherwise? – in the flush of the Enlightenment and, particularly, nineteenth-century rationalism, this was suddenly seen with horror. Much was invested in the notion that Historians were craftsmen – not a gender-neutral term – who dealt *only* with "the facts." Storytellers of various stripes were free to invent at their pleasure; historians were bound to *the* Truth, a conviction subsequently picked up by the social sciences – in pursuit, obviously, of "science" – which has dominated the discourse to this day.

If it is our biology that makes us human (a not uncontested claim), it is our stories that define us as people. Stories divide us and, however ineffectually at times, bind us together; in either case, we use them to forge community. And it is in these communities that we seek to, among other things, resist change, build a "better" life, redress our grievances, and find meaning. A significant part of who we are and how we define ourselves in the world is the supposition that we have the ability and capacity for creating an environment of shared feelings and symbolic meanings and to act upon them, often in conjunction with others. The innovation of bands bound together not simply by need or necessity but by their stories creates bonds of a different sort, and seems equally a part of our evolution.

Human communities were created, and then sustained and extended by webs, networks of stories, shared in song, in dance, in verbal story form. Some of these mutated into celebration or commemoration and grew to be associated with ritual; most were simply woven into the fabric of everyday life. Relationships, expectations, concerns, cares, and even conceptions of time and space all came to be bound up in the meanings, spoken or not, transmitted between and among the members of these communities. The problems of "reading" history and place and time from the present are myriad. We are cognizant of these and proceed at our own risk, reasonably expecting that careful and serious scholars will take such into account. Still, it would seem that from the very earliest times we are able to reasonably claim we can discern the connections between social, political, and economic institutions; and the consciousness, for want of a better term, of society is deep and abiding. This consciousness – and, I suspect, the inevitable concomitant, and contemporaneous unconscious(ness) – is revealed in and through story.

There is a (hi)story that is repeatedly related, often commencing in some form or another with "the word" or "the act," perhaps even the two together, a speech act. People are "social beings, with mutual relations and responsibilities to each other, acting historically, materially, and in groups" (Lipschutz 2001: 323), and it is stories that bind them together. And these "once (or twice or three or four million) upon a time" words and songs and symbols of people and places and action are indispensable to creating the world we know.

There is an increasing recognition that social scientists, too, tell stories (see Büthe 2002), though the social sciences, as a rule, do not look kindly on stories. Charles Tilly, who, it must be said, tells a *great* story, has highlighted some of his concerns in an engaging jeremiad "The Trouble With Stories" (2002). I am anxious to sign on for his rediscovery of "the centrality of social transactions, ties, and relations to social processes and to investigate connections between social relations, on the one side, and social construction on the other" (2002: 5) and pleased to note his proposition that people commonly understand their lives as stories which "do crucial work in patching social life together" and his allowance that stories capture "compelling accounts of what has happened, what will happen, or what should happen" (2002: 26) and thus "do essential work in social life, cementing people's commitments to common projects, helping people make sense of what is going on, channeling collective decisions and judgments, spurring people to action they would otherwise be reluctant to pursue" (2002: 27).

Despite their antiquity and some degree of "standardization," Tilly warns, stories are often transitory and profoundly localized. Yet, there are "standard stories": "sequential, explanatory recounting of connected, self-propelled people and events that we sometimes call tales, fables, or narratives ... explanatory accounts of self-motivated human action" (2002: 26). Because of a body of work awash in stories, however, Tilly has learned that while storytelling is central to human life, the "causal structure between most standard stories and most social processes" is simply incompatible (2002: 32). Thus, Tilly succinctly summarizes his position as "In most circumstances, standard storytelling provides an execrable guide to social explanation ... . Most social processes involve cause–effect relations that are indirect, incremental, interactive, unintended, collective, and/or mediated by the nonhuman environment" (2002: 35). Thus, stories are, at the end of the day, entertaining but of little real use.

Stories (and storytelling) may well prove problematic guides to social analyses. Yet the stories under consideration here are precisely those which reflect people's recognitions of what Tilly earlier called the indirect, incremental, and often unintended elements and aspects of their stories and lives, people's consciousness (and unconsciousness) of the profoundly interactive and deeply collective nature of their stories and lives, and the often exceptional degree of contingency people afford to the(ir) environment.

To paraphrase Churchill's trenchant observation about democracy: a focus on stories may be the least useful approach we have, except for all the others. In other words, if the best of our social science methods have failed to provide compelling or even satisfying answers to the questions we pose about revolutions – their provenance, their production, and their process – perhaps we should consider others. The "objective" and reassuring methods of social science analysis have not provided the instruments necessary for fully exploring and explicating the puzzle of revolutions; they seem particularly ill-equipped at capturing the look in someone's eyes, the tones in their voice, the passion with which, for them, Zapata's white horse, Che's beret, Sandino's hat, Ho's pith helmet, bamboo walking stick, and wispy beard, or Cabral's knit cap are redolent with meanings and freighted with significance, their invocation and deployment consequential.

No matter how contested, the stories people tell – and the parts they assign themselves, the symbols they imbue with meaning, the talismans they invoke, and the references they weave – matter. It is possible to access these stories people tell about revolution and through them decode a set of revolutionary matters that are most commonly set in national terms, and make them legible as much as they can be to outsiders. This is not, nor can it be, some sort of "objective" enterprise; no endeavor is genuinely free of some sort of bias. Cognizant that we all start from somewhere, the commitment must be to be rigorous, systematic when appropriate, radically open, and, as it were, to play fair.

The endeavor here then is to tell a story about stories of resistance, rebellion, and revolution, the tales that are told (and retold), the songs that are sung or played, or the places or objects that are shown, quietly, confidently, with commitment and conviction and, sometimes, but not always, with passion or something even harder to describe but which anyone who has talked to someone who has been involved in a revolutionary process has seen, heard, and felt: an expression on someone's face, a swell or catch in their voice, a shift in posture, a gesture with the head or hands, perhaps a lapse into silence in reverie or a frustration, of sorts, at trying to convey to an interloper something so profound. How does one articulate to a stranger, an acquaintance, even a friend or loved one, a matter at once so complex and simple? Often simply by asking, repeatedly, if their tale makes any sense, if you understand, if it is clear even as they (and you) know it never really will be or can. Stories rooted in, constitutive of, and constructing cultures, genealogies,[2] and veritable webs of resistance, rebellion, and revolution serve to attract and recruit, to create, maintain, and extend commitment, deepen collective identity, and empower those who heed the call. These same stories also provide powerful critiques of the way things are and have been (and perhaps a vision of what once was) as well as normative or programmatic guides to action and where to go.

In short, revolution does not occur without the articulation of compelling stories that enable, ennoble, and empower people who seek to change the material and ideological conditions of their lives. People draw on the past to explain the present and predict the future, forecast a future predicated on the present, and refashion the past as necessary to fit the exigencies they face. The result is an array of stories which compete to become the story of the moment, a process in which people rely on a complicated and complex combination of myth, memory, and mimesis which they use – consciously or not – to tell a story of who they are and where they have been, of who and where they are now, of who and where they want to go and be, and of how they will get there.

"The Uprising of the Anecdotes" (Benjamin 1999: 846)

Revolutions do not just come, as structural theorists would have it, but are intentionally made by people consciously seeking to change their world – though inevitably with unintended consequences they are unlikely and perhaps unable to imagine, and under circumstances over which they may have little control – and the primary vehicle for this is the articulation of compelling stories with engaging and empowering plots. That such change is highly contingent, perhaps even ephemeral, is less important than it might seem. The legions of failures often result in change and add to the store of revolutionary tales – as with so much in the lives of so many, little is left to waste – whose universal premise and basic promise is "better must come," in the words of Delroy Wilson's reggae song which was adopted by Michael Manley's movement in Jamaica in the early 1970s.

A crucial component of the revolutionary potential in any population is perception of the options available and plausible to them; these constitute "repertoires of collective action" (Tilly 1978: 143) and a "'tool kit' of symbols, stories, rituals and world-views," which provide the resources necessary for constructing "strategies of action" (Swidler 1986: 273). Thus there is a repository of knowledge that people maintain collectively and, to the extent possible, on their own, as part of their conception of what is imaginable and, hence, feasible. In societies where revolution is considered a viable response to oppression – due to a long-standing history of rebellious activities being celebrated in folk culture, or to revolutionary leaders having fashioned, restored, or magnified such traditions in the local culture or some combination of these – revolutionary activities are more likely to be undertaken, to receive broad popular support, and to conclude successfully.

Leaders of revolutionary processes consciously set out to (re)construct narratives predicated upon aspects of the stories which emphasize both the local relevance and universal nexus. The ability of revolutionaries to articulate compelling stories is critical to the success of any revolutionary enterprise. But revolutionaries do not articulate their stories to sheep; "dialogue with the people is radically necessary to every authentic revolution" (Freire 1970: 122). The population may respond to these revolutionary stories or not; often they may begin to (re)write their own tales or simply appropriate the revolutionaries' stories into their own (see Martin 1992). People have their stories, their narratives, and revolutionaries (or the counter-revolutionaries opposed to them) either find a way to accord with these or not; when they do, it is more likely that a revolutionary situation can be forged, will emerge, and, more rarely still, succeed. The revolution is not made for them by the revolutionaries, nor can they make the revolution without the revolutionaries.

Stories help develop, maintain, rewrite, valorize, rework, renovate, and reconfigure history and memory, both popular and personal. If in some sense revolution has no center but is rather a vast socio-political and cultural organization awash in and with culture, the most plausible way to capture this labyrinth (assuming it is possible) is by mapping the stories. Revolutions, in this conception, are intrinsically storied processes.

To this end it is possible to construct several stories of revolution which capture most of the revolutionary tales extant. Some of these might be thought of as elite stories that come from above or are articulated by those who are in their service or pay, such as public intellectuals and academics. These stories often feature famous characters, invoke large processes, and are marked by big events. Others might be thought of as popular stories that emerge from below or are articulated by those who seek to lead or energize the population at large, a group which might also include public intellectuals and academics. These are often smaller stories, built around local figures or, if famous, figures who are plausibly read as popular rather than elite; they less commonly mention or recognize processes as such, and imbue small events with great significance. In every story, the narrative must be rooted in the familiar or risk being rejected or ignored. An inauthentic narrative not only betrays the story, but may even serve as a narrative that indicates the tellers' alienation from their culture and society or at least the socio-political-economic realities of the day. What follows is an attempt to trace out a few of the more notable stories of revolution that can be discerned in an array of places; not surprisingly, they overlap to some degree.

The Civilizing and Democratizing Revolutionary story

This tale, with allowances for local color, takes as its starting point notions of citizenship and democracy attributed to the Greeks (circa the mid-fifth century BCE), may make a nod to Rome's Senate, and on occasion to the Exodus story. From there the story may touch on local heroes and struggles throughout post-Middle Ages Europe, which broadly reflect efforts to break the grip of the Roman Catholic Church and hold sovereigns more accountable. This culminates, depending on the storyteller and when and where the story is told, in passing mention of England's seventeenth-century "Glorious Revolution" (albeit not the Levellers, Diggers, and other antinomians) but more often the "American" revolutions and the French Revolution and the storming of the Bastille on July 14, 1789, an anniversary celebrated in a huge number of at times rather disconcerting places around the world. In this story, these three "liberal" and democratic revolutions share a great deal. Democracy – and, hence, "civilization" in its "modern" (read, European/North American) formulation – having thus been brought to the very belly of the beast (Europe's patchwork quilt of earldoms, duchies, principalities, kingdoms, and empires), the "revolution" was complete, the "setbacks" of the next hundred and fifty years or so aside.

Most subsequent revolutions, in this story, are measured and found (considerably) wanting. Still, one sometimes encounters references to the 1848 largely "bourgeois" revolutions in much of Europe with demands for greater enfranchisement and more democracy (interpreted somewhat more radically in other versions; see below), and such "modernizing" revolutions as Japan's 1868 Meiji Restoration and Turkey's "Young Turks" (1908) even if their import in this tale has to do with "civilizing" rather than democratizing. This vein sometimes also produces references, usually laments, to the possibilities unrealized of the 1905 revolutions in Iran and Russia, Sun Yat Sen (Sun Zhongshan) and the early Chinese Revolution (1911) and the potential squandered of Mexico's Revolution from 1917 or 1920 onward. More recently, there are versions of this story which see the 1989 Eastern European "revolutions" as modern day instances, even if they may be more fruitfully captured by the portmanteau term "refolutions."[3]

The central tropes here are ones of civilization, progress, democratization, and, rather ironically, nobility, in the sense of both sacrifice of one's position and, associated with this, a certain *noblesse oblige* on the part of elites who extend the franchise. This civilizing and democratizing revolutionary narrative tracks with the triumph of the Enlightenment and is often employed and deployed by states and elites in pursuit of the legitimacy and authority it presumably connotes. It is, ultimately, an essentially "liberal," and hence cautionary, revolutionary tale about revolution.

The Social Revolutionary story

Another familiar elite story, beloved of generations of scholars of revolution not to mention both Francophiles, who glory in all that is France, and Francophobes, who see France and its revolution as the root of much modern evil or at least mischief in the world. Here the French Revolution transforms the very conception of revolution – no more simply another turn of the wheel; henceforth profound socio-cultural transformation of the nation, the state, perhaps of the world. France represented, in Arendt's compelling formulation, "an entirely new story, a story never known or told before, is about to unfold" (1965: 28).[4] In Sewell's estimation, some ten days during this time – July 12–23, 1789 – represent "an extraordinary period of fear, rejoicing, violence, and cultural creativity that changed the history of the world" (1996: 845). Seeking two hundred years later to explain what was so revolutionary about the French Revolution, Darnton refers to "possibilism" (1989: 10), evoking the nineteenth-century French historian, Michelet, who said of France in 1789: "On that day everything was possible ... the future was present ... that is to say time was no more, all a lightening flash of eternity" (Kimmel 1990: 186). In this story of social revolution, people find themselves presented with what seem like boundless opportunities to transform the material and ideological conditions of their everyday lives and reshape their world and themselves.

For the next hundred plus years, those inspired tell a tale of struggling with how best to proceed, while those terrified by them tell tales of excesses wrought. At least in some tellings, other French upheavals (occasionally 1830, often 1848, most rarely 1871) are noted; less commonly the doomed 1905 Russian and Iranian efforts may appear, and, somewhat more commonly (though not often), Mexico, the first great social upheaval of the twentieth century. In every version we arrive next at the Russian Revolution followed by the Chinese and, for many, end with Cuba; for a time, Vietnam and Algeria were occasionally, if not comfortably, included. More commonly, later cases such as Nicaragua and Iran were invoked to provide a neat end point to a period, or are meant to bespeak a certain degradation – "From France to Nicaragua ... [Sigh] ... Look how far we have fallen!" The focus is on struggle for control of state power, and, echoing Skocpol, fast and fundamental transformations of a society's state and class structures driven in part by class-based revolts which alter the political, social, and economic systems in a "contemporaneous and mutually reinforcing fashion" (1979: 5). This narrative is popular with elites, public intellectuals and academics in both groups, and has some resonance with people in general, among whom France in particular retains a (certain) place of prominence and preeminence.

The Freedom and Liberation Revolutionary story

A somewhat looser and longer saga, this often begins with Spartacus's slave revolt in 73–71 BCE against the Romans, and various smaller anti-slavery, anti-colonial, and anti-imperialist revolts and rebellions strewn across the globe in which people sought either their freedom or liberation from sundry oppressors and overlords. Rather than the more cautionary, "liberal," elite-friendly Civilizing and Democratizing Revolutionary story, this is a more popular/ist-based account of historical events and processes. Some of these are from Arabia, at times by way of India (and vice versa), and others Persian. This narrative often features the resistance by indigenous peoples to the Spanish conquest of the Americas, as early as 1519, continuing through Tupac Amaru, and Tupac Amaru II, and sometimes various slave revolts across the Americas.[5] Here too the French Revolution is important, though less for the introduction of democracy than for egalitarianism, even the extreme version associated with St. Just, Rabat St. Etiennes, and the radical left of the revolution. Later instances such as China's Cultural Revolution (1966–1976), Kampuchea under the Khmer Rouge (1975–1979), and the vision of Peru's Sendero Luminoso (Shining Path, 1980–1995) made their fealty clear, weaving this into the liberatory story of freedom (though their visions of egalitarianism were undermined by their obsessions with charismatic leaders and the methods they employed to achieve it, highlighting the problems involved with translation and transmission of the revolutionary heritage).

From France this narrative often meanders to Haiti (1791–1804), one of the first and most important of the anti-colonial revolutions,[6] and at times elsewhere in the Caribbean (e.g. Fedon in Grenada 1795–6). This sets a tenor of sorts, as slave revolts (and occasionally anti-slavery struggles) in the Americas and nineteenth-century anti-colonial efforts become woven in. Among the slave revolts, Antigua 1736, the 1739 Stono Rebellion in Great Britain's Carolina colony, and a series in the early United States – Prosser's Rebellion (1800), the misnamed Andry's Rebellion (1811), and those led by Vesey in 1822 and Nat Turner in 1831 – get attention as does the insurrection at La Resouvenier in what is now Guyana in 1823 and the saga of John Brown and his anti-slavery rebellion is (far) more widely known now than it was when it happened (1855–1859). At times the Exodus story was (and is) invoked; it was the centerpiece of Prosser's and Vesey's uprisings.

Coexistent with the slave revolts and reasonably construed as related activities were anti-colonial struggles. In a surprising number of cases this vein begins with the "American" revolution and the *Declaration of Independence*, a radical document and an inspiration to anti-colonial activists still. Less often people include the 1780 Great Andean Rebellion of Tupac Amaru II, Tupac Katari, and others, and fewer still the wars to liberate South America from Spain. More pick up again with the 1857 Sepoy Rebellion against British colonial rule of India (the best known of such efforts, it was preceded by others still known in the region: Kerala 1793–1797 and 1800–1805; 1808–1809 in Travancore which featured the Kundara Declaration of Independence; the 1831 Kol uprising; the 1855 Santhal uprising; and the 1816–1832 Kutch Rebellion); the heroes and heroines of the Sepoy Rebellion have become folkloric staples in India, evoked and deployed in India's contemporary struggles. Less well known, but circulating still, are tales of the 1880s Mahdi Rebellion in Egyptian Sudan (under Ottoman suzerainty but administered by the omnipresent British) and contemporaneous revolts against colonial rule in Algeria, Dahomey (Benin), Ashantiland (both the Ndebele and the Shona in southern Africa), Sierra Leone and in the Fulani-Hausa states (northern Nigeria). Revolts persisted on the African continent since by the 1910s only Ethiopia and Liberia were not colonized.

Somewhat better known is the saga of China's "Fists of Righteous Harmony" (popularly known in the West as "Boxers"), who tried to drive out the various foreign powers occupying parts of their country from 1900–1901. From there the next stop is most often the Americas, with the Cubans battling the Spanish first in 1868–1878 (the Ten Years War or the Big War) still celebrated as a national holiday *Grito de Yara*, then in 1879–1880 (the

Small War), and, more famously, in their War of Independence 1895–1898, which brought the United States actively into the region. It is well remembered in Latin America that the three-month U.S. intervention resulted in the U.S. flag – not the Cuban – being raised over Havana. The next thirty-five years in Central America and the Caribbean were marked by assorted struggles against U.S. occupation of various countries, including Sandino in Nicaragua, 1926–1934. This period is also marked by the first great social upheaval of the twentieth century, the Mexican Revolution. Far from a monolithic event, this multi-act, multi-faceted, heavily populated story has countless tales. More notable appearances tend to be the rise of Zapata (and Zapatismo), radical urban workers, Villa's transformation from (social) bandit to revolutionary (and, for some, back), Aguascalientes and Article 27 of the 1917 Constitution, and the U.S. intervention at Tampico.

This story now picks up speed as the promises of the First World War victors to those in the colonized world of "self-determination of peoples" proved hollow. It is hard to imagine that moment not so very long ago when nationalists throughout the colonial world – including in Europe (with the example of 1916 Irish Rebellion) – heard and heeded the call, so full of promise and possibility. Dashed by the Great Powers' assertion of their prerogatives, anti-colonial struggles began. In the spring of 1919 alone (and influencing each other) there were revolts of varying lengths and degrees in Egypt (March), Korea (the March First Movement), Gandhi's *Satyagraha* (passive resistance) movement in "British India" (April), and in not-quite-colonized China (the May Fourth Movement). These in turn inspired a global surge, from the (Dutch) East Indies to the (British) West Indies. These struggles were interrupted by a second, again largely European, "world war." Once again colonized peoples were called upon to fight for democracy and freedom, and, this time, against fascism and subjugation; copious and generous promises were again made if they did so. In an eerie replay, the post-war victors moved to reassert their jurisdiction and authority, to continue the subjugation of "their" colonies.

An array of struggles, many armed and more often revolutionary as well as anti-colonial or anti-dictatorial, emerged across three continents (Africa, Asia, Latin America and the Caribbean) and Oceania. With varying degrees of success, struggles arose in Algeria, Tanzania, Ghana, Kenya, South Africa, Namibia, Iraq, Iran, Vietnam, Malyasia, Trinidad and Tobago, Colombia, Costa Rica, Indonesia, the Philippines, and East Timor. All served to reinforce and strengthen each other at a variety of levels, relationships recognized as early as the Bandung Conference and later in the Non-Aligned Movement and the Tri-Continental, but not least among people in the various locales who increasingly came to identify their aspirations with those of others and reassure themselves that if they can do it there, we can do it here.

For some, this story then turns back to the very belly of the beast, finding sustaining stories in the support of solidarity groups in the colonial and neo-colonial states. Even more, there begin to be stories of liberation within these countries as those marginalized and dispossessed due to ethnicity, sex, gender, indigeneity, or religion fed off the liberatory struggles of people elsewhere to embolden their struggles even as some of those in the powerful countries saw their liberation fundamentally intertwined with the liberation of those elsewhere. In this long, rambling, loose narrative, people forge a number of small stories into a popular story of liberation and freedom that elites are prone to downplay or invoke only when it is to their advantage.

The Revolution of the Lost and Forgotten story

If the Liberation and Freedom Revolutionary story is a long and loose one, it is however largely chronological, building toward an end and with, arguably, a discernable plot; it is, at least in contrast to the Revolution of the Lost and Forgotten story, clear and concise. While clear, concise, and chronological are convenient, they are also illusory, especially in the context of stories. All three of the previous stories are arguably as notable for what they omit as for what they include. Here we will find still "smaller," more obscure, more local, more narrow, more provincial, more insular, more limited stories. Which does not mean familiar faces are absent: France 1789 is here, albeit more as a moment lost; Russia for similar reasons, captured here by Kronstadt and the Ukraine; and the innumerable lost moments of Mexico duly noted. But here these stories are framed not by the "larger" process, but rather by the smaller, the more local and specific, and what was lost. And this only reflects the ones "we" "know" – it is impossible to tell what we have and are missing and may never know or, if we did, not know what to do with the information. This then, is a much longer, much looser, much vaguer and impressionistic story of struggles largely lost to us for a variety of reasons, some intentional and conscious, some not. This story is built on stories of everyday resistance, rebellion, and revolution, of which almost every people have their own version. Some are at least vaguely familiar if, for many of us, hard to place. The Assassins of Arabia in the Middle Ages have left us little more than their name but they once denoted much more, and resonate still. Various eighteenth-century pirate enclaves provided glimpses of democracy, social welfare, and the modern insurance system. The 1871 Paris Commune weaves in and out of history with a sinuosity worthy of the most meandering river. Multiracial struggles for justice in the Americas, such as the 1741 New York Conspiracy of African-American, "Spanish," and Irish sailors and dock workers as well as multiracial isolate/drop-out communities have left local legacies throughout North America and the Caribbean. Cubans can tell you about various revolutionary landings, "lightings" of the cane fields, and the mythos of the Sierra across decades. In North America, Chicago's May 1, 1886, Haymarket martyrs and indigenous North American ghost dancers of the 1890s crop up, sometimes even together. In Mexico you find the 1911–1914 Red

Battalions of the Casa del Obreros Mundial, "carpenters, bricklayers, stonecutters, tailors, typesetters, etc." who opposed both Zapata and Villa as "forces of reaction" (McLynn 2000: 344) and Oklahoma was home to the socialist Green Corn Rebellion in 1917.

Sometimes it is simply about places and spaces such as the 1534–1535 Anabaptist reign in Münster, Westphalia, the roughly seventy year seventeenth-century Republic of Palmares in northeast Brazil that resulted from a massive slave revolt, or the nine day Revolt of Masaniello in 1647 Spanish Naples. Temporary autonomous zones were provided by pirate enclaves as well as some of the "new world" religious and political movements and experiments such as the socialist Llano del Rio community in California (1914–1918) and after the New Llano Colony in Louisiana (1918–1938); so too Berlin in 1918 and the short-lived 1919 Soviets in Munich and Hungary. There were the twenty years of "Red Vienna" between the world wars (1918–1938) and Shanghai from 1925 onwards and the 1927 Guangzhou (Canton) "Three-Day Soviet" ("the Paris Commune of the East"), the Autumn Harvest uprising in Hunan, and Hamburg, Germany, in the 1920s. Chile's 1931/2 (no one can seem to agree!) 12-day socialist republic under Air Force General Marmaduke Groves left its small mark, while much greater space if little more impact is accorded to Spain where there was Asturias as early as 1934 and 1936–1939 in Madrid, "Red Barcelona," and Andalucía. In South Asia there were the 1946–1951 Telangana movement in Hyderabad (a princely state in India) and the Naxalbari subdivision of the Darjeeling district of West Bengal in 1967. The People's Republic of Greenwich Town in 1980 in Jamaica is known to few in the Caribbean and fewer outside.

Connections between and among those lost and forgotten episodes and the larger process of which they are part are not simply borne on the breezes. Whether hierarchical or lateral, direct or indirect, active agitators or more passive communicators, there are people who, in the vernacular, walk the walk and talk the talk, though at times more one than the other. Many of these people are local or national figures, largely unknown but important; Fedon at the end of the eighteenth century in Grenada and Mexico's revolutionary era Flores Magón brothers come to mind here, as in Egypt do Mustafa Kamil and Muhammad Farid of Egypt's 1919 uprising. Some of these people, while remaining in their locale, became regional or even international figures, as with Cape Verde's Amilcar Cabral or Vietnam's Ho Chi Minh in the 1970s. There is literally a cast of thousands over the centuries.

But there are those Hobsbawm describes, via anti-fascist German playwright Bertolt Brecht, as those who "change countries more often than their shoes" (1988: 12). Again, a few examples should suffice. England's Tom Paine contributed to eighteenth-century revolutionary processes in the United States, France, and the Caribbean. Franco-Peruvian Flora Tristan fought for socialism and feminism in Peru and France in the 1830s. The Italian Giuseppe Garibaldi fought for Uruguayan and Italian liberalism before turning his energies to the Socialist International. Once upon a time, albeit briefly, there really was an international communist conspiracy and people such as the peripatetic and ubiquitous Indian Marxist M.N. Roy led a Marxist rebellion in India, helped found communist parties in Mexico and India, and played significant roles in places as diverse as Germany, the Middle East, Russia, Indonesia, and China. German radical Olga Benärio (Prestes) made her presence felt in Germany, Russia, France, the United States, and Brazil; her erstwhile husband Otto Braun, another German Marxist was active throughout Europe but most famous for his role in the Chinese Revolution. The modern avatar here is Che Guevara, the Argentine doctor who participated in Guatemala's democratic experiment, worked with radical social democrats and nascent Marxists in Mexico where he connected with exiled Cubans, helped lead the Cuban Revolution, moved on to the Congo, and decamped for Bolivia, where he died in one of the few joint cold war efforts of the United States and the Soviet Union.

A few more evanescent instances may help convey the sense I am trying to capture here. There were the Ukraine's Makhnovist anarchists of 1918–1921 and the 1921 Kronstadt Rebellion which shook the nascent Soviet leadership in Russia. In Latin America, among the many, there were the Prestes Column in Brazil 1924–1927 (the original "Long March"), Sandino in Nicaragua 1926–1934, Farabundo Martí in El Salvador 1932, the Wobblies in early 1920s' Chile, and *la violencia* in Colombia circa 1948 but lasting a decade (or more) longer, its legacy alive today. The Vietnamese defeat of the French at Dienbienphu in 1954 resonates still as do Kenya's 1952–1956 *mau-mau* rebellion and the "epic" 1987–1988 battle of Cuito Cuanvale; these latter two are potent totems in sub-Saharan Africa just as the ongoing struggles of the Polisario in the Western Sahara is in the north. 1968 – in France, but especially Paris, in Italy (*il sessantotto* followed by the *autunno caldo* of 1969), in the United States, in Mexico City, in Tokyo, in the eastern Caribbean – resonates still in ways which are often alluded to if little considered and understood. Jackson State and Berkeley's "People's Park Riots" or New York's Stonewall Riot or Seattle's WTO riots all have an underground status of sorts. Mexico's now widely known modern-day Zapatistas and Nepal's less known Maoist revolutionaries are but the most recent iterations along the rhizomes of the lost and forgotten.

Some will quibble with the cases listed or be befuddled by the choices – I hope so. And I trust you will note, with some irritation, the "obvious" cases left out. Consider all the cases you know, those that hover around the edge of your consciousness, and therefore ours, that are part of your memory/ies and thus part of our collective memory/ies, that lurk just beneath the surface, waiting to be (re)animated. All are here, part of the rhizome of resistance and rebellion and revolution, part and parcel of the story/ies we tell.

All of these tales of resistance, of rebellion, and of revolution form what one student of revolutionaries has referred to as a "rich trove of stories all ... hold dear" (Anderson 1992: xii). There is, in this sense, a corpus of stories which people around the world draw on, rewrite, and make their own, as they create a narrative, their narrative, of their life and their struggle. A narrative that in its very construction (re)constructs the past, (re)mediates the present, and produces the future. A story of revolution.

Our story so far: a conclusion of sorts

If stories are tools, then it seems reasonable to construe them as a form, perhaps even the primary form, of socio-political struggle. This entails taking these stories in their contexts but also out of them; it also means recognizing in ways that are too often elided over, that context denotes more than "simply" "situation." Symbolic politics, collective memory, and the social context of politics are central to understanding and exploring revolutionary processes and stories provide us access – not just to the local and specific.

While what is mapped out here reminds us that revolution is profoundly local, it is equally clear that revolution is global. Revolution has long been global, some two hundred years is the common consensus, the stories above suggest far longer. Opposing the local and the global or the transnational to the national is not useful. Popular contention has long been a focal point not only in any given society but in all societies and the most common types of collective action – social movements, civil disobedience, demonstrations – attract attention beyond their immediate locale. While this may be particularly true of the late twentieth century (see Bleiker 2000: 1), such internationalization of revolution and revolutionary sentiments is long and storied, spread for eons over previous eras' versions of the cellphone and the Internet. "Denationalizing" these stories allows us to internationalize (but *not* globalize) them and find common themes which suggest that, while all matters revolutionary are local, they also reflect broader and deeper rules we write across times and spaces and cultures about who we are, how we behave, and what is possible in our world.

Humanity has long built infrastructures such as public waterworks, roads, buildings, etc. In more recent times, we have come to understand other human constructs, justice systems, for example, or health systems or information systems as infrastructures as well. While we too rarely think about them, these and myriad other facets of infrastructures enable our lives on a daily basis – when they are maintained, sustained, and functioning. If the biological world lacks an identical term to infrastructure, it is not because one does not exist. Long before human history, plants and animals and minerals and the elements developed what might be termed an eco-structure roughly analogous to infrastructure and equally foundational/fundamental to daily life (Warshall 1998). In much the same manner, humanity has created a story-structure, a repository of stories, which undergirds and shapes our daily lives. We (re)compose stories and (re)configure them in an effort to (re)connect with each other and to build community. Such stories inevitably feature stock characters and tend to the redundant lest the points be lost. Often meandering, perhaps taking hours or days to tell, as the tellers balance various aspects and elements, weave in characters and events, and project a process that is whole in the context of those listening. Whether they are strictly true or not is unimportant; what matters is the extent to which they are an expression of the people or are able to capture what it is people feel.

The point is not to privilege stories to the exclusion of other sources, nor to suggest that it is only stories that compel people to act. The focus here risks turning stories and culture into *things* as abstract as economic processes and political forces.[7] The sheer number of factors that one might reasonably consider in assessing why revolutions happen here and not there, now and not then, these folk and not those is simply overwhelming, and there have been many efforts of varying success. People go through an array of experiences ranging from oppression to hunger to emotions, and so forth. What far too few of these analyses consider, mediated as they often are by elite or establishment or intellectual discourse – all charges I am vulnerable to here – is the extent to which the articulation of compelling stories may provide the key. That any given story may have multiple meanings for both the tellers and the listeners, all of whom speak with many voices from multiple positions and listen from many positions and hear a multitude of voices.

None of this is meant to suggest some simple substitution of stories for rigorous intellectual analysis, though I think they are more than fair game for us to incorporate and even rely on as heuristics. Recognizing the power and importance of stories and the information they may provide and the access they may give us should not diminish our ability to "report" our "findings" (what we "know") in the (quasi-)objective, analytical terminology that defines social science in this day and age. But that is our story; inevitably our whole language of understanding, the very essence of the social science project, and our understanding is limited by what we can suss out from the stories we collect and then (re)tell. While I will leave it to my more talented postmodernist colleagues to tease out all the implications of this, the critical point here is that stories offer us a way in and thus another tool of the trade which can be turned to building a better understanding of who we are and what we are about and thus what we are up to and perhaps where we are going.

With many contemporary theorists of revolution, I believe the key to answering questions about revolutions lies with a dual focus on people and structures. I am equally certain that far more attention needs to be paid to people and their conscious, intentional efforts to make revolutions. How and why and where they do so are the questions; increasingly it seems to me that some important answers – for there are undoubtedly far more than one answer to such questions – have to do with culture, have to do with the stories that people tell, and as a result have to do, at least in part, with myth, memory, and mimesis.

There are stories, if not *a* story, of the past that are, somehow, held in common. These often resemble richly woven tapestries of myth and "fact" (i.e. the officially sanctioned myths) are demonstratively and even intensely mimetic, and draw on a reservoir of memories which themselves may be real or imagined but in either case are created. It is not History or even the past itself which binds us together (or, just as surely, splits us asunder), but the stories of that history, of *the* past that we recount to ourselves and others in the present; stories about the past inevitably in the service of the present and the future. These stories, shared stories rooted in and both reflective and refractive of collective memories are creations, reflecting conscious and intentional choices of what is to be included and what is to be omitted. The creation of these stories and thus of usable and hence manipulable pasts – as History or history – is as essential as it is inevitable. The story of revolution we can "know" now, today, reaches as far back as we can see and as far into the future as we can imagine and offers us more than we can possibly work with.

Notes

1 But see Marx's (Marx and Engels 1975–2005: XI, 104, 103) famous dismissal of borrowed "names, battle-cries, and costumes," the "traditions of all the dead generations ... weigh[ing] like a nightmare on the brain of the living."
2 See Hooks' (1995: 148) "cultural genealogy of resistance" which helps us to learn from and build "on present strategies of opposition and resistance that were effective in the past and are empowering in the present."
3 The term "refolution" is meant to connote "a non-revolutionary revolution" and convey democratic-minded, largely urban events with little or no violence, marked by civil disobedience led by opposition or "reformed" elites adept with media and technology and willing to negotiate (see Ash 1989a: 1; 1989b: 9).
4 People, Arendt argues, believe "they are agents in a process which spells the end of the old order and brings the birth of the new world" (1965: 42).
5 Most "famous" was the seventy year slave revolt in Brazil centered around the republic of Palmares in the northeast which by the 1690s had some 20,000 inhabitants who were forced to fight off Dutch and Portuguese invaders; in 1696, overwhelmed by the invaders, the leaders leapt to their deaths from a high cliff rather than surrender; see Meltzer (1993: 86). Their choice links Palmares with those across time and places as distant as Masada in ancient Israel, Carib's Leap in Grenada, and the Communards who chose to die rather than submit and go back to the life they had been forced to lead.
6 The intensity, drama, and import of Haiti seems to have largely been lost to the mists of time – perhaps no accident when one considers the circumstances: slaves, uneducated at least by the Western bourgeois liberal standards of the time, inspired by the revolution in France (their colonial taskmasters) rise up not only to throw off their masters but win their independence and defeat the world's three great colonial powers (France, Britain, and Spain) to maintain it. Haiti represents a number of things: the greatest, first, and only successful slave revolt

in the Western hemisphere; the first "black" republic and only the second independent republic in the hemisphere; and, "the first *free* nation of *free* men (sic) to arise within, and in resistance to, the emerging constellation of Western European empire" (Lowenthal 1976: 657). The only black, independent state in the Western hemisphere stood as both "a spiritual heir to the French Revolution" and "provided a serious challenge as the first non-European postcolonial state in the modern world" (Fauriol 1996: 520). Dubis (2004) is one recent effort to rectify this dearth of attention.

7 This salutary admonition comes courtesy of John Foran (2001); emphasis in original.

Part III

Globalization and the possible futures of revolution

10 What does revolution mean in the twenty-first century?

Alex Callinicos

Few subjects in social and political theory pose greater difficulties today than that of revolution. This is, of course, in large part a consequence of the upheavals of 1989 and 1991 that destroyed the Soviet empire. When I was growing up in the 1950s and 1960s, whatever one thought of the Russian Revolution of October 1917, there was no doubt that it was one of the defining events of the twentieth century. Today October 1917 and the state to which it gave birth have been reduced to a caesura: according to the prevailing opinion, they belong to the "short twentieth century" (1914–1991), an interlude during which totalitarian distractions diverted the world from its destiny of becoming the receptacle of the liberal capitalism inaugurated by the British Empire that it is the task of the United States to complete.[1]

In this era of restored normality what had been some of the main terms in the political vocabulary of the left have been appropriated by the neo-liberal right. "Reform," for example, no longer refers to measures designed to limit the operation of market capitalism in order (as T.H. Marshall's classic analysis had it) to expand citizenship rights. Today, in Britain or Germany or Brazil, reforms are measures designed instead to expand the scope of the market, and in particular to subject public services to the logic of commodity exchange, thereby removing them from the domain of collective decision making by citizens. Similarly "revolution" has become the watchword of Washington neo-conservatives who seek to use American military power simultaneously to expand their empire and to bring the benefits of a version of democracy, identified primarily with the protection of private property and individual freedom, to peoples previously denied them (see Zakaria 2004 and Callinicos 2003d: 23–34).

Not, of course, that the U.S. marines are a *sine qua non* of regime change. The dynamic at work in the "velvet revolution" that swept away Stalinism in Eastern and Central Europe in 1989 – for all their manifest limitations, upheavals that took the world by surprise and destroyed regimes that had long lost any right to exist – has been distilled into a technique of imperial rule, the means by which, in Georgia, Ukraine, Lebanon, and Kyrgyzstan, U.S. geopolitical interests and rivalries within local oligarchies have converged (thanks in part to the mediation of a network of foundations and NGOs) to help effect political changes congenial to Washington (Almond 2004). The importance of favorable geopolitical conditions in making possible the recent "colored revolutions" is underlined by the contrasting case of Uzbekistan, where in May 2005 the Karimov regime, confident in the support of Russia and China, crushed mass protests and subsequently reacted to Washington's criticisms by ordering the United States to withdraw from the airbase it had been allowed to use after September 11, 2001.

No wonder that those seeking to contest liberal imperialism from the left tend to avoid the language of revolution. John Holloway, who has made himself the theorist of one of the landmark struggles against neo-liberal globalization, the movement in Chiapas initiated by the Zapatistas, is disarmingly honest: "Revolutionary change is more desperately urgent than ever, but we do not any more know what revolution means" (Holloway 2002: 215). Daniel Bensaïd, a more orthodox revolutionary Marxist, has commented on the "strategic degree zero" faced by the contemporary radical left (Bensaïd 2004: 463). Even when the classical revolutions receive serious study (as opposed to the remythologizations practiced by fashionable historians such as Simon Schama), it is often the nature and effects of the counter-revolutionary attempts to destroy them that capture the imagination – as in, for example, Arno Mayer's *The Furies.*

In this context, it seems sensible to consider, in as sober and objective a fashion as possible, what, if anything, revolution could mean today in the era of neo-liberal imperialism. Plainly this requires some thought about how the word "revolution" is to be used. If one takes the great revolutions of modernity as one's benchmark, the occurrence of a revolution requires the coincidence of two distinct registers, social and political: that is, a revolution involves (1) the rapid and forcible transfer of state power that contributes to (2) a decisive acceleration in a process of broader social transformation. Both these conditions are necessary. To equate revolution merely with social transformation would be to license banalities about the "IT revolution" and the like. Unless deeper structural conflicts give rise to a convulsive and decisive struggle over the direction of state power that in turn contributes to the resolution (in some form or other) of these conflicts, then one should refuse to apply the term "revolution" to the changes under discussion. But without such structural conflicts any political transformation, however rapid, violent, and dramatic it may be, does not count as a revolution. As Theda Skocpol puts it, "[w]hat is unique to social revolution is that basic changes in social structure and in political structure occur together in a mutually reinforcing fashion" (1979: 4–5). A compromise strategy might be to distinguish between social revolutions that meet conditions (1) and (2) and political revolutions that merely involve an abrupt and forcible change of state power. For the purposes of this chapter, I will use "revolution" to refer to social revolutions. I appreciate that all this is stipulative rather than reflecting usage (particularly the kind of usage typified by the Bush administration's proclamation of "democratic revolution"); however, what makes revolution an interesting concept in social theory is that it offers a means of thinking about the interrelations between long-term, protracted processes of social transformation and the relatively rapid changes in state power that these processes may provoke or be shaped by.[2]

A third possible condition of revolution is given by Trotsky: (3) "the forcible entry of the masses in the realm of rulership over their own destiny" (Trotsky 1967: I, 15). Despite this excellent pedigree, I don't think that we should treat (3) as either a necessary or sufficient condition of revolution. To do so would be to narrow down the scope of the concept: in particular it would rule out a priori the possibility of revolution from above – what Gramsci called "passive revolution." It should at least be open to discussion whether or not events such as German unification, the Meiji restoration, the transformation of the USSR under Stalin, and the socio-political transformations undergone by the ex-communist states of Eastern and Central Europe and the former Soviet Union count as cases of revolution. Nevertheless, surely an important claim to be made for the political significance of the "great" revolutions – 1640, 1776, 1789, and 1917 – is that the mobilizations from below that they involved widened the sense of the potential of political agency. These were, as Perry Anderson puts it, "collective projects which have sought to render their initiators authors of their collective mode of existence as a whole, in a conscious program aimed at creating or remodelling whole social structures" (Anderson 1980: 20). It is this aspect of revolution that continues to have a grip on the collective imagination: it is some kind of tribute to this that the empire-expanding "democratic revolutions" of recent years have involved carefully staged managed public rituals of mass participation.

Revolutions thus can (even if they don't have to) be occasions for experiences of mass collective agency directed at effecting political and social transformation. Toni Negri has indeed sought to rewrite the history of modern political thought as the gradual emergence of the idea of constituent power – of the creative power of the multitude to make and remake concrete constitutional orders (Negri 1997). Whatever we may think of the highly suggestive reconstruction of classical republicanism that Negri offers, his argument has the merit of reminding us of how the topics of democracy and revolution intersect. This brings us to Marxism. For what is distinctive to the Marxist conception of socialist revolution is the proposition that all three conditions fuse in the overthrow of capitalism (Draper 1977–1990). What, if any, content has this conception today?

Revolution and contemporary capitalism

One can isolate three kinds of consideration here – roughly speaking: normative justification, structural context, and agency. The first is straightforward enough: can revolution, in the sense gestured towards above, be morally justified today? The legitimacy of revolution is, of course, a huge subject that played a major part in the very constitution of modern Western political thought (Skinner 1978, II). I want simply to sidestep this literature here. Approaching the problem instead in a fairly crude and common-sense fashion, one might seek to weigh up the undoubted evils of revolution with the evils that it would remove or prevent. Thus contemporary socialist critiques of capitalism focus on the system's present body count – 18 million preventable deaths a year caused by poverty or poverty-related reasons – and the prospect of even greater catastrophes induced by the processes of environmental destruction driven by the global accumulation process. In recent discussions the felicific calculus has been complicated by the problem of transition costs: the output losses resulting from the disruption caused by the transition to a new system might either eliminate the income gain produced by the abolition of exploitation or to reduce it so low as to make participation in revolution irrational (Przeworski 1985: ch. 5; see also Brighouse and Wright 2002 and Callinicos 2003c).

But while this argument is undoubtedly pertinent, the real problem with morally justifying revolution today is essentially the same as one of the standard requirements made of any claim to be embarking on a just war – namely, can it achieve the desirable objectives assigned to it? In the case of socialist revolution this problem of feasibility takes a dual form: (a) Can we imagine a reproducible social system with which such a revolution could replace the present system and that would represent an improvement according to mutually agreed criteria – let's say, democracy, efficiency, justice, and sustainability? (Callinicos 2003b: ch. 3) There would be no point in striving for revolution if its goal were unattainable. (b) Even if there were such a system, what is the probability of a revolution capable of installing it actually occurring? If the probability were sufficiently low, then assuming the costs of even striving for revolution might be unjustified.[3] In the 1980s and 1990s it was problem (a) that dominated discussion as the crisis of the command economies in the East and the renaissance of economic liberalism in the West created a climate in which it seemed that the superiority of the market over planning could be definitively established. This impression has indeed been entrenched as a dogma that sustains the Washington Consensus and the politics of the third way and of American neo-conservatism.

For all that, it is contestable: radical economists such as Michael Albert and Pat Devine have constructed models of democratically planned economies (called, respectively, participatory planning and negotiated coordination) that go a long way towards showing how the requirements set out above might be met (Devine 1988; Albert 2003; see my discussion of Devine's work in Callinicos 2003b, ch. 3, and my debate with Albert on Znet 2003). Of course, this relatively technical work isn't enough on its own seriously to budge the widespread assumption, on the left as well as the right, that some kind of market economy is the inescapable material basis of any modern society worth living in, but it has, in my view, established an intellectual bridgehead that is sufficiently robust for me to concentrate on problem (b) in the rest of this chapter: even if Albert and Devine are right, and democratic planning is feasible and would represent an improvement on capitalism, how likely is it that the necessary socio-political transformation will occur any time soon? "Not very," would be the most charitable answer just about everyone would give. In the hope of making addressing the reasons behind this response vaguely manageable, I want to focus on the other two kinds of consideration distinguished above, both of which bear on this particular problem of feasibility.

Is revolution feasible today?

There is, then, second, the question of the structural context that may facilitate or impede revolutions. In her classic study Skocpol isolated two main transnational dimensions of this context – the capitalist world economy and the modern state system (Skocpol 1979: ch. 1). Since, as Skocpol emphasizes, historically revolution has involved the seizure of control of a state within the interstate system, the critical issue here involves measuring the impact of globalization. Have conditions decisively turned against revolutionary seizures of state power? Two main reasons are given for thinking that they have, even though they are at least potentially in conflict with each other. First, the qualitative increase in global economic integration over the past generation means that states have lost the degree of autonomy they previously enjoyed: more specifically, any attempt to pursue socio-economic policies other than those mandated by the Washington Consensus will be ruthlessly punished by the financial markets and by international institutions such as the IMF and the World Bank. This argument is put forward by the boosters of neo-liberal globalization, but a version of it is to be found in Michael Hardt's and Toni Negri's argument that national sovereignty has been supplanted by empire, which marks the emergence of a new form of transnational network capitalism (Hardt and Negri 2000, 2004). Secondly, since the end of the cold war the state system has fallen under the unchallenged hegemony of the United States, which possesses resources, economic, military, and ideological unparalleled by those enjoyed by any earlier imperial power. The effect is not simply to confront any deviant state (and what could be more deviant than one that was the product of a socialist revolution?) with the might of the Pentagon but also to remove the kind of space that, during the cold war partition of the world into rival superpower blocs, gave at least some states the room for maneuver to play one side off against another. These two reasons are potentially in conflict since the first implies a general weakening of states whereas the second asserts that one state in particular has become much stronger. There are ways around this – for example, by distinguishing between the capacities common to all states (which may have declined) and the powers that states have relative to one another (where, despite the alleged general reduction in state capacities, the power of the United States may have grown with respect to that of other states). Or one might see the United States as a kind of global enforcer, imposing the conditions of neo-liberal globalization on recalcitrant states (Hay 2005 offers a thorough assessment of the impact of globalization on state capacities that is critical of the more extreme claims made for this impact).

In any case, I am not sure that either claim really stands up as a marker of a qualitative change in the structural context favoring or impeding revolutions. This is partly because, as everyone knows, the problem of survival in a hostile interstate system has always confronted revolutionary states. They have faced the direct threat of counter-revolution imposed by, or with the strong support of one or more great powers. But they have also had to deal with the more subtle danger that consists in adapting to meet this threat and thereby increasingly reproducing many of the characteristics of the socio-political order that the revolution was intended to destroy. It is this latter form of external pressure that, in my view, mainly explains the tragedy of the Russian Revolution: developing the heavy industries necessary to give the USSR military capabilities comparable to those of Britain and Germany implied an internalization of the imperative of capital accumulation and a concentration of economic and political power more extreme than in Western capitalism. This case is particularly striking because the decisive phase in this process of adaptation/counter-revolutionary transformation – the so-called "Stalin revolution" in the ten years that began in 1927–1928 – occurred during the Great Depression of the 1930s, when the world market shrank and fragmented, and in response all states capable of doing so pursued strategies of economic autarky. The pressure to adapt to a transnational environment dominated by competing imperialist powers made itself brutally felt even when global economic integration was at its weakest (see James 2001; Cliff 1988; and Callinicos 1991: 20–40).

So a hostile transnational context has always been a problem facing revolutions and the regimes they produce. Of course, greater global economic integration and American supremacy may have made the problem worse. But it does not follow that these changes have produced an impermeable world system with no cracks or crannies that a revolutionary regime could exploit. The case of the regime of Hugo Chávez in Venezuela suggests the opposite. To say this is not to engage in the cult of Chávez and the "Bolivarian Revolution" into which much of the Latin American left has fallen. Whatever changes have taken place in Venezuela under Chávez do not amount to a revolution in the sense in which I use the term here. Chávez himself, for all his courage, guile, and oratorical powers, falls into a not unfamiliar pattern of the Latin American military ruler who uses radical and in particular anti-American rhetoric in order to cultivate a popular base that is not allowed too close to the real levers of power. All the same, we have in Venezuela a regime that has implemented significant social reforms with the active support of the poor and against the bitter opposition of the local oligarchy, supported openly if often ineptly by the Bush administration. And the rhetoric of Chávez has become more radical recently, with calls to "transcend capitalism" and to explore what socialism might mean in the twenty-first century (Gott 2005; Chávez and Harnecker 2005). This suggests, among other things, that states aren't quite as impotent as they are widely represented as being. A sufficiently determined regime has been able to become a major focus of resistance to the United States. To the extent that the appeal of Holloway's slogan "change the world without taking power" depends on the claim that states are impotent, Venezuela should offer pause for thought.

Of course, it is quite possible to explain why Chávez has been able to get away (so far) with tweaking Bush's nose and defying the Washington Consensus. Venezuela as a major oil producer has benefited from the recent rise in the oil price: this, plus Chávez's success in defeating the 2002–2003 bosses' strike and regaining state control of the oil industry, has given him the extra revenues to finance the reforms that have helped to cement his popular base. Meanwhile, Washington has been distracted by the Middle East adventure that has contributed to the rise in the oil price. Finally, thanks to the resurgence of the left in a number of countries (Brazil, Argentina, Bolivia, Uruguay) and the more active presence of potential "peer competitors" of the United States (the European Union and China), Latin America is less securely under Washington's thumb than it was a decade ago, and this has allowed Chávez to use, for example, the Lula government in Brazil as a counterweight to the Uribe administration in Colombia, probably the Latin American regime most closely aligned with Washington. All this is true enough, but it merely points to the fact that, certainly geopolitically and, arguably, economically as well, the present global constellation of forces is considerably more fluid than one-sided portrayals of American dominance sometimes suggest. Chávez certainly has found enough cracks to give him the room for maneuver to survive and prosper, at least for the time being. Of course, the reasons for his relative success are quite specific: most obviously, very few states have the potential asset offered by being a major oil exporter. But it would be a ridiculously strong demand to require that *all* states should enjoy the same room for maneuver. Their circumstances necessarily differ, placing greater or lesser obstacles or advantages to revolutionary movements seeking to seize control of them. But precisely what politics is about as a practice is creatively responding to the specific, and changing causal constellation that confronts a particular group of actors sharing common goals – to borrow the language of Machiavelli, still the master of politics in this sense, of striving to align *virtù* and *fortuna*.

At least as long as global economic and political processes remain subject to what Trotsky called the law of uneven and combined development – which means certainly as long as capitalism exists, this will continue to be the case. But whatever space variations in circumstances give individual revolutionary states, it is a wasting asset. Consider, for example, the way in which the regional and global balance of forces that had allowed the Assad dynasty in Syria (by no means in any serious sense a revolutionary regime but undoubtedly one that has pursued a course in conflict with United States and Israeli interests and strategy) considerable leverage long after the end of the cold war has now moved dramatically against it. Closely connected is what remains one of the chief lessons of the Russian Revolution: the very struggle by a revolutionary regime to survive will in all likelihood produce adaptations that make it harder for the revolution to secure the objectives for which it was made in the first place.[4] Chávez and his supporters will no doubt have to confront both these truths in the coming years. The conclusion drawn by classical Marxists was, of course, the necessity of world revolution. A precondition of any attempt at addressing the question of whether or not this even more demanding transformation than the seizure of political power in an individual state has become more or less feasible (even less feasible, most would no doubt say) in the era of neo-liberal imperialism (something I do not undertake here) is dealing with the third consideration that I distinguished earlier on – agency.

Agency

It is here that, in my view, any attempt to pursue the socialist revolutionary project faces the greatest difficulty. During the twentieth century the kind of collective agency required to transform capitalism was imagined and constructed against the background of the development of the labor movement. The traditions of organizing and the ideological styles formed within this movement provided the most important single reference point for revolutionaries – even where their social base was far from proletarian (this was the most plausible, though in my view insufficient reason for describing the regimes in China, Cuba, and Yugoslavia, for example, as "workers' states"). To drop, once again, briefly into an autobiographical mode: when I was a young, revolutionary socialist thirty years ago, imagining the transformation for which I was striving took place within three main coordinates – the conception of revolution developed by the classical Marxist tradition, the events of May–June 1968 in France, and the forms of proletarian organization and militancy developed by the most militant groups of workers in contemporary Britain – the miners, dockers, car-workers, and engineers whose struggles brought down the government of Edward Heath in 1972–1974. Others' imaginings would have involved a somewhat different mix – in which, for example, guerrilla movements in Latin America, symbolized in the martyred figure of Che Guevara, might loom much larger – but the patterns of working-class struggle forged between the 1930s and 1960s in the giant plants of the Second Industrial Revolution remained a general reference point: the concept of the "mass worker" developed by Italian *operaismo* is a case in point.[5]

That working class has, of course, gone, dismembered by the neo-liberal offensive pioneered by Reagan and Thatcher and the process of capitalist restructuring that was initiated by the onset of, what Robert Brenner has called, the "long downturn" in the mid-1970s and that continues today with the emergence of China as a major industrial producer (Brenner 1998, 2002). We are still measuring the consequences of this enormous socio-political change. One consequence has been to deprive the concept of a revolutionary subject – of the collective agent capable of carrying through systemic transformation – of any obvious class referent. The potential revolutionary subject has been hollowed out socially, which poses, of course, an apparently fatal blow to the classical Marxist tradition since Marx's and Engels's conception of socialist revolution was intended to think the fusion of the social and political registers that I made a necessary condition of revolution *tout court* in a specific way – one where the working class being formed in industrial capitalism would complete the political project of human emancipation that the French Revolution had begun, but left unfinished.[6]

Now one response is simply to draw a line. This is in effect what Hardt and Negri do in their two books *Empire* and *Multitude*. Though they are ambivalent over whether or not the industrial working class has simply ceased to exist, they offer the concept of the multitude as that of a "new revolutionary subject," rooted in the class relations of contemporary trans-national capitalism but broader, more inclusive than the classical Marxist concept of the proletariat. It is worth noting the element of continuity here with Marx: Hardt and Negri are still trying to think the fusion of the social and political – thus they insist that the multitude is "a class concept" (Hardt and Negri 2004: 102). But the discontinuity is at least as important: they argue that transformations in capitalism – in particular the growing impor-tance of what they call "immaterial labor" – means that Marxist value theory no longer provides (as Marx thought it did) the key to under-standing class structure. The theory of the multitude can be assessed at two levels. The first involves asking how successful it is as a case of class analy-sis. The answer must be: not very. Marx's theory of value does not require commodities to take the form of material products – they may instead be services, and he was perfectly well aware that office and retail workers could be subjected to the same conditions of economic insecurity and work dis-cipline suffered by industrial laborers. Moreover, the break-up of the forms of proletarian collectivity specific to the Second Industrial Revolution has been accompanied, not by the marginalization of wage labor, but by a powerful tendency towards its generalization on a world scale (see, on the theory of the multitude as class analysis, Harman 2002 and Harribey 2004). But I am more interested here with the second level of assessment. This concerns the politics of the multitude as a revolutionary subject. As Ernesto Laclau has observed, Hardt and Negri effectively argue that the resistance of the multitude will develop into a constituent power essentially through the spontaneous coordination of the singularities composing it: "There is an actual historical subject of what they conceive as the realization of a full immanence: it is what they call the "multitude"" (Laclau 2004: 24). Consequently, "for them the unity of the multitude results from the spontaneous aggregation of a plurality of actions that do not need to be articulated between themselves .... . What is totally lacking in *Empire* is a theory of *articulation*, without which politics is unthinkable" (Laclau 2004: 26).

Laclau's critique is made from his own distinctive post-Marxist perspective, but what he highlights is the absence of any place for *strategy* in Hardt's and Negri's theory of the multitude. As Bensaïd has argued with great brilliance, strategy is necessary for a politics that does not assume that the outcome of historical struggles is determined in advance. Strategy concerns itself with the necessarily hazardous calculations that political actors must make as they grapple with an objective context (including the strategies and actions of others) whose current state and future course are riddled with uncertainties, in part because the interactions among the antagonists produce unexpected transformations. "A strategic thought is a thought of crises and of historical conditions, a comprehension of the connection between the event and its historical conditions" (Bensaïd 2003: 182). But if, as Hardt and Negri argue, capital both "operates on the plane of *immanence*," and tends to realize it, deterritorializing, breaking down national barriers to its free movement, producing a "general equalization or smoothing of social space" where the division of the world between North and South disappears, then strategy is beside the point (Hardt and Negri 2000: 226, 236; the economic analysis implied by such assertions has been powerfully criticized by Giovanni Arrighi 2002). In this non-hierarchical "smooth world" there is no longer any unevenness, any "weak links," any specific points where contradictions accumulate and capital is particularly vulnerable. Consequently, accordingly, strategy no longer has any leverage. The reason why this doesn't matter too much is that liberation is always-already here. This optimism, whose roots lie ultimately in the vitalist ontology for which Hardt and Negri are indebted to Gilles Deleuze, helps to explain one of the most puzzling features of *Multitude*, namely the way in which it simply juxtaposes empire as a transnational "network power" with contemporary realities – for example, the existence of strategic competitors to the United States and the nationalist global policy of the Bush administration – that apparently contradict the idea of Empire (Callinicos 2006: ch. 4).

The contradiction is resolved because the logic of both production and war today implies a "distributed network structure" whose "guiding principles" require "an absolutely democratic organization" (Hardt and Negri 2004: 87, 88). The evidence to the contrary, most obviously the global state of war proclaimed by the Bush administration, isn't a mere illusion, but is a secondary and waning phenomenon relative to the dominant tendency towards "absolute democracy" striving to assert itself in the shape of the multitude:

In the era of imperial sovereignty and biopolitical production, the balance has tipped such that the ruled now tend to be the exclusive producers of social organization. This does not mean that sovereignty immediately crumbles and the rulers lose all their power. It does mean that the rulers become ever more parasitical and that sovereignty becomes increasingly unnecessary. Correspondingly, the ruled become increasingly autonomous.

(Hardt and Negri 2004: 336)

Towards the end of *Multitude*, Hardt and Negri do briefly gesture towards a more strategic and interventionist approach: "What we need to bring the multitude into being is a form of grand politics that has been called realpolitik, or political realism." And they characterize realpolitik, in terms that acknowledge the problem of strategy, as including "the capacity to separate oneself from the immediate situation and tirelessly construct mediations, feigning (if necessary) coherence, and playing different tactical games into the continuity of strategy." But the book ends by conjuring up the prospect of "a strong event, a radical insurrectional demand. We can already recognize that today time is split between a present that is already dead and a future that is already living. ... In time, an event will thrust itself like an arrow into that living future. Thus will be the real political act of love" (Hardt and Negri 2004: 356, 358). This seems to commend a stance of passive waiting rather than the understanding implied by a strategic conception of politics that a new revolutionary subject will not spontaneously emerge but must be actively constructed.

But where to begin this process of construction? I have already suggested that the restructurings of capitalism that provided the structural context in which one working-class collectivity ceased to exist have led, not to the disappearance of wage labor, but to its tendential generalization. The implication is that the antagonism between capital and wage labor is, if anything, a more dominant global reality than it was during the great epics of the modern labor movement. In that sense, the working class, as it exists today and will further develop in the future out of the current global patterns of capital accumulation, remains the social basis from which any new revolutionary subject might be formed. But there is a fundamental difference between a class as an objectively existing set of common places in given production relations and a class collectivity – in other words, the participation of a significant number of members of a class thus objectively defined in collective action on the basis of a shared sense of common identity (Callinicos 2004a: chs. 4 and 5). The construction of a class subject, let alone a revolutionary subject, involves crossing the gap between the two. The gap is now wider than it has been for a long time, living as we do amid the ruins of a working-class collectivity that has been shattered by the transformations of the past generation. But this does not mean that beginning to imagine and construct a new one is simply impossible.

Let me conclude then by considering briefly what role the movement for another globalization might play in this process. Even though it was formulated before the great confrontations at Seattle and Genoa, Hardt's and Negri's theory of the multitude might be thought of offering a way of theorizing the spontaneous ideology of this movement. There is not much distance between the idea that the multitude "acts on the basis of what singularities share in common" and the self-conception of the *altermondialiste* movement as diverse social subjects acting together (Hardt and Negri 2004: 100). I have already highlighted one respect in which the theory of the multitude is misleading, namely that it implies that this convergence of singularities occurs spontaneously; in fact creating and sustaining a transnational movement since the late 1990s has involved an intense, and often highly conflictual political effort (see, for example, the highly polemical memoir by one of the founders of the World Social Forum: Cassen 2003).

Nevertheless, the impact of the movement for another globalization and the other movements associated with it, notably against the war in Iraq, has been far from negligible: most notably, in the early months of 2003, they mobilized, according to one cautious estimate, 35.5 million people around the world to protest against the invasion of Iraq (Reynié 2004; see also Callinicos 2003b and Callinicos 2004b). Efforts by European activists to achieve cross-border protests against economic measures such as the Bolkestein directive intended to liberalize services in the European Union have produced less spectacular, but nevertheless solid results, and the French wing of the *altermondialiste* movement played an important role in the successful campaign against the European Constitution during the referendum of May 2005. Despite the growing political divergences within its ranks and the high overhead costs imposed by its consensual decision-making procedures, this movement provides the main political terrain on which any attempt to revive a genuinely anti-capitalist left and a serious revolutionary project is likely to take place today. What shape any collective subject that emerges will take is extremely hard to say. This is in part because it involves developing new forms of working-class collectivity to replace those largely dismantled by the neo-liberal offensive that began at the end of the 1970s. The leaders of the existing trade union movement on both sides of the Atlantic tend to respond to the continual press of demands from neo-liberal governments and business executives themselves under the whip of international competition with corporatist tactics designed to negotiate the preservation of some kind of place for them in the socio-political order, even if this is at the price of the continued long-term decline in the power and social weight of the movement. It seems reasonable to expect that at some stage this pattern will be broken through some combinations of elemental rebellions and the molecular development of forms of proletarian collectivity more appropriate to the conditions of work and life in twenty-first century capitalism. But despite some anticipatory outbursts, notably in France, such as the great public sector strikes of

November–December 1995 and the protests of spring 2006 against the First Employment Contract (CPE)[7] law intended to reduce the rights of young workers, the hold of the past remains very largely to be broken.

In all probability, the new forms of collectivity will differ significantly from those of the recent past at least. The closest to a revolutionary experience that the neo-liberal era has seen – the popular insurrections in Bolivia in October 2003 and May–June 2005 that ejected two presidents from office and created the conditions in which Evo Morales could be elected in their place and order the renationalization of the hydrocarbon industry – has seen the emergence of hybrid forms of organization in which Bolivia's poor have drawn on both native American tradition and the modes of proletarian militancy developed by mining workers (Gonzalez 2005; Hylton and Thompson 2005). Maybe this kind of popular self-organization, based more on community (for example, El Alto, the vast city of the poor above La Paz) than on workplace, fits a social environment where the wage-form is spreading, but in conditions of growing "precarity" that condemn many to, at best, casual employment or the highly insecure forms of self-employment known as the informal sector. The role played by university and school students as the militant driving force of the CPE protests in France, limiting the room for maneuver of the trade-union officials in negotiating a compromise with the government, is another example of how the traditional forms of organizing of the labor movement are having other ways of acting grafted on to them. These forms of resistance have in any case begun to undermine the idea that there is no alternative to neo-liberal globalization. But at most some of the raw materials of a new collective subject currently exist. Imagining and constructing it is likely to be a long and laborious task – but, for all that, given how the world is, an essential one.

Notes

1 Niall Ferguson's recent books (2003, 2004) offer a good example of this kind of teleology. Eric Hobsbawm (1994) helped to invent the idea of the "short twentieth century." Alain Badiou (2005) offers some coruscating reflections on this era and on the contemporary reaction against it. I am grateful to all the participants in the original conference that gave rise to this book, and especially to David Lane for his very helpful comments on the original version of my paper.

2 All this talk about "processes of social transformation" is, I know, very vague. Much more needs to be said about the kind and extent of change involved. Skocpol's influential book ties social revolutions to transformations of agrarian class relations (1979, ch. 3). This is surely much too restrictive, and reflects Skocpol's inductive historical method, as Michael Burawoy (1989) has shown. More generally, should "revolution" be restricted to political ruptures associated with systemic transformations – from a Marxist perspective, from one mode of production to another? And must revolutions be events that contribute to historical movements in a progressive direction (assuming we have some means of

saying what counts as progress)? I evade these questions here, but for some relevant discussion, see Callinicos 1989 and 1995, ch. 4.

3 I say "might" here because the revolutionary case is often supported by the thought that, even if the struggle failed to meet its objective, the resulting pressure on the ruling class might produce genuine reforms that made the existing system easier to bear. Reforms, in other words, are often the by-product of revolutionary movements. One important issue here is the strategy used by such movements. There is much historical evidence to show that political terrorism, certainly (though not only) when used in liberal democracies, not only fails to meet the desired goal of systemic transformation but actually makes the immediate situation worse – by inducing repression, helping to isolate and weaken the revolutionary movement, and so on. It is partly for this reason, but also because of the elitism typical of terrorist organizations, that classical Marxism has always opposed terrorism: see, for example, Trotsky 1974.

4 The use of quasi-Darwinian language is intentional: for a pioneering attempt to deploy a non-teleological and non-Social Darwinist conception of natural selection in social theory, see Runciman 1989 and the discussion in Carling 2004.

5 See Wright 2002 for a critical history of *operaismo*. Daniel Bensaïd's autobiography illustrates the importance of Latin America for many of the 1968 generation: e.g. 2004, ch. 10. It is a symptom of how distant the working-class militancy of the 1960s and 1970s now seems that Microsoft's Word's spellcheck for UK English rejects the word "docker." Truly history is written by the victors.

6 Stathis Kouvelakis offers a fascinating, if problematic, reconstruction of the formation of this conception of revolution: Kouvelakis 2003.

7 The "contrat première embauche" is a contract with a two-year probation period that allows the employer the right to sack the employee without having to give a reason.

11 Revolution and empire

Robin Blackburn

"Empire" only became a dirty word in the twentieth century. Prior to this, educated Europeans and North Americans believed that while there were certainly bad empires (usually Eastern and despotic in character), there were also good empires – notably that of Rome, the cradle of Christian civilization and a model for enlightened later monarchies and republics. The Catholic Church always had an affinity with empire and saw even the heathen variety as providential if there was any chance of converting the ruler, as had happened with such prodigious consequences with Constantine in fourth-century Rome. Charlemagne, Frederic II, Charles V, Philip II, Louis XIV, Napoleon – all dreamt of re-establishing the universal empire. Republicans, too, admired the emancipatory vigor of the Roman Republic, seeing its imperial reach as proof of the special virtue of this form of government, even as they worried about the danger that a republican empire could be undermined by its own successes and capsize (as Rome did) into militarism and monarchy.

Under the circumstances, it is not so surprising that the idea that there might be something wrong with empire caught on very slowly – a process worth reviewing in more detail.

The triple success of colonial rebels in the Americas – of the North American revolutionaries in 1776–1783, the Haitian revolutionaries in 1791–1804, and the Spanish-American revolutionaries in 1810–1825 – should have impressed on all thoughtful observers the vanity of empire and, for a time, it did play a part in discouraging overseas expansion. The terms Jefferson used in 1811 to denounce European imperialism also stressed its absurdity:

> What in short is the whole system of Europe towards America? One hemisphere of the earth, separated from the other by wide seas on both sides, having a different system of interests flowing from different climates, different soils, different productions, different modes of existence and its own local relations and duties, is made subservient to all the petty interests of the other, to their laws, their regulations, their passions and wars.
>
> (Jefferson 1811)

The implications were ironic, however. For Jefferson's anathema left open a path for the United States to further extend its own institutions in its own continent.

For much of the U.S. republic's first one hundred and forty years, its leading statesmen would find it natural to talk of an American empire – an "empire of liberty," as it was sometimes called – and to see no tension between this and the revolutionary tradition of 1776. This was good republican empire, not bad monarchical empire. John Quincy Adams and Martin Van Buren opposed the unfolding of empire and the wars and displacements it involved, but this stance led them to defeat or isolation. The removal of Indians and the acquisition of territory were justified in the name of a "manifest destiny" that would spread good order and good husbandry, prosperity, and republican institutions. Thus domestic disorder in Mexico in the 1840s was seen as a sufficient threat to warrant a wholesale military invasion and the seizure of extensive territory. Though the actions of statesmen – especially the Louisiana Purchase and the Mexican war – were decisively important to U.S. expansion in the nineteenth century, these could only be effective because they expressed the dynamic of a whole social formation, with its increasingly commercial farming and new manufacturing, its canals and railways, its slave plantations, and its celebration of liberty and race. When Spain and France acquired Louisiana by treaty, each could make nothing of it. Within a few decades of its acquisition by the United States it comprised eleven flourishing states. Empire was felt to be a projection of the republic's native virtues and, like the republic, was rooted in revolution.

The victory of the North in the Civil War was a striking victory for republican empire, just as the defeat of the Confederacy was a defeat for the right of self-determination. The slave emancipation policy lent a needed idealistic dimension to the Union cause. Elsewhere in the Americas, attempts were made to construct monarchical empires – in Mexico (Iturbide, 1823–1824; Maximilian, 1863–1865), Haiti (Dessalines, 1804–1806; Soulouque, 1849–1859), and Brazil (Pedro I and II, 1821–1889). With the exception of the Brazilian empire, which boasted many "liberal" and parliamentary features, these attempts foundered quite quickly. The imperial idea fared better in the Old World: Napoleon III helped to unify Italy and was himself defeated by the formidable new German empire. Russia consolidated a transcontinental empire even larger than that of the U.S. republic.

Following the Berlin conference of 1884–1885, the European great powers carved up what was left of Africa and Asia. This was empire not simply as a monarchical style, but as a program of overseas territorial expansion and rule. The Europeans claimed they were acquiring colonies in order to stamp out the slave trade, to improve the condition of women, and to extend the benefits of free trade and civilization. The republics of Central and South America were spared outright colonization, but were still the objects of debt-collecting gunboat diplomacy. The United States had not claimed any prizes in the scramble for Africa – though it did support the Belgian king's claim to the Congo, citing his supposed abolitionist credentials (Hochschild 1999). Notwithstanding the anti-slavery claims made by the European imperialists, the spread of European rule in Africa in the late nineteenth century led to a horrendous expansion of slavery and forced labor in the newly acquired territories as the new rulers and their favored enterprises recruited labor for public works, plantations, and mines. While cynicism, racism, and cruelty contributed to this result, it was also brought on by colonial entrepreneurs whose efforts to recruit paid labor attracted little response. The Atlantic slave trade had created large-scale slave raiding and trading complexes. With its end, large numbers of slaves were available on the African market at low prices.

Still, attitudes toward empire were changing. The implicitly positive charge of the term was challenged around the turn of the century by three spectacles of colonial bloodletting: in 1895–1898, Spain suppressed Cuban opposition to its rule; in 1899–1902, Britain put down the Boer republics in South Africa; and in 1901–1904, the United States stamped out Filipino resistance to colonization. This moment witnessed the rise of an anti-imperial movement in the United States that attracted such illustrious supporters as Henry Adams and Mark Twain. In Britain there was radical and liberal opposition to the groundswell of imperial jingoism. J.A. Hobson's *Imperialism* elaborated a thoroughgoing critique of the new imperialism.

But in neither the United States nor the United Kingdom did the anti-imperial movement prevail. The British imposed their rule on the Boers. Washington clung on to the Philippines and Puerto Rico, extended its grip on Hawaii, established naval stations in the Pacific and the Caribbean, and schemed to promote a canal in the Isthmus of Panama. The U.S. military occupation of Cuba ended in 1902 with the establishment of a Cuban republic, which was obliged, by the terms of the Platt Amendment, to lease back Guantánamo and to accept a constitutional clause allowing for U.S. intervention if Washington deemed good order or U.S. property to be at risk. The nominal independence given to Cuba stemmed from the fact that the United States had supposedly gone to war to help the plucky Cubans in their valiant struggle to free their country. There was, indeed, some danger that the Cubans might revolt once again if denied the form of independence. Washington was also aware that the government and people of the war-devastated island would be more likely to be accommodating if treated with a little respect.

However, in the case of the Philippines and Puerto Rico, the openly imperial reflex triumphed, because President McKinley and Vice President Theodore Roosevelt believed that the United States could not stand aside from the global scramble for territory and coaling stations. Unlike Jefferson and Jackson, McKinley proposed overseas, not continental, acquisition: it was America's sacred duty to rule over its "little brown brother." The president famously claimed to a visiting delegation of Protestant pastors that he had gone down on his knees to the Almighty in his perplexity as to what to do – and then it came to him that the Philippines should not be given back to Spain, nor turned over to Germany or France, "our commercial rivals," but should rather be taken into American custody to "uplift and civilize and Christianize" its inhabitants (Wolff 1992).

The sanctimonious rhetoric of imperial statesmen was belied by the results of the new colonialism that included a huge loss of life among native peoples, as well as wholesale plunder and great cruelty. Whether monarchical or republican, liberal or conservative, parliamentary or presidential, the new imperialism was based on racial oppression and economic exploitation. In this species of imperialism, the ownership of railways, loans, plantations, and mines counted as much as territory, harbors, and coaling stations. Indeed, J.A. Hobson defined the new imperialism by its mobilization of extra-economic means to gain complex economic ends – its willingness to use gunboats or garrisons to secure supplies of tropical produce and scarce mineral deposits, to control overseas markets, and to guarantee the most secure investment conditions for the export of capital. It was this, rather than the seizure of territory, that defined the new capitalist imperialism (Hobson 1976: 71–109).[1]

The British empire drew great profit from plantations in the Americas, Africa, and the Far East; it balanced its international trade thanks to its grip on India; and it staked out strategic claims to oil in the Middle East. The British built railways and harbors but their aim was to facilitate the movement of grain and troops. While the troops were to deter native unrest, the grain was to move to where it could be sold. In Ireland and India, even in times of dearth, huge quantities of grain were sold to the metropolis, and thus were not available to feed the starving subjects of the Queen-Empress. Indian textiles enjoyed global primacy when the British arrived, but the commercial arrangements of the Raj rendered the entire subcontinent a captive market for English manufacturers. In 1750, India produced 24.5 per cent of global manufactures; by 1900 this number had sunk to 1.7 per cent (Davis 2001: 279–340; Hobsbawm 1968; Saul 1960; Tomlinson 1990).

The famines that brought many millions of deaths to India in 1876–1878 and 1896–1897 were not widely reported in Europe, where they were seen as unavoidable natural disasters. But while Britain was not responsible for the drought cycle, it was for the agricultural and commercial policies that aggravated the impact of the dearth. Native irrigation systems were neglected, and, in deference to *laissez-faire* doctrines, huge quantities of wheat were sold for export to Britain. Some U.S. observers blamed these devastating events on British arrogance, thirst for revenue, and lack of concern for native peoples.

The Indian elite, upon whom British rule depended, protested the destruction of native manufacturing and the flaunting of racial privilege. When the Indian National Congress called for a boycott of British manufactures in 1905–1906, it was speaking for an anti-colonial movement that was well organized, respectable, popular, and modern, at a time when the Raj, under Lord Curzon, was mounting such pseudo-feudal displays of vice-regal splendor as the Delhi Durbar.

During the same period, reports of pitiless repression and concentration camps in Spanish Cuba, British South Africa, and the U.S.-occupied Philippines in the years 1897–1903 showed that armies supposedly answerable to presidents and parliaments could act with great brutality. Imperial rivalries made it difficult to conceal news of atrocities. In the 1900s the revelation of the terrible consequences of King Leopold's rule in the Congo, and of the extermination of indigenous peoples by German forces in southwest Africa, made a mockery of the claims of the powers that had met in Berlin two decades earlier. Indeed anyone who cared to look into the matter would discover that, since empire was everywhere plagued by a lack of legitimacy, colonial authorities would typically resort to naked violence when challenged. But in these cases the victims were "colored" and seen as savages or heathens of the "lower races."

The Great War of 1914–1918 was different. It showed that the rival empires were also prepared to slaughter white Christians, and to do so on an industrial scale. The carnage of the First World War discredited the new imperialism in the eyes of many citizens of the belligerent states. It was also marked by nationalist stirrings in the colonial empires. In Russia, the Bolsheviks sought to make themselves the standard-bearers of the anti-imperial idea. They gained power in 1917 by insisting that Russia would withdraw from the war, and they kept their promise. Leon Trotsky, the first commissar for foreign affairs, published the secret treaties between France, Britain, and Russia that outlined their aim to dismember the Hapsburg and Ottoman Empires (Deutscher 2003). President Wilson, notwithstanding his willingness to enter the conflict in alliance with the Entente powers, saw the need to redefine the aims of the war. To the considerable discomfort of his new allies, he declared in early 1918 that the United States was aiming for a peace that would embody the self-determination of peoples.

Wilson's brandishing of the right of peoples to self-determination reflected an understanding of the power of nationalism and aimed to head off any revolutionary appropriation of the anti-imperial cause. As a Southerner, Wilson was keenly aware of the bitterness and resentment that could be provoked by alien occupation. He also sensed that the United States had no need of a territorial empire – a conclusion also belatedly reached by Theodore Roosevelt. The U.S. president was able to wield great leverage in 1918–1920 because of the utter exhaustion of Europe and the booming state of the U.S. economy. In the difficult year or two following the end of the war, the United States denied succor to those states that were reluctant to fall into line with its plans. Bela Kun's revolutionary government in Hungary was brought down by a food blockade and a Western-backed Romanian military intervention. Herbert Hoover, the "Food Tsar," saw it as his duty to prevent radical socialists from seizing power as a result of the German revolution and to offer support only to moderates, even though they had earlier backed the war. Arno Mayer has shown that the U.S. ability to orchestrate a blockade of Central Europe, threatening millions with starvation, was as much the key to its arbitrating role in 1918–1919 as General Pershing's divisions (Mayer 1967: 3–30, 266–273, 510–514, 716–852). But Wilson's hope that the United States would continue to exercise world leadership was not shared by Congress, which declined to ratify the League of Nations. The Treaty of Versailles dismembered the German and Ottoman Empires, chiefly to the advantage of Britain and France, though in deference to Wilsonian rhetoric the latter acquired "trusteeships," not colonies.

Wilson had sent a punitive expedition to Mexico in 1913, and his immediate successors routinely ordered U.S. marines to occupy any Caribbean or Central American state whose government was deemed to be slacking in its duties to U.S. companies or creditors. Franklin Roosevelt believed there were better and more effective ways to promote U.S. interests. When the military strongman Fulgencio Batista put an end to Cuban revolutionary turmoil in 1933–1934, the U.S. government formally revoked the Platt Amendment while retaining the lease on Guantánamo. The Second World War and the cold war were to consolidate the emergence of a *de facto* U.S. global empire based on financial and military power rather than territorial conquest. The expansion of Japan had swept Western colonialism out of Southeast Asia, its defeat opening the path for indigenous nationalism. But Washington had the resources to bid for leadership of the multiplying ranks of the United Nations.

The U.S. sway over the greater part of the world's peoples was embodied in the special role of the dollar, the structures of the IMF and the World Bank, the power to open or deny access to the U.S. domestic market, the power of Wall Street and Hollywood, and, last but not least, the global network of alliances and military bases. From Roosevelt onward, U.S. presidents once again took to decrying territorial colonialism and to proclaiming a Wilsonian faith in national self-determination. But the bases and alliances meant that there was still a territorial dimension to U.S. global ascendancy. While the United States refused to back a crudely colonialist Anglo-French power play at Suez in 1956, it often contrived to integrate strategic assets that had previously been exploited by the former colonial powers.

The collapse of the Soviet Union in 1989–1991 boosted U.S. global power to new heights, prompting a redefinition and extension of its informal empire. If the Soviet bloc had crumbled almost bloodlessly, then it might have seemed rational to rely on the existing apparatus of sanctions and incentives, and the new alliance with Russia, against lesser threats. But the opportunity to act with less constraint could not be resisted. Both the elder Bush and Bill Clinton advanced the idea of a new world order led by the United States, and structured by an expansion of the old system of alliances – in particular, a NATO that spread eastward, surrounding Russia. The new NATO, spurning help that Russia and the Organization for Security and Cooperation in Europe would willingly have furnished, took unilateral action against Serbia and was prepared to act out of theater.[2] According to Clinton's secretary of state Madeleine Albright, the United States was the "essential nation" because only it possessed decisive military might.

Those wishing to impress by their realism already spoke of a U.S. empire. But it was George W. Bush and his response to the 9/11 attack that gave the term "empire" wide currency through the writings of Max Boot, Niall Ferguson, and Michael Ignatieff, who all supported the second Iraq war. Capitalizing on the global wave of sympathy elicited by 9/11, the United States acted with needless unilateralism, first in Afghanistan, and then by seeking long-term advantage by establishing new bases in Central Asia. The invasion of Iraq in 2003 was a more brazen act of empire, responding to no direct aggression or threat. Washington rubbed salt in the wound by first soliciting UN help and then flouting a Security Council veto.

The new imperialists held that the UN Charter doctrine that one member state had no right to attack another was obsolete and dangerous in a world menaced by rogue states, failed states, terrorist networks, and proliferating weapons of mass destruction. A global gendarme, equipped with the power to intervene pre-emptively, was needed. Only the United States could play this role, and it could not allow others to determine its actions. Washington's willingness to overthrow governments and establish occupation authorities was saluted by some as the unveiling of a new empire. However, most of those who endorsed the Iraq war still shrank, as did the administration itself, from using the "e" word: "empire" was not a term that Samuel Huntington or Colin Powell wanted to use, for reasons I will explore later.

The recent turn to overt empire talk stems as much from frustration at the state of the planet as it does from the unprecedented power of the United States. The misery of Africa and the dismal condition of the Middle East and of parts of South Asia and Latin America generate frustration and despair among *bien pensant* observers of every description. Neocon advocates of the big stick acquire liberal allies who also believe that the answer is for the world's most powerful state to lead and to take matters into its own hands. The often deeply disappointing results of decolonization lead to a revisionism that forgets why colonialism was discredited in the first place. Niall Ferguson made himself an outstanding exponent of this revisionism with the publication of *Empire: How Britain Made the Modern World* in 2003 and *Colossus: The Price of America's Empire* in 2004.

Ferguson is to be commended for calling empire by its name, and for not shrinking from spelling out its logical corollaries. His message is that Britain did much to invent capitalism and, with it, the most valuable ideas and institutions of the modern world – the English language, private property, the rule of law, parliamentary institutions, individual freedom, and Protestant

Christianity. This British self-regard easily segues into endorsement for
American national messianism, with the Anglo-American imperial formula –
handily termed "Anglobalization" – offering the colonized the best hope of
capitalist success. As a historian of the English-speaking peoples, Ferguson
seeks to rescue Winston Churchill's narrative from its contemporary fate –
that of being entombed in countless forbidding leather-bound volumes. He
offers a pacier narrative, garnished with excellent quotes from the great man
and many shafts of his own droll wit (his one-liners are too reliant on puns to
be fully Churchillian).

Still, Ferguson's subtitle to *Empire* – "How Britain Made the Modern
World" – should have given him some pause, considering the sad state of
our world. Many of the most intractable and bloody communal divisions we
live with today were fostered, if not invented, by Britain's imperial policy of
divide and rule. Any list of the world's most dangerous and difficult communal conflicts would include the standoff between Pakistan and India and
the Arab/Israeli clash. The partition of Cyprus, the still unresolved conflict
in Northern Ireland, and the deep racial tensions in Guyana and Fiji would
also figure in such a list. In the post-apartheid era, the racial legacy of
empire and colonization is being gradually dismantled in South Africa, but
problems remain in many other parts of Africa.

Ferguson urges that ethnic sentiment and division long preceded colonization. He rightly observes that expatriate colonizers were often the driving
force behind injurious racial privileges and distinctions. Yet liberal imperial
strategists from Locke to Gladstone went along with colonial racism
because that is what empire was based on. Nor does Ferguson register the
fondness of imperial administrators for cultivating the so-called martial
races at the expense of other colonial subjects, or the deliberate fostering of
poisonous divisions – between Muslims and Hindus in India, Jews and
Arabs in Palestine, Turks and Greeks in Cyprus, Protestants and Catholics
in Ireland, Indians and natives in Fiji, blacks and (East) Indians in British
Guyana. The communal fault lines were not always of the imperial administrators' making, but those administrators nevertheless have much to
answer for – after all, they were in charge. (Likewise, today's neo-imperial-
ists are partly responsible for aggravating communal divisions in the Bal-
kans and Iraq.)

Today the division of the world between rich and poor regions roughly
follows the former division between imperial and colonized areas, even
though it has sometimes been partially counteracted or qualified by resistance to empire, or by prior institutional or natural endowments. The
colonial experience weakened the ability of the colonized to negotiate an
advantageous relationship to the emerging capitalist world market and
often condemned them to subordination and neglect. Ferguson cites the
disappointing performance of most ex-colonies as part of his case for
empire, when it would be more logical to conclude that the empires did not,
in fact, really equip the colonized with survival skills. The poor record of

Britain's former African colonies leads him to plead that "even the best institutions work less well in landlocked, excessively hot or disease-ridden places" (2004: 197). He concedes that, at 0.12 per cent, India's overall annual rate of growth between 1820 and 1950 was pitifully low, but he won't hold selfish imperial arrangements responsible because "[t]he supposed 'drain' of capital from India to Britain turns out to have been surprisingly modest: only 1 per cent of Indian national income between the 1860s and the 1930s, according to one estimate of the export surplus" (2004: 195). But obviously a country growing at only 0.12 per cent a year would have had many good uses for that lost 1 per cent of national income. Ferguson himself points out that in 1913 Britain's school enrollment rate was eight times that of India's.

Empires did not invent the uneven development of capitalism, but, having inherited or established a hierarchical structure of advantage, they reinforced it. For example, plantation slavery certainly brought great wealth to some in the plantation colonies and states. But it did not generate sustained and independent growth in the plantation zone, as the post-emancipation experience of the U.S. South, the Caribbean, and the Brazilian northeast testify. Empires tended to encourage only those infrastructure improvements that facilitated the movement of troops and the export of commodities. In the process that Davis calls "the origins of the third world," Western incursions into China from the Opium War onward weakened the Qing authorities and prevented them from maintaining the country's vital system of hydraulic defenses. With its customs service run by a consortium of foreign powers, China suffered a deindustrialization almost as severe as that of India (Davis 2001: 279–310).

At the same time, Ferguson's neo-liberal agenda and British focus lead him to miss the way that non-Anglo-Saxon empires promoted economic integration and coordination by non-market means. In an off-the-cuff remark explaining "why it was that Britain was able to overhaul her Iberian rivals," he fails to explain the source of Spanish wealth, but says that Britain "had to settle for colonizing the unpromising wastes of Virginia and New England, rather than the eminently lootable cities of Mexico and Peru" (2003: 369).[3] Both the Spanish and the British certainly looted American silver and gold. But Ferguson does not explain how this Spanish, rival species of empire worked, and seems to regard it as economically less impressive than the record of British settlement. Spanish administrators were, in fact, innovators who mainly relied on wage labor to mine and process the silver ore. In place of simple "looting" they adopted a tribute system, echoing Inca and Aztec arrangements that required the native villages to supply either labor, foodstuffs, or textiles to the royal warehouses. The king claimed a royalty of a fifth of the silver mined. But he garnered much more by selling mining concessions and the tribute food and clothing in his warehouses to the wage-earning miners. It was this ingenious system, not looting, that sustained a highly productive system of exploitation

for nearly three centuries. This is just one example of the productive organization promoted by Iberian imperialism that explains why the Mexican
and Peruvian elite were so reluctant to break with empire. But with Spanish
American independence, all such coordination ceased and entry into Britain's informal empire of free trade led to economic stagnation or regression.

Empires could promote a limited and usually self-interested species of
colonial development. Often, as today, the imperial impulse stemmed from
overweening confidence and a missionary impulse as much as from a sober
calculation of material gain. When empires spread, they did so partly
because they could, partly because they engaged in a rivalrous multistate
system, and partly because, in metropolitan regions where capitalism was
taking hold, consumers wanted colonial products. Starting with the Portuguese, the European maritime empires entered the lists partly because they
saw an advantage they did not want to yield to others, and partly because
those newly in receipt of rents, fees, profits, and wages had a thirst for exotic
commodities.

But there was still another more paradoxical and perplexing factor. This
was the role that revolutionary changes within the metropolitan societies
played in boosting the impulse to empire. Since Ferguson does not much
address the connection between the domestic and overseas articulation of
power, it will be necessary to pursue the argument without his help.

There have been at once real and fantastic connections between empire
and revolution. The real connection is that societies that had been internally
transformed by revolution thereby acquired social capacities that made
economic, cultural, and territorial expansion possible. But the fantastic
connection was just as important, in that a deluded revolutionary conceit
dreamt that empire might elevate and redeem otherwise benighted, recalcitrant native peoples. Such notions as the "elect nation," the "new Zion,"
and the republic "one and indivisible," prepared the ground for the "Anglo-
Saxon race," jingoism, or chauvinism.

In areas where the native peoples were largely wiped out by settlers and
disease, as in North America and Australia, something approaching the
replication of the metropolis – or of those elements of the metropolis that
were compatible with modernity – was achieved. The land was appropriated
in a way that echoed Europe's own social arrangements as they had been
shaped by the Neolithic revolution, the Roman Empire, the territorial expansion of Christendom, and the rise of commercial society in England. The
relationship of settlers to the land was defined by displacement of the original inhabitants, deforestation, exhaustive exploitation, and absolute property
rights (Crosby 1986; Bartlett 1993; Cronon 1983). The resulting transformations nourished the mistaken idea that the metropolis in other areas as
well would eventually transform the colonized into replicas of the colonizers, namely, self-governing, individualist Anglo-Saxons (Horsman 1981).

The rise of the absolutist states had been based on the defeat of rebellious
peasants and independent towns, on a military and administrative revolution,

and on the raising of sufficient revenue and credit to pay for this. Absolutist monarchs embodied an administrative transformation and socio-political formula that easily carried over into empire (Anderson 1974). Despite set-backs and reversals, England's Tudors and Stuarts emulated enough of this to make a contribution to the imperial organization of the British state. When clerics beholden to Henry VIII first spoke of a "British empire," the term certainly gestured at a wish to rule the whole of the British Isles. But the charge of the term "empire" was also theological and political. It was a declaration of independence from the Pope, and an insistence that the ruler of Britain had direct access to the Almighty – a foible more forgivable in a sixteenth-century monarch than in George W. Bush.

While several British monarchs, notably James II, made a contribution to the foundations of empire, the real substance came from elsewhere. England's "new merchants" of the mid-seventeenth century took their cue from Dutch businessmen, not the Spanish kings. They were interested in catering to mass consumption, not in supplying the court or aristocracy with rare silks and fine wines. Both the civil war of the 1640s and the Glorious Revolution of 1688 carried forward a fateful link between domestic trans-formation and overseas expansion (Brenner 1993). As in nineteenth-century America, military victories and diplomatic treaties could only lead to per-manent results where the ground had already been prepared by pioneering settlers and entrepreneurial merchants. This explains the very different fates of England's seventeenth-century acquisitions of Virginia and Algeria: while the former became a self-financing tobacco plantation, the latter had to be abandoned as a costly encumbrance.

The colonial impulse fed on the notion that native barbarism and back-wardness demanded civilized intervention. The colonial mission was a transformative one. Indeed, the nature of modern empire, with its commer-cial impulses, cannot be grasped unless its relationship to revolution – real and surrogate – is understood. The process classically known as the "bour-geois revolution" – and the tremendous boost it gave to the polities it transformed – helps us to identify one of the dynamic components of modern imperialism, from the seventeenth to the twentieth century and beyond, or, if you can forgive the bathos, from Cromwell to Karl Rove (both of them champions of free labor). If colonialism had a partly revolu-tionary impulse, it also invariably marked the limits of the transformative power of revolution, the geographical and social spaces that the bourgeois revolution could not penetrate.

The Dutch war of independence against Spain could not be confined to the Low Countries and eventually encompassed an attempt to take on, and take over, Iberian imperial strong points in the Americas and Africa. Gro-tius's *Mare Liberum* was both a cry of Dutch defiance and a charter of commercial expansion. The Dutch East and West India Companies established a global network of trading posts and colonies. But the disinclination of many Dutch to emigrate and the vulnerability of the Dutch state in Europe led to the loss of Dutch Brazil and North America. The English Puritans who had opposed the Stuarts did so in the name of a more forward policy against Spain in the New World. The Commonwealth period in Britain organized a new navy, checked Dutch power, and confronted Spain. It gave birth to the "Western Design," the capture of Jamaica, and the first version of the empire-fostering Navigation Acts. British colonial rule in Ireland was extended and reinforced. The Glorious Revolution of 1688 confirmed the imperial orientation and scope of the British state.

The American Declaration of Independence in 1776 certainly enunciated momentous principles of self-determination but, as we have seen, these soon spilled over into the project of a new empire. The Continental Congress, the Northwest Ordinance, and the Louisiana Purchase all bear witness to the imperial urge of many of America's Founding Fathers, their wish to expand their sway over all of North America. Long before the French Republic was transformed into Napoleon's empire, the revolutionary Convention, by hurling itself against the old order in both Europe and the Caribbean, enunciated some of the themes of an "emancipatory" empire radiating from the republic "one and indivisible." In each of these cases there were countercurrents that saw the urge to empire as a betrayal of the true ideals of the revolution – but the countercurrents did not prevail.

These revolutions did much to shape the world in which we live. But their best results were at home, not overseas. They could export goods much more easily than social arrangements. The Dutch intensified an odious slave traffic, while the English Puritans resorted to barbaric reprisals against the stubbornly Catholic and alien Irish. The Americans repeatedly failed to turn Indians into "Americans" and instead sought to remove or extirpate them. Following the Civil War, America's "Second Revolution," the North failed to modernize the South and instead allowed it to remain for a century in the grip of Jim Crow, landlordism, and rapacious supply merchants. Under pressure from a tenacious slave uprising in Saint Domingue, the French enacted the first comprehensive emancipation in 1794, but within less than a decade Napoleon's forces were trying to reintroduce slavery.

In 1848 and 1871 Europe was again haunted by the specter of revolution. In the wake of the suppression of revolutionary movements, the governments of France, Belgium, Germany, and Italy turned to a new wave of colonial expansion, partly in the hope that it would furnish an outlet for those who were discontented, and partly to display the potency of newly established polities – the French Third Republic, newly reunited Italy and Germany – but overseas these newly constitutional states resorted to a grim repertoire of land clearances, forced labor, racial privilege, and, where resistance was encountered, native extermination.

The national historiography of empire stresses each state's unique features and destiny. In reality the different empires ceaselessly borrowed from one another. The Spanish borrowed from the Incas and Aztecs, drawing on their tribute systems to extract silver, textiles, and foodstuffs in the Andes and

Central America. The Portuguese discovered that they could make a profit by trading slaves along the African coast and drew on this trade to establish sugar plantations. The Dutch improved on Iberian seamanship and trading; they also passed on expertise to English and French planters and merchants. The English refined and developed their own slave plantations and colonial system while the French brought to both a new pitch of intensity. The colonialism of the late nineteenth and early twentieth centuries was even more imitative and reflexive, with each power trying to pre-empt the other. The United States was drawn into colonial acquisition in part because it believed that it had to have its own coaling stations and secure territory in the Caribbean and Pacific to compete with European rivals. Most of today's far-flung U.S. military outposts are relics of bygone battles with bygone empires. The imperial practices that prevailed were those that inspired imitation and stood the test of time – which often meant the tests of war, revolution, and economic competition.

The retreat of empire was often impelled by national revolutions that trumped the imperial imports – as in China, Cuba, Algeria, and Vietnam. However, none of the European empires collapsed simply from internal resistance. The two world wars were watershed events, rendering them very vulnerable. But there was one empire – the Soviet – of which this was less true. While it was obviously weakened by economic failure and the strain of Afghanistan, it was also undermined by its relative success in fostering nation-states. Stalin's rise at the expense of Bolshevik internationalism, and the Red Army's advances in the "great patriotic war," seemed simply to boost the old Russian empire, albeit in communist disguise. Yet the Soviet constitution entrenched a right of secession to its constituent republics, while the autarchic economy nourished a species of nation building. In Eastern Europe, where Yalta brutally aligned national groups with new borders, the "peoples' democracies" were allotted the trappings of sovereignty, and Moscow's often heavy-handed tutelage nourished a countervailing nationalism (Suny 1991). The peaceful break-up of the Soviet empire was owed partly to the strength of such processes, partly to Gorbachev's idealism, and partly to the Russian people's disinclination to defend an empire that brought more burdens than privileges. No other empire yielded with such readiness.

Today the major international question is whether, for a similar mixture of motives, the people and government of the United States can also be induced to give up empire. The optimist must hope that a similarly mild quietus can be administered to the new imperialism. While the new lurch to empire will certainly join the heap of discards sooner or later, there are many in U.S. ruling circles who still cannot read the writing on the wall, even though that wall is in the land of ancient Babylon. Their dream is that neo-liberalism, with its market fundamentalism, and neoconservatism, with its jingoism and Old Testament certainties, can impose on the whole world what Ferguson calls "Anglobalization."

In the aftermath of twentieth-century decolonization and the break up of the Soviet bloc, some neo-conservatives and liberal imperialists, led by Niall Ferguson, have got a frisson from rehabilitating the "politically incorrect" language of empire. It underlines the hard-headedness and candor of those who use it and allows them to urge even greater boldness on Washington. But if we scan the speeches of George W. Bush or the National Security Document of September 2002, we find a repeated invocation of the need for "liberation," understood not just as national independence but as a further commitment to what the president called "democratic revolution" in his speech in the Banqueting Hall, London, in November 2003. Given that he was the guest of the English monarch, it is understandable that he did not remind his listeners of the Banqueting Hall's previous rendezvous with history – the execution of Charles I. While acknowledging that the time for alliance with absolutist monarchs and dictatorships in the Middle East was over, the president found himself in the predicament that these discredited regimes remained his only allies, apart from Israel, in the region.

The echo of revolution and the promise of democracy may have proved to be utterly deluded, but it would be wrong to neglect it just the same. It allowed Bush and Blair to sell their subsequent war, at least for a while, to their own electorates and to some sectors of liberal opinion. When the charge that Saddam Hussein possessed weapons of mass destruction was discredited, it was the subsidiary claim that regime change would open the way to democracy in the Middle East that took its place.

Bush's address to the United Nations in September 2004, in the midst of the presidential election, returned to the theme that the U.S. mission was to advance liberation, rights, and democracy. By contrast John Kerry, the Democratic contender, urged that "stability," not democracy, was the best that could be hoped for in Iraq. While President Bush appealed to a naïve but idealistic belief among voters that their country could and would promote democracy, Kerry implicitly favored the argument from realpolitik and a deal with the strongmen who run so much of the Arab world. In their different ways both policies were imperial: they were based on the idea that Iraq should be occupied for many years to come, with the occupier determining the scope of the country's politics. Prior to its departure in June 2004, the Coalition Provisional Authority (CPA) had dismantled much of the apparatus of the Iraqi state, with dire consequences for the delivery of basic public services. It had seized and spent oil revenues and had handed out large contracts to foreign, mainly U.S., firms. Tens of billions disappeared into the bank accounts of corrupt contractors and politicians. Resistance from Shi'ite leaders obliged the CPA to abandon an attempt to entrench in Iraq's basic law the wholesale privatization of national property. The CPA, and the puppet government led by Allawi, chose to prepare for elections by seeking to silence or arrest critics of the occupation, closing newspapers and TV stations that reported awkward news or opinion. Those who challenged the continuing occupation would not be able to take part in elections. Even so Allawi's party received less than an eighth of the votes cast.

Karl Rove, George W. Bush's chief political strategist, has said that the book that most influenced him as a graduate student was Eric Foner's classic study of the origins and rise of the Republican ideology in the 1840s and 1850s, *Free Soil, Free Labor, Free Men*. There can be little doubt that Bush sees himself as the man ordained to complete the neo-conservative revolution of Ronald Reagan and Margaret Thatcher, and to bring it home to the "axis of evil" and to any other countries that stand in the way (China, Vietnam, Cuba, and Venezuela being candidates here). The vision is both an imperial and a revolutionary one, since it seeks to reshape the whole social formation of target countries. That vision seeks to dismantle the local state and to entrust its essential functions to foreign corporations linked to the military-industrial, and, as Abu Ghraib made clear, prison-industrial complexes (Ali 2004; Wacquant 2002; Meiksins Wood 2004). The whole awkward structure is to be guaranteed, as Chalmers Johnson stresses, by a multiplication of military bases in the Middle East, Afghanistan, and Central Asia (Johnson 2004). Once acquired, such dubious "assets" are difficult to give up, further swelling the hugely expensive, provocative – and ultimately indefensible – global U.S. military establishment.

The emphasis that Niall Ferguson places on the imperial export of a neo-liberal institutional package places him squarely in the camp of those who believe that democratic revolution can be introduced from outside. Ferguson believed that the overthrow of Saddam Hussein and the occupation of Iraq would help bring Middle Eastern terrorism under control – he still argued this as justification for the war in his book *Colossus*. But instead of wiping out those he calls Islamo-Bolsheviks, the occupation gave them perfect conditions to recruit and grow. The willingness of the main Shi'a parties to collaborate with the occupiers, and the vicious sectarian fury of Sunni radicals, set the scene for appalling communal violence. This is extremely unwelcome to most Iraqi nationalists, and compromises the gains of the long-oppressed Shi'a majority. But since it is the occupation that helps the jihadists, it is absurd to expect Iraqis to rally around the occupiers. On two occasions several hundred thousand have dared to demonstrate openly against the United States – the first time on the second anniversary of the overthrow of Saddam Hussein in April 2005 and the second time following the Israeli assault on Lebanon in July and August 2006. The hostility of huge numbers of Iraqis who loathed Saddam shows how extraordinarily misconceived and counterproductive the imperial expedition has been. So far as the scourge of terrorism is concerned, the U.S. presence is part of the problem, not part of the solution. Only a government fully representative of Iraqi opinion and beholden to no outside power – especially a power interested in Iraqi assets – can hope to defeat the jihadists. The jihadists are neither numerous nor popular, but they can only be isolated by an unimpeachably Iraqi government.

The old empires eventually yielded to, or pre-empted, a rising tide of nationalism. The agitations of the Irish and the Indians, the pitched battles fought by Vietnamese and Algerians, the need to crush rebellious Malays and Kenyans – all prompted the metropolitan elite to undertake a rigorous cost-benefit analysis and to explore decolonization as a new form of indirect rule. While particular colonial ventures could be very profitable (I have given examples above), the costs tended to rise as other empires sought to enter the field, acting as competitors or spoilers.

As the British found out as early as the 1780s, decolonization did not need to be an economic disaster. In fact, Anglo-American exchanges soon boomed. After the Second World War, Western Europe discovered extraordinary prosperity as it shed colonies. There is a message here for the United States today. Those who really believe in market forces should conclude that it makes no sense to secure control of oil-producing states at great cost since, in the end, the oil will have to be purchased and sold at market prices. If there are energy shortages in store, then fuel efficiency will be cheaper in the long run than expeditions that require a down payment of $200 billion, followed by heavy running costs.

The new imperialism is a very much more flimsy entity than the old. The dreadful condition of Iraq, and the sad state of Afghanistan, Kosovo, and Bosnia – plagued by differing combinations of insecurity, arbitrary rule, drug trafficking, and warlordism – is no advertisement for it. Few will again be prepared to pay a price in blood and money to achieve such results. The number of problems that the United States can solve by flexing its muscles is diminishing. China and India must soon be recognized as great powers, and Brazil and Iran as worthy of a place at the top table. Bullying these countries would be folly, just as it is perilous and provocative to encircle China and Russia with bases. Eventually, it must be hoped, the United States will acquire a president who will understand and see the advantages of a less exposed and overweening stance.

The defeat of the neo-imperial project will not consolidate the old order in the Middle East. We can be quite sure that indigenous democratic revolutions will sweep the Arab lands, Iran, and China. They will arise sooner rather than later, and advance notions of liberty without any "made in USA" label. The overwhelming case for home-grown democracy does not mean that each state and people should simply be allowed to sink or swim. Today states are ceaselessly, if often ineffectively, coerced into approved capitalist behavior. A just international order remains to be built (Archibugi 2003). It would require a fundamental reshaping of global institutions that today function simply as relays for the Washington–Wall Street consensus. It might contain a new international agency that would credit less-developed countries with a portion of the per capita annual consumption of fossil fuels and other scarce resources that they currently forgo. The agency could be financed by a tax on fossil fuels and a small tranche of the levy applied to multinational corporations.

Ferguson accurately perceives many of the weaknesses of the modern state. But his key prescription – an even larger dose of Anglobalization – will make the problem worse. What is required is institutional innovation, and a democratic, new "cosmopolitics" that nourishes the social and economic capacities of its constituent states.

Notes

1 Hobson's sharp attention to the "economic taproot of imperialism" is complemented by a vigorous discussion of the "moral and sentimental factors" mobilized by imperialist policy: see Wolff 1992: 196–222.
2 I explain my reasons for believing this, based in part on observations made by Gorbachev during a visit to Cambridge, England, in March of 1999, in Blackburn 1999.
3 I have a more extended critique of Ferguson's books in Blackburn 2005.

12 Virtual revolution?

Information communication technologies, networks, and social transformation

Andreja Zivkovic and John Hogan

"Modernity" and "revolution:" both terms denote a radical rupture with the past, the idea of historical progress, and a vision of the future as open horizon. They are also radically opposed to one another. As Perry Anderson reminds us, each has a distinct temporality:

> The characteristic time of "modernity" is continuous, and all encompassing, like the process of industrialization itself: at most its most extended, nothing less than the totality of the epoch itself. The time of revolution is discontinuous, and delimited: a finite rupture in the reproduction of the established order, by definition starting at one conjuncture and ending at another.
>
> (1994: 30)

For Marx, the experience of capitalist modernity was one of "[c]onstant revolutionizing of production, unceasing disturbance, everlasting uncertainty and agitation" (Marx and Engels 1975–2000: vi, 487). The concept of modernity as this constant revolutionizing of all social relations is to be distinguished from that of revolution as a political event "compressed in time and concentrated in target" (see Anderson 1994) – notwithstanding the common substratum of both in the contradictions of capitalist modernization, that is, the capitalist system was both the product of social and political revolutions, e.g. 1789, and their matrix, the contradictions of capitalism's uneven and combined development generating bourgeois and socialist revolution across the globe.

Today this dialectical interrelation between modernity and revolution is widely considered to have been undone. In the wake of the revolutions of 1989, conventionally viewed as revolutions ending the modern era of revolution, and of the profound transformations effected by globalization, with the emergence of highly integrated and mobile financial markets and the tendency for the production and distribution of commodities to be organized across national frontiers – all of which appear to radically question the modern, territorial nation-state as the space and object of political and economic power – the modern concept of revolution as the conquest of state power appears to have exhausted itself. Indeed, precisely in response to the transformations association with globalization, we have recently seen the efflorescence of theories of (informational) technological revolution that confuse the "permanent revolution" of capitalist reproduction with the concept of social revolution, dissolving the latter into what Benjamin called the "empty, homogenous time" of capitalist modernization, of modernization theory.

This chapter seeks to examine contemporary "networked" or "informational" theories of revolution which privilege IT (information technology) or ICT (information communication technology) networks. We examine Castells's concept of "informational capitalism" and argue that there is no technological logic beyond capitalism, that theories of the "IT revolution" dissolve the properly political space of revolution into the linear, homogenous time of technological rationalization under capitalism. Castells's concept of the "network society" finds an uncanny echo in postmodern, networked theories of revolution, which see ICT networks as the very model for new revolutionary movements against global, neo-liberal capitalism (e.g. the Zapatistas). We argue that, by ignoring the character of revolution as a discontinuous event within the fabric of capitalist modernization, such theories dissolve revolution into a logic of immanence, of process and of movement, thus placing revolution beyond the time and space of politics. Nevertheless we are not dismissive of the potentiality of ICTs to generate transformations in the temporal and spatial dynamics of political agency. We conclude by reflecting on how the potential supplementary powers that ICTs afford agents may be realized in real time and space.

The "IT revolution" as post-capitalism?

For Castells the "IT revolution" of the last quarter century has led to a qualitative break in socio-economic development associated with a new "informational capitalism." In Castells the development of a new technology (IT) is accompanied by a new "mode of development" (informationalism), based on a new source of wealth creation ("the action of knowledge upon knowledge") and a new "performance principle" (technological innovation) (1996: 17–18). The IT revolution is also linked to a new flexible, decentralized, interdependent mode of organization, the networking logic. ITs have played a decisive role in "the expansion and rejuvenation of capitalism:" in the emergence of a flexible, innovation-based, globalized capitalism by providing the tools for networking, distant communication, storing/processing of information, coordinated individualization of work, and simultaneous concentration and decentralization of decision making (1998: 368).

Indeed in Castells's view the IT revolution has also enabled capitalism to overcome its tendency to crisis. Castells sees a fundamental modification of the market logic at work in global, integrated financial markets operating in real time via electronic and informational technology. The "annihilation of time and space by electronic means" has enabled capital to successfully "colonize the future" (1996: 435–7, 1998: 374–5).

On the other hand, Castells also appears to be saying that the new "informational capitalism," while based on a new source of wealth creation and performance principle, remains capitalist. Indeed,

> for the first time in history, the capitalist mode of production shapes social relationships over the entire planet. But this brand of capitalism is profoundly different from its predecessors. It has two fundamental characteristics: it is global, and it is structured to a large extent around a network of financial flows. Capital works globally as a unit in real time, and as it is realized, invested and accumulated mainly in the sphere of circulation, that is, as finance capital.
>
> (1996: 502)

Castells's discussion of informational capitalism, like Bell's post-industrial society, is linked to "a periodization of modes of development based on changes in the primary factor of production for wealth creation" (Jessop 2000: 2). From this perspective the key transition is from industrialism to an informational mode of development, from an industrial system orientated to maximizing growth to a knowledge-based economy orientated to technological innovation. The thrust of Castells's argument is that, while the informational mode of development has contributed to the emergence of an informational capitalism, informationalism cannot be reduced to the logic of capital accumulation.

It is for this reason that, at the end of the final volume of his trilogy, in terms that recall those of Marx, Castells inveighs against:

> the extraordinary gap between our technological overdevelopment and our social underdevelopment. Our economy, society and culture are built on interests, values, institutions, and systems of representation that by, and large, limit collective creativity, confiscate the harvest of information technology, and deviate our energy into self-destructive confrontation.
>
> (1998: 467)

For Marx, of course, this state of affairs derived from the contradiction between the forces and relations of production under capitalism, between an increasingly socialized, interdependent, knowledge-driven process of production and the privatized appropriation of the social product. Castells is not so sure and hesitates. On the one hand, the production of wealth in informational capitalism derives from knowledge-driven innovation (1996: 66–7, 1998: 369, 372). On the other hand, we are told that "[p]rofitability and competitiveness are the actual determinants of technological innovation and productivity growth" (1996: 81). In this case it is a specifically capitalist logic of valorization and competition rather than technological change that shapes informationalism. As Callinicos points out, this incoherence reflects the unstable and internally contradictory character of the concept of "informational capitalism," a hybrid of Marx's theory of the capitalist mode of production and the theory of the post-industrial society, an opposition which tends to dissolve in favor of the latter (2001a: 54–5). Castells nevertheless raises the interesting question of whether the increasing socialization of the productive forces in a knowledge-driven economy is coming into conflict with the capitalist nature of the social relations of production:

> we are already witnessing the development of alternative information networks, around non-capitalist and anti-capitalist values, which interact with dominant networks in an increasingly conflictive space of flows. Thus while, the network society, as a specific social structure, has been constituted around current forms of social domination (informational capitalism), its logic goes well beyond these specific interests: [information-communication] networks can be re-programmed by deliberate social action.
>
> (2000: 138)

For Marx, by setting in motion the powers of scientific knowledge and social cooperation (what Marx, in the *Grundrisse*, calls "the general intellect"), capitalism ultimately undermines itself. Market competition forces rival capitals to introduce productivity enhancing technologies to cut costs and thereby reduce relative prices. This tendency to replace "living labor" (wage labor) by "dead labor" (means of production) raises the rate of surplus value extraction for individual capitalists but, insofar as it also increases the organic composition of capital for the system as a whole, places a downward pressure on aggregate rates of surplus value and profit and thereby leads to frequent, ever deeper and more widespread economic crises.

But how might the "general intellect," like Prometheus, be unchained from the capitalist order that consumes it? Braudel and Mumford argue that technology has definite technical properties, but these are deeply molded and shaped by society and culture. Castells's concept of "informational capitalism" collapses the discontinuous temporality of revolution into the continuous, homogenous, undifferentiated time of modernity; that is the temporality of "creative destruction" under capitalism as understood by modernization theory and its logic of technological rationalization. Whilst rejecting the notion of a logic of technology à la Castells, we will consider below how technology might contribute to a revolutionary transformation in a manner consistent with the modern concept of revolution. For the moment, we will examine whether or not Castells can answer his own question: namely, the possibility of an informational mode of development beyond capitalism.

Network society, informational politics and symbolic power

For Castells, the central cleavage of the informational age is that between the abstract, calculating, timeless, placeless logic of the space of flows and the historically, culturally and geographically rooted identities of social actors. The decoupling of dominant processes from the space of places is the cause of a terminal crisis in the institutions and "legitimating identities" of industrial society – the nation-state, government, labor movements, the patriarchal family and the political ideologies of modernity. Emerging in the place of these shared identities is "a world exclusively made of markets, networks, individuals and strategic organizations" dominated by the identityless, individualistic logic of the self-centered calculations of the global networks (1997: 354–5). In response to global flows and radical individualism, defensive resistance identities are activated which "retrench in communal heavens" around the traditional values of God, nation and family, but also around non-traditional values, as with the feminist, sexual liberation and environmental movements (1997: 356). To the extent that resistance identities are able to project themselves beyond communal "trenches" set up outside and against network flows into society at large they cease to be purely reactive and develop transformative power. The reason why such resistance is transformative relates to the importance of identities in the new system of power.

> Power … is no longer concentrated in institutions (the state), organizations (capitalist firms), or symbolic controllers (corporate media, churches). It is diffused in global networks of wealth, power, information and images which circulate and transmute in a system of variable geometry and dematerialized geography … The new power lies in the codes of information and in the images of representation around which societies organize their institutions, and people live their lives, and decide their behavior.
>
> (1997: 359)

The significance of these arguments is that they enable Castells to establish an isomorphism between the informational, network structure of the "Information Age" and that of transformative identities. It is only as decentralized, informational networks, as networked nodes and hubs subverting the individualistic, abstract, identityless, timeless codes of the network of flows that resistance identities can become transformative. But, equally, it is only as place-based identities anchoring power to some area of the social structure that they are able to engage in symbolic warfare and so transform institutions. Thus we can say that the concept of the "informational politics" is consistent with the "logic of technology" that we have argued underpins the theory of the network society – such that flows of power, money and information void the state and representative government of power and legitimacy.

It is arguable, even in Castells's own terms, that the theory of informational politics ignores the problem that power in modern societies does not merely reside in the control of information, is not purely "immaterial" in the sense of a symbolic capacity to frame life experience, but is also embedded and embodied in the ownership of capital and the coercive power of the state. This is, of course, not exactly news to Castells, but it is remarkable to what degree his theory of informational politics appears to dissolve the space of economic and political power, market and state, into the flux of informational, dematerialized networks. Rather than capitalist states being simply bypassed by immaterial flows of money, power and information, based on "variable geometries and dematerialized geographies," the construction of global markets in capital, goods and services, and the neo-liberal institutional architecture regulating them, is in fact highly dependent on the cooperation and coercive power of the advanced capitalist states. Ignoring his own empirical analyses, Castells, in the manner of Althusser's theory of history, paints a picture of networked "processes without a subject" based on a "logic of technology." This makes it hard for Castells to answer his own question of how the promise of the Information Age, "the unleashing of unprecedented productive capacity by the power of the mind," might be fulfilled. Castells rules out revolution since there are "no Winter Palaces" to seize in a network society of dematerialized, placeless flows (1998: 352). Generally he talks of the reconstruction of institutions to enable them to mitigate the effects of a "hardened capitalism" (globalization and social exclusion) through social integration and the construction of "new institutions [to] bridge the split between the Net and Self" (2000: 147). But he is aware of the scale of the problem. For example, "[s]hould institutions of society, economy, and culture truly accept environmentalism they would be essentially transformed ... it would be a revolution" (1998: 383).

But this is a revolution that, since it is founded on an opposition between the timeless time and placeless space of flows and the place-based experience of singular identities, exists outside of time and space (the capital relation, world economy, the interstate system). Castells offers no guide as to how resistance movements might transform really existing socioeconomic structures and power relations in modern capitalist society. Nor is it obvious within the terms of reference of the concepts of "informational politics" and "network society" what the solution to this problem might be.

Network autonomy as revolution

By contrast, in postmodern, networked theories of revolution, the crisis of the nation-state and modern politics in the face of globalization is the matrix for a new type of revolution. These theories can be seen as either side of Castells's coin, each proceeding from one side of the constitutive cleavage of network society; on the one hand, the "information revolution" and its space of flows and, on the other, the cultural resistance of communicational networks to it. Thus, on the one hand, the autonomous space of informational-communicational flows and its rhizomatic, nomadic logic is itself revolutionary and points to a networked society beyond Empire (Hardt and Negri 2000); on the other, ICT networks are the very model for a revolutionary movement against neo-liberal globalization that could "change the world without taking power" (Holloway 2002). Let us now examine the first path.

The origins of Hardt and Negri's concept of Empire lie in Negri's genealogy of the capitalist system, which locates its dynamics in the struggle of the working class to wrest productive autonomy from the command of capital. The insubordination of the working class leads to struggles over "class composition," forcing capital to elaborate a politics of regulation, to develop reflexivity in its struggle to decompose proletarian self-valorization in order to continue to expropriate the latter's cooperative productivity. Historically, the skilled craft worker of the late nineteenth century forced capital to deploy Taylorist systems of regulation from which the "mass worker" emerged; the insubordination of the latter in the period of the New Deal led to the development of the state as "collective capitalist" (Keynesian demand management and the welfare state) and subsequently to the emergence of the "social worker" at the point at which all forms of labor became subsumed under capital, became proletarianized; the "social worker," now baptized as the "multitude," is the figure of informational capitalism, and to its socialized, networked, affective, immaterial labor today corresponds "Empire." "The multitude called Empire into being" (2000: 43). As such the structure of Empire is isomorphic to that of the multitude: it is a decentralized, network power. As such it has no center and no boundary; it has no territory or outside, it is a "non-place:"

> In contrast to imperialism, Empire establishes no territorial centre of power and does not rely on fixed boundaries or barriers. It is a *decentered* and *deterritorializing* apparatus of rule that progressively incorporates the entire global realm within its open, expanding powers. Empire manages hybrid identities, flexible hierarchies, and plural exchanges through modulating networks of command. The distinct national colors of the imperialist map of the world have merged and blended in the imperial global rainbow.
>
> (2000: xii-xiii)

The "smooth space" and "non-place" of Empire are analogous to the "variable geometries and dematerialized geographies" of Castells's space of flows, while Empire as networked power corresponds to the emergent global network state that Castells tentatively identifies as *one* of the key networks within the space of flows. Both the space of flows (including the global network state) and Empire distribute power via rhizomatic informational-financial flows by means of the supercession of space and timeless time or "time outside measure" (2000: 357). In the informational mode of development, the space of places is bypassed by a global space of flows (global financial markets, global information networks, the global network state, global criminal networks, etc.), resulting in the resistance of place-based identities; whereas in Empire, the *biopolitical* immanence of informational capital is fully realized (in the Foucauldian sense), that is, the whole of social reproduction is subsumed in "imperial nexuses of the production of language, communication and the symbolic," so that "[t]he political synthesis of social space is fixed in the space of communication," resulting in the biopolitical production of subjectivities as subjects proper to the reproduction of imperial biopower (2000: 32, 32–3). Whereas for Castells, cultural singularities must transform themselves into informational networks if they are to reprogram symbolic codes and rebuild institutions, in Negri productive singularities are not merely "always already" networks but are also the "general intellect" itself: "the powers of labor are infused by the powers of science, communication, and language," and "life is what infuses and dominates all production" (2000: 364). Thus, for Hardt and Negri, the constituent power in Empire is the immaterial labor of the cooperative informational-communicational networks of a multitude of productive singularities. These networks are directly generative of social life, including communication and affects, and thus biopolitical; and Empire as constituted power, is merely the "negative residue," the parasitic shell of the ontological creativity, of the strength and desire of the multitude. Empire is the "communism of capital." With the real subsumption of labor by capitalism, intelligence and affect become the primary productive powers, the collective social intelligence becoming coextensive with the process of social reproduction itself, so that labor breaks free from the value relation, is increasingly self-valorizing, increasingly autonomous of capital, which, as Empire, is now an imperial command structure that expropriates the "mass intellectuality" of the collective laborer from without since it can no longer extort surplus value from within the process of production. It is in this sense that the "general intellect" is "outside measure," is "virtual," both "irreducible innovation and revolutionary machine" (2000: 357). Where Marx saw the era of the "general intellect" in terms of an explosive contradiction between the productive powers of the social, cooperative brain and their limitation within capitalist relations of production, a contradiction that prepared the way for the revolutionary transformation of society, for Negri the formation of the "general intellect" indicates that the real subsumption of labor to capital has been reversed. Negri, like Castells, posits an autonomous logic of technology beyond capitalism based on an informational mode of production. The criticisms addressed above to Castells apply *a fortiori* to Negri. Here we will confine ourselves to some observations on the implications of the "always already" autonomous character of the multitude for Negri's theory of revolution.

Let us return to the non-space of Empire, this "empty shell," this "corruption" of the ontological creativity of a multitude of communicating networks. The biopolitical subsumption of the political sphere (government, the nation-state, international state system) into this decentralized network power, "integrated world capitalism", erases the revolutionary space characteristic of modernity:

> The decline of any autonomous political sphere signals the decline ...
> of any independent space where revolution could emerge in the national
> political regime, or where social space could be transformed using the
> instruments of the state. The traditional idea of counter-power and the
> idea of resistance against modern sovereignty in general thus become
> less and less possible.
>
> (2000: 307–8)

With the biopolitical penetration of social life by capitalism there is no outside to the realization of its immanence, but this merely generalizes struggle and resistance across the entire social bios: "Politics is given immediately: it is a field of pure immanence" (2000: 354). As in the "disciplinary society" of Foucault (to which Negri appeals), power is everywhere and nowhere, it is a "non-place." And also as in Foucault, resistance is the "always already" of power; that is, resistance precedes power. The ontological immanence of the "general intellect" of the multitude to Empire, its virtual autonomy from capital as self-programming informational network, means that the assertion of its constituent power, its autonomy, is equivalent to the overthrow of Empire. Hence the assertion of autonomy by the multitude is "always already" revolutionary:

> the construction of Empire, and the globalization of economic and
> cultural relationships, means that the virtual centre of Empire can be
> attacked from any point. The tactical preoccupations of the old revo-
> lutionary school are thus completely irretrievable – the only strategy
> available to the struggles is that of a constituent counter-power that
> emerges from within Empire.
>
> (2000: 59)

By dissolving the space of politics into the non-space of communicative capitalism, Negri erases the distinct temporality of revolution as discontinuous event, as rupture in the continuum of homogenous, irreversible, and empty time of capitalist modernization. We have already criticized Castells's notion that informational, network capitalism has deterritorialized the space of power. Here we note that Negri's equation of autonomy (the "constituent event") with revolutionary transformation annuls revolution as an event in time and space, the time of the destruction and reconstruction of a state structure and the space of the political. Revolution must then become a mystery, must exist everywhere and nowhere, both within and beyond space and time, a hidden God. Hence it is not surprising that for Negri revolution is no more than the outgrowth of the "[constituent] power of generation, desire and love" of the multitude, *"a project of love"* (2000: 388, 413).

If we follow the chain of reasoning back to its source in the ontological creativity of the multitude, that is, of the "general intellect" unchained, we find that this short-circuiting of the political is the result of a logic of technology à la Castells, of a logic of biopolitical immanence. As many commentators have pointed out, Negri lacks a theory of political mediation, of the articulation of political subjects (Callinicos 2001b: Laclau 2001; Žižek 2001; Bensaid 2002). Political strategy, as the construction of a prince through the mastery of time, of *fortuna* by revolutionary *virtù*, has no place in the smooth space of Empire.

Change the world without taking power?

In the second type of postmodern revolution ICT networks are the very organizational model for a revolutionary movement against neo-liberal globalization that aims to "change the world without taking power."

The most celebrated example of such a movement is the Zapatista revolt against neo-liberalism and for the rights of indigenous peoples. For Castells the success of the Zapatistas was largely due to their "communication strategy." In this sense they are "the first informational guerrilla movement" (1997: 79). The ability to communicate with the world through decentralized ICT networks enabled the Zapatistas: to evade and undermine elite and commercial media control of information; to organize virtual international solidarity networks that encircled and undermined the repressive capacity of the Mexican state, forcing it to negotiate; to export their revolution against neo-liberalism into the very fabric of Mexican society and throughout the world; to shake Mexican politics to its foundations, accelerating the break-up of one-party rule, and wresting constitutional reform guaranteeing the rights of indigenous peoples in 1996; and to powerfully contribute to the creation of a critical discourse and a diverse planetary movement against neo-liberal globalization (Castells 1997: 79–83, Cleaver 1998: 81–83). As Castells perceptively notes, ICT "propelled a local, weak insurgent group to the forefront of world politics" (1997: 81). It was exactly this that troubled the advisers to the powers that be. In the opinion of the Rand Corporation, the Zapatista revolt is the "prototype transnational social netwar of the 21st century" (see Arquilla and Ronefeld 1993, 1996). Castells concurs:

> New communication technologies are fundamental for these movements to exist: indeed they are their organizational infrastructure . . . . The revolutionary cells of the information age are built on flows of electrons.
>
> (1997: 107)

This is also the starting point of theorists of networked revolution, which identify three main revolutionary potentials in ICT networks. First, their character as distributed discourse enables marginalized social actors to evade territorial or organizational control of information. Hence the potential for ICTs to generate an unofficial and decentralized public sphere in which open and informed deliberation and discussion, based on a wide variety of media sources, from the official to the unofficial, from the revolutionary to the counter-revolutionary, flourishes (Cleaver 1998, 1999). Second, ICT is seen as a tool for *cyber-activism* (see Kellner 2003) where ICT as a decentralized network is paradigmatic of the organizational structure of new social movements based on decentralized, participatory democracy, like the "anti-globalization" movements:

> Rather than a single movement, what is emerging is thousands of movements intricately linked to one another, much as "hotlinks" connect their websites on the Internet. This analogy is more than coincidental and is in fact key to understanding the changing nature of political organizing. Although many have observed that the recent mass protests would have been impossible without the Internet, what has been overlooked is how the communication technology that facilitates these campaigns is shaping the movement in its own image. Thanks to the Net, mobilizations are able to unfold with sparse bureaucracy and minimal hierarchy; forced consensus and labored manifestos are fading into the background, replaced instead by a culture of constant, loosely structured and sometimes compulsive information-swapping.
>
> (Klein 2002: 4)

Thus, third, ICT as distributed discourse enables the emergence of decentralized networks of struggle in real time that are able to evade and thus challenge the centralized and bureaucratic territorial and organizational structures of modernity. Postmodern theorists of revolution often cite approvingly the view of the Rand Corporation that, thanks to the Internet, the "war of the flea" of the Zapatistas turned into a "war of the swarm." The problem facing centralized state apparatuses and bureaucratic organizations is that the swarm has no "central leadership or command structure; it is multiheaded, impossible to decapitate" (Klein 2002: 8; see also Hardt and Negri 2004). These three potential applications of ICTs to the formation of revolutionary movements have generated a new concept of revolution "as a struggle, not for power, but against it" (Holloway and Peláez 1998: 5).

The Zapatistas are once again paradigmatic of the new concept of revolution. The Zapatista revolution, unlike all previous revolutions, does not aim to take power – either through the ballot box or the seizure of power. Hence it is the first "postmodern" revolution (Burbach 2001: 116). This concept of revolution is based on two premises. First, a loose form of the postmodern suspicion of the state; that is, a politics of difference, hybridity and fluidity that challenges the modern state as an apparatus of power-knowledge. Consequently, any attempt to transform state power will succeed only in replacing one apparatus of power-knowledge with another. Thus, second, the premise that the organization forms of struggle must prefigure the political forms of the emancipated society; that is, the future abolition of the state must be prefigured in a decentralized, anti-state power.

The Zapatistas reject the authoritarian, vanguard organizational forms of traditional guerrilla movements in favor of "commanding obeying," the principle that those who lead should be effectively subordinated to the rule of those who are led; that is, the federated, revolutionary leadership is mandated to act on the basis of decisions made by communal assemblies of the different ethnic communities. This commune form of direct democracy is a "revolution which makes the revolution possible," a revolution which overcomes the separation between "political society" and "civil society" by dissolving the former into the latter, thus prefiguring the stateless self-managing society of the future (Lorenzano 1998: 131) Hence, according to the Zapatistas, the future revolution:

> will not be the product of one kind of action. That is, it will not be, in the strict sense either an armed or a pacific revolution. It will primarily be a revolution resulting from struggle on various fronts, using many methods, using various social forms, with various degrees of commit-ment and participation. And its result will not be the victory of a party, an organization or an alliance of triumphant organizations with their own specific social proposal, but rather a democratic space for resolving the confrontation of various political proposals. This democratic space will be based upon three fundamental, historically inseparable premises: democracy to define the dominant social proposal; the freedom to endorse one proposal or another; and justice as a principle that must be respected by all proposals.
> (Zapatista proclamation of January 20, 1994, quoted in Lorenzano 1998: 131–2)

It is precisely this indeterminacy in the concept of revolution that is cele-brated by authors like Holloway (2002: 165, 168, 171–2, 198). If the revo-lution is not only to achieve radical democracy as its end, but is radically democratic in its struggle, then it is impossible to predefine its path, or indeed think of a definite point of arrival. Echoing Eduard Bernstein, the revolution is the movement itself, is the "openness of uncertainty." Drawing directly on the negative dialectics of Adorno, revolution lies in the movement of the non-identical, movement "in the mode of being denied" (Holloway 2002: 210, 212):

> The problem of struggle is to move onto a different dimension from capital, not to engage with capital on its own terms, but to move

forward in modes in which capital cannot even exist: to break identity, break the homogenization of time.

(Holloway 2002: 213)

But this is to pretend that "one can abolish capitalist relations of production by pretending they aren't there" (Callinicos 2003a). It is to ignore the problem of the space of power in modern societies, that is, in the final instance, the coercive power of the state. Returning to the case of the Zapatistas, ICT enabled them to escape a "space of enclosure" (Foucault), the Lacandon jungle, and more generally, the peripheral region of Chiapas, and virtually project their movement into the space of Mexican and world politics, thus effecting transformation in real time. However, the problem of the state has not gone away and the Zapatista revolution remains under military siege, imprisoned within the jungles of Chiapas. Thus, virtual, decentralized networks do not completely escape their physical embodiment in space. We may say then that networked theories of revolution pose a problematic isomorphism between (and thus conflate) networked, informational models of organization and the revolutionary event and/or with post-capitalist society.

The iron law of oligarchy?

We have argued that theories of networked revolution pose a problematic isomorphism between virtual networks and the real world that effaces the politics of time and space under global capitalism. Nevertheless, our intention is not to throw the baby out with the bath water. ICTs have technical properties that have the potential to contribute the formation of political subjects that can challenge the spatial and temporal characteristics of organizational life characteristic of modernity. Here we hope briefly to clarify some of these technical properties by means of a discussion of Michels's iron law of oligarchy.[1]

Michels (1915) argued that there is an iron law of oligarchy inherent to all forms of organization, such that even formally representative organizations, such as political parties and trade unions, are dominated by oligarchies. Notwithstanding the ahistorical and teleological character of the idea of an "iron law" of oligarchy, the great strength of Michels's work lies in its introduction of communication structures into the paradigm of domination. Michels identifies five key inequalities contributing to oligarchy:

- inequality of knowledge
- differential control over the means of communication
- uneven distribution of skill in the art of politics
- low levels of culture and sophistication
- time, energy, and space poverty.

Under each of these headings we will briefly examine the ways in which the technical properties of ICTs may enable the formation of counter-hegemonic political subjects.

The relatively low cost of online communication and publication renders less credible any claim that the presentation of decisions, processes and action must be subject to the rule of informational parsimony (Hogan and Greene 2002). What is more, flows of information are now much harder to retain within institutional boundaries, while the distribution of points of entry into the force field of communication allows for unsanctioned and unofficial communicative pathways to be opened, where organizational performance may be observed and indexed (Grieco, Hogan and Martinez-Lucio 2005). Visibility and transparency are sharpened, with consequences for the processes of auditing individual and institutional performance, enabling the development of forms of meta-governance (Grieco 2002) through the deployment of a *reverse panopticon* in relation to leaders, with significant implications for tracking and thereby resisting their maneuvers (Hogan and Grieco 2000). With the diffusion of the technologies and skills for the faster and more extensive marshaling of materials revealing organizational and leadership performance, the bargaining power of the led over those who lead is strengthened. By allowing for the rapid and low cost collation of information, the e-form allows actors to trace the points of origin and moments of translation and distortion as particular narratives pass across interfaces. This is significant not only in tracing the violation of ideal speech, but also in showing the paths of linkage which are traveled upon in the process of constructing power discourses (Greene, Hogan and Grieco 2001).

Moreover, with the ever wider distribution of transmission technologies, the contribution of a multitude of voices to such processes can be recorded in a disintermediated way, free from institutionalized policing (Hogan and Greene 2002). The e-form, by taking collective decision-making processes out of traditional physical spaces of power, provides a safer space within which to deploy and develop communicative skills. This is because intervention can be rehearsed in safe spaces and then delivered when the participant is confident. In traditional physical spaces of power the pressures of time mean that even the most politically committed individual is unable to realize the aim of participation. When one adds the tendencies towards what Hyman has referred to as the bureaucracy of dependency (Hyman 1979), as manifest in the differential distribution of expertise and experience, as well as the problems associated with white, male, heterosexual, able-bodied domination, then the physical meeting place represents an unlikely arena in which a plethora of voices might be heard. ICT also promotes continuous learning. In allowing skill development to take place by small increments, e.g. online questions, statements, calls for information, etc., the acceleration of information transfers become part of the educational process for participants. Indeed, every development in user-friendly technology is a contribution to communicative competence (Greene, Hogan and Grieco 2001).

Imaginative communicative strategy can be developed to service and organize participants outside of the spatial dominion of managerial and bureaucratic oligarchies and to resist the logic of residential dispersal (Hogan and Nolan 2005). Furthermore, the capacity to meet and organize in virtual time and space, outside of physical spaces of enclosure, erodes dependency upon employer and state sponsorship, enabling the maintenance of collective counter-organization outside of spaces of bureaucratic forms of domination (Hogan and Nolan 2005). Through allowing for asynchronous communicative exchanges, communication technologies can be used to alleviate time–space poverty and provide alternative points of entry into modes of deliberation and decision making, thus providing for the possibility of intervention and extended participation in collective organization and action, along with new ways of collective identity and action formation (Greene, Hogan and Grieco 2003).

Thus within the realm of organization, tendencies towards oligarchy (sustained by control over the flow of information, access to superior knowledge, skill in the art of politics and a membership diverted by the pulls of work, family and leisure) are challenged by the possibility for greater equality of knowledge, distributed control over the means of communication, enhanced communicative skills and a reconfiguration of the time–space dimensions of communicative practice (Carter, Clegg, Hogan and Kornberger 2003).

That ICT has the potential to confer *supplementary powers* on social actors is already in evidence. From the Liverpool dockers' dispute to the "penguin revolution" of school students in Chile, from the general strikes organized by the South Korean Confederation of Trade Unions to the Seattle protests again neo-liberalism, from the Zapatista revolution to the worldwide demonstrations against the Iraq war, from the anti-corruption campaigns of "rogerlyons.com" in the UK trade union AMICUS and of "Pro-Veritas" at BBC Monitoring to the anti-Lieberman U.S. senatorial campaign, from the "No Sweat" and fair-trade movements to the campaigns against the exploitation of the global south by the Western pharmaceutical giants – social actors are transforming the time–space dimensions of collective action through innovative use of the new technologies.

Let us take the case of the Liverpool dockers' dispute of 1995–1998 against the Mersey Docks and Harbour Company over casualization. The distributed technologies of communication enabled the Liverpool dockers to sustain strike action without the full institutional support of their own trade union body, the Transport and General Workers Union (TGWU), or of the International Transport Workers Federation (ITF). The qualities of virtual adjacency, and of high speed, low cost, global communication, enabled the dockers to coordinate global action, including two international stoppages spanning 27 countries, reported to have been the most widespread international solidarity actions in labor movement history. Major capitalist assets were tracked as they moved across the globe. Reception protests were quickly assembled across the different links of the international transport chain to prevent the loading and unloading of cargo ships associated with the opponents of the Liverpool dockers. Leadership behavior, promises, alleged betrayals and dissembling, were showcased, made transparent, indexed, audited and archived in Web forums, providing a valuable reference point for measuring performance and marshaling arguments during the conduct of the action; and as a means for retaining memories and lessons that might enrich future actions. Through showcasing the dispute, the Liverpool dockers were also able to construct globally visible narratives of injustice, free from institutionalized cognitive policing, as a plethora of worker voices were broadcast and retained within the web spaces of solidarity (Carter, Clegg, Hogan and Kornberger 2003).

As we have demonstrated, ICTs allow social actors to stretch and deepen the time–space dimensions of communicative practice and political action, with greater levels of reflexivity, deliberation, intervention, participation and action.

Let us now conclude our argument. ICT demonstrates the *potential* for the formation of revolutionary movements across time and space that challenge the reified and bureaucratized figures of modernity, but there is no technological fix to the problem of politics and thus of the revolutionary transformation of state power.

We have argued that networked theories of revolution dissolve the properly political space of revolution since they either posit an informational logic of technology beyond capitalism, as in the case of Castells; or, as with Negri, they argue that with the real subsumption of labor, collective social intelligence becomes co-extensive with the entire process of social reproduction, breaking free from capitalist relations of production as a multitude of communicating, networked singularities, leading to an immanent logic of revolution; or, as with the theorists of *Zapatismo*, they conflate networked, informational models of organization with the revolutionary event and/or with post-capitalist society. In this way they either dissolve revolution, as discontinuous event into the homogenous, evolutionary time of capitalist rationalization (as in the idea of an "information technology revolution"); or they place a logic of revolutionary (biopolitical) immanence outside of the dimensions of time and space, as an ontological apparatus beyond measure, absolute procedure without foundation; or they dissolve revolutionary rupture into pure process or movement.

But this is to misrepresent the novelty and singularity of the revolutionary event. Revolution is neither the inevitable culmination of a teleology of technology nor the intrusion of messianic time into the empty, homogenous time of "creative destruction," of capitalist modernization, but is constituted within the discontinuous time of politics and strategy; a discontinuous temporality that unfolds within the widening aperture of systemic contradictions and crises driven by the uneven and combined development of planetary capitalism, but a temporality which itself overdetermines and thus constitutes revolutionary crisis as revolution. Thus our journey through "evolutionary revolutions" driven by a "logic of technology" or informational networking leads us back to the political and its constitutive role in the formation of political subjects, in the widening of discontinuities in the fabric of evolutionary, capitalist time into revolutionary ruptures and in the determination of revolutionary outcomes. ICT provides agents located in the space and time of capitalist relations of production with supplementary powers that afford them a greater degree of mastery over the time–space dynamics of political action. The extent to which these supplementary powers are realized and contribute to the formation of new revolutionary subjects is, however, a purely political question.

Note

1 The heuristic of deploying Michels's iron law of oligarchy for the purpose of examining the dynamic implications and possibilities of ICTs for the erosion and challenge to extant organizational forms and politics has been used previously in relation to the specific domain of trade unionism (see Hogan and Grieco 2000; Greene, Hogan and Grieco 2001; Hogan and Greene 2002; Greene, Hogan and Grieco 2003; Hogan and Zivkovic 2004; Zivkovic and Hogan 2005).

13 Explaining revolutionary terrorism

Jeff Goodwin

The terrorist attacks of September 11, 2001, have spurred many social scientists to explore the dynamics of terrorism, most for the first time. Before 9/11, terrorism research was the exclusive preserve, with very few exceptions, of small networks of political scientists and non-academic "security experts," relatively few of whom were interested in social science theory. Descriptive case studies abound, replete with *ad hoc*, case-specific explanations of terrorism. Curiously, most scholars of rebellion and revolution, broadly defined, have had virtually nothing of significance to say about terrorism. More generally, the *strategic choices* of revolutionary movements – of which terrorism is one – have received much less scholarly attention than the causes and consequences of revolutions. To be sure, many scholars have examined the use of terrorism by revolutionaries in power – including the Jacobin "reign of terror" and Stalin's show trials and forced collectivization of agriculture – but there has been no systematic study of the use of terrorism by revolutionary movements that are struggling to take power.

In this chapter, I begin with a definition of terrorism and revolutionary terrorism; I then discuss several extant theories of terrorism, noting their insights and shortcomings; and I outline my own theory of "categorical" terrorism, a type of terrorism that has been employed by revolutionaries with increasing frequency in recent years. Although my theory requires more rigorous empirical testing than I can provide here, I believe that it helps to explain better than extant approaches why some revolutionary movements, *but not others*, employ or try to employ a strategy characterized by the use of violence against anonymous civilians or non-combatants. It is terrorism in this sense which today alternately fascinates, repels, and inspires women and men across large parts of the globe.

What is terrorism?

Like "democracy," "power," "class," "revolution," and so many other "essentially contested concepts," there is no commonly accepted definition of "terrorism." And yet explanation requires a clear analytic definition or demarcation of the phenomenon to be explained, even if, empirically, terrorism is not always easily distinguished from cognate phenomena. "Leaving the definition implicit is the road to obscurantism" (Gibbs 1989: 329).

Several representative definitions of terrorism are presented in Table 13.1. The *deliberate use of violence or threats in order to influence some audience (or audiences)* is common to most of these definitions, but there are also several areas of divergence. First, there is no consensus as to who can *practice* terrorism: Can states as well as oppositional groups engage in terrorism? Several definitions (Hoffman 1998; the U.S. State Department, cited in Hoffman 1998; Black 2004; Bergesen and Lizardo 2004) seem to imply that "state terrorism" is either a misnomer or at least something that needs to be distinguished from terrorism proper and presumably analyzed in its

Table 13.1 Definitions of terrorism

Terrorism is "1. Government by intimidation as directed and carried out by the party in power in France during the Revolution of 1789–94 ... 2. A policy intended to strike with terror those against whom it is adopted; the employment of methods of intimidation" (Oxford English Dictionary).

Terrorism "means an activity that ... appears to be intended to (i) intimidate or coerce a civilian population; (ii) to influence the policy of a government by intimidation or coercion; or (iii) to affect the conduct of a government by assassination or kidnapping" (U.S. Code cited in Chomsky 2001: 16).

Terrorism is "the deliberate creation and exploitation of fear through violence or the threat of violence in the pursuit of political change" (Hoffman 1998: 43).

Terrorism is "asymmetrical deployment of threats and violence against enemies using means that fall outside the forms of political struggle routinely operating within some current regime" (Tilly 2004: 5).

Terrorism is "the contemporary name given to, and the modern permutation of, warfare deliberately waged against civilians with the purpose of destroying their will to support either leaders or policies that the agents of such violence find objectionable" (Carr 2003: 6).

Terrorism is "the premeditated use or threat of symbolic, low-level violence by conspiratorial organizations" (Crenshaw 1981: 379).

Terrorism is "organized political violence, lethal or nonlethal, designed to deter opposition by maximizing fear, specifically by random targeting of people or sites" (Turk 1982: 122).

"Terrorism is the intentional use of or threat to use violence against civilians or against civilian targets, in order to attain political aims" (Ganor 1998).

Terrorism is "premeditated, politically motivated violence perpetrated against noncombatant targets by subnational groups or clandestine agents, usually intended to influence an audience" (U.S. State Department cited in Hoffman 1998: 38).

"Pure terrorism is self-help by organized civilians who covertly inflict mass violence on other civilians" (Black 2004: 16).

Terrorism is "the use of violence by nonstate groups against noncombatants for symbolic purposes, that is, to influence or somehow affect another audience for some political, social, or religious purpose" (Bergesen and Lizardo 2004: 50).

own right. Second, there is disagreement as to who can be the *target* of terrorist threats or violence. Can *anyone* be a target of terrorism – or just civilians (or "non-combatants")? Several definitions (Carr 2003; Ganor 1998; the U.S. State Department, cited in Hoffman 1998; Black 2004; Bergesen and Lizardo 2004) suggest that only civilians or non-combatants can be the targets of terrorism, properly understood. Finally, there is disagreement as to whether terrorism necessarily produces *terror* – that is, extreme fear or timidity. Several definitions (Tilly 2004; Crenshaw 1981; Ganor 1998; the U.S. State Department, cited in Hoffman 1998; Black 2004; Bergesen and Lizardo 2004) make no mention of terror or fear (Carr is more ambiguous, defining terrorism as intending to "destroy the will" of civilians to support certain leaders or policies); these definitions imply that terrorism may not always terrorize and hence may in fact influence audiences by other means.

I believe that (non-state) terrorism is most usefully defined as follows: *Terrorism is the strategic use of violence and threats of violence by an oppositional political group against civilians or non-combatants, and is usually intended to influence several audiences.* This definition, which is fairly conventional, accords with those which suggest that terrorism involves violence or threats *by civilians against other civilians*, thus differentiating terrorism from guerrilla warfare, on the one hand, and state violence, on the other. This definition is also agnostic as to whether terrorism is intended literally to terrorize. What we must explain in order to explain terrorism is not why people sometimes resort to violence, but why they employ violence against civilians or non-combatants in particular (Goodwin 2004). Following this definition, *revolutionary terrorism* may be defined as *the strategic use of violence and threats of violence by a revolutionary movement against civilians or non-combatants, and is usually intended to influence several audiences.* I employ the concept of "revolutionary movement" broadly here, meaning any organization or network, and its supporters, which seeks to change the political, but not necessarily the socio-economic, order in more or less fundamental ways.

These definitions by no means imply that state violence or "state terrorism" does not exist or should not be studied. On the contrary, state terrorism is an enormously important subject; it is incontestable, for example, that state terrorism has claimed many more victims than has terrorism, in the sense in which I am defining it here (see, e.g. Herman and O'Sullivan 1989: chs 2–3; Gareau 2004). But state terrorism and oppositional forms of terrorism need to be clearly distinguished, if only to understand better the relationship between the two – a relationship, I will suggest, which does indeed exist. The preceding definitions allow us to make just such a distinction.

My definition of revolutionary terrorism also has the advantage of demarcating a widely recognized political strategy that has been employed by revolutionary groups with some frequency, especially since the 1960s – a strategy clearly distinct from, albeit sharing family resemblances with, such violent oppositional strategies as *coups d'état*, conventional and guerrilla warfare (directed at a state's armed forces), and economic sabotage. Indeed, at least since the 1960s terrorism has become part of the "repertoire of contention" (Tilly 1995) which is culturally available to virtually all revolutionary groups around the globe, irrespective of their specific goals.

Finally, my definition of revolutionary terrorism emphasizes, conventionally, that the groups that employ terrorism are oppositional *political* groups which view terrorism as, at least in part, a *political* strategy. These groups may also be nationalist, ethnic, religious, cultural, economic, or even criminal in nature (in some sense of these terms), but they seek – whatever else they may seek – to change the political (and perhaps socio-economic) order more or less fundamentally. Revolutionary groups that employ terrorism as a strategy (like those which eschew it) seek, minimally, to overthrow or terminate a state's power within a specific territory (including colonial and military occupations) or to secede from a political order and set up a new state (or join a pre-existing one). Thus, my definition of revolutionary terrorism does *not* include the violence of pro-state vigilantes or paramilitaries, although these groups obviously can (like states themselves) attack civilians.

Two types of terrorism need to be analytically differentiated, both of which differ from conventional and guerrilla warfare, insofar as the latter are directed against a government's armed forces, hostile paramilitaries, and armed civilians (see Table 13.2).[1] Of course, as Donald Black points out, "those popularly known as guerrillas may sometimes engage in terrorism [when they attack civilians], and those popularly known as terrorists may sometimes engage in guerrilla warfare [when they attack military facilities or personnel]" (2004: 17). One type of terrorism, which we may call "selective" or "individualized," is directed against non-combatants who are targeted

Table 13.2 Three types of armed struggle

| Combatants | Targets of revolutionaries | |
	Non-combatants	

Defense forces
Security forces
Paramilitaries/
  armed civilians
	Politicians
	State administrators
	Leaders/activists of
	  competing oppositions
	Presumed collaborators
	Common criminals
		Anonymous members
		of an ethnicity, religion,
		nationality, social class,
		etc.

Type 1 Conventional/ guerrilla warfare	*Type 2* Selective/ individualized terrorism; i.e. targeted assassination	*Type 3* Categorical/ indiscriminate terrorism

because of their individual identities or roles; in fact, these individuals are typically known *by name* to at least some members of the revolutionary movement. These individuals typically include politicians and (unarmed) state officials, usually those held responsible, directly or indirectly, for the institutional arrangements and policies that the revolutionaries oppose (including "counterterrorist" policies). They may also include competing oppositional leaders and political activists, presumed government collaborators and spies, unsympathetic intellectuals and journalists, and, sometimes, common criminals. This type of terrorism – essentially a strategy of "targeted assassination" – was employed by some nineteenth-century Russian revolutionaries, a number of anarchist groups, and several radical European groups of the 1960s and 1970s, such as Italy's Red Brigades. Terrorism of this type, especially when targeted at real or imagined collaborators whom the government cannot (or will not) protect, may result in an exceedingly large number of casualties, as in Peru during the 1980s and Algeria during the 1990s (see, e.g. Kalyvas 1999).

Targeted assassination or selective terrorism is very different from "indiscriminate" or what I term "categorical" terrorism, which is directed against anonymous individuals by virtue of their belonging (or seeming to belong) to a specific ethnic or religious group, nationality, social class, or some other collectivity. This type of terrorism – the focus of this chapter – is typically called indiscriminate or "random" terrorism because it makes no distinctions among the *individual* identities of its targets. In another sense, however, such terrorism is *very* discriminate, being directed against specific categories of people and not others. For this reason, "categorical terrorism" is a more accurate label than "indiscriminate terrorism" for this strategy. (Revolutionaries who practice terrorism, whether selective or categorical, also display varying degrees of tolerance for harming anonymous bystanders, that is, people who are not the individuals, or who do not belong to the category targeted for violence. U.S. military officials refer to such casualties as "collateral damage.")

Following the general definition of terrorism given above, *categorical terrorism* may be defined as *the strategic use of violence and threats of violence, usually intended to influence several audiences, by oppositional political groups against civilians or non-combatants who belong to a specific ethnicity, religious or national group, social class, or some other collectivity, without regard to their individual identities or roles.* In much if not most popular discourse, and for many scholars (e.g. Turk 1982; Senechal de la Roche 1996; Black 2004), "terrorism" fundamentally *is* categorical terrorism in this sense. Indiscriminate violence, that is, is seen by many as an essential property of terrorism. Terrorism in this sense, particularly as it is practiced (or not) by revolutionary movements, is what I seek to explain with my own theory of categorical terrorism.

There is substantial variation in the extent to which revolutionary movements employ categorical terrorism as a strategy. Table 13.3 lists some of the more important revolutionary groups that arose during the period since the Second World War as well as their principal violent strategies (excluding economic sabotage). Of course, revolutionary groups generally employ a number of both violent and non-violent strategies in pursuit of their goals, and their mix of strategies typically changes over time. Hence, it can be quite misleading to describe some such groups as "terrorist organizations" (or others as "guerrilla groups"). These labels are unhelpful insofar as they falsely "essentialize" revolutionary movements not just in terms of their strategic orientation – a rather limited view of what any movement is all about – but also in terms of just *one* of their strategies.

The first five sets of revolutionary groups listed in Table 13.3, whatever other strategies they pursued or pursue, perpetrated or continue to perpetrate extensive categorical or indiscriminate terrorism. The other listed organizations were (or are) generally much more selective or individualized in their use of terrorism, and in at least one case (the Sandinistas in Nicaragua) employed virtually no terrorism to speak of. The Irish Republican Army (IRA), the Basque nationalist group Homeland and Freedom (Euskadi ta Akatasuna or ETA), and the Tamil Tigers (LTTE) are borderline cases. Before it went on ceasefire in 1997, the IRA typically engaged in attacks on security forces as well as some selective terrorism, but it also occasionally carried out indiscriminate bombings in both Northern Ireland

Table 13.3 Coercive strategies of revolutionary organizations

Country	Main organization(s)	Dates
Algeria	National Liberation Front (FLN)	1954–1962
Categorical as well as selective terrorism; guerrilla warfare		
Palestine/Israel	PLO, PFLP, Hamas, PIJ	1964–present
Extensive categorical as well as selective terrorism; guerrilla warfare		
Sri Lanka	Liberation Tigers (LTTE)	1983–2002?
Categorical as well as selective terrorism; conventional and guerrilla warfare		
Various countries	Al Qaeda	1988–present
Extensive categorical as well as selective terrorism; guerrilla warfare		
Chechnya/Russia	Chechen separatists	1996–present
Categorical as well as selective terrorism; guerrilla warfare		
Nicaragua	Sandinistas (FSLN)	1961–1979
Very limited selective terrorism; guerrilla warfare		
South Africa	African National Congress	1961–1990
very limited categorical terrorism; some selective terrorism; guerrilla warfare		
Basque Country/Spain	ETA	1968–present
Limited categorical terrorism; selective terrorism; guerrilla warfare		
Northern Ireland (UK)	Irish Republican Army (IRA)	1969–1997
Limited categorical terrorism (esp. mid-1970s); selective terrorism; guerrilla warfare		
El Salvador	FMLN	1980–1992
Very limited selective terrorism; guerrilla warfare		

and Britain and sectarian killings of Protestants, especially during the height of "the Troubles" in Northern Ireland during the mid-1970s (see, e.g. English 2003). Historically, ETA has directed most of its violence against the Spanish military and police presence in the Basque region and against politicians of parties that oppose Basque independence. However, it has also engaged in occasional indiscriminate bombings and attempted bombings (Clark 1984). The Tamil Tigers have likewise engaged in occasional indiscriminate attacks on ethnic Sinhalese in Sri Lanka, including suicide bombings, but the vast majority of suicide bombings carried out by the Tigers have been targeted at the military and political leaders (Pape 2005: Appendix I).

Clearly, any adequate theory of categorical terrorism needs to explain the wide variation shown in Table 13.3. That is to say, it is necessary but not sufficient to explain why some revolutionary movements have practiced categorical terrorism; an adequate theory must also explain why other revolutionary movements have *not* carried out categorical terrorism or have done so relatively infrequently.

Extant theoretical approaches

When social scientists *have* attempted to explain why revolutionaries employ terrorism, how have they done so? Here, I briefly review three theoretical claims: (1) terrorism is a product of the *weakness and desperation* of revolutionaries; (2) terrorism is a response to *state terrorism*; and (3) terrorism is a result of extreme *"social polarization"* between groups. While these claims do offer important insights into terrorism, they are ultimately unsatisfactory.

Before examining these claims, however, I should note that a typical explanation for terrorism in much public discourse, and by many scholars, is *grievance-based* (e.g. Stern 2003). That is to say, many people suggest that the causes – or "root causes" – of terrorism are to be found in the grievances of those who utilize terrorism as a strategy. But this argument is extremely problematic. It is certainly true that the removal of the grievances that presumably motivate revolutionaries would end terrorism. But those who make this argument never explain which grievances or which kinds of grievance, if any, *require or somehow cause terrorism* to be utilized by revolutionaries as opposed to other political strategies. Grievances may be a necessary cause of collective action, but it is less clear that they explain *how* people act collectively. In fact, ends do not explain means any better than they justify them. Thus, as they are typically articulated, grievance-based accounts of terrorism are at best incomplete and at worst quite misleading.

After grievance-based explanations, perhaps the most frequently cited hypothesis for why revolutionaries might choose a strategy of terrorism is that they are very weak and even desperate to redress their grievances. (This claim – or rationalization – also seems very popular among many groups that employ terrorism.) The core idea here is that groups that lack the capacity to wage conventional or even guerrilla warfare against repressive governments, not to mention non-violent protest, or which fail to attain their goals even when they *do* employ these strategies, will turn to terrorism as a "last resort." Martha Crenshaw, for example, suggests that "Terrorism is the resort of an elite when conditions are not revolutionary"; "terrorism is most likely to occur precisely where mass passivity and elite dissatisfaction coincide" (1981: 384). (For these reasons, Rubenstein (1987) calls terrorists "alchemists of revolution.")

Disaffected elites, in Crenshaw's account, turn to terrorism because it is easier and cheaper than strategies based on mass mobilization, especially when government repression makes mass mobilization difficult if not impossible. "In situations where paths to the legal expression of opposition are blocked, but where the regime's repression is inefficient, revolutionary terrorism is doubly likely, as permissive and direct causes coincide" (Crenshaw 1981: 384). Revolutionary groups will presumably employ categorical terrorism, moreover, because it is generally even cheaper than selective terrorism (Kalyvas 2004). There may be only so many opportunities available for killing a particular politician or competing opposition leader, for example, but setting off a bomb in a pub or bus may be relatively simple and will also produce more casualties. "The observation that terrorism is a weapon of the weak," Crenshaw concludes, "is hackneyed but apt. At least when initially adopted, terrorism is the strategy of a minority that by its own judgment lacks other means. When the group perceives its options as limited, terrorism is attractive because it is a relatively inexpensive and simple alternative, and because its potential reward is high" (1981: 387; for similar views, see Rubenstein 1987; Irvin 1999: ch. 2; Pape 2005: 92–4; Bloom 2005).

There are two logical and empirical problems with this theory of terrorism. Most importantly, this theory by itself does not explain why attacking or threatening ordinary civilians would be perceived as beneficial as opposed to detrimental for the revolutionaries. Terrorism may be cheaper than some other strategies, but why employ it at all? We need to know what revolutionaries believe they will gain by attacking specific categories of civilians. What are their strategic goals and expectations? Would not attacks on civilians simply undermine the popularity of revolutionaries or their own morale? To say that the revolutionaries are weak begs these questions.

Second, many weak revolutionary organizations have eschewed terrorism. Perhaps the best example of this is the armed wing of the African National Congress (ANC) in South Africa. In 1961, as many of its leaders were being arrested and many others driven into exile, the ANC established an armed wing called Umkhonto we Sizwe ("Spear of the Nation," or MK). The ANC explicitly adopted "armed struggle" as one of its main political strategies. By most accounts, however, MK failed to become an effective guerrilla force, as the South African Defense Forces (SADF) were simply too strong and effective. And yet MK did *not* adopt a strategy of terrorism, despite the fact, as Gay Seidman points out, that "In a deeply segregated society, it would have been easy to kill random whites. Segregated white schools, segregated movie theaters, segregated shopping centers meant that if white deaths were the only goal, potential targets could be found everywhere" (2001: 118). However, as Stephen Davis notes, "since the exile leadership sought to portray the ANC as a principled and responsible contender for power, it imposed restrictions against terrorist tactics that specifically targeted non-combatant whites" (Davis 1987: 121). The then president of the ANC, Oliver Tambo "even went to the extent of signing a protocol of the Geneva Convention which legally bound the ANC to avoid attacks on civilian targets, and to 'humanitarian conduct of the war,' marking the first time a guerrilla group had ever done so" (Davis 1987: 121–2).[2]

In short, weak revolutionary groups do not necessarily adopt a strategy of terrorism, and strong revolutionaries do not necessarily eschew this strategy. As Turk concludes:

> Because any group may adopt terror tactics, it is misleading to assume either that "terrorism is the weapon of the weak" or that terrorists are always small groups of outsiders – or at most a "lunatic fringe" ... . Terror is organized violence, but the nature of the organization cannot be specified in defining terror.
>
> (1982: 122)

Some of the many investigations of the socio-economic backgrounds of "terrorists," to the extent that they bother to address issues of causation, also point to a type of weakness as the source of terrorism. One idea in this literature is that poor and poorly educated people are especially likely to become terrorists because they are desperate for status, power, or resources, but lack the ability to use other strategies for securing these. The evidence for this claim, however, is indeed quite weak. In fact, as Crenshaw's thesis suggests, much research demonstrates that the members of revolutionary groups that practice terrorism are just as likely, if not more likely, to come from elite social strata as from working- or lower-class backgrounds (see, e.g. Krueger and Maleckova 2003).

The insight of the "weakness theory" of terrorism is that oppositional groups *do* generally seem to take up arms because they have concluded that non-violent politics does not work or works too slowly or ineffectively to redress urgent grievances. But notice that this does not tell us why armed groups would employ terrorism as opposed to guerrilla warfare. Moreover, the argument that attacking "soft" targets like unprotected civilians is cheaper and easier than waging guerrilla warfare against government forces does not explain why *all* oppositional groups do not engage in terrorism.

Another hypothesis claims that terrorism is a response to *state terrorism*. Leftist analysts of terrorism often make this claim, and it is mentioned, although not much developed, by Herman and O'Sullivan (1989). They suggest that the "retail" terrorism of oppositional groups is caused or provoked by the "wholesale" or "primary" terrorism of states, especially powerful Western states, above all the United States. (The terms "wholesale" and "retail," which have also been employed by Noam Chomsky (2001), are meant to remind readers that state terrorism has been much more deadly than oppositional terrorism.) This claim certainly has an intuitive plausibility. Why else would oppositional groups turn to violence except when they confront a government or state that is itself unmoved by and indeed uses violence against peaceful protesters? Avenging such state violence might be reason enough for opposition groups to employ violent strategies. And yet, as an explanation of terrorism, this hypothesis is also beset by both logical and empirical problems.

It is certainly true that indiscriminate state violence, especially when perpetrated by relatively weak states, encourages the development of revolutionary movements (see, e.g. Goodwin 2001). But why would these movements attack and threaten ordinary *civilians* as opposed to the state's armed forces? In other words, if they are in fact responding to *state* terrorism, why wouldn't revolutionaries target *the state* – and just the state? State terrorism would seem to be a better explanation for a strategy of guerrilla (or conventional) warfare than for a strategy of terrorism.

Empirically, one can also point to revolutionary organizations that have arisen in contexts of extreme state violence which have nonetheless eschewed the strategy of terrorism. For example, Central American guerrilla movements of the 1970s and 1980s, including the Sandinistas (FSLN) in Nicaragua and the Farabundo Martí National Liberation Movement (FMLN) in El Salvador, confronted states that engaged in extensive violence against non-combatants, yet neither revolutionary group engaged in categorical terrorism, and the Sandinistas engaged in virtually no terrorism of any type. Another such example is, once again, the ANC in South Africa. Interestingly, Herman and O'Sullivan's book devotes considerable attention to both South African and Israeli state terrorism (1989: ch. 2). And yet, while they note the "retail" terrorism of the Palestine Liberation Organization (PLO) during the 1970s and 1980s – emphasizing that Israeli state terrorism was responsible for a great many more civilian deaths during this period – they do not discuss the oppositional terrorism in South Africa which their theory would seem to predict. In fact, as I have noted, the ANC simply did not carry out much terrorism. State terrorism, clearly, does not always cause or provoke categorical terrorism.

Having said this, it is indeed difficult to point to a revolutionary group that has carried out extensive terrorism which has *not* arisen in a context of considerable state violence. Leaving aside for the moment the case of Al Qaeda (which I discuss below), all of the groups in Table 13.3 which have engaged in extensive terrorism are drawn from, and claim to act on behalf of, populations that have themselves suffered extensive and often indiscriminate state repression (in French Algeria, the West Bank and Gaza, and

Chechnya). The question is what to make of this correlation. Why, in these particular contexts, have revolutionaries attacked certain categories of civilians as well as government forces? My own theory of categorical terrorism, outlined below, attempts to answer this question.

A final hypothesis worth considering is that terrorism is the result of extreme "social polarization" between groups. Such polarization is said to exist when such groups are relationally distant (i.e. they have little if any intimate contact), culturally distant (i.e. they differ in terms of language, religion, dress, and other "expressive" characteristics), functionally independent (i.e. they do not cooperate with or depend upon one another for their well-being), and extremely unequal in terms of wealth, status, and power (Senechal de la Roche 1996). "Enduring grievances" against, or "intractable offenses" by, socially distant groups allegedly provide the motive for organizing terrorist attacks against them. Thus, "terrorism is most likely in polarized conflicts where the grievance endures" (Senechal de la Roche, 1996: 120; see also Black 2004: 18). By contrast, "closer civilians such as those of the same or similar ethnicity are largely immune to terrorism, especially its deadlier forms. If closer collective conflicts lead to violence at all, they produce different forms with fewer civilian casualties, such as riots, assassinations, kidnappings, and guerrilla warfare" (Black 2004: 20).

This theory is also intuitively plausible. It is indeed difficult to imagine that two populations would engage in a violent conflict if they have extensive face-to-face contact, belong to the same ethnic group, speak the same language and worship the same gods, depend upon one another for their livelihoods, and are more or less equal in terms of wealth, status, and power. In fact, we would presumably not recognize two such populations as distinct "groups" at all. Furthermore, it is quite *easy* to imagine that members of a subordinate group would come to hate, and even view as inherently evil, members of a dominating group with whom they have little intimate contact and who belong to a different "race," speak a different language, practice a different religion, and are much wealthier and more powerful. (My own theory of categorical terrorism draws upon this insight.) Empirically, furthermore, there does indeed seem to be a huge "social distance" separating those revolutionaries who practice categorical terrorism (and those they claim to speak for), on the one hand, and their civilian targets, on the other. The conflicts in French Algeria, Palestine/Israel, and Chechnya were or are characterized by extreme polarization – in terms of wealth, status, and power – between the primarily ethnically self-defined antagonists.

Nonetheless, the social-polarization theory of terrorism is plagued by a number of ambiguities. To begin with, how could "enduring grievances" or "intractable offenses" arise between groups that are in fact "functionally independent," that is, groups which do not "cooperate with one another economically, politically, militarily, or otherwise" (Senechal de la Roche 1996: 111)? Indeed, would not functional independence actually *discourage* violence between groups by making it difficult for one group to plausibly blame the other for its grievances? If my own livelihood really does not depend in any way on some other group, why would I care if its members have more money than me or dress differently or do not recognize me on the street? *Extremely* socially distant groups typically know little about one another, so why would they fight one another?

Proponents of the social-polarization thesis are vague about the precise forms of social distance that encourage extreme hatred, moral repulsion, or at least callous indifference between groups – sentiments that would seem to be necessary for groups to support terrorist violence against civilians. They speak in very general and rather vague terms when describing the goals of revolutionary groups, and they say virtually nothing about the strategic goals of terrorist violence. Accordingly, it is difficult to determine from this literature precisely *why* revolutionary groups would indiscriminately attack civilians, be they "socially distant" or otherwise, instead of employing other means to attain their goals. Will just any type of "enduring grievances" lead to terrorism? According to Senechal de la Roche, "Invasions, military dictatorships, and other patterns of domination provide fertile conditions for terrorism" (1996: 119). But would not military invasions and military dictatorships encourage their opponents to adopt a strategy of conventional or guerrilla warfare against military forces? Why attack civilians in these contexts? "Terrorists typically demand a restoration of the past," claims Donald Black, "such as political independence, lost territory, or a customary way of life" (2004: 18). But, again, why attack civilians indiscriminately in pursuit of such goals? How do these goals require or encourage terrorism?

Finally, there have in fact been situations in which groups have massacred people who are seemingly "socially close" to them, even neighbors. Jan Gross (2001), for example, recounts how the Christian residents of the Polish town of Jedwabne brutally and indiscriminately killed their Jewish neighbors (or stood by silently) in July 1941 – 1,600 men, women, and children in all.[3] Previously, according to at least one (non-Jewish) resident, the Jews of Jedwabne were "on good terms with the Poles. Depending on each other. Everybody was on a first-name basis, Janek, Icek .... Life here was, I would say, somehow idyllic" (quoted in Gross 2001: 18). There seem to have been extensive economic relations between Jedwabne's Jewish and non-Jewish residents (most Jews were craftsmen and merchants), as well as considerable residential integration.

A theory of categorical terrorism

We can begin to move toward a better understanding of categorical terrorism by considering the precise categories of civilians which revolutionaries (sometimes) target for violence. How revolutionaries "socially construct" their enemies is something which the theories discussed above generally do not examine. Yet, clearly, revolutionaries do not indiscriminately attack just *any* civilians or non-combatants. Indeed, revolutionaries are also usually interested in winning the active support or allegiance of certain civilians. So which are the "bad" civilians whom they attack?

When they employ a strategy of categorical terrorism, revolutionaries generally threaten and attack what we might call "complicitous civilians."[4] Revolutionaries view these categories of civilians as complicitous insofar as they are believed to (1) routinely *benefit from* the actions of the government or state that the revolutionaries oppose, (2) *support* the government or state, and/or (3) have a substantial capacity to *influence* or to direct the government or state. Such complicitous civilians are akin to what Charles Tilly calls "polity members," that is, groups which "can routinely lay claim to the generation of action or yielding of resources by agents of the government" (Rule and Tilly 1975: 55).

The precise categories of civilians which revolutionaries view as complicitous depends in turn on how revolutionaries construe the extant political regime that they are trying to displace. Different types of complicitous civilians are generally associated with different regime types (see Table 13.4). Precisely how revolutionaries construe or socially construct political regimes, hence complicitous civilians, is itself a complex process, one which depends, among other things, on an organization's ideology and practical experience (as filtered through its ideology). One group might view the United States, for example, as a genuine democracy in which the general citizenry is complicit in government policies, whereas another group might view the U.S. as a "bourgeois democracy" in which only the bourgeoisie or wealthy business people are complicitous. To take another example, some Palestinians believe

Table 13.4 Targets of categorical terrorism: "complicitous civilians"

How do revolutionaries construe the extant political regime?	
Political regime (ideal types)	*Complicitous civilians* (i.e. the politically influential supporters and/or beneficiaries of the regime)
Autocracy	The cronies of the autocrat (usually not anonymous), the wealthy
Oligarchy or "bourgeois democracy"	The dominant economic class, business people, the wealthy
Single-party authoritarian regime	Party members
Ethnocracy	The dominant ethnic group
Settler regime	Settlers
Colonial or neocolonial ("puppet") regime	Expatriate and comprador bourgeoisie, the metropolitan bourgeoisie, the general citizenry of the metropolis
Democracy	The general citizenry

that Israeli Jewish settlers in the West Bank and Gaza are the complicitous civilians of a settler regime, understood in one sense, while other Palestinians believe that *all* Israeli Jews, including Jews living within Israel's pre-1967 borders, are the complicitous civilians of a settler regime, understood in a very different sense. In any event, one will not be able to understand why certain revolutionary groups target particular categories of civilians without grasping the revolutionaries' understanding of the political order that they confront and the complicitous civilians associated therewith.

But why indiscriminately attack or threaten complicitous civilians? To answer this question, we need to understand not only how revolutionaries socially construct specific civilians as enemies but also how they weigh the costs and benefits of violently attacking such civilians. What, then, are the potential strategic benefits of terrorist attacks against complicitous civilians? The main strategic objective – the primary incentive – of categorical terrorism is *to induce complicitous civilians to stop supporting, or to proactively demand changes in, certain government policies, or the government itself.* Categorical terrorism, in other words, mainly aims to apply such intense pressure to complicitous civilians that they will demand that "their" government change or abandon policies that the revolutionaries oppose. Research on terrorism suggests that there are several other strategic objectives behind indiscriminate attacks on complicitous civilians, including to:

- Provoke a violent overreaction by the government against the revolutionaries and their presumed supporters, ultimately benefiting the revolutionaries.
- Seize or recover territory from the government.
- Undermine efforts at peace or reconciliation between the government and competing oppositional groups, ultimately benefiting the revolutionaries.
- Attract, retain, and/or boost the morale of the revolutionaries and their supporters.
- Avenge specific acts for which complicitous civilians are held responsible.

The fact that a group or movement may have one or more of these strategic objectives or incentives does not automatically "cause" categorical terrorism. Whether such goals will actually induce revolutionaries to adopt a strategy of categorical terrorism depends on a number of other factors, including whether revolutionaries believe they actually have the capacity to wage an effective campaign of terrorism. More generally, the strategic choice of revolutionaries to employ categorical terrorism is much complicated by the fact that this strategy also has many potential costs as well as benefits. Research on terrorism suggests that there are several reasons why revolutionaries might reject a strategy of categorical terrorism:

- Complicitous civilians may be potential members or allies of the revolutionary movement.

- Non-violent appeals or protests may influence complicitous civilians more effectively than threats or violence.
- Terrorism may anger or repel the members or supporters of the revolutionary movement.
- Terrorism may harm or prevent alliances with actually or potentially sympathetic third parties.
- Terrorism may provoke state repression for which the revolutionaries will be blamed by their constituents.
- Terrorism may provoke state repression that will severely weaken or even destroy the revolutionary movement itself.

Because there are often very good reasons, in one and the same social context, to both employ *and* reject a strategy of terrorism, revolutionaries usually confront a number of "strategic dilemmas" (Jasper 2004: 7–10). There may be no simple solutions to these dilemmas, in part because revolutionaries may have very imperfect information about the political regime, complicitous civilians, or even their own presumed constituents and thus cannot easily predict future flows of interaction. Because these dilemmas are not always easily resolved, moreover, they do not clearly direct revolutionaries along a particular line of action. This may help account for the sheer unpredictability of some terrorist attacks as well as the seemly quixotic or self-defeating character of others.

One strategic dilemma, which Jasper labels "naughty or nice" (2004: 9), has to do with whether collective action is more effective when it involves friendly persuasion or coercion. For revolutionaries, one concern is whether complicitous civilians will be more effectively influenced by non-violent appeals or protests, on the one hand, or by violence and threats, on the other. Non-violent appeals are relatively cheap, but they may not work; and violence, even when efficiently executed, may backfire, inducing complicitous civilians, for example, not to pressure "their" government to change its ways but to redouble their support for it. The less familiar revolutionaries are with the cultural beliefs and assumptions of complicitous civilians (i.e. the greater the cultural distance between these groups), the more likely they are to strategically miscalculate.

Another strategic dilemma, which Jasper calls "reaching out or reaching in," concerns the "issue of whether to play to inside or outside audiences once they are defined" (2004: 10). As noted above, one reason why revolutionary groups sometimes employ terrorism is to attract, retain, and/or boost the morale of their members, but this may serve only to alienate potential allies. Heeding such allies, on the other hand, and rejecting terrorism may undermine the morale of members and risk losing the political initiative to more violent organizations (Bloom 2005: ch. 4). This dilemma is very evident among Palestinian groups. Terrorism against Israeli Jews has sometimes won the approval of many Palestinians (and other Arabs), but at the cost of alienating potential allies outside the Middle East.[5]

Revolutionaries' calculations about whether they should employ categorical terrorism as a strategy are not of course made in a vacuum, outside of
any social, political, or cultural context. A theory of categorical terrorism
needs to specify the key contextual factors that create incentives or disin-
centives for revolutionaries to engage in such terrorism. Sometimes these
factors pull in both directions, but sometimes they may convince revolutionaries that their strategic dilemmas may be more or less adequately
resolved by a consistent course of action.

Logically, I propose, the key factors in a theory of categorical terrorism
must be those that either *blur* or *brighten* the conceptual and moral distinctions between the political order that a revolutionary group seeks to
change, on the one hand, and the civilians who live under that political
order, on the other. Factors that *blur* this distinction encourage categorical
terrorism, insofar as the latter rests upon the revolutionaries' failure or
refusal to draw a moral or even conceptual distinction between a hated
political regime and "its" citizens, or some subset of them. Factors that
brighten this distinction discourage terrorism by dissociating civilians from
the targeted regime and its policies.

My theory proposes that three key contextual factors strongly influence
the decision of revolutionaries either to employ or not to employ categorical
terrorism (see Table 13.5). (I leave aside, for present purposes, consideration
of the variable *capacity* of revolutionary groups to carry out terrorist
attacks.) First, and most importantly, terrorism is encouraged when revolutionaries perceive that certain categories of civilians – complicitous civilians,
as I call them – benefit from, support, demand, or tolerate *extensive and*

Table 13.5 Key variables affecting revolutionaries' use of categorical terrorism

	(+)		(−)
1	Complicitous civilians support extensive, state violence/state, terrorism	vs.	State violence is limited and/or opposed by complicitous civilians
	(a) Blurred boundaries between the state and citizens	vs.	State autonomy from society
	(b) Blurred boundaries between the military/combatants and civilians/non-combatants	vs.	Military autonomy from society (and/or the political regime)
2	Complicitous civilians are numerous and relatively unprotected	vs.	Complicitous civilians are few and well protected
3	Weak or absent political alliances/ cooperation between revolutionaries and complicitous civilians (i.e., strong linguistic, religious, territorial segregation)	vs.	Significant political alliances/ cooperation between revolutionaries and complicitous civilians

indiscriminate state violence or state terrorism against themselves (the revolutionaries) and their presumed constituents. This perception is more or less strongly encouraged by the ideologies of revolutionary organizations, but also by institutional arrangements that (1) blur the boundaries between the government and these complicitous civilians (e.g. elections) and/or (2) blur the boundaries between the military and complicitous civilians (e.g. universal conscription). In other words, practices that tend to elide the distinction between state and citizen, or between combatant and non-combatant, also tend to elide the willingness or even capacity of revolutionaries (and others) to make moral and political distinctions between these categories.

I noted earlier that revolutionary groups that have employed a strategy of categorical terrorism are usually drawn from, and claim to act on behalf of, populations that have suffered extensive and often indiscriminate state repression (in French Algeria, the West Bank and Gaza, and Chechnya). In each of these cases, moreover, there was or is a perception by the revolutionaries of *substantial civilian support* for (or at least passive toleration of) that repression (by European settlers, Israelis, and Russians, respectively). Indeed, the governments which have carried out the repression in these cases had or have a substantial measure of democratic legitimacy among complicitous civilians. Democratic rights and institutions in general, in fact, are often effective at creating an impression, especially at a distance, of substantial solidarity between citizens and "their" states. When extensive and indiscriminate state violence is seen to be supported by civilians and/or directed by democratically elected governments, it is hardly surprising (other things being equal) that revolutionaries would tend to view both repressive states *and* the civilians who seem to stand behind them as legitimate targets of counter-violence, typically justified as "self-defense." Nor is it surprising that *retribution* for such violence would be directed at civilians as well as the state's armed forces. And it would also be reasonable under these circumstances for revolutionaries to conclude that attacking civilians might cause the latter to put substantial pressure on "their" states to change their ways. Extensive state ("wholesale") terrorism begets extensive oppositional ("retail") terrorism, in other words, *only when there exists a citizenry with significant democratic rights.* The latter would appear to be a necessary precondition for categorical terrorism (see Pape 2005 and Goodwin 2006).

A second contextual factor that encourages categorical terrorism, other things being equal, is simply a large and relatively unprotected population of complicitous civilians. By contrast, categorical terrorism is discouraged when complicitous civilians are few and far between and/or well protected (usually because of their wealth and/or political status). Hence, categorical terrorism is much more likely when an entire ethnic group or nationality is viewed by revolutionaries as complicitous as compared, for example, to a small social class or the cronies of an autonomous, "above class" dictator.

And, in fact, all major cases of categorical terrorism seem to have entailed the use of violence and threats against a large ethnic or national group.

This factor helps to explain why the Sandinistas (FSLN) in Nicaragua carried out virtually no terrorism during their armed conflict with the personalistic Somoza dictatorship, an otherwise bloody insurgency during which some thirty thousand people were killed (see, e.g. Booth 1985). Complicitous civilians in this political context consisted only of a tiny number of Somoza cronies and a loyal elite opposition, which was drawn mainly from Nicaragua's small bourgeoisie. Virtually all other civilians in Nicaragua, from the lowliest peasant to Somoza's bourgeois opponents, were viewed by the Sandinistas as potential allies, and indeed many would become such (Everingham 1996).

The third main contextual factor that encourages terrorism is a particular *type* of "social distance," namely, the weakness or absence of political alliances between revolutionaries and their presumed constituents, on the one hand, and complicitous civilians, on the other. In fact, where one finds this type of *political* distance as well as mass-supported state violence, ideologies and/or cultural idioms that depict complicitous civilians as inherently evil are especially likely to resonate among the victims of that violence. Simply put, these victims will not have experienced any positive political interactions with complicitous civilians to weigh against the palpable evil that the latter are seen to countenance. There has in fact been a huge political distance – in this particular sense – separating those revolutionaries who practice categorical terrorism (and those they claim to speak for), on the one hand, and their civilian targets, on the other.

By contrast, categorical terrorism is *discouraged* when there *are* significant political alliances or forms of cooperation between revolutionaries and complicitous civilians (for a similar argument about ethnic rioting, see Varshney 2002). When revolutionary groups and their constituents, that is, have a history of collaborating politically with complicitous civilians, they are not likely to classify as enemies complicitous civilians as such. To attack such civilians would jeopardize politically valuable alliances and the resources and legitimacy attached thereto.

I believe that this last factor is extremely important for understanding why the ANC in South Africa rejected a strategy of categorical terrorism. As I noted earlier, the ANC eschewed this strategy even though there was very extensive state violence against the opponents of the apartheid regime. This violence, moreover, was palpably supported (or tolerated) by large segments of the white, especially Afrikaner, population. The Nationalist Party governments that unleashed the security forces against the apartheid state's enemies were elected by the white population. So why did the ANC adhere to an ideology of "multiracialism" and refuse to view whites as such as enemies? The answer lies, I believe, in the ANC's long history of collaborating with white South Africans, especially of British background – as well as with Indian and "colored" South Africans – in the anti-apartheid struggle. Perhaps especially important in this respect was the ANC's long collaboration with whites in the South African Communist Party. Tellingly, an important, long-time leader of MK, the ANC's armed wing, was Joe Slovo, a white communist. (Try to imagine an Israeli Jew leading Hamas's armed wing, or an American directing Al Qaeda.) For the ANC to have indiscriminately attacked South African whites would have soured this strategic relationship, which, among other things, was essential for securing substantial Soviet aid for the ANC. In sum, given the long-standing multiracial – including international – support for the anti-apartheid movement, a strategy of categorical terrorism against complicitous (white) civilians made little strategic sense.

In sum, my theory of categorical terrorism predicts – and seems to ret-rodict accurately – that when revolutionaries indiscriminately attack civilians, they generally attack those large and unprotected categories of civilians or non-combatants, and only those categories, which are perceived as benefiting from, supporting and/or having a substantial capacity to influence states that are themselves seen to employ extensive, indiscriminate violence against revolutionaries and their constituents. However, if significant numbers of these "complicitous civilians" are perceived by revolutionaries as potential supporters (or as capable of being influenced by nonviolent appeals or protests), then they will not be attacked. Whether specific categories of civilians will be perceived as potential allies by revolutionaries depends mainly upon the prior history of political interaction and cooperation between these civilians and the revolutionaries. Categorical terrorism is most likely where there has been little such interaction or cooperation, resulting in weak political alliances between the revolutionaries and complicitous civilians – for example, where the revolutionaries and complicitous civilians speak different languages, practice different religions, claim the same homeland, and/or are physically highly segregated or even live in different national societies.

This theory can be represented by means of a conceptual space, akin to a two-by-two table, which is defined by two variables (see Figure 13.1). The first variable is a measure of perceived civilian support for (and/or toleration of) extensive and indiscriminate state violence or state terrorism against revolutionaries and their constituents. This variable can be said to be "extensive" if state violence is great *and* revolutionaries believe that large numbers of civilians support or tolerate it; this variable would be measured as "limited," on the other hand, if state violence itself is limited *or* if revolutionaries believe that relatively few civilians support it, however extensive or limited it may be. The second variable is the strength of the cross-cutting political alliances that connect (or fail to connect) revolutionaries and their constituents, on the one hand, and complicitous civilians, on the other. Categorical terrorism occurs, to repeat, when and where revolutionaries perceive extensive civilian support for extensive state violence *and* cross-cutting political ties between the revolutionaries and complicitous civilians

		Cross-cutting political alliances/cooperation between revolutionaries and complicitous civilians	
		Weak	**Strong**
Perceived civilian support for extensive state violence/terrorism	**Extensive**	French Algeria Israel/Palestine Sri Lanka Chechnya *categorical terrorism* Northern Ireland (1970–80s)	South Africa under apartheid Basque country
	Limited	El Salvador (1980s)	Nicaragua (1970s)

Figure 13.1 A theory of categorical terrorism.

are weak (i.e. when revolutionary groups fall into the upper-left region of the conceptual space in Figure 13.1). Otherwise, revolutionaries will adopt strategies of conventional and/or guerrilla warfare and/or targeted assassination.

Conclusion: Al Qaeda and 9/11

By way of conclusion, let me turn to the question of whether the theory outlined here explains why Al Qaeda and affiliated Islamist groups have carried out extensive terrorism, including the attacks of September 11, 2001. I believe that it does. To be sure, Al Qaeda and its affiliates do differ from other revolutionary organizations that have practiced categorical terrorism insofar as they represent a genuinely *transnational* revolutionary movement. That is to say, Al Qaeda not only has followers in more than one national society, which is by no means unusual among revolutionary groups, but it also opposes and seeks to overthrow not just one, but several political orders (Gunaratna 2002).

Al Qaeda has a pan-Islamic revolutionary project, viewing itself as the vanguard and defender of the transnational *umma* or Muslim community. Unfortunately, in Al Qaeda's view, this multi-ethnic, transnational community is currently balkanized and violently oppressed by "apostate" secular and "hypocritical" pseudo-Islamic regimes, from Morocco to Mindanao, as well as by the "Zionist entity" in Palestine. And standing behind these regimes – and now occupying Iraq – is the powerful U.S. government. This perception that the United States is the ultimate power which is propping up repressive, un-Islamic regimes in the Muslim world is the fundamental source of Al Qaeda's conflict with the U.S. Al Qaeda believes that until the U.S. government – the "far enemy" – can be compelled to end its support for these regimes – the "near enemy" – and withdraw its troops from Muslim countries, local struggles against these regimes cannot succeed (Anonymous 2002; Doran 2001).

But why kill ordinary Americans in addition to U.S. armed forces? Why would Al Qaeda target the World Trade Center, for example, in addition to U.S. military installations? Shortly after 9/11, Osama Bin Laden described the rationale for the attacks in an interview that first appeared in the Pakistani newspaper *Ausaf* on November 7, 2001:

> The United States and their allies are killing us in Palestine, Chechnya, Kashmir, Palestine, and Iraq. That's why Muslims have the right to carry out revenge attacks on the U.S .... The American people should remember that they pay taxes to their government and that they voted for their president. Their government makes weapons and provides them to Israel, which they use to kill Palestinian Muslims. Given that the American Congress is a committee that represents the people, the fact that it agrees with the actions of the American government proves that America in its entirety is responsible for the atrocities that it is committing against Muslims. I demand the American people to take note of their government's policy against Muslims. They described their government's policy against Vietnam as wrong. They should now take the same stand that they did previously. The onus is on Americans to prevent Muslims from being killed at the hands of their government.
>
> (quoted in Lawrence 2005: 140–1)[6]

Bin Laden seems to be saying here that because the United States is, in his view, a genuine democracy, ordinary citizens are responsible for the violent actions of "their" government (and, indirectly, of governments supported by the United States) in Muslim countries (see Wiktorowicz and Kaltner 2003: 88–9). Al Qaeda views ordinary American citizens, in other words, as complicitous civilians – morally culpable for the U.S.-sponsored "massacres" of Muslims in a number of countries. This idea was also expressed by Mohammad Sidique Khan, one of the four suicide bombers who killed more than 50 people in London on July 7, 2005. In a videotape broadcast on Al-Jazeera television on September 1, 2005, Khan said, "Your democratically elected governments continuously perpetuate atrocities against my people all over the world. And your support of them makes you directly responsible, just as I am directly responsible for protecting and avenging my Muslim brothers and sisters" (BBC News 2005).

To be sure, Al Qaeda's precise strategic goal in attacking U.S. citizens remains unclear: Was 9/11 a reprisal for massacres carried out or supported by the United States? Was 9/11 meant to "wake up" Americans to what their government was doing in the Islamic world, in the hope that they would force it to change its policies? Or was the goal perhaps to provoke a violent overreaction by the U.S. government, luring it into Afghanistan, where it would become bogged down (like the Soviet Union before it) in an unwinnable war? What is certain, however, is Al Qaeda's belief that it is logical and indeed just to attack ordinary Americans in order to bring about change in "their" government's policies.

As in other cases in which revolutionaries have turned to a strategy of terrorism, Al Qaeda perceives that the state violence and oppression which it suffers and opposes has widespread civilian support in the United States. At the same time, Al Qaeda and its Islamist sympathizers obviously do not have the type of history of political collaboration with American citizens which might lead them to reject a strategy of categorical terrorism; language, religion, and geography have created a formidable chasm between the two. The confluence of these factors, as elsewhere, has strongly encouraged, and continues to encourage, Al Qaeda's terrorist strategy.[7]

In sum, I have argued that revolutionaries do not employ terrorism simply because they are weak or desperate, confront extensive state terrorism, or are socially distant from others. These monocausal arguments are inadequate. I have argued instead that revolutionaries do indeed employ terrorism against civilians whom they view as complicit in extensive state violence, but only when and where revolutionaries do not have political alliances or a history of cooperation with some segment of that civilian population. Cross-cutting ties of this sort are unlikely where revolutionaries and complicitous civilians practice different religions, speak different languages, claim the same homeland, and/or live in different areas or even countries.

Notes

1 Some authors seem to assume that the tactic of suicide bombing is inherently terrorist in nature (e.g. Bloom 2005; Pape 2005). This is incorrect. Suicide bombings may either be part of a strategy of conventional or guerrilla warfare (if they are aimed at military and/or political targets) or a strategy of terrorism (if aimed at ordinary civilians or non-combatants) (Goodwin 2006).
2 A few indiscriminate bombings were carried out by ANC cadres during the mid-1980s, contrary to ANC guidelines, but these caused relatively few casualties and were publicly denounced by the ANC leadership. There were also many incidents of violence against cadres in ANC camps outside of South Africa, including the killing of dissidents and presumed dissidents. But these were targeted killings, not the kind of indiscriminate violence that I wish to explain in this chapter.
3 Of course, I do not mean to claim that this massacre is an example of categorical terrorism. It was not perpetrated by an oppositional political group; on the contrary, it was encouraged by the governing Nazi occupation forces in Poland. Accordingly, the Jedwabne massacre is not a case of terrorism as I am using the term, although it clearly has affinities, like other state-sanctioned atrocities, with terrorism.
4 My thanks to Steven Lukes for suggesting this term.

5 See the various polls conducted since 1993 by the Palestinian Center for Political and Survey Research (www.pcpsr.org/index.html).
6 Prior to 9/11, in a December 1998 interview that appeared on Al-Jazeera television, Bin Laden remarked, "Every American is our enemy, whether he fights directly or whether he pays taxes. Perhaps you have heard the recent news that three-quarters of the American people support Clinton in attacking Iraq. This is a people whose votes are won when innocents die, whose leader commits adultery and great sins and then sees his popularity rise – a vile people who have never understood the meaning of values" (quoted in Lawrence 2005: 70).
7 The group, known as Al Qaeda in Iraq, and other Sunni Islamist groups have targeted U.S. and allied forces in Iraq, but they have also indiscriminately attacked Shi'a (and some Kurdish) Iraqis, whom they view as supporters and beneficiaries of – hence, complicit in – the U.S. occupation. Many if not most members of Al Qaeda in Iraq and similar groups seem to be non-Iraqis and/or sectarian Sunnis who view Shi'a Muslims as apostates; they certainly have no history of political cooperation with Shi'ites (Cordesman 2005). Hence, recent terrorism in Iraq accords with my theory of categorical terrorism.

14 The future of revolution

Imitation or innovation?

Krishan Kumar

"The West has long since found itself unable to think the category of the 'great collective project' in terms of social revolution and social transformation .... [A] fundamental structural and ideological limit on our Utopian imagination is surely demonstrated by this lack of alternatives."

Fredric Jameson (2002: 211–12)

"Before 1989 it was fashionable to say that revolution was a thing of the past. I incline to the view even now that revolutions are highly improbable in developed industrial societies with established systems of liberal democracy .... There are less than two dozen countries in the world which meet this criterion. In other words, for the great majority of the 169 states in the world, the conditions under which revolutions can occur still prevail."

Fred Halliday (1991: 151)

"There seems to be almost nothing completely new in writings on revolution!"

John Foran (1993a: 9)

The power of the past

"The social revolution of the nineteenth century," said Marx (Marx and Engels 1975–2005: XI, 106), "cannot draw its poetry from the past, but only from the future." This urging has largely been in vain. Nineteenth- and twentieth-century revolutions repeatedly and unvaryingly looked backwards. Their principal theorists and practitioners were steeped in the history of revolutions, from what was retrospectively baptized as "the English revolution" of the seventeenth century, through the American Revolution (again guardedly so-called by contemporaries) of the eighteenth century, to the great sequence of French revolutions that began in 1789 and continued in 1830, 1848, and 1871. No one was more aware of this than the Bolshevik leaders, struggle as they might to go beyond the inheritance of these revolutions. "A Frenchman has nothing to renounce in the Russian Revolution," wrote Lenin to a French comrade in 1920, "which in its method and procedures merely recommences the French Revolution" (quoted in Kumar

1971: 3). Trotsky, in exile, wrote his great *History of the Russian Revolution* (1929–1930) with the fullest awareness of where that revolution stood in the sequence of past European revolutions and their particular histories – down to the melancholy description of "the Soviet Thermidor."

Even the supposed innovations of the twentieth century introduced nothing truly original. The newer thing was the non-urban peasant revolution that took place in Mexico, China, Vietnam, Cuba, and other Third World countries (Wolf 1971; Dunn 1989a).[1] Mao, Giap, Castro, and Guevara were certainly aware of the pitfalls of imitating past European revolutions, most notably in the avoidance of dependence on the city and the urban classes; "the city," observed Castro, "is the graveyard of revolutions and revolutionaries" (quoted in Debray 1968: 67). But not only was the model of peasant revolution a revamping of the traditional form of "social banditry" that was common in peasant societies (Hobsbawm 1959). The leaders of these revolutions were for the most part Western-educated intellectuals who developed most of their ideas in dialogue with Western theorists, dead or alive, and whose goals were shaped by those of earlier revolutions. What after all is Marxism, the working ideology of most of those Third World revolutions, but a Western invention and export? When Fidel Castro defended himself at his trial for his part in the 1953 raid on the Moncada barracks, he ransacked the Western revolutionary tradition, going back to the French Revolution, in defense of his actions (Castro 1967: 95–6).

"1789 and 1917 are still historic dates but they are no longer historic examples." Thus, in the spirit of Marx, Camus in 1946, contemplating the future of revolution amidst the ruins of Europe (quoted in Kumar 1971: 303). So again we are warned of the dead hand of the past. But what do we have apart from the past? What are the elements of the future revolution, and where do they come from? In what way would we still be talking and thinking of revolution if what is conceived is so novel that we cannot discern any continuity with the past? No one, it is true, has any proprietary right to revolution, as the car manufacturers who every year announce a new revolutionary design ("the Volvo revolution," etc.) regularly remind us. But there have, it seems, to be some real elements of persistence if we are to feel that we are dealing with the same, or a similar, phenomenon. With the advances in biotechnology and computer science anyone with a little imagination can dream up transformations in human life with mind-blowing qualities – the immortal "human robot" of Robin Williams's *Million Year Man*, for instance, or Donna Haraway's disembodied cyborgs meeting and merging on the Internet. No doubt it might be plausible to call these revolutions, if they were to come about on a sufficiently large scale. But might it not be better to call them something else altogether – why be shackled with a word that has a particular history, and a meaning or meanings given by that history?

To some extent we have been even here before. Convinced that earlier attempts to achieve freedom through revolution had been hampered by insufficient attention to the largely unconscious mechanisms of repression and subordination, a whole tradition of thinking from the Frankfurt School to Fanon attempted a reconceptualization of revolution that would attend as much to the psychological and cultural residues of domination as to its political and social aspects (Kumar 2001c: 183–90). Had a revolution in the name of Reich, Marcuse, or Fanon – not to mention Dali or the Dadaists – actually been carried out, the result would certainly have been something very different from 1789 or 1917 (perhaps closer to the revolution dreamed of by the Marquis de Sade). May '68 in Paris of course attempted something of this sort (and there were some faint echoes in the revolutions of 1989). The Situationist slogans and writings of this time give us an exhilarating sense of what such a revolution might look like. But the attempt was too short-lived, and perhaps not even sufficiently seriously intended, to give us a workable model of such a revolution (see Kumar 1988: 190–9; Ross 2002).

Moreover, even the '68-ers and the theorists who inspired them were conscious of working within a tradition. Reich wrote as a critical disciple of Freud, and Freud himself implicitly or explicitly engaged in a critical dialogue with the rationalism and optimism of the Enlightenment. Marcuse and Fromm looked back to Hegel and the young Marx for their critiques of the received ideas of revolution. The heritage of the "utopian socialists" – Fourier especially – and of nineteenth-century utopianism generally was important to the '68-ers, as was the anarchism of Proudhon and Kropotkin, and the inspiration of the commune of 1871 and the soviets of 1917. Strands of the revolutionary tradition, many of them buried or long ignored, were disinterred and reworked into new concepts of revolution. The past was not renounced; it was selectively retrieved.[2]

There is a tradition of revolution, and the starting point for thinking about the future of revolution must be to ask what that tradition is and what has become of it. The future cannot be wholly determined by the past, else we would never have moved out of the Stone Age. But the future is, by definition, unknown and unknowable. The past is all we can know. What does the past tell us about revolution, and its prospects today? What were the conditions that gave rise to revolution, and how likely are they to recur in current circumstances? What are the varieties of revolution, and to what extent do they point to new forms that, with all their differences, remain recognizably members of the same species? Or should we conclude that, to use the distinction of Pierre Nora (1996), revolution is no longer "memory" – a living presence and possibility in the minds and lives of communities – but merely "history" – an object to be dissected and discussed by scholars?

The family history of revolution

Without engaging directly or in detail with the question of definition – best left, as Weber said, to the end of a study rather than its beginning – it is possible to say that we can discern a group of revolutions which have the necessary "family resemblances" that are all we can hope for with social and political phenomena. These include the so-called "great revolutions" of England, America, France, Russia, and China, as well as a host of lesser ones between the seventeenth and twentieth centuries. There is a lineal or genealogical connection between them, in the sense that they acknowledge their membership in the family by showing devotion to its memory and by keeping a well-thumbed family album. They are also aware that, as in all families, there are some problematic members, members who slur the reputation of the family by their dubious or deviant character. There is no question of disowning these members, and in any case we can even learn from their bad or misguided actions.

Knowing the family history, we can seek to avoid its mistakes and add lustre to its name by fresh deeds of heroism. The communards of the Paris Commune of 1871 sought to throw off the Jacobin heritage with its excessive centralization and bureaucratization. The communists in 1917 Russia wished to go beyond the bourgeois revolution of the nineteenth century by adding the goal of economic and social emancipation to that of political and legal equality. The Maoists and the student radicals of the 1960s wished to add cultural and psychological liberation to the more traditional goals of political and social liberation. With a somewhat different reading of the family history, the revolutionaries of 1989 sought to avoid the somewhat unruly and disorderly examples of the twentieth century and return to the more staid and respectable principles of the older generations, the people who made the revolutions of 1688, 1776, and, at least in its earlier phases, 1789.

Family knowledge can be disabling as well as enlightening. Knowing the plot of earlier revolutions, as Hannah Arendt (1963: 51) says, revolutionaries often try to abridge it, or to avoid the dénouement of the final act.[3] This can lead to desperate efforts to escape what, through the regularity of its occurrence, seems almost foredoomed, the implacable logic of the revolutionary process. Trotsky spoke of the liberals of the 1848 revolutions as being "shabbily wise with the experience of the French bourgeoisie" of 1789 (quoted Kumar 1971: 4). They knew that there would be – to use Crane Brinton's (1965) well-known terms – "the rule of the moderates," "the rise of the radicals," "the Terror," "the Thermidorean reaction," the military dictatorship. They thought their understanding of the "natural" course of revolution would help them forestall its more unpleasant stages. This knowledge cost them dear. They opposed all "leftward" movements of the revolution, fearing that these would lead inevitably to the Jacobin dictatorship and the Terror. In France, the workers were brutally suppressed in the "June Days" and the national workshops disbanded. Marx, in *The Eighteenth Brumaire*, showed the irony of this understanding of revolution. In protecting themselves against their rivals on the left, the liberals delivered themselves into the hands of Louis Bonaparte, so ending up with the dictatorship it had been their main aim to avoid.

If the revolutions of the seventeenth to the twentieth centuries are linked by a continuity of ideas and influences, they are also linked by a rough similarity of the conditions that gave rise to them and allowed for their success. Here two thinkers, Plato and Tocqueville, supply the key insights. Tocqueville tells us that revolutions are not the expression of absolute but of relative deprivation. Revolutions tend to occur when people, experiencing or expecting betterment, find their hopes and expectations disappointed (reforming monarchs therefore being the most subversive of agents) (Tocqueville 1873: 322–3). This also explains why the most revolutionary classes tend not to be those at the very bottom of society – who ought in justice to be the most eager – but middling groups who have, or at least feel that they have, the most to lose (hence the regular appearance of the "middling peasant" in twentieth-century revolutions as among the most militant of revolutionaries) (Wolf 1971; but see also Wickham-Crowley 1992).

Tocqueville's generalization, derived from the experience of the French Revolution, applies quite well to most of the revolutions we have been considering. But it needs to be complemented by another insight, Plato's observation that revolutions break out only when there is disunity within the ruling class. So long, Plato insists, as that class is united it will, however small, be able to resist popular threats to its rule (Plato 1941: 262). This generalization, too, stands up very well in the face of the evidence – better perhaps even than Tocqueville's, or at least with greater consequence (Kumar 1971: 40–70). It is difficult to think of a single example of successful revolution where what we might call the "opportunity" – the "space" – for revolution was not offered by the struggles for power between warring factions of the ruling class or ruling elites. All revolutions, in this sense, have the character of *frondes*, at least in their crucial initial stages (what happens afterwards has a lot to do with the "logic" or "natural history" of revolution). We should remember, too, that this breaking of the unified power of the ruling stratum can sometimes come from outside: as in the American State Department's antipathy, and active opposition, to the Batista regime in the case of Cuba, or Gorbachev's sympathetic "nod" to the opposition within the ruling communist parties of most of the East European states (Kumar 2001a: 43–6, 268–73).[4]

It is true, of course, that the divided ruling class is easier to see in the French and Russian revolutions than it is, say, in the case of China, whose revolution can be said to have stretched gigantically from 1911 to 1949. In general Third World revolutions show a number of distorting or deviant factors, accounted for usually by the fact they occur within imperial structures, formal or informal (many though not all of the features of Third World revolutions can be observed in the case of the eighteenth-century American Revolution, the first of the anti-colonial revolutions). The conditions that bring them about are heavily influenced by forces and agents outside the societies in which they occur.[5] But it is not too difficult in most cases to see, and to show, the operation of the principles advanced by Tocqueville and

Plato (including, for instance, the role of war in destabilizing regimes, as true for eighteenth-century France as for twentieth-century Russia, China, Vietnam, and a host of other examples).

It is wrong to think that Third World revolutions are "international," and therefore very different, from earlier "national" Western revolutions. All revolutions, from the English seventeenth-century revolution to the 1989 revolutions in Eastern Europe, can be thought of as "international civil wars," to use Sigmund Neumann's term (Neumann 1949; see also Halliday 1999). In every case, in their causes, course, and consequences, they were affected by the play of international forces, whether through ideological or military competition, covert or open support to rival parties, or direct military intervention by foreign powers. It is an unfortunate trait of many of the leading theories of revolution, including that of Marx's, that they put such exclusive emphasis on the antagonistic forces internal to national societies (though later Marxists did much to rectify the narrowness of this approach).

Revolution in a postmodern world

A tradition can enable and empower as much as it, necessarily, limits and constrains. The tradition, or ideology, of revolutionism that began in seventeenth-century Europe reached out to the whole world in the wake of the American and French revolutions, encouraging and educating a host of movements across the globe. The impact was evident as late as 1989: the Chinese students who constructed the "Goddess of Democracy" in Tiananmen Square in 1989 paid explicit homage to the French Revolution of 1789, as did several of the participants in the 1989 revolutions in Eastern Europe (Tu 1992: 282; Hobsbawm 1990: xi). Mindful of the force of Chou En-Lai's celebrated (if perhaps apocryphal) response to a question about the consequences of the French Revolution, that it was "too early to tell," we should not be surprised if the example of that revolution, or any other from the past, is invoked yet again on some future occasion.

Nevertheless, even in the commentaries on the 1989 revolutions there were numerous statements to the effect that these were the "last" revolutions, that perhaps they were not even revolutions, and that in any case they pointed to the exhaustion of the revolutionary tradition, at least in the West. Some even called them "postmodern" revolutions, by which they meant a variety of things but which collectively amounted to the view that, while we might still call them revolutions, they were not revolutions as we had customarily understood that term (Kumar 2001a, 2001b). They had scrambled the revolutionary inheritance, mixing past, present, and future in novel yet incoherent ways. Given that many of the participants themselves seemed uncomfortable in their roles as revolutionaries, the 1989 revolutions did not seem to offer themselves as models for the future in any real sense. On the contrary, it seemed as if the inhabitants of the region hoped to bury revolution once and for all, blaming on it many of their past woes. Revolution, to quote the title of a famous collection of reflections by disillusioned Western communists in the 1940s, was "the god that had failed."

The condition of the world as expressed in theories of postmodernity would certainly be one starting point for thinking about the future of revolution, at least in Western societies. Among other things, it suggests, at least at the level of everyday life, a degree of fragmentation and segregation that militates against collective action of the kind that made revolutions in the past. It is not so much the retreat from the world of work, or the decline of occupational or trade union solidarities, that mark the change here. The workplace was the site of many bitter struggles in the past but few of them had to do with, or caused, revolution. Trade union consciousness, as Lenin rightly pointed out, does not equal revolutionary consciousness. The sphere of consumption can be as much the arena of conflict as the sphere of production – as pre-industrial bread riots make amply clear.

What is more important in recent times is the relentless drive towards the privatization of everyday life, a direction in which every development in technology – from the computer-based "electronic cottage" to iPods – seems to propel us. Life becomes life increasingly lived in and for the home or, at least, in highly privatized places (Kumar 1997). Public spaces are evacuated, whether of the more traditional kind based on the square or the piazza, or of the kind associated with the spheres of sociability – pubs, clubs, cafés, theatres, opera houses (vital in the case of many revolutions, including several in East–Central Europe in 1989). In the new towns and "exurbs" where many people now live – the urban strips strung out along major routes of communication – the public spaces do not even exist in a physical sense; they are airbrushed out of the architect's plan. Why provide central places in the cities for people to shop or to socialize when a custom-built mall, replete with shops, restaurants, cinemas, and even a concert hall, is a 30-minute drive away down a freeway? Leszek Kolakowski once spoke of the difficulties for modern revolutionaries of storming "the palace of alienation." Is it any easier to storm the palaces of consumption? And what would be gained in doing so?[6]

Postmodern theory points to fragmentation of another kind: that brought about by the retreat from the centralized structures of the nation-state. Both globalizing and localizing forces have united to disengage effort and action from the centralized state ("think globally, act locally"). The operations of multinational capital converge with the stress on identity politics, environmentalism, and "heritage" to direct action either at the level of supranational institutions – the European Union, the World Bank, human rights organizations – or at the level of the locality. In neither case is it easy to describe what kind of model of revolution would be adequate to the situation. "World revolution" *à la* Trotsky is certainly one candidate, but that remains as much of a fantasy now as it did in the time of the Fourth International. Hardt and Negri (2000; 2004) in various works have offered a somewhat similar model, based not so much on an international working class as on all the dispossessed and rejected cast adrift by the forces of the global "empire." This too seems to be more a metaphoric or symbolic gesture than any realistically-based hope.[7] At the other end anarchism and utopianism, with their tradition of the small-scale, experimental, radical community – New Harmony, Navahoo, Twin Oaks – offer somewhat more reliable models. But, despite the expressed aims of many of their founders and members, it was never clear how such small-scale communities formed, as it were, in the interstices of larger ones, were ever going to be able to challenge the power of their more formidable neighbors. Education by example was an appealing strategy, and it had some significant victories, not least in the attitudes towards women and in the upbringing of children. But nowhere did it usher in the New World dreamt of by its advocates (Kumar 1987: 69–98; 1991: 64–85). Nor, despite the fervent hopes placed on them by some, did the radically decentralized units – the *sociétés populaires*, clubs, communes, *soviets, räte* – thrown up by a succession of revolutions from 1789 to 1968.[8]

The changes noted in Western societies are of course occurring, in varying degrees, all over the world. What they seem to have brought forth is not so much a new model of revolution as the revival or re-invention of various movements of resistance at a relatively local or regional level. With, say, the Zapatistas of Chiapas, we are on fairly familiar territory, though the skillful use of the Internet does add an intriguing new ingredient (though perhaps more in scale than substance: the pamphleteers, pornographers, lampoonists, and cartoonists that played their part – according to Robert Darnton (1982) – in undermining the ancien régime of eighteenth-century France seem to have been pretty effective in much the same way). Locally based resistance leaders, with a relatively "safe haven" of peasant villages, have led peasant rebellions throughout the ages, often for long stretches of time, as with the Pugachev rebellion in eighteenth-century Russia or the Taiping rebellion in nineteenth-century China. There does not really seem anything new in the Chiapas case, except perhaps the unusual degree of world attention that it has been able attract, and which gives it some undoubted leverage in its engagement with the Mexican government.[9]

Elsewhere, again fairly plausibly related to the changes that go under the heading of "globalization," we have seen the rise or renewal of armed ethnic risings among a number of groups: Basques, Chechens, Tamils, Sikhs, Timorese, Kurds, and a host of ethnic groups in Africa. Their goals are mostly fairly clear: independence or autonomy, preferably in their own state. Whether it is helpful to attach the label "revolution" to these struggles is a moot point.[10] We are prepared to call the forcible American secession from the British state a revolution (the "American Revolution"); and certainly if these newer ethnic movements achieve their ends this would point to what could be major transformations in the lives of these groups. But what they clearly do not offer is a new model of revolution. Their goals and tactics are similar to a host of other "national liberation" struggles that have occurred in the past two centuries.

Is that also true of the most spectacular of the recent revivals, that of the great religious movements among Muslims, Hindus, Christians, and Buddhists? Several of these movements have taken the form of armed uprisings. In some cases, as most notably in Iran in 1979, they have achieved their goal of creating a new state based on religious principles.[11] Something similar was attempted by the Taliban in Afghanistan. A transformation so complete – insofar as any major social change can be complete – surely deserves the name of revolution (cf. Kampwirth 2003: 227–8, 239–40). If the Islamists in Algeria had succeeded in their armed struggle (one that followed the stealing of their electoral victory), might we not now be talking of a second Algerian revolution?

The concept of "religious revolution" has always been problematic. For one thing the goal – unlike the case with ethnic or national conflicts – is often unclear. Is it some form of religiously based national liberation, in which case the Iranian Revolution shows some strong parallels with the "revolution of the saints" (Walzer 1968) of seventeenth-century England (and perhaps sixteenth-century Holland)? Or is the victory in one country or society merely to be the beginning of a worldwide revolution that aims to regenerate the world according to the principles of the true religion? In this case the religious revolution would be more akin to the millenarian movements that frequently convulsed medieval Europe, such as that of the Taborites of Bohemia or the Anabaptists of Münster. This certainly seems to be the character – if not the ideology – of some of the Islamic revolutionary movements that are currently attracting so much of the world's attention.

There is a further problem with the concept of the religious revolution. The modern concept of revolution, as it emerged during the course of the French Revolution, was definitively linked to a secular project. It meant the victory of science and reason over superstition. It proclaimed the goals, on earth and in our time, of liberty, equality, and fraternity. It might, as in the case of the "worker-priest" movement and the "liberation theology" of Latin America, have support from religious thought and religious officials. It might have its religious martyrs, as with the murdered Catholic Archbishop Oscar Romero of San Salvador. It might even, as with some socialists in nineteenth-century Europe, conceive of the revolution in terms akin to religion. But it remained a secular idea with secular goals.

To speak of a religious revolution therefore always runs the risk of confusing a number of things that are perhaps better kept separate. It may, for purposes of analysis, sometimes be useful to compare revolutions with religions, and revolutionary transformation with religious transformation. The "revolutionary personality," as Bruce Mazlish has shown, is a type that fits a Luther as much as a Lenin.[12] But ultimately the ends of religions and religious movements are different from those of revolutions and revolutionary movements. However much, therefore, the Iranian Revolution has changed Iranian society, it remains unclear ("it is too early to say") how much it will, in the end, deserve the designation revolution.[13]

Has revolution a future?

The conditions, and to some extent the language, that made the classic revolutions of the seventeenth to the twentieth centuries both conceivable and possible have been changing. The major objective fact is the growing interconnectedness of the world, or globalization. Revolutions have always had global aspirations – the French and Russian revolutions unmistakably and uncompromisingly so – and were in most cases affected by international developments. "Revolution in one country" was always something of a myth. But the change in scale and intensity of the global context has brought in something new. Movements for change now exist under the scrutiny of the global media and are monitored closely by the large powers and supranational agencies. This severely curtails their independence. The United States in particular has now on a number of occasions asserted its right, and certainly its power, to intervene in the internal conflicts of societies virtually anywhere in the world. If certain observers are right, it has even formulated for itself a policy of the "modular democratic revolution" whereby it equips selected oppositions and non-governmental organizations in a given country with techniques for exploiting democratic opportunities. These can then be handed on in relay-fashion to other groups in other countries so as to further the goal of "democratizing the world" – in the belief of course that this will benefit America as well as those freed from autocratic rule. The Bulldozer Revolution in Serbia that toppled Milosevic in the autumn of 2000, the Rose Revolution of November 2003 that forced Georgian President Shevarnadze's resignation, and the Orange Revolution of November 2004 that handed over the presidency of Ukraine to Yushchenhko, are all seen as the first fruits of that policy.[14]

If this is the revolution of the future, we have come a long way from 1789 and 1917, though perhaps not so far from 1989. But is the guided, state-directed, revolution the only form of the future? Are there other models, other ideas that might inspire the revolutions of the future? While isolated cases of old-style revolution within states cannot be ruled out, it is clear that any worthwhile concept of revolution must face up to the realities of globalization – or, to put it in a less insistent way, of the international context (cf. Dunn 1980: 228–9; 1989a: xix-xxi; 1989b: 350; Foran 2003a). This means that however local the action – and all action must have local origins – it must conceive of itself in global terms. Trotsky and Camus were right: all revolution now must be world revolution. But it cannot be thought of as some synchronization of national revolutions, nor of some global proletariat gathering itself for an epic encounter with empire.

If one were to look to contemporary ideas and movements, the sources for a new conception of revolution are most likely to be found in the environmental or ecological movements, sometimes linked to the anti- or alter-globalization movements (cf. Wallerstein 2002). Only here does one find that linking of the local and the global, the human and the non-human, the personal with the political, that must mark any new concept. Of course there will be precedents here too – one thinks, say, of the utopian vision of William Morris, whose socialist society owed as much to the Romantic poets as to Marx, and whose idea of revolution was of a society living in harmony with nature as well as with itself. But utopian visions are only one part, though maybe a necessary part, of reformulating concepts of revolution. What has characterized recent ecological thought as much as ecological action is an admirable concreteness, a hard-headed understanding of the facts of the case and a determination to work through each case. Ecologists are fully aware – no one more so – of the global significance of their actions. Their ability to link up with each other on an international scale has been demonstrated on several occasions. But they remain properly skeptical of the grand gesture. The work that has to be done demands patience and resolution. If the world is to be changed, it will not be through some cataclysmic event – unless that comes in the form of ecological disaster – but rather through a war of attrition.[15]

This may not look like revolution to many people, and perhaps it does not seek, or deserve, the name. But the realization of the ecological program, with its far reaching consequences in every aspect of our personal and political lives, would be a revolution of a kind never yet achieved. Call it revolution, call it religion; it would certainly measure up to the dream of human emancipation that has been at the heart of all concepts of revolution in modern times.

To return to the question posed at the beginning of this essay, in the terms of Pierre Nora (1996). Is revolution still "memory" – a way of thinking and acting that remains alive and active in contemporary society, a tradition that has not exhausted its possibilities? Or is it merely "history," a record of past events that can be contemplated instructively but that has lost its potency to stimulate feeling and action? Writing in 1980, John Dunn, reflecting on the future of revolution, and the inevitability that some revolutions will occur "at some time somewhere" (not excluding the Soviet bloc), concluded that "what we may be *certain* lies ahead for us in future decades of revolutionary experience is surprises" (Dunn 1980: 239). The 1989 revolutions in East–Central Europe were indeed "surprises" to most people and do much to vindicate the prognoses of those such as Dunn who feel that revolution as an aspiration and example to imitate still has a lively future – even though they may feel highly ambivalent about the likely outcomes of such revolutions, as in the past (see also Foran 2003b: 274).

This view may be accepted even by those, such as Jeff Goodwin, who believe that the "age of revolutions" – specifically the period from 1945– 1991 – is now over, mainly due to the worldwide victory of democracy in recent years. "The ballot box has been the coffin of revolutionaries"

(Goodwin 2001: 302; see also Goodwin 2003). For there are clearly places where democracy, formally instituted or not, is extremely thin and often no more than a fig leaf for authoritarian rule. Such states remain vulnerable to revolutionary change, as the recent examples of Georgia and Ukraine indicate. And of course there are many states in Africa and Asia that have stubbornly resisted the latest "wave of democratization" that many scholars have charted (e.g. Huntington 1991). Moreover, as Goodwin himself admits, "past waves of democratization, alas, have in fact been regularly followed by anti-democratic waves" (2001: 306). There thus seems plenty of space in the future for the recurrence of revolution, if we understand revolution primarily as the overthrow of authoritarian or dictatorial rule.[16]

The real problem indeed has to do with the meaning of revolution, and the extent to which this may have changed so extensively in recent times as to make the very use of the word questionable and perhaps unhelpful in analysis. Definitions are of no help here, for revolution, as a human creation, has a history and, as Nietzsche (1956: 212) says, "only that which has no history can be defined." The further away in time and space we move from the original events – the eighteenth-century Western revolutions – that gave revolution its modern meaning, the more diffuse becomes its meaning and the less certain that we are dealing with the same phenomena.[17] We cannot legislate about this, but we can at least try to be clear about what people might mean when they use the term, especially in accounting for their actions. Revolution will have a future so long as there are people who think that what they are doing is making a revolution. Whether, and to what extent, what they aim for and what they achieve measure up to past instances of revolution is however surely something that as students of revolution we are entitled to judge.

Notes

1 "Non-urban" is perhaps too strong; urban intellectuals such as Mao and Ho Chi Minh, as well as certain groups of urban workers, clearly played important roles in these Third World revolutions. The urban poor also played a significant part in Peru's Sendero Luminoso (Shining Path) movement. See Goodwin (2001: 142–79) on Central American revolutions; and generally Foran (1993a: 8). But the contrast with the essentially urban character – at least in the crucial opening stages – of European revolutions from 1789 to 1917 nevertheless remains.

2 The Situationists were the most prominent group during the "May Events," chief among them Guy Debord, especially in such works as *The Society of the Spectacle* (1967). On Debord and his circle see Jappe (1999), Hussey (2001), and Merrifield (2005).

3 Benedict Anderson has noted an interesting parallel here between revolution and nationalism. Both are, in Anderson's terms, "modular," constructed of standardized elements that make them "capable of being transplanted, with varying degrees of self-consciousness, to a great variety of social terrains." But the degree of repetition and imitation is affected by "the process of modulation and adaptation,

according to different eras, political regimes, economies and social structures."
The knowledge of past occurrences and their outcomes is among the things that
influence the newer forms, making, therefore, the Cambodian Revolution as different from the French Revolution as Vietnamese nationalism is from French
nationalism. But the connection – the "filiation" – is still clear to all. See
Anderson (1991: 4, 156–7).

4 On the role of divided elites in bringing down the Soviet Union itself, see Lane
(1996).

5 Drawing on world-system theory, now often discussed under the label "globalization," Parker (1999; 2003: 43) gives a good account of the increasing difficulties
faced by Third World actors in attempting revolution, and of the reasons why so
many Third World revolutions fail or are blown off course.

6 Fred Halliday (2003: 305) makes a related point when, discussing the "vacuous
consumerism" that is one possible effect of the culture of the new communications technology, he comments: "One of the most pervasive, and demobilizing,
aspects of contemporary society is a radical, often narcissistic, individualism that
rejects collective responsibility or engagement."

7 For critical discussion of the ideas of Hardt and Negri, see Balakrishnan (2003).
It should be said that the idea of a world revolution can be conceived in different
terms from that of Trotskyism – not so much as a worldwide seizure of power as
a global "transformation of consciousness" based on movements for human
rights, increased assertiveness of the claims of gender, race, and ethnicity, etc. For
such a view see, for example, Paige (2003: 29) and Moghadam (2003: 168).

8 The *soviets* (councils) of the Russian Revolution of 1917, inspired to some extent
by Marx's writings on the Paris Commune of 1871, have to some been a model
of revolution that avoided the excessive centralization and statism of the Jacobin
model; so too the worker' councils of the Hungarian Revolution of 1956, and the
practice of *autogestion* in Paris May '68 – both harking back to the popular clubs
and societies of the early stages of the French Revolution. On all these as the
"lost treasure" of the revolutionary tradition, see Arendt (1963: 217–85) and
Kumar (1971: 14–26). Anarchists have also shown much interest in the various
social and political experiments of the Spanish Civil War – especially in
Catalonia – as possible models for the future organization of society. See on
these, and generally on anarchist views of revolution, Hobsbawm (1973: 57–91);
Guerin (1970: 73–143); Marshall (1993: 430–535).

9 On the rebellion in Chiapas as simply the latest phase of a long-running tradition
in Mexico which constantly reinterprets the legacy of the 1910 revolution, see
Benjamin (2000) and Harvey (1998).There are indeed several authors who have
seen in the Zapatista movement a new kind of "postmodern revolution," pos-
sessing several features – a concern with the role of women and the rights of
indigenous peoples, certain forms of democratic organization, strong international linkages and much international publicity – that might make it a model for
the revolution of the future. See, among the contributors to Foran (2003a),
especially Parker (2003: 50), Selbin (2003: 94 note 12), Kellner (2003: 184),
Kampwirth (2003: 232–7), Collier and Collier (2003), Foran (2003b: 275–9); also
Foran (1997: 804–7; 2001: 131–7). See also, for a similarly optimistic reading,
(Mason 2004: 264–73). But there remain grounds for skepticism on the score
both of novelty and the potential to act as a realistic model for future
revolutions – see, again in the Foran volume, for instance Vilas (2003: 99, 104),
Goodwin (2003: 63), Halliday (2003: 308). There is also Parker's earlier
assessment (1999: 174), that this is a case of old wine in new bottles, that "the
Zapatista insurgency reasserts older forces of revolution even though it does so
on a new stage." That the Zapatistas have become an "icon of revolution" – in
the virtual absence of any other compelling instances today – cannot be doubted;

but they have so far not made much headway in Mexico itself, which casts doubt on their ability to act as a model for the rest of the world, though that does not mean that they cannot inspire would-be revolutionaries.

10 Parker (1999: 155–9, 178–83) suggests that the revival of nationalism in the late twentieth century should be regarded as a *substitute* for and *alternative* to revolution, faced as the latter is with the absence of a credible "collective subject" today.

11 Perhaps it might be more accurate to say that the theocratic Iranian state was the outcome, rather than the original goal, of the revolution. As many have pointed out, there were important secular strands in the movement that overthrew the Shah (see, for example, Foran 1993a: 14, and Kurzman 2004).

12 See Mazlish (1976). Tocqueville (1873: 17–23) was one of the first to note the parallel between revolutionary and religious movements: "The French Revolution was ... a political revolution, which in its operation and its aspect resembled a religious one," etc. For later reflections on the parallels and borrowings, see Walzer (1968, 1985) and Lasky (1976).

13 Eric Hobsbawm sees the Iranian Revolution of 1979 as "one of the major social revolutions of the twentieth century" but notes its peculiar features. "The novelty of this revolution was ideological. Virtually all the phenomena commonly recognized as revolutionary up to that date had followed the tradition, ideology and, in general, the vocabulary of Western revolution since 1789; more precisely: of some brand of the secular left, mainly socialist or communist .... The Iranian Revolution was the first made and won under the banner of religious fundamentalism and which replaced the old regime by a populist theocracy whose professed program was a return to the seventh century AD" (1995: 453). See also Halliday (2003: 306–7), Parker (1999: 92–96), and, for a similar view, broadly applied to recent movements in the Middle East, Fromkin (2005).

14 On "the modular democratic revolution" I have learned much from Beissinger (2005). Specifically on Georgia's "Rose Revolution" see Ascherson (2004); on Ukraine's "Orange Revolution," see Wilson (2005). An uprising in April 2005 that forced Kyrgyzstan's autocratic ruler Aksar Akayev into exile was initially hailed as another round of the "modular democratic revolution" but doubts on this score soon surfaced – see Smith (2005). The continuing troubles in Ukraine, with the possibility of the reversal of the achievements of 2004, indicate the difficulty of assessing how much real change these "modular revolutions" have brought about.

15 The possibilities of ecological disaster, and in the not too distant future, are well spelled out in Hansen (2006), specifically in relation to global warning – a looming problem now highly publicized in Al Gore's film, *An Inconvenient Truth* (2006).

16 A recent example, indicating future possibilities, is the success of the popular movement in Nepal in April 2006 in forcing King Gyanendra to restore parliamentary democracy. As with Georgia and Ukraine, the question remains as to how far the designation "revolution" is appropriate to these events. Similar questions still hover over 1989. But at the very least we can say that the Nepalese movement, involving large numbers of people risking their lives in the face of armed police who showed themselves willing to use their weapons against the demonstrators, was at least as revolutionary as the anti-communist movements of 1989. For brief details, see BBC (2006).

17 Halliday (2003: 309) observes that "the very category of 'Revolution' with a capital 'R' may turn out to be a product of a particular phase of modernity, associated with the two centuries following the twin revolutions, political and ideological, of the late eighteenth century." This, he argues, throws into question both the inevitability and the desirability of revolution today.

15 New political cultures of opposition
What future for revolutions?

John Foran

If it is true that revolutions are the product of both structural conditions and human agency, and that they are born out of both political economic and cultural causes, then we may ask: In the current structural, political economic conjuncture of globalization, what are human and cultural dimensions of revolutionary social change in the modern world? Certainly, in the post-cold war, post-September 11, 2001, world, the space for revolutionary projects seems constrained by the collapse of older ideals and models. The socialist vision of the twentieth century has been tarnished by the authoritarian shape it took under the Soviet Union and in Eastern Europe, the return of savage forms of capitalism to China's new economy, the reversal of the Sandinista revolution in Nicaragua in the 1990s, and the uncertain future that lies ahead in a post-Castro Cuba. Zimbabwe, Mozambique, Angola, Vietnam, and Algeria all experienced anti-colonial social revolutions in the latter half of the twentieth century, and now find their prospects circumscribed by global capitalism and leaderships whose socialist credentials have given way to a hunger for power and money. The end of dictatorships in Haiti, the Philippines, and Zaire through political revolutions has not been accompanied by economic growth or betterment of life for their populations. Even the momentous toppling of apartheid in South Africa in 1994 has not been matched by any measurable gains for much of the black social base whose sacrifices brought it about.

Yet to conclude from this survey of broken dreams and promises that the path of revolution has failed for good, and that the future offers little prospect for positive social change, seems premature. For since the early 1990s a variety of new projects of radical social change have emerged, particularly in Latin America, where the left has been elected in Venezuela (1998), Brazil (2002), Uruguay (2004), and Bolivia (2005), joined in 2006 by Ecuador and Nicaragua and a second term for the left in Brazil and Venezuela, and was quite probably robbed of victory in Mexico in 2006, where the Zapatistas continue to build autonomous communities in Chiapas. And on a global scale, a vast "movement of movements" has emerged in the last ten years to counter neo-liberal capitalism in the form of the global justice movement, transnational feminist networks, the gatherings of the World Social Forum, and the spirited protests at meetings of the World Trade Organization and the G-8 nations, in Seattle, Genoa, Cancún, and elsewhere.

The confluence of the demise of twentieth-century social revolutions and the emergence of radical new struggles in the twenty-first suggests that the present moment is one of transition in the revolutionary tradition, in which armed struggle led by a vanguard in the name of socialism is yielding to more inclusive, democratic struggles in the name of something else. Students and proponents of revolution alike would do well to attend to the forms of this transition in seeking to understand and further the prospects for deep social change in an age of globalization and crisis. The present essay will offer one way of thinking about the changes that are underway, by focusing on the ways in which revolutionary cultures are shifting from older forms to newer ones.

Political cultures of opposition: a lens on how people become agents of revolution

My own work on the history of twentieth-century revolutions led me to explore the link between the structural conditions that figure in their origins and the coming together of a coalition of social forces broad enough to take power. In a look first at the Iranian Revolution of 1979 (Foran 1993b), and then at a wider set of cases (Foran 2005), I came to see this in terms of the articulation of political cultures of opposition and resistance (see Reed and Foran 2002). This refers to the process by which both ordinary citizens and revolutionary leaderships came to perceive the economic and political realities of their societies, and to fashion a set of understandings that simultaneously made sense of those conditions, gave voice to their grievances, and found a discourse capable of enjoining others to act with them in the attempt to remake their societies. The complexities of this process, and the several elements that work together to create a viable political culture of opposition, are suggested in Figure 15.1.

The origins of revolutionary political cultures lie in the experiences of people, in the subjective emotions and dynamics that animate their politics. At the same time, revolutionary discourses in the form of consciously articulated ideologies travel from revolutionary groups into local settings, as well as circulate between revolutions. Meanwhile, more popular "idioms" also circulate in communities, putting people's concerns in everyday terms such as fairness, justice, or freedom. Political cultures are forged out of the encounter of these different elements, and can become generalized when groups of people organize themselves into networks and organizations seeking to change the established order. It should be pointed out that in any given society, there may exist more than one political culture of opposition, for people do not necessarily share the same experiences, speak the same idioms, or respond to the same formal ideologies. The most effective revolutionary movements find ways of tapping into whatever political cultures emerge in

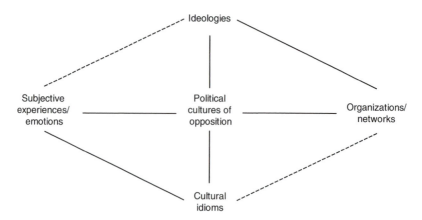

Figure 15.1 The making of political cultures of opposition.

their society, often through the creation of a common goal – "the regime must step down" – or through an ability to speak to people's experiences and cultural understandings in a way that acknowledges and builds upon their diversity. When this happens, a revolutionary movement can gain enough committed followers to contest power with the state. The forging of a strong and vibrant political culture of opposition is thus an accomplishment, carried through by the actions of many people, and, like revolutions themselves, is rare in human history.

"Old" political cultures of opposition in the record of the twentieth-century revolutions

To test our thesis that political cultures of opposition may be undergoing important changes in the current conjuncture, we should begin with an attempt to characterize the political cultures that animated the great social revolutions of the twentieth century, in Mexico, Russia, China, Cuba, Iran, and Nicaragua. What follows is necessarily a great simplification of the complexity and historical uniqueness of these events, and is done for the purpose not of suppressing that uniqueness, but for exploring possible patterns of similarity across them.

In each of these cases, the economic process of dependent development and the internal political structure of dictatorship produced experiences of exploitation and political exclusion, in turn eliciting emotions of anger and rage. The subjective side of these revolutions drew on an enormous reservoir of human aspiration and courage, difficult to document, and impossible to present in this (or any) space. As the Cuban revolutionary Enrique Olutski put it, "No book can ever convey the greatness of a people in revolt" (2002: n.p.). One of the emotions at work in each case was surely a combination of anger and indignation at the conditions imposed. Teodor Shanin's work on the Russian Revolution gives it expression: "At the very centre of revolution lies an emotional upheaval of moral indignation, revulsion and fury with the powers-that-be, such that one cannot demur or remain silent, whatever the cost" (1986: 31).

The formal discourses that revolutionaries put forward varied from case to case, from the radical agrarian programs of Zapata in Mexico to the militant Islam of Khomeini in Iran. One core discourse was that of nationalism, the notion that foreign influence over the economy and national politics must come to an end. A second, in the cases of Russia, China, Cuba, and Nicaragua, was a more or less formal appeal to socialism (present also in an inchoate form in Mexico and as a minor current in Iran, and more subterranean in Cuba until after the movement came to power). A third strand, in Nicaragua and Iran especially, was a radical interpretation of religion, in the form of liberation theology in the first case, and an activist Islam in the second.

Identifying the less formal, popular idioms that animated revolutionary action is more difficult. The distrust of foreign power can be discerned across these cases, a visceral hatred for the alliance of the government with rapacious outsiders: "Death to America" was a prominent slogan at the mass demonstrations against the Shah, as was "Mexico for the Mexicans" in the 1910s. This extended to dislike of the dictator's monopoly of power, a factor which brought middle-class groups into opposition in Mexico, Russia, Cuba, Nicaragua, and Iran. Behind these lay a sense that social justice should be served: "Land, Liberty, and Freedom" in Mexico was one slogan that embodied this, the peasantry's desire for land reform in China another measure of it.

The organizations that emerged in five of the six cases – all but Iran – consisted of armed insurgents who directly engaged the state, though these were aided in all cases by non-armed groups and organizations who engaged in support activities of many kinds (on Cuba, see Klouzal 2005). In Russia and China, and more loosely in Nicaragua, political parties existed alongside the armies and gave direction to them. In Iran, the network of mosques and clerics, most of them loyal to the Ayatollah Khomeini, provided the organizational base for the mass demonstrations and general strike that undermined the shah's government without taking up arms. A common thread across cases is the hierarchical structure of the movements, with well-identified individuals at their head – Emiliano Zapata and Pancho Villa, Vladimir I. Lenin and Leon Trotsky, Mao Tse-Tung, Fidel Castro and Che Guevara, Khomeini, and the Sandinista leadership under the Ortega brothers and other commanders. This hierarchical nature of guerrilla militaries, socialist parties, and of religious leadership meant that influential figures – always male, and usually privileged in background – would lead in the name of the people.

Despite the variations from case to case, we may discern a rough but common pattern among the "old" political cultures of opposition that made the great revolutions of the twentieth century, as suggested in Figure 15.2.

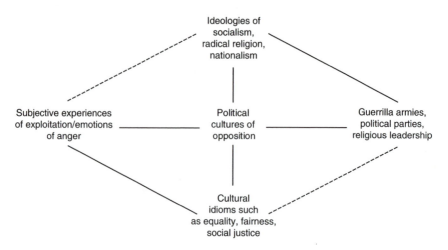

Figure 15.2 The making of "old" political cultures of opposition in the major twentieth-century revolutions.

These political cultures produced broad and powerful revolutionary movements, all of which took state power (in Mexico, power fell to less radical forces, but the dictatorship of Porfirio Díaz was definitively toppled). Once in power, all the movements encountered internal and external pressures, and each produced new states whose leaderships held power close: Mexico's Party of the Institutionalized Revolution for eight decades, the Communist Party of the Soviet Union for almost as long, Castro's reign of almost 50 years, the Chinese Communist Party's monopoly of power since 1949, the strong hold of the Islamist leadership in Iran down to the present. Only in Nicaragua was a polity created which ran the risk of ceding power, and there the Sandinistas did indeed yield power in the 1990 elections; their subsequent presidential campaigns, all under Daniel Ortega, indicate that the party did not democratize internally, however, and this shared characteristic with the other cases has been an obstacle to their return to power. Ortega would win the November 2006 elections, aided by a change in the electoral rules enabling a candidate with 40 per cent of the vote to win in the first round.

I am not suggesting that the limits of these revolutions can be laid entirely at the feet of the political cultures which made them. For one thing, all of the revolutions produced gains for the population of some depth and duration (most notably in Russia and Cuba, for a short time in Nicaragua, and for a long time in China). For another, the fashioning of powerful political cultures was a remarkable accomplishment, and each possessed admirable features, particularly in the phase of the insurrection. These were not always preserved by the winners afterward, who faced the daunting task of holding together broad and heterogeneous social forces, typically with divergent interests. Of substantial weight in the outcomes of each were other factors that acted independently of political culture and human agency: external intervention and disadvantageous positions in the world economy chief among them (see Foran and Goodwin 1993). We see here, as attested at the outset of this essay, the profound intersection of political economy and culture, of impersonal structures and human agency.

But the possibility remains that the strength and solidity of these revolutionary political cultures, so crucial in overthrowing the states they opposed, yet possessed features – especially the combination of the leaderships' emphases on ideology over popular idiom, and the hierarchical nature of the organizations that came to power – which must be counted among the Achilles heels of the outcomes that followed. If we compare them with the emergent shape of their counterparts in the twenty-first century, we may find further clues to the nature and power of political culture in revolutions.

The emergence of "new" political cultures of opposition in the twenty-first century

The Zapatista uprising of 1994, the election of left governments in a number of Latin American countries, and the emergence of a movement for global justice have also been animated by resilient political cultures of opposition. While retaining the same elements as older political cultures, they accord different weights to them, with different contents and novel forms in some of them. They have also experienced a variety of outcomes to date, coming to power in Venezuela, Brazil, Uruguay, Bolivia, Ecuador, and elsewhere, establishing autonomous communities but not taking national power in Chiapas, and organizing across borders without a clear or singular goal in the case of the global justice movement. We should explore not only these variations, but also the ways in which as a group of movements they differ from their twentieth-century revolutionary counterparts.

A new left comes to power in Latin America

In Venezuela, Brazil, Uruguay, Bolivia, Ecuador and Nicaragua, left parties succeeded in gaining political power through elections (the following analysis is based in part on a reading of news media, including the *New York Times* and *Latinamerica Press*). The impact of globalization on the populations of each country has exacerbated social inequalities of class and ethnicity (the latter especially in Bolivia and Ecuador), such that people's experiences of exploitation were sharply felt. Anger against established political elites animated the bases of the left parties – the Workers Party (PT) in Brazil, the aptly named Frente Amplio (Broad Front) coalition in Uruguay, the Movement Toward Socialism (MAS) in Bolivia, and the born-again Sandinistas in Nicaragua. The Argentine slogan – "*que se vayan todos*" (get all the politicians out) – resonated across working-class, indigenous, and middle-class communities and voters tired of the older parties in all four countries (cf. the *New York Times* reference to "a strong throw-the-bums-out sentiment" in Nicaragua: November 7, 2006).

There was less emphasis also on an ideological appeal to socialism by the leaderships: Brazil's Luis Inacio da Silva (universally known as "Lula"), Uruguay's Tabaré Vázquez, and Bolivia's Evo Morales. When asked what he and the MAS understood by "socialism," Morales replied:

> To live in community and equality .... It is an economic model based on solidarity, reciprocity, community, and consensus. Because, for us, democracy is a consensus. In the community there is consensus, in the trade union there are majorities and minorities .... And beyond that, [it means] respecting Mother Earth, the Pacha Mama.
>
> (Dieterich 2006)

The notion of democracy as a consensus comes out of the popular idiom of the indigenous communities of Bolivia, and has its deepest expression in the rebellion in Chiapas, as we shall see. In Uruguay, the Frente Amplio has governed with an emphasis on documenting the human rights abuses of the 1970s' dictatorship and on strengthening worker participation in wage negotiations (Long 2005). Lula's campaigns for the presidency of Brazil stressed social programs and relief for the landless. In all three cases, socialism was translated into concerns close to those of the populations who brought the left to power. Daniel Ortega's 2006 campaign in Nicaragua did not refer to socialism, instead emphasizing peace and reconciliation, choosing pink as the symbolic color of his candidacy, and adapting John Lennon's "Give Peace a Chance" as his anthem (*New York Times*, November 7, 2006).

Nationalism has persisted as a revolutionary current as well, again inflected away from any formal, ideological focus and more rooted in popular idioms. In the era of globalization, its content has shifted from confrontation with outside powers such as the United States to the newer targets of the transnational corporations. Lula proclaimed "The victory is Brazil's," when he was elected to a second term in October 2006; during the campaign he told the IMF to "keep its nose out of Brazil's affairs" (paraphrased in the *New York Times*, October 30, 2006). This has been evidenced most spectacularly in Bolivia, where it has been conjoined with the rise and acceptance of indigenous demands expressed in a new political idiom that has not had a national-level voice in the past. The Bechtel Corporation was forced to withdraw its bid to privatize water in Cochabamba in 2000. Starting in 2003, a movement to reclaim Bolivia's extensive natural gas holdings began to press for control against the Spanish, British, Argentine, and Brazilian corporations that operated the gas fields. On May 1, 2006, Morales declared, "The looting by the foreign companies has ended" (Zuazo 2006), passing a decree requiring them to deliver their production to the Bolivian state and to renegotiate their contracts to pay 82 per cent of their profits to Bolivia (*Latinamerica Press*, May 17, 2006). Felipe Quispe, an Aymara indigenous leader who is critical of all politicians, including Morales, puts it this way: "The foreigners can stay as long as we get 90 percent of the power. If not, there will be war .... We will rewrite history with our own blood. There will be a new sun, and even the rocks and the trees will be happy" (Parenti 2005: 18). In this there are echoes of previous indigenous movements which argued: "*Ya es otro tiempo el presente* (The present is a new time)" (Hylton and Thomson 2004: 19). Carlos Laime, a 33-year-old tailor, makes this connection: "I feel more Bolivian since an Aymara is in power. Now we can talk about majorities, and in [public] offices the people who are served are not only those wearing ties" (Manrique 2006: 8).

In Venezuela, an even more striking shift toward new political cultures of opposition crystallized with the election of Hugo Chávez in 1998. Coming out of a military tradition, and after engaging in a failed coup in 1992 Chávez remade himself into a political candidate who again challenged the legitimacy of the existing parties. In the course of the decade, Chávez came to articulate an original political culture based on what he termed "Bolivarianism" – an appeal to the vision of Simon Bolívar for liberation from foreign powers and the development of a unity of purpose among Latin American nations, especially in the Andean region. This has also translated into calls for improving the lives of rural residents and the urban poor, integration of the indigenous and black populations into the national project, and using Venezuela's oil wealth for development and investment in human capital (Gott 2005).

Even in power, his relationship with the population was more loosely organized than the formal political parties of Brazil, Uruguay, Nicaragua, and Bolivia. His original organization, the Bolivarian Revolutionary Movement, became a political party, the Fifth Republic Movement (MVR), that participated in an alliance of left parties to bring him to power in 1998 (Gott 2005: 134–9). After that he moved away from both the established left parties and his own organization to establish a more personal link to his social base. The new constitution that enshrined the principles of Bolivarianism into law was passed by a non-partisan referendum. Chávez addresses the nation in a weekly radio program in which he speaks with humor and candor in a popular idiom, with a language reminiscent of "an evangelical preacher, invoking pain and love and redemption" (Gott 2005: 137). Institutionally, the government has also reached deeply into communities in the form of social campaigns known as "missions" charged with addressing critical needs in health, education, housing, food, and jobs (Boudin *et al.* 2006: 65–77). The depth of this new political culture was proven in the events of the April 2002 coup attempt, which against almost all precedent in Latin American history, saw the restoration of a deposed president through popular mobilization and the loyalty of a part of the military. It was reaffirmed with the president's re-election in the 2006 election.

The November 2006 election of left-leaning Rafael Correa in Ecuador with support from leading indigenous organizations further illustrates the current trend in Latin America. Correa campaigned against global capital ("It is necessary to overcome all the fallacies of neo-liberalism"), the U.S. military base ("If they want, we won't close the base in 2009, but the United States would have to allow us to have an Ecuadoran base in Miami in return"), and prioritizing spending on social programs over debt repayment (Kozloff 2006). Correa also enjoyed the close support of Hugo Chávez, and took much of the indigenous vote (40 per cent of the population of 13 million) with the backing of CONAIE (the Confederation of Indigenous Nationalities of Ecuador).

The left governments of Brazil, Uruguay, Bolivia, Ecuador, and Venezuela tap into a political culture that differs in some key respects from the older revolutionary tradition. Chief among these are the democratic route to power and the effort to build a more participatory political system on the parts of significant sectors of their populations. In this, the relative weight of formal ideology and popular idiom can be seen as shifting in the direction of popular demands for social justice and national sovereignty, more loosely expressed in terms of the socialist tradition. Perhaps better put, the current of socialism is being reworked in subterranean directions in the post-cold war era, and the depth of the democratic ideal is arguably proving a more solid barrier to external and internal intervention than in the more polarized era of the Allende experiment with this form of revolution in the 1970s.

The future may be now: the Zapatistas and the global justice movement

The most radical developments in political cultures of opposition have occurred further from the limelight of elections on a national stage, at levels both above and below it. The Zapatista movement in Mexico offers one instance of this, and its genesis and subsequent trajectory are instructive. When student intellectuals sought to organize resistance in the indigenous south of Mexico after the government's massacre of their movement in 1968, they came to the local communities with Marxist ideas of socialism, tinged with a new left respect for non-authoritarian organizing. After many stumbles and little success in the 1980s, the group that included future Zapatista spokesperson Subcomandante Marcos began to learn from the indigenous Mayan communities of Chiapas, rather than try to lead them from above or outside (Kampwirth 2002: 107–9; Womack 1999).

This encounter was shaped by practices and visions that had never been incorporated in the visible or official histories of revolutionary struggle in Mexico. Drawing on their own political idioms, indigenous communities provided such core Zapatista principles as *mandar obedeciendo* – "to rule, obeying" – the view that leaders serve the community and the struggle for its issues, rather than the community furthering the vision of the leadership.

This would be embodied after 2002 in the institution of the "Juntas de buen gobierno" (Councils of Good Government), chosen on a rotating basis within each community to work with members to determine their goals and projects. The assumption behind these was that every community member possessed the ability to lead the group, and that the community is strengthened when all are given this opportunity. The charismatic non-indigenous Subcomandante Marcos is the most well-known figure among the Zapatistas by virtue of his gift for powerfully evocative political writing and speech, but he himself acknowledges the higher rank of the indigenous leadership of the guerrilla army: he is a *sub*comandante.

Another innovative Zapatista practice is expressed in the phrase *dar su palabra* (literally, to have one's say). One way this has been expressed is "allowing your true word to speak to my true word" (Martínez and García 2004: 215). This speaks to the effort to include all members of a group in the discussions which concern the group's plans. Behind this lies the respect that is accorded to each, and the value attached to the views of differently situated members of a community. The goal is to make decisions that benefit from the unique insights of all present, to find solutions which have eluded them in the past. Such discussions can take much longer than formal debates followed by votes, but they endow the group's choices with a broader legitimacy. When a consensus does not emerge, the process has the merit of identifying where the points of disagreement lie.

The degree to which women have been truly empowered in the autonomous communities remains an open question, but it is worth considering whether their role in the Zapatista struggle may also portend a new face of revolution. Women have been prominent since before the movement publicly declared its existence, advocating and obtaining passage of the ten-point Women's Revolutionary Laws, giving women the right to work and own land, to choose their partners and the number of their children, to be educated and to receive health care, and to take positions of revolutionary leadership. Women serve at the highest level of the Zapatista army and indigenous leadership; as Comandanta Ramona put it in 1994: "We [women] demand respect, true respect as Indians. We also have rights ... and my message to all women who feel exploited, ignored, is take up arms as a Zapatista" (Collier 1994: 60, quoting *Tiempo*, February 6, 1994). Blanca Flor, a member of the group Kinal Antzetik (Women's Territory), points to the emotions driving women's participation: "Every day the women get madder. And the madder they get, the stronger they get" (quoted in Flinchum 1998: 31).

For Javier Eloriaga, a member of the National Coordinating Commission of the FZLN (the unarmed, civil society, political wing of the Zapatista movement until it became inactive in the fall of 2005), "We have to do politics in a new way. You can't accept only what is possible because it will bring you into the hands of the system. This is a very difficult struggle. It is very, very difficult" (quoted in Zugman 2001: 113). Part of this involves "walking at a slower pace," acknowledging that change is a long and slow process, not secured with the mere seizure of power or electoral victories. Indeed, Zapatistas have said that they do not aspire to *take* state power in the traditional sense, but rather, to create "a free and democratic space for political struggle" (EZLN 2002: 226). To this end, they have engaged in campaigns of international solidarity against neo-liberalism, and in gathering together the many groups in Mexico who feel excluded from the political system. And above all, they have worked to implement their own visions of autonomy in those parts of the Lacandón forest of Chiapas where they have enough support to keep the Mexican government and military at bay, even in the face of continued violence and low-intensity warfare.

The movement, though formally armed at the level of the Zapatista Army of National Liberation, has concerned itself not with fighting but with building positive alternatives to the capitalist exploitation of Chiapas and its inhabitants. While some of the rebels initially said that their goal is "for socialism, like the Cubans have, but better" (*New York Times* January 4, 1994), their demands have been for such things as land, health care, education, autonomy for indigenous peoples, and deeper forms of democracy than elections. The rebellion thus marks very clearly the movement away from ideologies and toward idioms of resistance and opposition. The terms introduced above, along with others, are evidence of the depth of this shift: *dignidad y esperanza* (dignity and hope); *caminamos preguntando* (we walk asking); *nunca jamás un mundo sin nosotros* (never again a world without us); and *todo para todos y nada para nostros* (everything for everyone and nothing for ourselves). Manuel Callahan (2004: 218) believes we should see these as personal and communal conceptions rather than political slogans.

The Zapatistas emerged in tandem with and as part of an international movement of resistance to capitalist globalization that has many parts and its own history. While its first prominent manifestation was arguably the spectacular shutting down of the meetings of the World Trade Organization (WTO) in Seattle in late 1999 (Cockburn *et al.* 2000), its roots go deeper and further, ranging from actions that started in the late 1980s in South Korea, Venezuela, India, Germany, and many other countries on campaigns against Third World debt and structural adjustment plans, environmental struggles against states and corporations, new labor movements, women's actions, indigenous organizing, and anti-war demonstrations. They range forward to the militant protests at subsequent meetings of the WTO and the G-8 nations from Genoa in 2001 to Gleneagles, Scotland in 2006 and include the millions of people throughout the world who went to the streets on February 15, 2003, to protest the imminent U.S. attack on Iraq (key works include Notes from Nowhere 2003; Mertes 2004; Solnit 2004; Starr 2005; Yuen *et al.* 2004). And they include the considerable grassroots organizing that takes place without attention from either the media or academics, much of this being done by women and people of color.

As Kevin Danaher and Roger Burbach suggest:

If we look closely we can see the pieces of the first global revolution being put together. Every revolution up until now has been a national revolution, aimed at seizing control of a national government. But the blatant corporate bias of global rule-making institutions such as the IMF, World Bank and WTO have forced the grassroots democracy movement to start planning a global revolution. It is a revolution in values as well as institutions. It seeks to replace the money values of the current system with the life values of a truly democratic system.

(2000a: 9)

If we focus on the political cultures that animate the global justice movement, we can see some novel features, many of them parallel with the Zapatista rebellion, but coming from movements with many distinct locations around the world and occasionally gathering in one place for action or reflection.

On the subjective side of experience and emotion, it is useful to point out that love – of life, of people, of justice – often provides the vital force that impels ordinary people into extraordinary acts. Expressing hope and optimism, it provides a constructive counterpoint to those other powerful animating emotions, hatred and anger. I am not arguing here that a change has been wrought in the emotional tenor of revolutions per se, but suggesting that this thread may be gaining in prominence as movements come together in new ways. L.A. Kauffman, who has participated in anti-WTO protests, describes it this way:

the central idea behind the carnival is that protests gain in power if they reflect the world we want to create. And I, for one, want to create a world that is full of color and life and creativity and art and music and dance. It's a celebration of life against the forces of greed and death.

(Shepard and Kaufmann 2004: 380–1)

Compassion, caring, and creativity have roles to play. To this, we may add the subjective experience of hope (is it an emotion?). In David Solnit's words: "Hope is key. If our organizations, analysis, visions and strategies are lanterns, then hope is the fuel that makes them burn bright and attracts people to them" (Neumann and Solnit 2004). Interestingly, the Zapatistas are sometimes referred to as "professionals of hope."

As with the Zapatistas, we can also discern a turn toward popular idioms over ideology. John Walton puts it thus: "The broader lesson is the emergence of a new global political consciousness ... which attempts to define a coherent code of global justice embracing indigenous people, peasants, the urban poor, labor, democrats and dolphins" (Walton 2003: 225). We have seen that a concern with social justice has not been absent in the great revolutions of the twentieth century; one can readily see it in the demands for "Bread, Land, and Peace" in 1917 Russia, "Socialism with a Human Face" in 1968 Czechoslovakia, and "a preferential option for the poor" in the 1970s' language of liberation theology in Central America. It has taken the form of demands for "Hope and Dignity" in Chiapas, and "Fair Trade" and "Democracy" in Seattle. For Patrick Reinsborough:

> When we say we want a better world, we mean it. We want a world that reflects basic life-centered values. We've got the vision and the other side doesn't. We've got biocentrism, organic food production, direct democracy, renewable energy, diversity, people's globalization, and justice. What have they got? Styrofoam? Neo-liberalism? Eating disorders? Designer jeans, manic depression, and global warming?
>
> (Reinsborough 2004: 178–80)

This vision includes radically different modes of struggle for an age of globalization where the location of the enemy is the increasingly interlocked institutions of global capitalism in the form of the WTO, World Bank, transnational corporations, and First and Third World states. These modes of struggle include sit-ins, boycotts, strikes, civil disobedience, occupation of land or factories, all forms of direct action aimed at uprooting the system rather than reproducing it. In a no doubt conscious echo of the Zapatistas, direct action activist David Solnit writes "The world cannot be changed for the better by taking power .... Capturing positions of state power, either through elections or insurrection, misses the point that the aim of uprooting the system is to fundamentally change the relations of power at the root of our problems" (2004b: xix).

Organizationally, new forms are being developed that depart from the past practice of revolutions. The global justice movement "has no international headquarters, no political party, no traditional leaders or politicians running for office, and no uniform ideology or ten-point platform" (Solnit 2004b: xii).

> This is a movement about reinventing democracy. It is not opposed to organization. It is about creating new forms of organization. It is not lacking in ideology. These new forms of organization are its ideology. It is about creating and enacting horizontal networks ... based on principles of decentralized, non-hierarchical consensus democracy.
>
> (Graeber 2004: 212)

Mexican artist and scholar Manuel De Landa suggests we use the term "meshworks" for such self-organizing, non-hierarchical, and heterogeneous networks. It is for this reason also that one name for the whole is "the movement of movements."

Figure 15.3 attempts to sum up this argument about the emergence of new political cultures of opposition, particularly those of the Zapatistas and the global justice movement (the elected left governments also share certain of these features, except for their organizational forms, as noted on the diagram).

Can these new political cultures produce some sort of revolution? The left has achieved state power or is on the verge of it in an important set of Latin American countries: does it have the will, internal support, and global room for maneuver to redirect resources to the poorest sectors of society? The Zapatistas have registered concrete gains on a local level: will they be able to generalize these accomplishments beyond Chiapas? The global justice movement has registered significant opposition to elite globalization projects, and has mustered its forces at the successive World Social Forums. It has also made gains in many local settings around the world. Can this movement reverse the tide of neo-liberal capitalism? No one can say. If millions of ordinary citizens around the world can be attracted to these movements, then maybe so (a big if and a modest maybe are to be read here).

Whether this can be done depends in some measure on how their new political cultures of opposition build on the past and how they read the lessons of each other's bold experiments. These cases have shown their ability to move beyond ideology in favor of the strengths of popular idioms demanding social justice; they have shown us some of the advantages of horizontal networks over vertical hierarchies. But how to fashion large-scale popular spaces for democracy, and how to articulate the discourses that will bring together the broadest coalition ever seen on a global stage, remain among their greatest challenges.

As the Zapatistas argue, and the disappointing experience of Lula and the Workers Party in Brazil (watering down their radical program once in

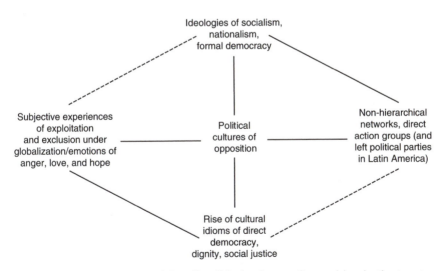

Figure 15.3 The emergence of "new" political cultures of opposition in the twenty-first century.

power) has shown, elections are not a magic solution to undoing fundamental structures of exploitation. But neither is direct democracy. Both can
be subverted by new forms of domination even as they seek to avoid old
ones. There are no guarantees that either can spread in conditions of crisis
and scarcity. Fighting a system is not as easy as overthrowing a state (and
the latter was rarely achieved in the past century in any case). Behind the
institutions of global capital lie other forms of internal oppression and
power: patriarchy, militarism, racism, fundamentalism, nationalism, environmental destruction, consumerism, media control, and the privileging of
cultures that oppress others. None of this is going to be undone swiftly or
without cost.

What, then, lies between direct action and elections? Do we have the
imagination to know? The tensions between the new left projects of taking
state power through elections, and the Zapatista goal of not taking power
but seeking to subvert it at the local level, are palpable. This was brought
clearly into focus in the July 2006 election in Mexico, where Andrés Manuel
Lopez Obrador, the candidate of the Party of the Democratic Revolution
(PRD), was narrowly defeated in the official vote count but claimed that the
government had engaged in massive fraud to retain power. If the Zapatistas
had not put forward sharp critiques of his revolutionary credentials, could
he have won outright? And if he had, could he have shifted the bases of
Mexican development to any meaningful degree in favor of the poor? What
common ground might be found between these two approaches to revolutionizing Mexico? In the immediate aftermath of the elections, Lopez
Obrador took his protest into the streets, pushing beyond the bounds
imposed by legal frameworks of opposition. The Zapatistas, for their part,
had been calling for an alliance of all progressive forces to challenge the
country's economic and political arrangements at their core. What are the
prospects for these currents to converge, and what might such a convergence
look like and accomplish? A strong grassroots movement of teachers,
workers, students, and ordinary citizens rose up in Oaxaca in the fall of
2006, shutting down the state capital and provoking a violent response from
the government. Mexico remains a very important site in the struggle to
cultivate effective new political cultures of opposition, and what happens
there will tell much about their potential for deep social transformation.

Meanwhile, the U.S. response to the September 11 attacks has effected
another large setback for a future of deep social change. It has militarized
the course of globalization from above by a transnational elite and opened
up a new and uncertain period in the global political economy. It has also
broken the growing momentum of the global justice movement by its "war
on terror" discourse. It has created facts on the ground in a shattered Iraq
that defy restitution and conjured paralyzing new fears and amorphous
threats in the United States where none existed before. Perhaps the Bush
administration has overplayed its hand, at home and abroad, as the
Democratic sweep of the 2006 midterm elections signaled. It has certainly

stumbled in terms of its prosecution of the war, its response to Hurricane Katrina, its wire-tapping of its own citizens, its budget priorities and massive indebtedness, and its inaction on global warming and peak oil. But can those who oppose it regain the initiative? The possibility for radical social change of a positive kind depends on a recovery from this enormous setback.

In a 2003 essay (Foran 2003: 282), I observed that the revolutionaries of the present and future are faced with a new set of paradoxes and challenges to:

- find a language capable of uniting diverse forces and allowing their not necessarily mutually compatible desires full expression
- find organizational forms capable of nurturing this expression and debate as well as enabling decisive action when needed, both locally and across borders
- articulate an economic alternative to neo-liberalism and capitalism that can sustain itself against the systemic weight of the past and the pervasive and hostile reach of the present global economic system
- make all this happen, in many places and at different levels (local, national, "global") over time, working with both the deep strengths and frailties of the experiences and emotions of human liberation.

These tasks remain as pressing as ever. The new revolutionary movements and the political cultures they repose upon have opened them up for consideration. The categories we have used to think about revolutions may be the same – economic, political, cultural – but the content is shifting in all these domains. We need a fresh look at the current conjuncture to take us from it toward the future – unknown, yes; unknowable, granted; but in need of our careful attention.

Acknowledgment

I thank my research assistant Molly Talcott for much of the material reported on the global justice movement, and Jordan Camp for tracking down the details of key references. I have learned much from the constructive comments of Jordan Camp and Eric Selbin on the first draft of this chapter.

Afterword

On the concept of revolution

Antonio Negri

The turning point between modernity and postmodernity

To speak of revolution (of political and social revolution – socialist or communist) today, under postmodern conditions, implies a *new vocabulary*. *Modern* political terminology (that designated sovereignty, the nation-state, imperialism, colonialism, etc., as fundamental concepts) has lost its capacity to refer to the reality of the current social condition, usually called *post-modernity*. In particular, it has lost touch with the new political subjects that inhabit this postmodern condition. The theme of revolution implies the analysis of subjectivity.

On the basis of this premise concerning the distinctive characteristics of our age, we would emphasize that any claim that there is a continuity between modernity and the contemporary condition is erroneous and, in our view, conceptually ineffective. We have in mind authors such as Bauman, Beck, or Giddens who, by making use of the concept of "hyper-modernity," still deem it crucial to ground the project of emancipation in the continuity of objectives and methods of political action specific to social democracy. In other words, these authors think that the project of emancipation should be connected to the realization of the values of "modernity;" they still assume a subjectivity in the making for the "working class" and its political organizations; they think that the State and its coercive apparatus are fundamental in constructing the synthesis of "civil society" as a whole and in overcoming its contradictions – or better, in overcoming the crisis of "bourgeois consistency" in the concept of "civil society."

This seems impossible. By talking about "postmodernity," our intention is to highlight a real and proper caesura between the paradigms of modernity and postmodernity. In the postmodern condition the quality of the political subject has been transformed. A new production of subjectivity has irreversibly come into play. New forms of knowledge and new productive activities, becoming more and more intellectual and cooperative, have constructed a new subject. Today production processes emerge from the activity of the "general intellect;" if this activity implies social production and also extends to biopolitical dimensions – affective, cognitive, cooperative, etc. –

of considerable range, we can infer from this that society and political life have profoundly changed, leading to a break in paradigms. Consequently, the new subject of production is submerged in a new temporality, entirely different to the modalities of the modern process of production and the classical working day, upon which our political economy still relies. The new temporality is accompanied by a new mobility in space. A further element in the characterization of this new subject – which is important for the concept of revolution – implies a new regime of desires emerging from this condition, amounting to a new potentiality for constituent power.

We have so far insisted on the fact that the subject of production is increasingly part of the "general intellect:" that the labor force is becoming, therefore, more and more intellectual and cooperative; that the valorization of commodities occurs by means of a permanent production of subjectivity; and, finally, we have inferred that this series of relationships constitutes a new biopolitical fabric, within which both the putting to work of society as a whole, and, in particular, the diffusion of productive and political intellectuality by the multitude, is determined.

If this is what contemporary politics is about, and if it is so profoundly different from modernity, then it is quite obvious that we ought to focus our attention on and entirely revisit the themes of "reform" and "revolution."

Perhaps it would be worth arguing that, if the transformation of the constitution of subjectivity is so deep, it would be just as well if we gave up the term "revolution," which is so indissolulably linked to the subjectivity of modernity. This would also be supported by the conceptual inflation inflicted upon the term "revolution." Over the last two hundred years it has meant everything and its opposite, the good and the bad, emancipation and terror, etc. And, as in all processes of inflation, the bad currency has expunged the good. Moreover, if we wanted to dispense with the term "revolution" in the political debate of postmodernity, we could also be encouraged by the suggestion that the term "revolution" is actually quite a recent one. In the Renaissance, "revolution" still referred to astronomical rather than social and political movements, the latter being designated by the term "reform." In the medieval and, especially, the Franciscan tradition, which includes even the Lutheran and Calvinist schism, "reform" is equivalent to and stands in place of the later concept of revolution.

If we still prefer today *to retain the term "revolution,"* we do so because it renders apparent a range of contents that, within and beyond the paradigm shift of postmodernity, we deem to be relevant to the problematic of contemporary politics. First, it will be of interest to capture the *new shape of the temporality*, entirely ontological, which accompanies the revolutionizing of power relations when, in postmodern conditions, we assume them to develop *a new biopolitical form*. From the perspective of this new biopolitical condition, the evolutionary account of the concept of "revolution" taken from the French Revolution (libertarian insurrection, Jacobin terror, bourgeois Thermidor), that is characteristic of revisionist schools, becomes completely unusable. The ontological scheme which postmodernity allows us to adopt, and biopolitics to make use of, does not allow for any malleability of the historical event. "Revolution" has become a more difficult, but also a tougher concept; the revolution is forced – by virtue of being biopolitical – to be loyal to itself. Thus, within this framework, we are able to speak anew of "revolution" without appearing to be talking about something else.

This depends first and foremost on the fact that in postmodernity subjectivity and its production hold center stage. When the "general intellect" becomes biopolitical, there can be no revolution that does not imply a reform of subjectivity, the recognition of its singularity, and the autonomous and common management of its power. Emancipation itself cannot be attained without revolutionizing subjectivity.

Approaching, in postmodernity, constituent power and revolution

What, under postmodern conditions, are revolution and constituent power?

In modernity, revolution is defined as a radical transformation of the constitution of a society on the basis of the exercise of a constituent will. As for the socialist revolution, it relies upon the exercise of a constituent will expressed by the working class and its allies, comprised in a hegemonic power. Therefore, under modern conditions, constituent revolutionary and socialist power is defined as the expression of masses exploited by capitalism that attempt to impose a dictatorship on bourgeois society and to reappropriate the structures of the capitalist state. Paradoxically, constituent revolutionary and socialist power tends to offer itself, by means of the *proclaimed seizure of power*, as the basis of something transcendental – as transcendental as the capitalist state, the legitimate monopolist of force, capable of unilaterally imposing its project of domination. It does not seem irrelevant to remark how different authors in modernity, be they reactionaries such as Carl Schmitt, liberals such as Max Weber, or communists such as Lenin, understand constituent power and the attendant definition of the state within a concept of sovereignty that reveals a profound *homology* with respect to the supreme monopoly of force. Accordingly, it is worth underlining that, in modernity, constituent power is opposed to constituted power only in dialectical terms, as totality against totality, while maintaining, in fact, the same nature.

By contrast, things are different in postmodernity. "Seizing power" makes little sense if the concept of power – redefined in biopolitical terms – is no longer homologous for both elites and for rebels. In postmodernity this point is finally obvious. If we accept the notion of the multitude and a concept of immaterial labor (cognitive, overabundant, and constitutive) as hegemonic within productive labor as a whole, any homology of power between elites and rebels, between exploiters and exploited, between domination and living labor, loses its significance. Rather than talking of seizing power, we could talk about the *expression of the strength of the multitude*: to the management of power by parts of the ruling class, and the homologous reversal of this power, we may oppose the *exercise of the common*; even better, the "management" of the common by parts of the exploited and oppressed classes, which amounts to saying by parts of the multitude.

These affirmations, which are usually effective through ideal opposition and alternative, are evidently insufficient to configure a concrete field of political struggle. In this sphere there are no pre-established formulas. Nothing that exists repeats itself, especially in a period of transition (such as the one in which we live), where paradigms of society and of power undergo processes of violent transformation. Constituent political struggle (democratic or socialist) must, therefore, be reconstructed on the basis of new, post-liberal and post-socialist, projects. We must insist on the fact that the growth of the revolutionary and constituent process and of the management of the common can be linked only to the decision to turn the multitude into a political body. That is to say, the revolutionary process is ever more bound up with the constituent process; or rather, it confounds itself with the latter, since it is a biopolitical process of production of subjectivity.

The multitude is not only a premise of the revolutionary process of managing the common: this is, as it were, an *external* aspect. But, if the multitude is neither a pre-constituted and preconfigured body nor a compact body, then it will also have an *internal* form: a machine of recomposition, ever open, which develops levels of encounter and intermediation, a mobile whole of intersubjective forms, which are proposed again and again. This "internal" aspect feeds the "external" one; recomposition feeds constituent strength.

When the old theories of constituent power and revolution, as well as of processes of socialist transition, went into crisis during the 1970s, the new "workers' science" (this was the way non-Stalinist communist groups in Western Europe defined their knowledge) proposed an image of constituent power, which moved between *tactical de-stabilization* of the functions of capitalist control and a permanent and profound *de-structuring* of this very same control. In fact, today we are way beyond this image of the revolutionary and constituent process. As a result of the experience of the movements, to the interplay of tactical de-stabilization and strategic de-structuring has been added (as an essential element for the definition of the revolutionary process) the *positive imagination of the construction of a new power*. This is an original expression of strength and the capacity to manage the common. We are not dealing simply with the de-stabilization or the breaking of the structures of power but with the construction of different "forms of life." The idea of the revolutionary event, therefore, is followed by the collective action of a common decision, which complements the ontological structure of the former. The untimeliness of the revolutionary political decision is followed by an effort to produce a new subjectivity as the capacity for a new social being. Rather than seeing it as an event, we can identify the revolutionary process now as a series of opportunities and of ruptures, but also of bifurcations and reconstructions. Rather than reward "virtù" with "fortuna," a horizon appears where "virtù" rewards "fortuna."

There has also been a considerable modification of the perspectives of contemporary political philosophy on the relations between the revolutionary process and the expression of constituent power. In postmodernity the paradigm of political action has been defined as *difference* (whereby difference is understood as the impossibility of ending the crisis of the constitutive capitalist order of the world in coherent, unitary, and rationally significant terms). Hitherto this process of constituent differentiation emerged – as understood, for instance, by Derrida and a few others – at the margins of social processes. Now it must be moved towards the center of the historical process: difference must present itself as *exodus*, and antagonism as the separation and construction of a new subjectivity.

In order to conclude this part of the conceptualization of revolution, an example may be useful. Today, one can say that the structure of power is constituted in a form that Marx would have called "communism of capital." Multinational, collective capital develops its global domination by unifying its various sections. It organizes an association of capitalists as financial investors, essentially linked to each other in those speculative groups which also encompass shareholders and the participation of entire sectors of the productive classes in Western countries. Profits and income have found new means of coexistence within biopower in its configuration as financial capital. The capitalist world (which once exalted its virtue in organizing direct production and in "profit making") is now dominated by a perverse recomposition and redistribution of revenue. Now, the revolutionary project (and that of constituent power which grows together with it) must answer the following questions: how is it possible to have a redistribution of wealth, which is valorized against the corporatism of capital, in the times and spaces of the common growth of the productive networks of the multitude? If constituent power today is a "common" decision concerning the "common" apparatus that regulates the "common" networks of production and distribution of wealth among all the active and productive subjects on planet earth, how will it be possible to express and realize this common strength?

Let us add a final consideration. When problems are posed at this global level, resistance cannot but appear at the global level as well. The act of transformation is possible only within the dimensions of globalization. Most recent political and social movements have indeed identified the global arena as the terrain on which any revolutionary transformation can occur. Yet they have failed at the level of defining a program adequate to this revolutionary intelligence. Therefore, it will be useful, in order to contribute to overcoming these programmatic insufficiencies (which we encounter in the very definition of the concept of revolution), to take up again, from the beginning, the discussion of "revolution, multitude, and the common."

Revolution, multitude and the common

Today, the fundamental terms of reference when speaking of "revolution" are *multitude* and *the common* (rather than class and modernity). The multitude is a *class* concept. In contemporary postmodernity, the definition of "class" cannot, however, be reduced to the definition given to it by modernity, be it from the perspective of the *extension* or *intension* of the concept. From the perspective of extension, the multitude is a broader concept than that of "working class" (and is also more articulated than the concept of the "mass" of workers), because the working subject is today exploited not simply in the factory (or in the system of factories) but at the scale of society as a whole; moreover, the working subject is exploited as productive subjectivity.

From the perspective of intension, the multitude is a concept that refers to the existence of (i.e. it is, rather than representing) a totality of cooperating singularities. We began by defining this totality as a biopolitical apparatus, a social dynamic that refers historical events back to the revolutionary decision, and finally, as a constituent machine.

Broadly speaking, this process depends on the fact that the deployments of the multitude act in a *regime of absolute immanence*. There is no longer any "outside" to this sequence, an "outside" that may turn the biopolitical into a constituent event; and, therefore, it is "inside" this phenomenological sequence that we will have to establish the matrix of the revolutionary process.

In fact, *the regimes of immanence are potentially manifold.* Some voices were raised to denounce the inadequacies of the concept of the multitude (in realizing the totality of virtualities of which it is the bearer). Laclau said: the concept of the multitude lacks internal articulation, that is to say, political mediation – therefore it is a useless concept in so far as it is prepolitical. Macherey added that it is difficult to see how the multitude *in itself* could become the multitude *for itself* in the absence of an engine that would transform the social dimension into a political one. Balibar added that, for the same reason, the concept of the multitude fails to qualify as anti-systemic, that is, it is in danger of being useless because it does not immediately express an antagonistic dimension. Other authors developed these critiques up to the point where Fukuyama – expressing his judgment in historical, political, and synthetic terms – arrived at the following conclusion: the concept of the multitude transcends the dimensions of the nation-state (and of the working class) – but these dimensions cannot be transcended – therefore the concept is useless because it is utopian.

These critiques are incorrect. They restate, for the multitude, the same epistemological schema that constituted the concept of the working class (in itself/for itself, contradiction/antagonism, immediacy/mediation, etc.). By contrast, we have emphasized at length that the *conceptual epistemology of modernity cannot be used any more in contemporary conditions*. And yet, despite their errors, these critiques should not be dismissed as completely worthless. Their contribution lies in inviting further clarification. It is indeed a matter of urgency that we define the internal articulation of the concept of the multitude, and the bonds that link, in immanence, the biopolitical apparatus to the constituent machinery. Now, we insist on the fact that the regime of immanence fundamental to the definition of the multitude is that which is based on the common, on the common network of desire and the production of singularity. The concept of the multitude invites – between sociological analysis which shows its extension, and ethical-political analysis which exposes its deployment (a deployment that is decisive-decisional) – an *ontological inquiry* into the mutual relations of the structure of the common. The multitudinal network is organized through the common. The common is a fabric of singular tensions, becoming ever more intertwined as a consequence of the double aim of producing wealth and subjectivity. The common of the multitude is what resists the exploitation that collective capital exercises over global society. The common of the multitude is the biopolitical existence that is both opposed to biopower and in exodus, thus affirming itself as something other than its violence.

We return now to the analysis of the concept of revolution today, under postmodern conditions. Fundamentally, revolution appears to consist in the exodus of the multitude of workers from the modern regime of production and capitalist domination. At the same time, the revolutionary process appears as the *exodus constitutive of a new world*, set up by the multitude in opposition to the structure of present-day capitalism. The exodus (that is, the very concept of the multitude) presents itself as a process of recomposition in the synthesis of this departure and of this reconstruction, as a deepening of the capacity to articulate productive identity, as well as its massification and social extension.

Defining the relationship between multitude, the common and revolution in this way, it seems that we once again remove the determinate nature of the event from revolutionary experience. That we seem to suffocate the revolutionary event in the movement, without any guarantee against reversal by tendencies of reformist consolidation of capitalist domination. Indeed, it was precisely Bernstein who declared that the movement was everything – i.e. the Bernstein who was the ideological culmination of reformism and who supported the massacre of revolution in Germany. It is not so. For us also, *the revolutionary event is central.* But we want to characterize the revolutionary event outside the modern homology of transcendental conceptions (sometimes transcendental, often mystical) of power. The revolutionary event does not appear to us as a sudden and untimely vicissitude – quite the contrary, its necessary radicalism (temporal and/or historical) consists of the strength of ontological *expression of a new, radically new, temporal constitution of being.* It consists in the declaration of an exodus already in the making, in the affirmation of new conditions of hegemony of the exploited against the exploiters.

The revolutionary event is not a leap into the abyss. Thus has the counter-revolution always characterized the revolution. Thus have reactionary ideologies always justified the violence of fascist repression. The revolutionary event is the revelation of a new being that fills the present void by launching a futuristic construction – an ontological bridge over/ against the abyss of the future.

On the basis of these observations, one can see just how close the relationship between event and decision is. The ontological growth of the exodus is demonstrated in the event so that, in *the exodus*, the event and the decision press together in one single flux the sense of being and the determinations of time.

On the question of violence and of war

Violence and war are once again brought into view and necessitate reflection. Let us be clear on this. Our definition of revolution does not involve the statement of the necessity of violent action. Whereas in modernity revolutionary strategy imposed an unrenounceable appreciation and affirmation of violence, today this is no longer true. The fact remains that violence and war can always reappear, not just as historical accidents, but as the expression of processes of indignation, resistance, and subversion.

It follows that strategy can no longer be defined in progressive or teleological terms, as the old socialism kept telling us. But even so, the fact remains that *there is no strategy without telos*: this *telos* will be constructed (or else it will not be) through the movements and the deadlines that these movements set for themselves. Strategy and tactics, however, march together. The more imperial dominion, in the absence of any rational perspective of development, relies exclusively upon violence and war, the more the problem of violence and war becomes important for the development of the movements. Strategy and tactics live one and the same adventure, the same adventure and a kind of mutual indistinction.

What does this mean, once the revolution is imagined as an exodus, as the management of the common, and as the reappropriation not so much of power but rather of the common strength? As the production of a common subjectivity? As the autonomous decision and strength that is constitutive of a surplus and alterity?

Speaking of *exodus* comes down to speaking of a *radical separation* of the desires of the multitude from what capital has succeeded in colonizing and reducing to dominion. The exodus is already taking place. However, it is confronted by capital through the mechanism of war. Politics as such is defined as the management of war. Even though, rather than war in the classical and traditional sense of the notion, it now consists of a policing exercise by collective capital against the global proletariat. If there is a fundamental problem that emerges at this stage from within the movement, then it is that of the use of violence to resist capitalist initiative during the exodus. Here we must insist on the fact that, if the problem of violence concerns the totality of the movement of opposition and antagonism, nevertheless this total valence of the problem does not make it ontologically central. *The revolutionary rupture has already occurred.* The multitude is everything, capitalist power nothing. This is the only transcendental that is still given today.

Tactically, it is a question of resisting the violence of power but strategically the question is one of continuing the exodus from power, of radically deepening the consciousness and practice of disconnecting the multitude's constituent power from capitalist repression. Already in Spinoza the consideration that the violence of power has total valence does not translate into the registering of an equally total historical efficacy: the central question remains, in any case, the capacity to constitute liberty and liberated desire, slipping through the holes in the fabric of power. *Being transcends its own historical actuality.*

As far as the theme of revolution as management of the common is concerned, we can now only repeat our earlier points: the management of the common is realized in the exodus. As regards overturning the concept of revolution as the re-appropriation of state/sovereign force, that today is crystallized in capitalist power, we can only reaffirm the same option: *reject it and walk out.* But, if necessary, respond with an ethical and democratic force adequate to the violence of this power; denounce its parasitical character, thus emptying it of any repressive capacity. Is it possible, and in what sense, to interpret today Lenin's adage: "turn the imperialist war into revolutionary war"? It is possible to answer in the positive only if for "revolutionary war" we substitute "constituent power," "constituent exodus."

In sum, today, at the center of the problem of defining strategy and tactics (which appear more and more unified), there lies a choice. The first alternative is traditional, even a little antiquated: it involves an act of resistance as the opening and realization of a process of conquering power. The second identifies, in the action of the multitude, an irreversible accumulation of strength that develops through a progressive emptying out and an irresistible occupation of capitalist spaces of power.

Following the second alternative, from a theoretical perspective (but one which is not devoid of influence on the dimensions of political action), a new International is forming itself. *For the time being,* it is unarmed. But it is not the multitude which is posing the problem of violence – when it suffers violence, it will propose tactical solutions that will be accompanied by a strategy that has by now become a natural part of its power.

Acknowledgment

Translated from Italian by Harald Wydra and Marina Frasca-Spada.

Bibliography

Abaza, M. (2001) "Shopping Malls, Consumer Culture and Reshaping of Public Space in Egypt," *Theory, Culture and Society*, 18 (5): 97–122.

Abrahamian, E. (1982) *Iran between Two Revolutions*, New Jersey: Princeton University Press.

—— (1989) *Radical Islam: Iran's Mudjahedin*, London: I.B. Tauris.

Ahmad, I. (2005) "From Islamism to Post-Islamism: Jama'at-i Islami of India," Ph.D. dissertation, Department of Anthropology, University of Amsterdam.

Alagha, J. (2006) *The Shifts in Hizbullah's Ideology*, ISIM Dissertations Series, Amsterdam: Amsterdam University Press.

Albert, M. (2003) *Parecon*, London: Verso.

Alexander, A. and Mbali, M. (2004) "'Have the Slaves Left the Master's House?' A Report on the Africa Social Forum." Alternatives. Online. Available HTTP: www.alternatives.ca/article1625.html (accessed January 3, 2006).

Ali, T. (2004) *Bush in Babylon*, 2nd edn, London and New York: Verso.

Almond, M. (2004) "The Price of People Power," *Guardian* (December 7).

Amin, A. and Thrift, N. (2002) *The City: Imagining the Urban*, Oxford: Polity Press.

Amin, G. (2000) *Whatever Happened to the Egyptians?* Cairo: American University in Cairo Press.

Amrane, D. (1991) *Les Femmes Algériennes dans la Guerre*, Paris: Plon.

Anderson, B. (1983) *Imagined Communities: Reflections on the Origin and Spread of Nationalism*, London: Verso.

—— (1991) *Imagined Communities: Reflections on the Origin and Spread of Nationalism*, revised edition, London: Verso.

Anderson, J.L. (1992) *Guerrillas: The Men and Women Fighting Today's Wars*, New York: Random House.

Anderson, P. (1974) *Lineages of the Absolutist State*, London: New Left Books.

—— (1980) *Arguments within English Marxism*, London: Verso.

—— (1994) *A Zone of Engagement*, London: Verso.

Anonymous. (Scheuer, M.) (2002) *Through Our Enemies' Eyes: Osama bin Laden, Radical Islam, and the Future of America*, Washington: Brassey's Inc.

Arendt, H. (1958) *The Human Condition*, Chicago and London: The University of Chicago Press.

—— (1963) *On Revolution*, London: Faber and Faber.

—— (1965) *On Revolution*, New York: Penguin.

—— (1990) *On Revolution*, London: Penguin.

Arjomand, S.A. (1988) *The Turban for the Crown: The Islamic Revolution in Iran*, Oxford: Oxford University Press.

Aron, R. (1962) *Dix-huit leçons sur la société industrielle*, Paris: Gallimard.

Arquilla, J. and Ronefeldt, D. (1993) "Cyberwar is Coming!," *Comparative Strategy*, 12 (2).

—— (1996) *The Advent of Netwar*, Santa Monica: RAND.

Arrighi, G. (2002) "Lineages of Empire," *Historical Materialism*, 10 (3): 3–16.

Ascherson, N. (2004) "After the Revolution," *London Review of Books*, 26 (5): 3–8.

Ash, T. G. (1989a) "Refolution: The Springtime of Two Nations," *New York Review of Books*, 36 (10): 3–10.

—— (1989b) "Revolution in Hungary and Poland," *New York Review of Books*, 36 (13): 9–15.

—— (2000) "Conclusions," in S. Antohi and V. Tismaneanu (eds) *Between Past and Future*, Budapest: Central European University Press, 395–402.

Ayubi, N. (1995) "Rethinking the Public/Private Dichotomy: Radical Islamism and Civil Society in the Middle East," *Contention*, 4 (3): 107–27.

Bach, A. (2004) "The Third European Social Forum." Online. Available HTTP: www.eurosur.org/wide/Globalisation/ESF_AB.htm (accessed October 14, 2004).

Badiou, A. (2005) *Le Siècle*, Paris: Seuil.

Badran, M. (1995) *Feminists, Islam and the Nation: The Making of Modern Egypt*, Princeton: Princeton University Press.

Balakrishnan, G. (ed.) (2003), *Debating Empire*, London: Verso.

Bartlett, R. (1993) *The Making of Europe, 950–1350*, Princeton: Princeton University Press.

Bayat, A. (1994) "Class, Historiography, and Iranian Workers," in Z. Lockman (ed.) *Workers and Working Classes in the Middle East: Struggles, Histories, Historiographies*, New York: State University of New York Press, 165–210.

—— (1997a) "Cairo's Poor: Dilemmas of Survival and Solidarity," *Middle East Report*, 202 (January–February): 2–6, 12.

—— (1997b) *Street Politics: Poor People's Movements in Iran*, New York: Columbia University Press.

—— (1998) "Revolution without Movement, Movement without Revolution: Comparing Islamic Activism in Iran and Egypt," *Comparative Studies in Society and History*, 40 (1): 136–69.

—— (2002) "Activism and Social Development in the Middle East," *International Journal of Middle East Studies*, 34 (1): 1–28.

—— (2005) "Islamism and Social Movement Theory," *Third World Quarterly*, 26 (6): 891–908.

—— (2007a) *Making Islam Democratic: Social Movements and the Post-Islamist Turn*, Stanford: Stanford University Press.

—— (2007b) "Does Islam Have an Urban Ecology?," *International Journal of Urban and Regional Research*.

BBC News. (2005) "London bomber: Text in full." September 1. Online. Available HTTP: http://news.bbc.co.uk/1/hi/uk/4206800.stm (accessed September 4, 2005).

—— (2006) "BBC News, Q & A: Nepal Crisis." April 25. Online. Available HTTP: http//news.bbc.co.uk./1/hi/world/south-asia/2707107 (accessed May 5, 2006).

Beal, A. (2000) "Real Jordanians Don't Decorate Like That: The Politics of Taste among Amman's Elites," *City and Society*, 12 (2): 65–94.

Behdad, S. and Nomani, F. (2002) "Workers, Peasants and Peddlers: A Study of Labor Stratification in Post-Revolutionary Iran," *International Journal of Middle East Studies*, 34 (4): 667–90.

Beissinger, M.R. (2005) "Modular Democratic Revolution: How Far Can the Bull-dozer/Orange Revolution Spread?" Unpublished paper.

Bell, D. (1973) *The Coming of Post-Industrial Society. A Venture in Social Forecasting*, New York: Basic Books.

Benjamin, T. (2000) *La Revolución: Mexico's Great Revolution as Memory and Myth and History*, Austin: University of Texas Press.

Benjamin, W. (1976) *Illuminations*, New York: Schocken Books.

—— (1999) "First Sketches: Paris Arcades," in W. Benjamin, *The Arcades Project*, trans. H. Eiland and K. McLaughlin, Cambridge: Belknap, 827–68.

Bensaïd, D. (2002) "Antonio Negri et le pouvoir constituant." Online. Available HTTP: www.espaimarx.org/3_19.htm.

—— (2003) *Un monde á changer*, Paris: Textuel.

—— (2004) *Une lente impatience*, Paris: Stock.

Berdyaev, N. (1961) *The Russian Revolution*, Ann Arbor: University of Michigan Press.

Bergesen, A.J. and Lizardo, O. (2004) "International Terrorism and the World-System," *Sociological Theory*, 22 (1): 38–52.

Berkovitch, N. and Moghadam, V.M. (1999) "Middle East Politics and Women's Collective Action: Challenging the Status Quo," *Social Politics* (Fall): 273–91.

Bernstein, T. and Lu, X. (2000) "Taxation Without Representation: Peasants, The Central and the Local States in Reform China," *The China Quarterly*, 163: 750.

Bianco, L. (2003) *Peasants Without the Party*, Armonk: M.E. Sharpe.

Black, D. (2004) "The Geometry of Terrorism," *Sociological Theory*, 22 (1): 14–25.

Blackburn, R. (1999) "Kosovo: The War of NATO Expansion," *New Left Review*, 235 (May–June): 107–23.

—— (2005) "Imperial Margarine," *New Left Review*, 35 (September–October): 124–36.

Bleiker, R. (2000) *Popular Dissent, Human Agency, and Global Politics*, Cambridge: Cambridge University Press.

Bloom, M. (2005) *Dying to Kill: The Allure of Suicide Terror*, New York: Columbia University Press.

Booth, J. (1985) *The End and the Beginning: The Nicaraguan Revolution*, Cambridge: Westview Press.

Borkenau, F. (1963a) *The Spanish Cockpit*, Ann Arbor: University of Michigan Press.

—— (1963b) *World Communism*, Ann Arbor: University of Michigan.

Bouatta, C. (1995) "Feminine Militancy: Moudjahidates During and After the Algerian War," in V.M. Moghadam (ed.) *Gender and National Identity: Women and Politics in Muslim Societies*, London: Zed Press, 18–39.

Boudin, C., Gonzalez, G. and Rumbos, W. (2006) *The Venezuelan Revolution: 100 Questions – 100 Answers*, New York: Thunder's Mouth Press.

Brenner, R. (1993) *Merchants and Revolution: Commercial Change, Political Conflict, and London's Overseas Traders, 1550–1653*, Princeton: Princeton University Press.

—— (1998) "The Economics of Global Turbulence," *New Left Review*, 229: 1–265.

—— (2002) *The Boom and the Bubble*, London: Verso.

Breslauer, G. (2002) *Gorbachev and Yeltsin as Leaders*, Cambridge: Cambridge University Press.

Brewer, J. (1989) *The Sinews of War: War, Money and the English State, 1688–1783*, London: Unwin Hyman.

Brighouse, H. and Wright, E.O. (2002) "Review of *Equality* by Alex Callinicos," *Historical Materialism*, 10 (1): 193–222.

Brinton, C. (1965) *The Anatomy of Revolution*, revised and expanded edition, New York: Vintage Books.

Bromley, S. (1994) *Rethinking Middle East Politics*, Austin: University of Texas Press.

Bunce, V. (1999) *Subversive Institutions*, Cambridge: Cambridge University Press.

Burawoy, M. (1989) "Two Methods in Search of Science: Skocpol versus Trotsky," *Theory and Society*, 18: 759–805.

Burbach, R. (2001) *Globalization and Postmodern Politics: From Zapatistas to High-Tech Robber Barons*, London: Pluto Press.

Burke, E. (1989) "Writings and Speeches Vol VIII," in L.J. Mitchell (ed.) *The French Revolution 1790–1794*, Oxford: Clarendon Press.

Burton, M.G. and Higley, J. (1987) "Elite Settlements," *American Sociological Review*, 52: 295–307.

Büthe, T. (2002) "Taking Temporality Seriously: Modeling History and the Use of Narratives as Evidence," *American Political Science Review*, 96 (3): 481–93.

Callahan, M. (2004) "Zapatismo beyond Chiapas," in D. Solnit (ed.) *Globalize Liberation: How to Uproot the System and Build a Better World*, San Francisco: City Lights Books, 217–28.

Callinicos, A. (1989) "Bourgeois Revolutions and Historical Materialism," *International Socialism*, 2 (43): 113–71.

—— (1991) *The Revenge of History: Marxism and the East European Revolutions*, Cambridge: Polity Press.

—— (1995) *Theories and Narratives*, Cambridge: Polity Press.

—— (1999) *Social Theory. A Historical Introduction*, Cambridge: Polity Press.

—— (2001a) *Against the Third Way*, Cambridge: Polity Press.

—— (2001b) "Toni Negri in Perspective," *International Socialism,* 92.

—— (2003a) "State of Discontent," *Socialist Review*, 272 (March). Online. Available HTTP: www.socialistreview.org.uk.

—— (2003b) *An Anti-Capitalist Manifesto*, Cambridge: Polity Press.

—— (2003c) "Egalitarianism and Anti-Capitalism: A Reply to Harry Brighouse and Erik Olin Wright," *Historical Materialism*, 11 (2): 199–214.

—— (2003d) *The New Mandarins of American Power*, Cambridge: Polity Press.

—— (2004a) *Making History*, Leiden: Brill.

—— (2004b) "The Future of the Anti-Capitalist Movement," in H. Dee (ed.) *Anti-Capitalism: Where Next?* London: Bookmarks, 96–119.

—— (2006) *The Resources of Critique*, Cambridge: Polity Press.

Camus, A. (1992) *The Rebel*, London: Penguin.

Carling, A. (2004) "The Darwinian Weberian," *Historical Materialism*, 12 (1): 71–95.

Carr, C. (2003) *The Lessons of Terror: A History of Warfare Against Civilians*, New York: Random House.

Carr, E.H. (1973) *The Bolshevik Revolution*, vol. 3, Harmondsworth: Penguin.

Carter, C., Clegg, S., Hogan, J. and Kornberger, M. (2003) "The Polyphonic Spree: The Case of the Liverpool Dockers," *Industrial Relations Journal*, 34 (4).

Cassen, B. (2003) *Tout a commencé à Porto Alegre ...* , Paris: Mille et Une Nuits.

Castañeda, J. (1993) *Utopia Unarmed: The Latin American Left after the Cold War*, New York: Knopf.

Castells, M. (1996) *The Rise of the Network Society*, Oxford: Blackwell.

—— (1997) *The Power of Identity*, Oxford: Blackwell.

—— (1998) *End of Millennium*, Oxford: Blackwell.

—— (2000) "Materials for an Exploratory Theory of the Network Society," *British Journal of Sociology*, 51 (1): 5–24.

Castro, F. (1967) *History Will Absolve Me*, London: Jonathan Cape.

Chan, A. (2000) "Globalization, China's Free (Read Bonded) Labor Market, and the Trade Union," *Asia Pacific Business Review*, 6 (3–4): 260–79.

Chávez, H. and Harnecker, M. (2005) *Understanding the Venezuelan Revolution*, New York, Monthly Review Press.

Cheng, T. and Selden, M. (1994) "City, Countryside and the Dialectics of Control: The Origins of China's Hukou system," *The China Quarterly*, 139: 644–68.

Cherifati-Merabtine, D. (1995) "Algeria at a Crossroads: National Liberation, Islamization, and Women," in V. M. Moghadam (ed.) *Gender and National Identity: Women and Politics in Muslim Societies*, London: Zed Press, 40–62.

Chomsky, N. (2001) *9–11*, New York: Seven Stories Press.

Clark, R.P. (1984) *The Basque Insurgents: ETA, 1952–1980*, Madison: University of Wisconsin Press.

Claudin, F. (1976) *The Communist Movement from Comintern to Cominform*, Harmondsworth: Penguin.

Cleaver, H. (1998) "The Zapatistas and the Electronic Fabric of Struggle," in J. Holloway and E. Peláez (eds) *Zapatista! Reinventing Revolution in Mexico*, London: Pluto Press, 81–103.

—— (1999) "Computer-linked Social Movements and the Global Threat to Capitalism." Online. Available HTTP: www.eco.utexas.edu/faculty/Cleaver/polnet.html.

Cliff, T. (1964) *Russia: A Marxist Analysis*, London: Socialist Review Publications.

—— (1988) *State Capitalism in Russia*, London: Bookmarks.

Cockburn, B., St. Clair, J. and Sekula, A. (2002) *Five Days That Shook the World: Seattle and Beyond*, Petrolia: Counterpunch.

Collier, G.A. (1994) *Basta! Land and the Zapatista Rebellion in Chiapas*, with E.L. Quaratiello, Oakland: Food First/Institute for Food and Development Policy.

Collier, G.A. and Collier, J.F. (2003) "The Zapatista Rebellion in the Context of Globalization," in J. Foran (ed.) *The Future of Revolutions: Rethinking Radical Change in the Age of Globalization*, London: Zed Press, 242–52.

Connell, D. (1998) "Strategies for Change: Women and Politics in Eritrea and South Africa," *Review of African Political Economy*, 25 (76): 189–206.

Cordesman, A.H. (2005) "New Patterns in the Iraqi Insurgency: The War for a Civil War in Iraq," working draft (September 27), Washington, DC: Center for Strategic and International Studies. Online. Available HTTP: www.csis.org/features/050927_civilwar.pdf (accessed February 4, 2006).

Crenshaw, M. (1981) "The Causes of Terrorism," *Comparative Politics*, 13 (4): 379–99.

Cronon, W. (1983) *Changes in the Land*, New York: Hill and Wang.

Crosby, A.W. (1986) *Ecological Imperialism: The Biological Expansion of Europe, 900–1900*, Cambridge: Cambridge University Press.

Dabashi, H. (1993) *Theology of Discontent: The Ideological Foundations of the Islamic Revolution in Iran*, New York: New York University Press.

Dallin, D. (1974) "The Outbreak of the Civil War," in L. Haimson (ed.) *The Mensheviks: From the Revolution of 1917 to the Second World War*, Chicago and London: The University of Chicago Press, 156–90.

Danaher, K. and Burbach, R. (2000a) "Introduction: Making History," in K. Danaher and R. Burbach (eds) *Globalize This! The Battle Against the World Trade Organization and Corporate Rule*, Monroe: Common Courage, 7–11.

—— (eds) (2000b) *Globalize This! The Battle Against the World Trade Organization and Globalized Rule*, Monroe: Common Courage.

Danton, G.J. (1910) *Discours de Danton*, A. Fribourg (ed.), Paris: Edouard Cornely.

Darnton, R. (1982) *The Literary Underground of the Old Regime*, Cambridge: Harvard University Press.

—— (1989) "What was Revolutionary About the French Revolution?" *New York Review of Books*, 35 (21/22): 3–6, 10.

Davis, J.E. (2000) "Introduction: Social Change and the Problem of Identity," in J.E. Davis (ed.) *Identity and Social Change*, New Brunswick and London: Transaction Books, 1–12.

Davis, M. (2001) *Late Victorian Holocausts: El Niño Famines and the Making of the Third World*, London: Verso.

Davis, S.M. (1987) *Apartheid's Rebels: Inside South Africa's Hidden War*, New Haven: Yale University Press.

DAWN (Development Alternatives for Women in a New Era) (2002) "Addressing the World Social Forum: A DAWN Supplement." Online. Available HTTP: www.dawn.org.fi (accessed 2004) (DAWN is now found at www.dawnorg.org/).

Debord, G. (1967) *La Société du Spectacle*, Paris: Buchel-Chastel. English translation: *Society of the Spectacle*, Detroit: Black and Red, 1970.

Debray, R. (1968) *Revolution in the Revolution? Armed Struggle and Political Struggle in Latin America*, trans. B. Ortiz, Harmondsworth: Penguin Books.

de Koning, A. (2005) "Global Dreams: Space, Class and Gender in Middle Class Cairo," Ph.D. dissertation, Department of Anthropology, Amsterdam University.

De Landa, M. (1997) *A Thousand Years of Nonlinear History*, New York: Zone Books.

Denoeux, J. (1993) *Urban Unrest in the Middle East*, Albany: SUNY Press.

Deutscher, I. (2003) *The Prophet Armed: Trotsky, 1879–1921*, London: Verso.

Devine, P. (1988) *Democracy and Economic Planning*, Cambridge: Polity Press.

Devji, F. (2006) *Landscapes of Jihad*, London: Hurst Books.

Dieterich, H. (2006) "Communitarian Socialism, and the Regional Power Block," *MRZine*. Online. Available HTTP: http://mrzine.monthlyreview.org/dieterich070106. html (accessed January 8, 2006).

Ding, X.L. (2000) "The Illicit Asset Stripping of Chinese State Firms," *The China Journal*, 43 (January): 1–28.

Doran, M.S. (2001) "Somebody Else's Civil War: Ideology, Rage, and the Assault on America," in J.F. Hoge, Jr. and G. Rose (eds) *How Did This Happen? Terrorism and the New War*, New York: Harper Collins, 31–52.

Draper, H. (1977–90) *Karl Marx's Theory of Revolution*, 4 vols, New York: Monthly Review Press.

Dubis, L. (2004) *Avengers of the New World: The Story of the Haitian Revolution*, Cambridge: The Belknap Press.

Duncan, P. (2000) *Russian Messianism: Third Rome, Revolution, Communism and After*, London: Routledge.

Dunn, J. (1972) *Modern Revolutions: An Introduction to the Analysis of a Political Phenomenon*, Cambridge: Cambridge University Press.

—— (1980) "The Success and Failure of Modern Revolutions," in J. Dunn (ed.) *Political Obligation in its Historical Context*, Cambridge: Cambridge University Press, 217–39.

—— (1985) *Rethinking Modern Political Theory*, Cambridge: Cambridge University Press.

—— (1989a) *Modern Revolutions: An Introduction to the Analysis of a Political Phenomenon*, 2nd edn, Cambridge: Cambridge University Press.

—— (1989b) "Revolution," in T. Ball, J. Farr and R.L. Hansen (eds) *Political Innovation and Conceptual Change*, Cambridge: Cambridge University Press, 333–56.

—— (1990) "Revolution," in J. Dunn, *Interpreting Political Responsibility*, Cambridge: Polity, 85–99.

—— (1993) "Conclusion," in J. Dunn (ed.) *Democracy: The Unfinished Journey*, Oxford: Oxford University Press, 239–66.

—— (2000) *The Cunning of Unreason: Making Sense of Politics*, London: HarperCollins.

—— (2003) "Revolutionary Movements in Comparative Perspective," *Archives Européennes de Sociologie*, 44: 279–83.

—— (2005) *Setting the People Free: The Story of Democracy*, London: Atlantic Books.

Dunn, R.G. (2000) "Identity, Commodification, and Consumer Culture," in J.E. Davis (ed.) *Identity and Social Change*, New Brunswick and London: Transaction Books, 109–34.

The Economist. (1997) "In Praise of the Davos Man," (February 2).

Eidlin, F.H. (1980) *The Logic of "Normalization": The Soviet Intervention in Czechoslovakia of 21 August 1968 and the Czechoslovak Response*, New York: Columbia University Press.

Einhorn, B. (1993) *Cinderella Goes to Market: Citizenship, Gender and Women's Movements in East Central Europe*, London: Verso.

Elias, N. (1996) *The Germans: Power Struggles and the Development of Habitus in the Nineteenth and Twentieth Centuries*, Cambridge: Polity Press.

Emad Eldin Shahin, E. (1994) "Secularism and Nationalism: The Political Discourse of Abd al-Salam Yassin," in J. Ruedy (ed.) *Islamism and Secularism in North Africa*, New York: St. Martin's Press, 167–86.

English, R. (2003) *Armed Struggle: The History of the IRA*, Oxford: Oxford University Press.

Eschle, C. (2005) "'Skeleton Woman': Feminism and the Antiglobalization Movement," *Signs: Journal of Women in Culture and Society*, 30 (3): 1742–69.

Escobar, A. (2001) *Encountering Development*, New Jersey: Princeton University Press.

European Commission. Online. Available HTTP: http://europa.eu.int/comm/enlargement/intro/criteria.htm#Accession criter. (accessed October 4, 2005).

Evans, G. (1996) "Social Class and Interest Formation in Post-communist Societies," in D.J. Lee and B.S. Turner (eds) *Conflicts about Class: Debating Inequality in Late Industrialism*, London and New York: Longman.

Evans, G. and Mills, C. (1999) "Are there Classes in Post-Communist Societies? A New Approach to Identifying Class Structure," *Sociology*, 33 (1): 42.

Everingham, M. (1996) *Revolution and the Multiclass Coalition in Nicaragua*, Pittsburgh: University of Pittsburgh Press.

Eyal, G., Szenenyi, I. and Townsley, E.R. (1998) *Making Capitalism without Capitalists: Class Formation and Elite Struggles in Post-Communist Central Europe*, New York and London: Verso.

EZLN (2002) "Second Declaration from the Lacandón Jungle: 'Today We Say: We Will Not Surrender!'" in T. Hayden (ed.) *The Zapatista Reader*, New York: Thunder's Mouth Press and Nation Books, 221–31.

Fauriol, G. (1996) "Haiti: The Failures of Governance," in H. Wiarda and H. Kline (eds) *Latin American Politics and Development*, 4th edn, Boulder: Westview, 517–40.

Ferguson, N. (2003) *Empire: How Britain Remade the Modern World*, London: Penguin.

Figes, O. (1996) *A People's Tragedy: The Russian Revolution 1891–1924*, London: Jonathan Cape.

Figes, O. and Kolonitskii, B. (1999) *Interpreting the Russian Revolution: The Language and Symbols of 1917*, New Haven and London: Yale University Press.

Fisher, W.F. and Ponniah, T. (eds) (2003) *Another World is Possible: Popular Alternatives to Globalization at the World Social Forum*, London: Zed Press.

Flinchum, R. (1998) "The Women of Chiapas," *The Progressive* (March): 30–1.

Foran, J. (1993a) "Theories of Revolution Revisited: Toward a Fourth Generation?" *Sociological Theory*, 11 (1): 1–20.

—— (1993b) *Fragile Resistance: Social Transformation in Iran from 1500 to the Revolution*, Boulder: Westview Press.

—— (1997) "The Future of Revolutions at the fin-de-siècle," *Third World Quarterly*, 18 (5): 791–820.

—— (2001) *Personal correspondence*. E-mail. (February 5).

—— (ed.) (2003a) *The Future of Revolutions: Rethinking Radical Change in the Age of Globalization*, London: Zed Press.

—— (2003b) "Magical Realism: How Might the Revolutions of the Future Have Better End(ing)s?" in J. Foran (ed.) *The Future of Revolutions: Rethinking Radical Change in the Age of Globalization*, London: Zed Press, 271–83.

—— (2005) *Taking Power: On the Origins of Third World Revolutions,* Cambridge: Cambridge University Press.

Foran, J. and Goodwin, J. (1993) "Revolutionary Outcomes in Iran and Nicaragua: Coalition Fragmentation, War, and the Limits of Social Transformation," *Theory and Society,* 22 (2) (April): 209–47.

Forsyth, M. (1987) *Reason and Revolution: The Political Thought of the Abbé Sieyès*, Leicester: Leicester University Press.

Foucault, M. (1984) "Nietzsche, Genealogy, History," in P. Rabinow (ed.) *The Foucault Reader,* London: Penguin Books.

—— (1987) "An Interview with Michel Foucault," *Akhtar*, 4 (Spring).

Fourest, C. (2004) *Frère Tariq: Discours, stratégie et méthode de Tariq Ramadan*, Paris: Grasset and Fasquelle.

Freire, P. (1970) *Pedagogy of the Oppressed*, trans. M. Bergman Ramos, New York: The Seabury Press.

Friedman, E., Pickowicz, P.G. and Selden, M. (2005) *Chinese Village, Socialist State*, New Haven: Yale University Press.

Fromkin, D. (2005) "A Wall of Faith and History," *New York Times*, March 24: A23.

Fukuyama, F. (1992) *The End of History and the Last Man*, London: Hamish Hamilton.

Furet, F. (1981) *Interpreting the French Revolution*, trans. E. Forster, Cambridge: Cambridge University Press.

—— (1998) "The French Revolution Revisited," in G. Kates (ed.) *The French Revolution*, London and New York: Routledge, 71–90.

—— (1999) *The Passing of an Illusion*, trans. D. Furet, Chicago: University of Chicago Press.

Gambetta, D. (ed.) (2005) *Making Sense of Suicide Missions*, Oxford: Clarendon Press.

Ganor, B. (1998) "Defining Terrorism: Is One Man's Terrorist Another Man's Freedom Fighter?" International Policy Institute for Counter-Terrorism. Online. Available HTTP: www.ict.org.il/ (accessed October 4, 2005).

Gareau, F.H. (2004) *State Terrorism and the United States: From Counterinsurgency to the War on Terrorism*, Atlanta: Clarity Press and London: Zed Press.

Gibbon, E. (1994) [1776–1788] *The History of the Decline and Fall of the Roman Empire*, 3 vols, D. Womersley (ed.), London: Allen Lane.

Gibbs, J.P. (1989) "Conceptualization of Terrorism," *American Sociological Review*, 54 (3): 329–40.

Giddens, A. (1987) *Social Theory and Modern Society*, Palo Alto: Stanford University Press.

Gleason, A. (1995) *Totalitarianism: The Inner History of the Cold War*, Oxford: Oxford University Press.

Gleijeses, P. (2002) *Conflicting Missions: Havana, Washington, and Africa 1959–1976*, Chapel Hill: University of North Carolina Press.

Goldstone, J.A. (1991) *Revolution and Rebellion in Early Modern Europe*, Berkeley: University of California Press.

Goldstone, J.A. (1998) "The Soviet Union: Revolution and Transformation," in M. Dogan and J. Higley (eds) *Elites, Crises and the Origins of Regimes*, Lanham: Rowman and Littlefield, 95–124.

Gonzalez, M. (2005) "Bolivia: The Rising of the People," *International Socialism*, 2 (108): 73–101.

Goodwin, J. (1997) "State-Centered Approaches to Social Revolutions," in J. Foran (ed.) *Theorizing Revolutions*, London and New York: Routledge.

—— (2001) *No Other Way Out: States and Revolutionary Movements, 1945–1991*, Cambridge: Cambridge University Press.

—— (2003) "The Renewal of Socialism and the Decline of Revolution," in J. Foran (ed.) *The Future of Revolutions: Rethinking Radical Change in the Age of Globalization*, London: Zed Press, 59–72.

—— (2004) "What Must We Explain to Explain Terrorism?" *Social Movement Studies*, 3: 259–62.

—— (2006) "What Do We Really Know About (Suicide) Terrorism?" *Sociological Forum*, 21 (2): 315–30.

Gorbachev, M. (1987) *Perestroika*, London: Collins.

Gott, R. (2005) *Hugo Chávez and the Bolivarian Revolution*, London: Verso.

Grachev, A. (1995) "Russia and the World," paper delivered at the annual conference of the British National Association for Slavic and East European Studies, Cambridge.

Graeber, D. (2004) "The New Anarchists," in D. Solnit (ed.) *Globalize Liberation: How to Uproot the System and Build a Better World*, San Francisco: City Lights Books, 202–15.

Greene, A.M., Hogan, J. and Grieco, M. (2001) "E-collectivism and Distributed Discourse: New Opportunities for Trade Union Democracy," paper presented at the TUC/LSE/HARVARD Conference on Unions and the Internet, May 11. Online. Available HTTP: www.geocities.com/unionsonline/e_discourse.htm.

—— (2003) "E-Collectivism and Distributed Discourse: New Opportunities for Trade Union Democracy," *Industrial Relations Journal*, 34 (4).

Grieco, M. (2002) "Introduction," in L. Holmes, D.M. Hosking and M. Grieco (eds) *Organising in the Information Age: Distributed Technology, Distributed Leadership, Distributed Identity, Distributed Discourse*, Aldershot: Ashgate.

Grieco, M., Hogan, J. and Martinez-Lucio, M. (2005) "Editorial Epilogue: The Globalisation of Labour: Counter-coordination and Unionism on the Internet," *Critical Perspectives on International Business*, 1 (2/3).

Gross, J.T. (2001) *Neighbors: The Destruction of the Jewish Community in Jedwabne, Poland*, New York: Penguin Books.

Gu, E. (1999) "Foreign Direct Investment and the Restructuring of Chinese State-Owned Enterprises 1992–1995: A New Institutionalist Perspective," *China Information*, 12 (3).

Gu, Y. and Yang, Y.Y. (2004) "New Trends in Income Distribution and Related Policy Recommendations," in X. Yu, X.Y. Lu, and P.L. Li (eds) *Analysis and Forecast on China's Social Development (2005)* [in Chinese], Beijing: Social Sciences Academic Press.

Guérin, D. (1970) *Anarchism*, trans. M. Klopper, New York: Monthly Review Press.

Guilhot, N. (2002) "The Transition to the Human World of Democracy: Notes for a History of the Concept of Transition, from Early Marxism to 1989," *European Journal of Social Theory*, 5 (2): 219–43.

Gunaratna, R. (2002) *Inside Al Qaeda: Global Network of Terror*, New York: Columbia University Press.

Habermas, J. (1986) *Autonomy and Solidarity*, London: Verso.

Haddad, Y. (1983) "Sayyid Qutb: Ideologue of Islamic Revival," in J. Esposito (ed.) *Voices of Resurgent Islam*, Oxford: Oxford University Press, 67–98.

Hafez, S. (2001) "The Terms of Empowerment: Islamic Women Activists in Egypt," M.A. thesis, Department of Sociology and Anthropology, The American University in Cairo.

Hall, S., Held, D., Hubert, D. and Thompson, K. (eds) (1995) *Modernity: An Introduction to Modern Societies*, Cambridge: Polity Press.

Halliday, F. (1978) *Iran: Dictatorship and Development*, New York: Penguin Books.

—— (1988) "Three Concepts of Internationalism," *International Affairs* (Spring).

—— (1991) "Revolution in the Third World: 1945 and After," in E.E. Rice (ed.) *Revolution and Counter-Revolution*, Oxford: Basil Blackwell, 129–52.

—— (1999) *Revolution and World Politics: The Rise and Fall of the Sixth Great Power*, Houndmills: Macmillan.

—— (2000) "Reason and Romance: The Place of Revolution in the Works of E.H. Carr," in M. Cox (ed.) *E.H. Carr: A Critical Appraisal*, Basingstoke: Palgrave, 258–283.

—— (2003) "Utopian Realism: The Challenge for 'Revolution' in Our Times," in J. Foran (ed.) *The Future of Revolutions: Rethinking Radical Change in the Age of Globalization*, London: Zed Press, 300–9.

Hansen, J. (2006) "The Threat to the Planet," *New York Review of Books*, July 13: 12–16.

Hardt, M. and Negri, A. (2000) *Empire*, Cambridge: Harvard University Press.

—— (2004) *Multitude: War and Democracy in the Age of Empire*, London and New York: Penguin.

Harman, C. (1990) "The Storm Breaks," *International Socialism*, 46: 82.
—— (2002) "The Workers of the World," *International Socialism*, 2 (96): 3–45.
Harribey, M. (2004) "Le Cognitivisme, nouvelle société ou impasse théorique et politique?" *Actuel Marx*, 36: 151–80.
Harvey, D. (2000) *Spaces of Hope*, Berkeley: University of California Press.
Harvey, N. (1998) *The Chiapas Rebellion: The Struggle for Land and Democracy*, Durham: Duke University Press.
Hatem, M. (1994) "Privatization and the Demise of State Feminism in Egypt, 1977–1990," in P. Sparr (ed.) *Mortgaging Women's Lives: Feminist Critiques of Structural Adjustment*, London: Zed Press, 40–60.
—— (2000) "The Pitfalls of the Nationalist Discourses on Citizenship in Egypt," in S. Joseph (ed.) *Gender and Citizenship in the Middle East*, Syracuse: Syracuse University Press, 33–56.
Havel, V. (1985) "The Power of the Powerless," in J. Keane (ed.) *The Power of the Powerless: Citizens Against the State in Eastern Europe,* London: Hutchinson and Co., 23–96.
Hawthorn, G. (1976) *Enlightenment and Despair: A History of Sociology*, Cambridge: Cambridge University Press.
Hay, C. (2005) "Globalization's Impact on States," in J. Ravehill (ed.) *Global Political Economy*, Oxford: Oxford University Press, 235–62.
Haynes, M. (1992) "Class and Crisis – the Transition in Eastern Europe," *International Socialism*, 50: 45–104.
Heinen, J. (1992) "Polish Democracy is a Masculine Democracy," *Women's Studies International Forum*, 15 (1): 129–38.
Held, D. (1987) *Models of Democracy*, Stanford: Stanford University Press.
Herman, E. and O'Sullivan, G. (1989) *The "Terrorism" Industry: The Experts and Institutions That Shape Our View of Terror*, New York: Pantheon.
Higley, J. and Burton, M.G. (1989) "The Elite Variable in Democratic Transitions and Breakdowns," *American Sociological Review*, 54: 17–32.
Hinton, W. (1966) *Fanshen: A Documentary of Revolution in a Chinese Village*, Berkeley: University of California Press.
Hirschman, A. (1991) *The Rhetoric of Reaction*, Cambridge: Harvard University Press.
Ho, P. (ed.) (2005) *Developmental Dilemmas: Land Reform and Institutional Change in China*, London: Routledge.
Hobsbawm, E. (1959) *Primitive Rebels*, New York and London: Norton.
—— (1968) *Industry and Empire*, London: Weidenfeld and Nicolson.
—— (1973) *Revolutionaries: Contemporary Essays*, London: Weidenfeld and Nicolson.
—— (1981) *Forward March of Labour Halted?* London: Verso.
—— (1988) "Working-class Internationalism," in F. van Holthoon and M. van der Linden (eds) *Internationalism in the Labour Movement 1830–1940*, Leiden: E.J. Brill, 3–16.
—— (1990) *Echoes of the Marseillaise*, London: Verso.
—— (1994) *Age of Extremes*, London: Michael Joseph.
—— (1995) *Age of Extremes: The Short Twentieth Century 1914–1991*, London: Abacus.
—— (2002) *Interesting Times: A Twentieth-Century Life*, London: Allen Lane.
Hobson, J.A. (1976) [1902] *Imperialism: A Study*, New York: Humanities Press.
Hochschild, A. (1999) *King Leopold's Ghost: A Story of Greed, Terror, and Heroism in Colonial Africa*, Boston: Houghton Mifflin Co.

Hoffman, B. (1998) *Inside Terrorism*, New York: Columbia University Press.

Hogan, J. and Greene, A.M. (2002) "E-collectivism: On-line Action and On-line Mobilization," in L. Holmes, D.M. Hosking and M. Grieco (eds) *Organising in the Information Age: Distributed Technology, Distributed Leadership, Distributed Identity, Distributed Discourse*, Aldershot: Ashgate.

Hogan, J. and Grieco, M. (2000) "Trade Unions on Line: Technology, Transparency and Bargaining Power," in M. Donnelly and S. Roberts (eds), *Future: Working Together for Change. Proceedings of the Second Scottish Trade Union Research Network* Conference, 58–68.

Hogan, J. and Nolan, P. (2005) "Prologue: The Globalisation of Labour: Counter-coordination and Unionism," *Critical Perspectives on International Business*, 1 (2/3).

Hogan, J. and Zivkovic, A. (2004) "Fire Fighting in Cyber Space: An Exploration of Distributed Discourse and Labour Movement Strategy," paper presented to the colloquium, "Union Renewal: Assessing Innovations for Union Power in a Globalized Economy," HEC Montreal, November 18–20. Online. Available HTTP: www.crimt.org/2eSite_renouveau/Theme3_ang.html.

Holloway, J. (1998), "Dignity's Revolt," in J. Holloway and E. Peláez (eds) *Zapatista! Reinventing Revolution in Mexico*, London: Pluto Press, 159–98.

—— (2002) *Change the World Without Taking Power: The Meaning of Revolution Today*, London: Pluto.

Holloway, J. and Peláez, E. (eds) (1998) *Zapatista! Reinventing Revolution in Mexico*, London: Pluto Press.

Holmes, L. (1997) *Post-Communism: An Introduction*, Cambridge: Polity Press.

—— (1998) "Russia as a Post-Communist Country," in G. Gill (ed.) *Elites and Leadership in Russian Politics*, Basingstoke: Macmillan and New York: St. Martin's Press.

Hont, I. (2005) *Jealousy of Trade*, Cambridge: Harvard University Press.

Hoogvelt, A. (1997) *Globalization and the Postcolonial World*, Baltimore: Johns Hopkins University Press.

hooks, b. (1995) "Black Vernacular: Architecture as Cultural Practice," in b. hooks, *Art on My Mind*, New York: New Press, 145–51.

Horsman, R. (1981) *Race and Manifest Destiny: The Origins of American Racial Anglo-Saxonism*, Cambridge: Harvard University Press.

Hourani, A. (1993) "Introduction," in A. Hourani, P. Khoury and M. Wilson (eds) *The Modern Middle East*, Berkeley: University of California Press.

Hsing, Y-t. (2006) "China's New Urban Politics and the Local State," *The China Quarterly*, 187: 575–91.

Hughes, M. (1998) "The British Battalion of the International Brigades and the Spanish Civil War, 1936–39," *RUSI Journal* (Royal United Services Institute for Defence Studies), 143 (April): 59–74.

Huntington, S.P. (1991) *The Third Wave: Democratization in the Twentieth Century*, Norman: University of Oklahoma Press.

—— (1996) *The Clash of Civilizations and the Remaking of the World Order*, New York: Basic Books.

Hussey, A. (2001) *The Game of War: The Life and Death of Guy Debord*, London: Cape.

Hylton, F., and Thomson, S. (2004) "The Roots of Rebellion: I: Insurgent Bolivia," *NACLA Report on the Americas*, 38 (3) (November/December): 15–19.

—— (2005) "The Chequered Rainbow," *New Left Review*, 35: 40–64.

Hyman, R. (1979) "The Politics of Work Place Trade Unionism: Recent Tendencies and Some Problems for Theory," *Capital and Class*, 8.

International Gender and Trade Network. (2002) "With Women, Another World is Possible." Online. Available HTTP: www.eurosur.org/wide/Globalisation/IGTN-State_WSF.htm (accessed January 6, 2006).

Irvin, C.L. (1999) *Militant Nationalism: Between Movement and Party in Ireland and the Basque Country*, Minneapolis: University of Minnesota Press.

James, H. (2001) *The End of Globalization*, Cambridge: Harvard University Press.

—— (2006) *The Roman Predicament*, Princeton: Princeton University Press.

Jameson, F. (2002) *A Singular Modernity: Essay on the Ontology of the Present*, London: Verso.

Jappe, A. (1999) *Guy Debord*, trans. D. Nicholson-Smith, Berkeley: University of California Press.

Jasper, J.M. (2004) "A Strategic Approach to Collective Action: Looking for Agency in Social-Movement Choices," *Mobilization*, 9: 1–16.

Jayawardena, K. (1986) *Feminism and Nationalism in the Third World*, London: Zed Press.

Jessop, B. (2000) "The State and the Contradictions of the Knowledge-Driven Economy." Online. Available HTTP:www.lancs.ac.uk/fss/sociology/papers/jessop-state-and-contradictions.pdf

Johnson, C. (2004) *The Sorrows of Empire*, New York: Metropolitan Books.

Kalyvas, S.N. (1999) "Wanton and Senseless? The Logic of Massacres in Algeria," *Rationality and Society*, 11 (3): 243–85.

—— (2004) "The Paradox of Terrorism in Civil War," *Journal of Ethics*, 8 (1): 97–138.

Kaminski, B. (1991) *The Collapse of State Socialism*, Princeton: Princeton University Press.

Kampwirth, K. (2002) *Women and Guerrilla Movements: Nicaragua, El Salvador, Chiapas, Cuba*, University Park: Pennsylvania State University Press.

—— (2003) "Marching with the Taliban or Dancing with the Zapatistas? Revolution after the Cold War," in J. Foran (ed.) *The Future of Revolutions: Rethinking Radical Change in the Age of Globalization*, London: Zed Press, 227–41.

Kandiyoti, D. (ed.) (1991) *Women, State and Islam*, London: Macmillan.

Katouzian, H. (1981) *The Political Economy of Modern Iran*, London: Macmillan.

Keck, M. and Sikkink, K. (1998) *Activists Beyond Borders*, Ithaca: Cornell University Press.

Kelliher, D. (1992) *Peasant Power in China*, New Haven: Yale University Press.

Kellner, D. (2003) "Globalization, Technopolitics and Revolution," in J. Foran (ed.) *The Future of Revolutions: Rethinking Radical Change in the Age of Globalization*, London: Zed Press, 180–94.

Kennan, G.F. (1961) *Russia and the West under Lenin and Stalin*, 3rd printing, Boston and Toronto: Little, Brown and Company.

Kenney, P. (1999) "What is the History of 1989? New Scholarship from East-Central Europe," *East European Politics and Societies*, 13 (2): 419–31.

—— (2002) *A Carnival of Revolution: Central Europe 1989*, Princeton: Princeton University Press.

Kepel, G. (2004) *Jihad: The Trail of Political Islam*, 2nd edn, London: I.B.Tauris.

Khafaji, E. (2005) *Tormented Births: Passages to Modernity in Europe and the Middle East*, London: I.B. Tauris.

Khan, A.R. and Riskin, C. (2001) *Inequality and Poverty in China in the Age of Globalization*, Oxford: Oxford University Press.

Kharkhordin, O. (1999) *The Collective and the Individual in Russia: A Study of Practices*, Berkeley: University of California Press.

Khilnani, S. (1993) *Arguing Revolution*, New Haven: Yale University Press.

Kimmel, M. (1990) *Revolution: A Sociological Interpretation*, Philadelphia: Temple University Press.

King, L.P. and Szelenyi, I. (2001) "The New Capitalism in Eastern Europe: Towards a Comparative Political Economy of Postcommunist Capitalisms," draft copy of a chapter later published as "Post-Communist Economic Systems" in N. Smelser and R. Swedberg (eds) (2005) *Handbook of Economic Sociology*, 2nd edn, New York: Russell Sage Foundation.

Klein, N. (2002) "Farewell to the 'End of History': Organisation and Vision in Anti-Corporate Movements," in L. Panitch and C. Leys (eds) *Socialist Register 2002: A World of Contradictions*, New York: Monthly Review Press, 1–14.

Klouzal, L. (2006) "Rebellious Affinities: Narratives of Community, Resistance, and Women's Participation in the Cuban Revolution (1952–1959)," Ph.D. dissertation, Department of Sociology, University of California, Santa Barbara.

Kolodko, G.W. (2000) *From Shock to Therapy*, Oxford: Oxford University Press.

Konrád, G. (1984) *Antipolitics: An Essay*, trans. R.E. Allen, New York: Harcourt Brace Jovanovich.

Kornai, J. (1998) *From Socialism to Capitalism*, London: The Social Market Foundation.

Koselleck, R. (1985) *Futures Past: On the Semantics of Historical Time*, Cambridge: The MIT Press.

Kotkin, S. (1995) *Magnetic Mountain: Stalinism as a Civilization*, Berkeley: University of California Press.

Kouvelakis, S. (2003) *Philosophy and Revolution*, London: Verso.

Kozloff, N. (2006) "The Rise of Rafael Correa: Ecuador and the Contradictions of Chavismo," *Counterpunch*. Online. Available HTTP: www.counterpunch.org/kozloff11272006.html (accessed November 27, 2006).

Krueger, A.B. and Maleckova, J. (2003) "Education, Poverty and Terrorism: Is There a Causal Connection?" *Journal of Economic Perspectives*, 17 (4): 119–44.

Kumar, K. (ed.) (1971) *Revolution: The Theory and Practice of a European Idea*, London: Weidenfeld and Nicolson.

—— (1987) *Utopia and Anti-Utopia in Modern Times*, Oxford: Basil Blackwell.

—— (1988) "Twentieth-Century Revolutions in Historical Perspective," in K. Kumar, *The Rise of Modern Society: Aspects of the Social and Political Development of the West*, Oxford: Basil Blackwell, 169–205.

—— (1991) *Utopianism*, Buckingham: Open University Press.

—— (1997) "Home: The Promise and Predicament of Private Life at the End of the Twentieth Century," in J. Weintraub and K. Kumar (eds) *Public and Private in Thought and Practice: Perspectives on a Grand Dichotomy*, Chicago: University of Chicago Press, 204–36.

—— (2001a) "The Revolutions of 1989: Socialism, Capitalism, and Democracy," in K. Kumar, *1989: Revolutionary Ideas and Ideals*, Minneapolis: University of Minnesota Press, 31–70.

—— (2001b) "The 1989 Revolutions and the Idea of Revolution," in K. Kumar, *1989: Revolutionary Ideas and Ideals*, Minneapolis: University of Minnesota Press, 104–41.

—— (2001c) "The Revolutionary Idea in the Twentieth-Century World," in M. Donald and T. Rees (eds) *Reinterpreting Revolution in Twentieth-Century Europe*, Basingstoke and Houndmills: Macmillan Press, 177–97.

Kurzman, C. (2004) *The Unthinkable Revolution in Iran*, Cambridge: Harvard University Press.

Kutsenko, O. (2003) "Samoidentifikatsii s klassami: proyavlenie obraza klassovoy structury postsovetskogo obshchestva," in S. Makeeva (ed.) *Klassovoe obshchestvo, Teoriya i empiricheskie realii*, Kiev: NAN Ukrainy.

Lachmann, R. (1997) "Agents of Revolution," in J. Foran (ed.) *Theorizing Revolutions*, New York and London: Routledge, 73–101.

Laclau, E. (2001) "Can Immanence Explain Social Struggles?" *Diacritics*, 31 (4).

—— (2004) "Can Immanence Explain Social Struggles?" in P.A. Passavant and J. Dean (eds) *Empire's New Clothes*, New York and London: Routledge, 21–30.

Lacroix, S. (2004) "A New Element in the Saudi Political-Intellectual Field: The Emergence of an Islamo-Liberal Reformist Trend," paper presented in Workshop "Saudi Futures: Trends and Challenges in the Post-9/11 Post-Iraq-War World," February 20–21, Leiden, Netherlands.

Lane, D. (1996) *The Rise and Fall of State Socialism*, Cambridge: Polity Press.

—— (2006) "From State Socialism to Capitalism: The Role of Class and the World System," *Communist and Post-Communist Studies*, 39: 135–52.

Lane, D. and Ross, C. (1999) *The Transition from Communism to Capitalism*, New York: St. Martin's Press.

Laqueur, W. (2003) *No End to War: Terrorism in the Twenty-first Century*, New York: Continuum International Publishing Group.

Lasky, M. (1976) *Utopia and Revolution*, Chicago: University of Chicago Press.

Lawrence, B. (ed.) (2005) *Messages to the World: The Statements of Osama bin Laden*, trans. J. Howarth, London: Verso.

Lee, C.K. (2002) "From the Specter of Mao to the Spirit of the Law: Labor Insurgency in China," *Theory and Society*, 31 (2): 189–228.

—— (2003) "Pathways of Labor Insurgency" in E.J. Perry and M. Selden (eds) *Chinese Society*, London and New York: Routledge, 71–92.

—— (2007) *Against the Law: Labor Protests in China's Rustbelt and Sunbelt*, Berkeley: University of California Press.

Lefort, C. (1986a) *Essais sur le Politique*, Paris: Seuil.

—— (1986b) *The Political Forms of Modern Society: Bureaucracy, Democracy, Totalitarianism*, Cambridge: Polity Press.

—— (1999) *La complication: Retour sur le Communisme*, Paris: Fayard.

Lenin, V.I. (1947) *Selected Works*, 2 vols, Moscow: Foreign Languages Publishing House.

—— (1964) *Collected Works*, 4th English edn, 42 vols, Moscow: Progress Publishers Press.

—— (1967) *On Proletarian Internationalism*, Moscow: Progress Publishers Press.

Lewis, B. (1954) "Communism and Islam," *International Affairs*, 30 (1): 1–12.

—— (1990) "The Roots of Muslim Rage," *Atlantic Monthly*, 266 (3): 47–60.

—— (2002) *What Went Wrong*, London: Phoenix.

Li, Q. (2000) *Social Stratification and Inequality* [in Chinese], Xiamen: Publishing House of Lu-Jiang.

Lipschutz, R. (2001) "Because People Matter: Studying Global Political Economy," *International Studies Perspectives*, 2 (4): 321–39.

Lipset, S.M. (1960) *Political Man: The Social Bases of Politics*, London: Heinemann, 1960.

—— (1994) "The Social Requisites of Democracy Revised," *American Sociological Review*, 59 (1): 1–22.

Lipton, D. and Sachs, J. (1992) "The Strategy of Transition," in D. Kennett and M. Lieberman (eds) *Economic Transformation in Eastern Europe and the Former Soviet Union*, Fort Worth: The Dryden Press, 350–54.

Lister, R. (1997) *Citizenship: Feminist Perspectives*, London: Macmillan.

Long, P. (2005) "Broad Front Strengthens," *Latinamerica Press* (May 18): 2–3.

Lorenzano, L. (1998) "Zapatismo: Recomposition of Labour, Radical Democracy and Revolutionary Project," in J. Holloway and E. Peláez (eds) *Zapatista! Reinventing Revolution in Mexico*, London: Pluto Press, 126–58.

Lowenthal, I. (1976) "Haiti: Behind Mountains, More Mountains," *Reviews in Anthropology*, 3 (6): 656–69.

Lubeck, P.M. and Britts, B. (2002) "Muslim Civil Society in Urban Public Spaces: Globalization, Discursive Shifts and Social Movements," in J. Eade and C. Mele (eds) *Understanding the City: Contemporary and Future Perspectives*, Oxford: Blackwell Publishers.

Lyotard, J.F. (1984) *The Postmodern Condition*, Manchester: Manchester University Press.

MacIntyre, A. (1973) "Ideology, Social Science and Revolution," *Comparative Politics*, 5 (2): 321–42.

Macpherson, C.B. (1977) *The Life and Times of Liberal Democracy*, New York: Oxford University Press.

Mahmood, S. (2005) *The Politics of Piety*, Princeton: Princeton University Press.

Maier, C.S. (2006) *Among Empires: America's Ascendancy and its Predecessors*, Cambridge: Harvard University Press.

Mandel, E. (1957) *Marxist Economic Theory*, London: Merlin.

—— (1990) "A Theory Which has not Withstood the Test of Facts," *International Socialism*, 49: 43–65.

Manrique, J. (2006) "Bolivia: Evo's Friends and Foes," *Latinamerica Press* (July 26): 8–9.

Markoff, J. (1998) "Violence, Emancipation, and Democracy," in G. Kates (ed.) *The French Revolution*, London and New York: Routledge, 236–78.

Marshall, P. (1993) *Demanding the Impossible: A History of Anarchism*, London: Fontana.

Martin, J. (1992) "When the People Were Strong and United: Stories of the Past and the Transformation of Politics in a Mexican Community," in C. Nordstrom and J. Martin (eds) *The Paths to Domination, Resistance, and Terror*, Berkeley: California, 177–89.

Martínez, E. (Betita) and García, A. (2004) "What Is Zapatismo? A Brief Definition for Activists," in D. Solnit (ed.) *Globalize Liberation: How to Uproot the System and Build a Better World*, San Francisco: City Lights Books, 213–16.

Marx, K. (1976) *Capital*, Volume 1, London: Penguin.

Marx, K. and Engels, F. (1968) *Selected Writings*, London: Lawrence and Wishart.

—— (1975–2005) *Collected Works*, 50 vols, London: Lawrence and Wishart.

Mason, T.D. (2004) *Caught in the Crossfire: Revolutions, Repression and the Rational Peasant*, Lanham: Rowman and Littlefield.

Mateju, P. and Rehakova, B. (1997) "Turning Left or Class Realignment? Analysis of the Changing Relationship between Class and Party in the Czech Republic, 1992–96," *East European Politics and Societies*, 11 (3): 501–42.

Mau, V. and Starodubrovskaya, I. (2001) *The Challenge of Revolution*, Oxford: Oxford University Press.

Mauss, M. (2001) *Sociologie et Anthropologie*, 9th edn, Paris: Presses Universitaires de France.

Mawdudi, A. (1982) "Nationalism and Islam," in J. Donohue and J. Esposito (eds) *Islam in Transition: Muslim Perspectives*, Oxford: Oxford University Press, 94–97.

Mayer, A. (1967) *The Politics and Diplomacy of Peacemaking: Containment and Counterrevolution at Versailles, 1918–1919*, New York: Knopf.

—— (2000) *The Furies: Violence and Terror in the French and Russian Revolutions*, Princeton: Princeton University Press.

Mazlish, B. (1976) *The Revolutionary Ascetic: Evolution of a Political Type*, New York: McGraw-Hill.

McLynn, F. (2000) *Villa and Zapata: A History of the Mexican Revolution*, New York: Carroll and Graf.

Melucci, A. (1996) *Challenging Codes*, Cambridge: Cambridge University Press.

Meltzer, M. (1993) *Slavery: A World History*, vol. 2, updated edition, New York: Da Capo Press.

Merrifield, A. (2005) *Guy Debord*, London: Reaktion Books.

Mertes, T. (ed.) (2004) *A Movement of Movements: Is Another World Really Possible?* New York: Verso.

—— (1915) *Political Parties: A Sociological Study of Oligarchical Tendencies in Modern Democracy*, New York: Free Press.

Michels, R. (1987) *Masse, Führer, Intellektuelle. Politisch-soziologische Aufsätze 1906–33*, Frankfurt and New York: Campus.

Moghadam, V.M. (1994) "Introduction: Women and Identity Politics in Theoretical and Comparative Perspective," in V.M. Moghadam (ed.) *Identity Politics and Women: Cultural Reassertions and Feminisms in International Perspective*, Boulder: Westview Press, 3–26.

—— (ed.) (1995) *Gender and National Identity: Women and Politics in the Muslim World*, London: Zed Press.

—— (1997) "Gender and Revolutions," in J. Foran (ed.) *Theorizing Revolutions*, New York: Routledge, 137–67.

—— (1998) *Women, Work and Economic Reform in the Middle East and North Africa*, Boulder: Lynne Rienner Publishers.

—— (2003a) *Modernizing Women: Gender and Social Change in the Middle East*, 2nd edn, Boulder: Lynne Rienner Publishers.

—— (2003b) "Is the Future of Revolution Feminist? Rewriting 'Gender and Revolutions' in an Era of Globalization," in J. Foran (ed.) *The Future of Revolutions in the Context of Globalization*, London and New York: Zed Press, 159–68.

—— (2005) *Globalizing Women: Transnational Feminist Networks*, Baltimore: The Johns Hopkins University Press.

—— (2007) "Feminism and Nationalism in the Middle East" in N. del Mel and S. Thiruchandran (eds) *At the Cutting Edge*, New Dehli: Women Unlimited.

Molyneux, M. (1982) "Socialist Societies Old and New: Progress Toward Women's Emancipation" *Monthly Review* 34 (3) (July–August): 56–100.

—— (1985) "Mobilization without Emancipation? Women's Interests, the State, and Revolution in Nicaragua," *Feminist Studies*, 11 (2): 227–54.

Moore, Jr., B. (1966) *Social Origins of Dictatorship and Democracy: Lord and Peasant in the Making of the Modern World*, Boston: Beacon Press.

—— (1978) *Injustice: The Social Bases of Obedience and Revolt*, Armonk: M.E. Sharpe.

Mottahedeh, R. (1986) *The Mantle of the Prophet: Religion and Politics in Iran*, New York: Pantheon.

—— (1987) *The Mantle of the Prophet: Religion and Politics in Iran*, Harmondsworth: Penguin.

Naples, N.A. and Desai, M. (eds) (2002) *Women's Activism and Globalization: Linking Local Struggles and Transnational Politics*, New York and London: Routledge.

Negri, A. (1997) *Le pouvoir constituant*, Paris: Presses Universitaires de France.

Neumann, R. and Solnit, D. (2004) "The New Radicalism." AlterNet. Online. HTTP: www.alternet.org/story/19308/ (accessed August 19, 2006).

Neumann, S. (1949) "The International Civil War," *World Politics*, 1 (3): 333–50.

Nietzsche, F. (1956) [1887] *The Genealogy of Morals*, trans. F. Goffing, New York: Doubleday Anchor.

Nisbet, R.A. (1959) "The Decline and Fall of Social Class," *Pacific Sociological Review*, 2: 11–17.

—— (1970) *The Sociological Tradition*, London: Heinemann.

Nolan, P. (1995) *China's Rise, Russia's Fall: Politics, Economics and Planning in the Transition from Socialism*, Basingstoke: Macmillan.

—— (2004) *China at the Crossroads*, Cambridge: Polity Press.

Nora, P. (1996) "General Introduction: Between History and Memory," in P. Nora (ed.) *Realms of Memory*, vol. 1, trans. A. Goldhammer, New York: Columbia University Press, 1–20.

Notes from Nowhere (2003) *We Are Everywhere: The Irresistible Rise of Global Anticapitalism*, London: Verso.

Offe, C. (1996) *Varieties of Transition*, Cambridge: Polity Press.

Oi, J. (1998) *Rural China Takes Off: Institutional Foundations of Economic Reform*, Berkeley: University of California Press.

Olutski, E. (2002) *Vida Clandestina: My Life in the Cuban Revolution*, trans. T. and C. Christensen, New York: Wiley.

Ost, D. (1995) "Labor, Class and Democracy," in B. Crawford (ed.) *Markets, States and Democracy*, Boulder: Westview Press, 177–203.

Ozkirimli, U. (2006) *Theories of Nationalism*, London: Palgrave.

Paidar, P. (1995) *Women and the Political Process in Twentieth Century Iran*, Cambridge: Cambridge University Press.

Paige, J. (1975) *Agrarian Revolution: Social Movements and Export Agriculture in the Underdeveloped World*, New York: Free Press.

—— (2003) "Finding the Revolutionary in the Revolution: Social Science Concepts and the Future of Revolution," in J. Foran (ed.) *The Future of Revolutions: Rethinking Radical Change in the Age of Globalization*, London: Zed Press, 19–29.

Pajetta, G. (1978) *La lunga marcia dell'internazionalismo*, Rome: Riuniti.

Pakulski, J. and Waters, M. (1996) *The Death of Class*, Thousand Oaks: Sage.

Palmer, R.R. (1959) *The Age of Democratic Revolution*, vol. 1, Princeton: Princeton University Press.

Pape, R.A. (2005) *Dying to Win: The Strategic Logic of Suicide Terrorism*, New York: Random House.

Parenti, C. (2005) "Bolivia's Battle of Wills," *The Nation* (July 4): 13–18.

Parker, N. (1999) *Revolutions and History: An Essay in Interpretation*, Cambridge: Polity Press.

—— (2003) "Parallaxes: Revolutions and 'Revolution' in a Globalized Imaginary," in J. Foran (ed.) *The Future of Revolutions: Rethinking Radical Change in the Age of Globalization*, London: Zed Press, 42–56.

Perry, E.J. (1985) "Rural Violence in Socialist China," *The China Quarterly*, 103 (September): 414–40.

—— (1994) "Shanghai's Strike Wave of 1957," *The China Quarterly*, 137: 1–27.

Perry, E.J. and Li, X. (1997) *Proletarian Power: Shanghai in the Cultural Revolution*, Boulder: Westview.

Petersen, R. (2001) *Resistance and Rebellion: Lessons from Eastern Europe*, Cambridge: Cambridge University Press.

Pilbeam, P. (2001) "Chasing Rainbows: The Nineteenth-Century Revolutionary Legacy," in M. Donald and T. Rees (eds) *Reinterpreting Revolution in Twentieth-Century Europe*, New York: St. Martin's, 19–40.

Pipes, R. (1998) *Three Whys of the Russian Revolution*, London: Pimlico.

Plato (1941) *The Republic*, trans. F.M. Cornford, Oxford: Clarendon Press.

Porter, B. (2006) *Empire and Superempire*, New Haven: Yale University Press.

Price, D.C. (1974) *Russia and the Roots of the Chinese Revolution, 1896–1911*, Cambridge: Harvard University Press.

Przeworski, A. (1985) *Capitalism and Social Democracy*, Cambridge: Cambridge University Press.

—— (1991) *Democracy and the Market: Political and Economic Reforms in Eastern Europe and Latin America*, Cambridge: Cambridge University Press.

Qian, Y. (1996) "Enterprise Reform in China: Agency Problems and Political Control," *Economics of Transition*, 4 (2): 427–47.

Qiao, J. and Jiang, Y. (2004) "An Analysis of Labor Demonstrations," in X. Yu, X.K. Lu and P.L. Li (eds) *Analysis and Forecast on China's Social Development (2005)* [in Chinese], Beijing: Social Science Academic Press.

Radosh, R., Haback, M. and Sevostianov, G. (eds) (2001) *Spain Betrayed: The Soviet Union in the Spanish Civil War*, New Haven: Yale University Press.

Reed, J.-P. and Foran, J. (2002) "Political Cultures of Opposition: Exploring Idioms, Ideologies," *Critical Sociology*, 28 (3) (October): 335–70.

Reinsborough, P. (2004) "Decolonizing the Revolutionary Imagination: Values Crisis, the Politics of Reality, and Why there's going to be a Common-Sense Revolution in this Generation," in D. Solnit (ed.) *Globalize Liberation: How to Uproot the System and Build a Better World*, San Francisco: City Lights Books, 161–211.

Resnick, S.A. and Wolff, R.D. (2002) *Class Theory and History* (Part 2), New York and London: Routledge.

Reynié, D. (2004) *La Fracture occidentale*, Paris: Editions de la Table Ronde.

Ricoeur, P. (1984) "The Political Paradox," in W.E. Connolly (ed.) *Legitimacy and the State*, New York: New York University Press.

Roederer, P.-L. (1853–59) *Oeuvres*, A.-M. Roederer (ed.), Paris: Firmin Didot Frères.

Rose, R., Tikhomirov, E. and Mishler, W. (1997) "Understanding Multi-Party Choice," *Europe-Asia Studies*, 49.

Ross, K. (2002) *May '68 and Its Afterlives*, Chicago: University of Chicago Press.

Rousseau, J.J. (1993) *The Social Contract and Discourses*, trans. and intro. G.D.H. Cole, reprinted, London: Dent.

Rowbotham, S. (1972) *Women, Resistance, and Revolution*, London: Allen Lane.

Rozelle, Scott. (1996) "Stagnation Without Equity: Patterns of Growth and Inequality in China's Rural Economy," *The China Journal*, 35 (January): 63–92.

Rubenstein, R.E. (1987) *Alchemists of Revolution: Terrorism in the Modern World*, New York: Basic Books.

Rueschemeyer, M. (ed.) (1998) *Women in the Politics of Postcommunist Eastern Europe*, Armonk: M.E. Sharpe.

Rule, J. and Tilly, C. (1975) "Political Process in Revolutionary France, 1830–1832," in J. Merriman (ed.) *1830 in France*, New York: Franklin Watts, 41–85.

Runciman, W.G. (1989) *A Treatise in Social Theory*, vol. 2, Cambridge: Cambridge University Press.

Sachedina, A. (1983) "Ali Shariati: Ideologue of the Iranian Revolution," in J. Esposito (ed.) *Voices of Resurgent Islam*, Oxford: Oxford University Press, 191–214.

Sakwa, R. (2001) "The Age of Paradox: The Anti-Revolutionary Revolutions of 1989–91," in M. Donald and T. Rees (eds) *Reinterpreting Revolution in Twentieth-Century Europe*, Basingstoke: Macmillan, 159–76.

Salama, G. (1990) "Strong and Weak States: A Qualified Return to the Moqaddimah," in G. Luciani (ed.) *Arab State*, Berkeley: University of California Press, 29–64.

Saul, S. (1960) *Studies in British Overseas Trade*, Liverpool: Liverpool University Press.

Shachtman, M. (1962) *The Bureaucratic Revolution*, New York: The Donald Press.

Schurmann, F. (1968) *Ideology and Organization in Communist China*, Berkeley: University of California Press.

Scott, J. (1990) *Domination and the Art of Resistance*, New Haven: Yale University Press.

Scurr, R. (2000) "Social Equality in Pierre-Louis Roederer's Interpretation of the Modern Republic, 1793," *History of European Ideas*, 36: 105–26.

—— (2004) "Pierre-Louis Roederer and the Debate on Forms of Government in Revolutionary France," *Political Studies*, 52: 251–68.

Seidman, G. (2001) "Guerrillas in their Midst: Armed Struggle in the South African Anti-Apartheid Movement," *Mobilization*, 6 (2): 111–27.

Selbin, E. (2003) "Zapata's White Horse and Che's Beret: Theses on the Future of Revolution," in J. Foran (ed.) *The Future of Revolutions: Rethinking Radical Change in the Age of Globalization*, London: Zed Press, 83–94.

Selden, M. (1979) *The People's Republic of China: A Documentary History of Revolutionary Change*, New York: Monthly Review Press.

Senechal de la Roche, R. (1996) "Collective Violence as Social Control," *Sociological Forum*, 11 (1): 97–128.

Sewell, Jr., W.H. (1994) "A Rhetoric of Bourgeois Revolution," in G. Kates (ed.) *The French Revolution*, London and New York: Routledge, 143–56.

—— (1996) "Historical Events as Transformations of Structures: Inventing Revolution at the Bastille," *Theory and Society*, 25 (6): 841–81.

Shahin, E. (1994) "Secularism and Nationalism: The Political Discourse of Abd al-Salam Yassin," in J. Ruedy (ed.) *Islamism and Secularism in North Africa*, New York: St. Martin's Press, 167–86.

Shanin, T. (1986) *The Roots of Otherness: Russia's Turn of the Century*, vol. 2, *Russia, 1905–07: Revolution as a Moment of Truth*, New Haven: Yale University Press.

Sharabi, H. (1988) *Neopatriarchy: A Theory of Distorted Change in Arab Society*, New York: Oxford University Press.

Shariati, A. (n.d.) *Shi'eh-ye Alavi and Shi'e-ye Safavi*, Tehran: n.p.
—— (1980) *Jahat-guiri-ye Tabaqati-ye Islam*, Tehran: n.p.
—— (1982) "Return to Self," in J. Donohue and J. Esposito (eds) *Islam in Transition: Muslim Perspectives*, Oxford: Oxford University Press, 305–7.
Shayne, J. (1999) "Gendered Revolutionary Bridges: Women in the Salvadoran Resistance Movement (1979–1992)," *Latin American Perspectives*, 26 (3) (May): 85–102.
—— (2004) *The Revolution Question: Feminisms in El Salvador, Chile and Cuba*, New Brunswick: Rutgers University Press.
Sheng, L.Y. (2001) "Changing Stages of the Rise in Peasant Income," in Z.D. Xian (ed.) *Major Issues in Chinese Rural Studies, 2001* [in Chinese], Beijing: n.p.
Shepard, B. and Kauffman, L.A. (2004) "A Short Personal History of the Global Justice Movement: From New York's Community Gardens, to Seattle's Tear Gas, Quebec's Fences, the 9/11 Backlash, and Beyond," in E. Yuen, D. Burton-Rose and G. Katsiaficas (eds) *Confronting Capitalism: Dispatches from a Global Movement*, Brooklyn: Soft Skull Press, 375–88.
Sieyès, E.J. (2003) *Political Writings*, M. Sonenscher (ed.), Indianapolis: Hackett.
Skinner, Q. (1978) *The Foundations of Modern Political Thought*, 2 vols, Cambridge: Cambridge University Press.
Skocpol, T. (1979) *States and Social Revolutions: A Comparative Analysis of France, Russia, and China*, Cambridge: Cambridge University Press.
—— (1994) *Social Revolutions in the Modern World*, Cambridge: Cambridge University Press.
Slomczynski, K.M. and Shabad, G. (1997) "Systemic Transformation and the Salience of Class Structure in East Central Europe," *East European Politics and Societies*, 11 (1): 155–89.
—— (2000) "Structural Determinants of Political Experience: A Refutation of the 'Death of Class' Thesis," in K.M. Slomczynski (ed.) *Social Patterns of Being Political*, Warsaw: IFiS Publishers.
Smith, A. (1976) *An Inquiry into the Nature and Causes of the Wealth of Nations*, 2 vols, R.L. Meek and A. Skinner (eds), Oxford: Clarendon Press.
—— (1983) *Theories of Nationalism*, 2nd edn, London: Duckworth.
Smith, C.S. (2005) "Kyrgyzstan's Shining Hour Ticks Away and Turns Out To Be a Plain, Old Coup," *New York Times*, April 3: 6.
Smith, J. and Johnston, H. (eds) (2002) *Globalization and Resistance: Transnational Dimensions of Social Movements*, Lanham: Rowman and Littlefield.
Solinger, D. (1999) *Contesting Citizenship in Urban China: Peasant Migrants, the State, and the Logic of the Market*, Berkeley: University of California.
Solnit, D. (ed.) (2004a) *Globalize Liberation: How to Uproot the System and Build a Better World*, San Francisco: City Lights Books.
—— (2004b) "Introduction: The New Radicalism: Uprooting the System and Building a Better World," in D. Solnit (ed.) *Globalize Liberation: How to Uproot the System and Build a Better World*, San Francisco: City Lights Books, xi–xxiv.
Sonenscher, M. (1997) "The Nation's Debt and the Birth of the Modern Republic," *History of Political Thought*, 18: 64–103, 267–325.
Staël, G. de (1819) *Considerations sur les principaux événements de la révolution française*, 3 vols, 2nd edn, London: Baldwin, Cradock and Joy.
Starr, A. (2005) *Global Revolt: A Guide to the Movements against Globalization*, London: Zed Press.

Stern, J. (2003) *Terror in the Name of God: Why Religious Militants Kill*, New York: Ecco.

Sun, L.P. (2004) *Imbalance: The Logic of a Fractured Society* [in Chinese], Beijing: Tsinghua University Press.

Suny, R. (1991) "Incomplete Revolution: National Movements and the Collapse of the Soviet Empire," *New Left Review*, 189 (September–October): 111–25.

Swidler, A. (1986) "Culture in Action: Symbols and Strategies," *American Sociological Review*, 51 (2): 273–86.

Szelenyi, I., Fodor, E. and Hanley, E. (1997) "Left Turn in Post-Communist Politics: Bringing Class Back in," *East European Politics and Societies*, 11 (1): 190–224.

Tackett, T. (1996) *Becoming a Revolutionary. The Deputies of the French National Assembly and the Emergence of a Revolutionary Culture (1789–1790)*, Princeton: Princeton University Press.

Tang, J. (2003–4) "Selections from the Report on Poverty and Anti-Poverty in Urban China," *Chinese Sociology and Anthropology*, 36 (2–3): 10–198.

Tarrow, S. (1998) *Power in Movement: Social Movements and Contentious Politics*, Cambridge: Cambridge University Press.

Taylor, J.R. and Hardee, K.A. (1986) *Consumer Demand in China. A Statistical Fact Book*, Boulder: Westview.

Therborn, G. (1989) "Revolution and Reform: Reflections on Their Linkages Through the Great French Revolution," in J. Bohlin *et al.* (eds) S*amhällsvetenskap, Ekonomi, Historia*, Göteborg: Daidalos, 197–220.

Thompson, E.P. (1963) *The Making of the English Working Class*, New York: Vintage Books.

Tilly, C. (1978) *From Mobilization to Revolution*, Reading: Addison-Wesley.

—— (1993) *European Revolutions 1492–1992*, Oxford: Blackwell.

—— (1995) "Contentious Repertoires in Great Britain, 1758–1834," in M. Traugott (ed.) *Repertoires and Cycles of Collective Action*, Durham: Duke University Press, 15–42.

—— (2002) "The Trouble With Stories," in C.Tilly, *Stories, Identity, and Political Change*, Lanham: Rowman and Littlefield, 25–42.

—— (2004) "Terror, Terrorism, Terrorists," *Sociological Theory*, 22 (1): 5–13.

Tocqueville, A. de (1873) [1856]. *On the State of Society in France Before the Revolution of 1789* [*L'Ancien Régime et la Révolution*], trans. H. Reeve, London: John Murray.

—— (1988) *L'ancien régime et la révolution*, Paris: Flammarion.

—— (2000) *Democracy in America*, trans. H. Reeve, 2 vols, New York: Bantam Classic.

Tomlinson, B.R. (1990) "Economics and Empire: The Periphery and the Imperial Economy," in A. Porter (ed.) *The Oxford History of the British Empire*, Oxford: Oxford University Press, 146–93.

Touraine, A. (1971) *The Post Industrial Society, Tomorrow's Social History: Classes, Conflicts and Culture in the Programmed Society*, New York: Random House.

—— (1988) *The Return of the Actor*, Minneapolis: University of Minnesota Press.

—— (1998) "Do Social Movements Exist?" paper presented to the World Congress of Sociology, Montreal, July 26 – August 1.

Trotsky, L. (1937) *The Revolution Betrayed,* New York: Doubleday.

—— (1958) *The Revolution Betrayed*, London: Plough Press.

—— (1967) *The History of the Russian Revolution*, 3 vols, London: Sphere Books.

—— (1974) *Against Individual Terrorism*, New York: Pathfinder.

Tu, W. (1992) "Intellectual Effervescence in China," *Daedalus*, 121: 251–92.

Tucker, A. (2000) *The Philosophy and Politics of Czech Dissidence from Patočka to Havel*, Pittsburgh: University of Pittsburgh Press.

Turk, A.T. (1982) "Social Dynamics of Terrorism," *Annals of the American Academy of Political and Social Science*, 436 (1): 119–28.

UNDP (2002) (United Nations Development Programme) *Arab Human Development Report 2002: Creating Opportunities for Future Generations*, New York: UNDP.

Unger, J. (2002) *The Transformation of Rural China*, Armonk: M.E. Sharpe.

Urban, M., Igrunov, V. and Mitrokhin, S. (1997) *The Rebirth of Politics in Russia*, Cambridge: Cambridge University Press.

Vargas, V. (2005) "Feminisms and the World Social Forum: Space for Dialogue and Confrontation," *Development*, 48 (2): 107–10.

Varshney, A. (2002) *Ethnic Conflict and Civic Life: Hindus and Muslims in India*, New Haven: Yale University Press.

Vilas, C.M. (2003) "Between Market Democracies and Capitalist Globalization: Is There Any Prospect for Social Revolution in Latin America?" in J. Foran (ed.) *The Future of Revolutions: Rethinking Radical Change in the Age of Globalization*, London: Zed Press, 95–106.

Voegelin, E. (1987) *The New Science of Politics: An Introduction*, London and Chicago: The University of Chicago Press.

Wacquant, L. (2002) "From Slavery to Mass Incarceration," *New Left Review*, 13 (January–February): 41–60.

Walder, A. (1986) *Communist Neo-Traditionalism: Work and Authority in Chinese Industry*, Berkeley: University of California Press.

—— (1996) "The Chinese Cultural Revolution in the Factories" in E. Perry (ed.) *Putting Class In its Place*, Berkeley: Institute of East Asian Studies, 167–98.

Walicki, A. (1988) *The Three Traditions in Polish Patriotism and Their Contemporary Relevance*, Bloomington: The Polish Studies Center.

Wallerstein, I. (2002) "New Revolts Against the System," *New Left Review*, 18: 20–39.

Wallis, W. (2006) "Fighting 'Has Dealt a Fatal Blow to Hopes of an Independent Lebanon,'" *Financial Times* (August 2): 6.

Walton, J. (2003) "Globalization and Popular Movements," in J. Foran (ed.) *The Future of Revolutions: Rethinking Radical Change in the Age of Globalization*, London: Zed Press, 217–26.

Walzer, M. (1968) *The Revolution of the Saints: A Study in the Origins of Radical Politics*, New York: Atheneum.

—— (1985) *Exodus and Revolution*, New York: Basic Books.

Warshall, P. (1998) "Modern Landscape Ecology: Patterns of Infrastructure, Patterns of Ecostructure, Visions of a Gentler Way," *Whole Earth Review*, 93: 4–5, 8–9.

Weber, M. (1961) "Class, Status, Party," in H.H. Gerth and C. Wright Mills (eds) *From Max Weber*, London: Routledge, 180–95.

—— (1980) *Wirtschaft und Gesellschaft*, 5th edn, Tübingen: Mohr.

White, S. (2003) "Rethinking Postcommunist Transition," *Government and Opposition*, 38 (4): 417–35.

Whitehead, L. (2002) *Democratization: Theory and Experience*, Oxford: Oxford University Press.

Wickham-Crowley, T.P. (1992) *Guerrillas and Revolution in Latin America: A Comparative Study of Insurgents and Regimes since 1956*, Princeton: Princeton University Press.

WIDE (Women in Development Europe) (1995) "From Copenhagen to Beijing," *WIDE Bulletin*, Brussels: WIDE.

—— (2003) *Transformation, Participation, Gender Justice: Feminist Challenges in a Globalised Economy*, Report of WIDE Annual Conference, Vienna, May 2003, M. Macdonald (ed.), Brussels: WIDE.

—— (2004) *Globalising Women's Rights: Confronting Unequal Development Between the UN Rights Framework and the WTO Trade Agreements*, Report of WIDE Annual Conference, Bonn, May 2004, Brussels: WIDE.

—— (2005) "Poverty, Inequality and Insecurity – What Answers Does Feminism Have?" Online. Available HTTP: www.eurosur.org/wide/Structure/publ.htm (accessed January 3, 2006).

Wiktorowicz, Q. and Kaltner, J. (2003) "Killing in the Name of Islam: Al-Qaeda's Justification for September 11," *Middle East Policy*, 10 (2): 76–92.

Williamson, J. (1990) "What Washington Means by Policy Reform," in J. Williamson (ed.) *Latin American Adjustment: How Much Has Happened?* Washington: Institute for International Economics, 7–20.

Wilson, A. (2005) *Ukraine's Orange Revolution*, New Haven: Yale University Press.

WLUML (Women Living under Muslim Laws) (2005) "WLUML Appeal Against Fundamentalisms: There is No Such Thing as the 'Clash of Civilizations': The Clash in the World Today Is Between Fascists and Antifascists." Online. Available HTTP: www.wluml.org/english/newsfulltxt.shtml?cmd%5B157%5D=x-157–103376 (accessed March 2006).

Wolf, E. (1969) *Peasant Wars of the Twentieth Century*, New York: Harper Colophon Books.

—— (1971) *Peasant Wars of the Twentieth Century*, London: Faber and Faber.

Wolff, L. (1992) *Little Brown Brother: How the United States Purchased and Pacified the Philippines*, New York: Oxford University Press.

Womack, J. (1999) *Rebellion in Chiapas: An Historical Reader*, New York: New Press.

World Economic Forum. Online. Available HTTP: www.weforum.org (accessed May 2006).

Wright, S. (2002) *Storming Heaven*, London: Pluto.

Wydra, H. (2006) *Communism and the Emergence of Democracy*, Cambridge: Cambridge University Press.

Yu, J.R. (2003) "Organized Peasant Resistance in Contemporary China," lecture delivered at Fairbank Center, Harvard University, December 4.

Yuen, E., Burton-Rose, D. and Katsiaficas, G. (eds) (2004) *Confronting Capitalism: Dispatches from a Global Movement*, Brooklyn: Soft Skull Press.

Yuval-Davis, N. (1997) *Gender and the Nation*, Thousand Oaks: Sage.

Zakaria, F. (2004) *The Future of Democracy*, New York: W.W. Norton and Co.

Zaslavskaya T. (1999) "Transformatsionny Protsess v Rossii: Sotsiostrukturny Aspekt," in T. Zaslavskaya, *Sotsial'naya Trayektoriya Reformiruyemoy Rossii*, Novosibirsk: Nauka.

Zhou, X.G. (2004) *The State and the Life Chances in Urban China: Redistribution and Stratification, 1949–1994*, Cambridge: Cambridge University Press.

Zivkovic, A. and Hogan, J. (2005) "The Implications of Informational Communication Technology for the Time-Space Dynamics of Collective Mobilisation: The Case of Post Communist Balkan Trade Unionism," *Critical Perspectives on International Business*, 1 (2/3).

Žižek, S. (2001) "Have Michael Hardt and Antonio Negri Rewritten the Communist Manifesto For the Twenty-First Century?" *Rethinking Marxism*, 13 (3/4).

Znet (2003) "Movement Building 2004: An Exchange between Michael Albert and Alex Callinicos." Online. Available HTTP: www.zmag.org/callinicosalbertdebate.htm.

Zuazo, A. (2006) "Bolivia's president orders army to natural gas fields after declaring nationalization," Associated Press (May 1). Online. Available HTTP: http://web.lexis-nexis.com (accessed August 18, 2006).

Zugman, K. (2001) "Mexican Awakening in Postcolonial America: Zapatistas in Urban Spaces in Mexico City," Ph.D. dissertation, Department of Sociology, University of California, Santa Barbara.

Zweig, D. (1989) "Struggling Over Land in China: Peasant Resistance After Collectivization, 1966–1986," in F.D. Colburn (ed.) *Everyday Forms of Peasant Resistance*, Armonk: M.E. Sharpe, 151–74.

—— (2002) *Internationalizing China: Domestic Interests and Global Linkages*, Ithaca: Cornell University Press.

Index

Engels, Friedrich 2, 68, 78, 79, 146n1, 182, 222
English, R. 205
Enlightenment 3, 13, 23, 27, 29, 31, 130, 132, 137, 224
Equador 236, 241–44
equality: class and inequalities 51; democratic equality 31; growth with equity in China 86–87; inequality in China, reformation of (1970–2005) 86–91, 95; total equality 29–30
Eschle, Catherine 124, 126
Escobar, A. 108
ETA (Euskadi ta Akatasunsa) 204, 205
Ethiopia 76, 124, 139
European imperialism, denunciation of 165–66
European Social Forum 124
European Union (EU) 60–61, 67, 157
Evans, G. and Mills, C. 51, 52
Evans, Geoffrey 50, 51, 52
Everingham, M. 216
exodus: constituent exodus 260; declaration of 258–59; difference and 256
Eyal, G. *et al.* 49

family history of revolution 224–27
famine: after Great Leap forward in China 83–84, 85; in India 168
Fanon, Frantz 224
Farid, Muhammad 142
Fauriol, G. 146–47n6
Fedon, Julian 139
feminism: in Central and Eastern Europe 115, 118; feminist economics 121; and global justice movement 120–27, 128; and nationalism, mutual suspicion between 118–19; second wave of 117–18; *see also* women
Feminism and Nationalism in the Third World (Jayawardena, K.) 116
Ferguson, Niall 163n1, 171–74, 178, 179, 181n3
Figes, O. 34
Figes, O. and Kolonitskii, B. 32, 33
Fiji 172
Finland 72
First International 68, 69, 70
First World War 69, 169–70
FLN (National Liberation Front) in Algeria 204
Flor, Blanca 245

Fodil, Abassia 117
Foner, Eric 179
Foran, J. and Goodwin, J. 241
Foran, John 1–13, 147n7, 222, 231, 232, 233n1, 234n9, 235n11, 236–51, viii
Forsyth, M. 18
Foucault, Michel 5, 40, 100, 190, 194
Fourest, C. 129n7
Fourier, Charles 224
Fourth International 228
France 143, 158, 166, 168, 169; *ancien regime* in 18, 19, 20; colonial expansionism 176; CPE (Employment Contract), protests against 162–63; ETA (Euskadi ta Akatasunsa) 204, 205; French Revolution 24–25, 27, 29–333, 40, 42, 44, 68–69, 73, 114–15, 136–38, 159, 222–23, 225–27, 230, 231, 253–54; Paris (1968) 143; Paris Commune 43, 141, 142, 225; revolutionary processes in 142; revolutionary tradition of democracy 32–33, 44
Franciscan tradition 253
Frasca-Spada, Marina 260
Frederic II 165
Free Soil, Free labor, Free Man (Foner, E.) 179
Freud, Sigmund 224
Friedman, E. *et al.* 85, 86
Friere, Paolo 135
Fromkin, D. 235n13
Fromm, Erich 224
Fukuyama, Francis 1, 17, 257
fundamentalist nationalism 118
Furet, Francois 17, 33
The Furies (Mayer, A.) 152
future of revolution 25–26; agents of revolution, paths to becoming 237–38; centralized structures, retreat from 228–29; in China 236, 238, 239, 240; classical concept of, future for 12–13; in Eastern Europe 228, 231–32, 236; elements of future revolution 223–24; family history of revolution 224–27; globalization and 9–13, 229–30, 231; ideas and influences, continuity of 226; imitation or innovation? 7, 222–35; Islamist Revolution 109–11, 112, 113, 115, 117, 118; Latin America, new left power in 241–44; meaning of revolution, change in 233; meaning of 'revolution' and whether a future

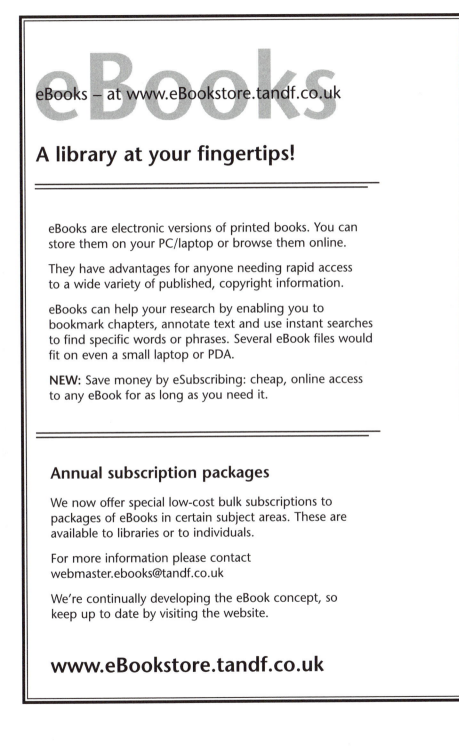